Indicopleustes Cosmas, John Watson McCrindle

The Christian Topography of Cosmas, an Egyptian Monk

Indicopleustes Cosmas, John Watson McCrindle

The Christian Topography of Cosmas, an Egyptian Monk

ISBN/EAN: 9783743422230

Manufactured in Europe, USA, Canada, Australia, Japa

Cover: Foto ©Lupo / pixelio.de

Manufactured and distributed by brebook publishing software (www.brebook.com)

Indicopleustes Cosmas, John Watson McCrindle

The Christian Topography of Cosmas, an Egyptian Monk

ΚΟΣΜΑ
ΑΙΓΥΠΤΙΟΥ ΜΟΝΑΧΟΥ
ΧΡΙΣΤΙΑΝΙΚΗ ΤΟΠΟΓΡΑΦΙΑ.

THE
CHRISTIAN TOPOGRAPHY
OF
COSMAS, AN EGYPTIAN MONK.

Translated from the Greek, and Edited, with Notes and Introduction

BY

J. W. McCRINDLE, M.A., M.R.A.S., F.R.S.G.S.,

LATE PRINCIPAL OF THE GOVERNMENT COLLEGE AT PATNA, AND FELLOW OF
CALCUTTA UNIVERSITY;

AUTHOR OF A SERIES OF WORKS ON ANCIENT INDIA, AS DESCRIBED BY THE CLASSICAL AUTHORS,
INCLUDING THE "INDICA" OF CTESIAS, MEGASTHENES AND ARRIAN; THE "PERIPLÛS
OF THE ERYTHRAEAN SEA"; PTOLEMY'S "GEOGRAPHY OF INDIA", AND THE
"INVASION OF INDIA BY ALEXANDER THE GREAT".

LONDON:
PRINTED FOR THE HAKLUYT SOCIETY.

M.DCCC.XCVII.

LONDON:
PRINTED AT THE BEDFORD PRESS, 20 AND 21, BEDFORDBURY, W.C.

COUNCIL

OF

THE HAKLUYT SOCIETY.

SIR CLEMENTS MARKHAM, K.C.B., F.R.S., *Pres. R.G.S.*, PRESIDENT.
THE RIGHT HON. THE LORD STANLEY OF ALDERLEY, VICE-PRESIDENT.
REAR-ADMIRAL SIR WILLIAM WHARTON, K.C.B., VICE-PRESIDENT.
C. RAYMOND BEAZLEY, ESQ., M.A.
COLONEL G. EARL CHURCH.
THE RIGHT HON. GEORGE N. CURZON, M.P.
ALBERT GRAY, ESQ.
ALFRED HARMSWORTH, ESQ.
THE RIGHT HON. LORD HAWKESBURY.
EDWARD HEAWOOD, ESQ., M.A.
ADMIRAL SIR ANTHONY H. HOSKINS, G.C.B.
VICE-ADMIRAL ALBERT H. MARKHAM.
A. P. MAUDSLAY, ESQ.
E. DELMAR MORGAN, ESQ.
CAPTAIN NATHAN, R.E.
ADMIRAL SIR E. OMMANNEY, C.B., F.R.S.
CUTHBERT E. PEEK, ESQ.
E. G. RAVENSTEIN, ESQ.
HOWARD SAUNDERS, ESQ.
CHARLES WELCH, ESQ., F.S.A.

WILLIAM FOSTER, ESQ., B.A., *Honorary Secretary.*

CONTENTS.

	PAGE
EDITOR'S PREFACE	IX-XII

INTRODUCTION :

    Sources of the Text.—Biography of the Author; His system of the world; Opinions about his work; His place in history . . . . . . i-xxvii

THE AUTHOR'S SUPPLICATION FOR DIVINE AID   1

PROLOGUE I .   2

PROLOGUE II   3

BOOK I :

    The Places and Figures of the Universe ; the heresy of affirming that the Heavens are spherical, and that there are Antipodes ; Pagan errors as to the causes of rain and of earthquakes 7

BOOK II :

    The position, figure, length and breadth of the earth ; the site of Paradise ; the Greek inscriptions at Adulê ; extract from Ephorus ; the ancient empires ; the Fall of Man and its effect on the Angels ; the circumscription of angels, demons and souls 23

BOOK III :

    The Tower of Babel; the Mission of Moses to the Israelites ; comments on his history of the Creation of the World ; the conversion of the nations to Christianity . 91

BOOK IV :

    A recapitulation of the views advanced ; theory of eclipses ; doctrine of the sphere denounced . . . 129

BOOK V :

    Description of the Tabernacle : Patriarchs and Prophets who predicted the coming of Christ and the future state ; the agreement of these with the Apostles . . 138

viii   CONTENTS.

                                                                    PAGE
BOOK VI:
    The size of the Sun : a dissertation on the two states   . 244
BOOK VII:
    The Duration of the Heavens .   . 263
BOOK VIII:
    Interpretation of the Song of Hezekiah ; the retrogression
    of the Sun ; ancient dials ; predictions referring to Cyrus 304
BOOK IX:
    Courses of the Sun and Moon and other heavenly bodies ;
    their movements effected by the angels   .   . 321
BOOK X:
    Passages from the Christian Fathers confirming the Author's
    views   .   .   . 331
BOOK XI:
    Description of certain Indian animals and plants, and of the
    island of Taprobanê (Ceylon)   .   .   . 358
BOOK XII:
    Old Testament narratives confirmed by Chaldaean, Baby-
    lonian, Persian and Egyptian records ; the island Atlantis 375
APPENDIX:
    Plates with figures illustrative of the Text, and explanations
    of them 387
INDEX   . 393

ERRATA.

Page ix, line 17, *for* *Theodosius*, *read* Theodorus.
  ,,   5, line 24, ,, *vail*,   ,, veil.
  ,,   23, note 2, ,, *ἐγκύκλιον*,   ,, ἐγκύκλιος.
  ,,   43, line 19, ,, *each of*,   ,, each pair of.
  ,,   76, line 4,   ,, *diameter*,   ,, dimensions.
  ,,   154, note 1, ,, *papilio*,   ,, papilio.
  ,,   213, line 5, ,, *Appolinarius*, ,, Apollinarius.

EDITOR'S PREFACE.

HE *Christian Topography* of Cosmas Indicopleustes is one of the prodigies of literature. The boldness and perverse ingenuity with which its author, from a long array of irrelevant scripture texts, seeks to construct an impossible theory of the universe can scarcely fail to astonish everyone who reads it. It made its appearance at that period in the world's history, when Christendom, fast losing the light of Greek learning and culture, was soon to be shrouded in the long night of mediæval ignorance and barbarism. The work reflects with singular distinctness this prominent characteristic of the age which produced it; for while Cosmas, on the one hand, held the principles of the Christian faith combined with others pervading the theology then current which led to the darkening of all true knowledge, he had, on the other hand, a somewhat considerable, if inexact, acquaintance with the philosophical and scientific speculations of the Greeks. He may thus not inaptly be compared to a two-headed Janus, with one face turned to the light of departing day, and the other to the shadows of the coming night.

In our Introduction will be found a statement showing the sources whence the text of this unique work has been derived. A biography of its author then follows; next, a synopsis of his cosmological views, and finally, citations of the opinions which have been passed upon his *system of the world* and the contents of his work generally.

The translation here presented is literal, as far as the exigencies of idiom would permit. It is the first that has been made of the whole work into English, or, indeed, into any other language except Latin and Norwegian. In its preparation we have lacked the advantage, generally enjoyed by translators of classical texts, that of having at hand for reference a variety of translations and commentaries to throw light on passages that are dark, dubious, or disputed, or otherwise perplexed. We have had, indeed, the assistance of Montfaucon's Latin version, but no commentary whatever to give us light where we found Cosmas dark. That good and learned Father is generally accurate, but, like the good Homer, he sometimes nods, and we give at the foot of the page a list of notes which refer to passages whereof his interpretations differ from our own.[1] Another list of notes follows, in which suggestions are offered for the correction of the Greek text.[2]

---

[1] N. 2, p. 2; n. 1, p. 19; n. 3, p. 24; n. 3, p. 71; n. 1, p. 85; n. 2, p. 92; n. 1, p. 94; n. 2, p. 106; n. 5, p. 119; n. 1, p. 123; n. 2, p. 131; n. 1, p. 138; n. 2, p. 183; n. 4, p. 192; n. 1, p. 264; n. 2, p. 277; n. 1, p. 279; n. 1, p. 322; n. 2, p. 336; n. 3, p. 341; n. 2, p. 361; n. 1, p. 363; n. 2, *ibid*.; n. 3, p. 364.

[2] N. 1, p. 12; n. 1, p. 13; n. 1, p. 16; n. 1, p. 29; n. 1, p. 50;

Cosmas tells us, in the outset of his work, that he has inserted notes (παραγραφαί) for the clearer exposition of the text (τὸ κείμενον). These notes he seems to have placed, not in the margin, but in the body of the work, after the text to which they refer. In our translation they appear in a similar position, but printed in a type somewhat smaller than that of the text.

Our rendering of the word "Ελληνες requires a word of explanation. In the days of Cosmas it was used, not so much to designate persons of Hellenic descent, as persons who clung to the old superstitions of Greece and Rome and rejected Christianity. Montfaucon's rendering is *Graeci*, but we have considered *Pagans* as preferable.[1] This class of persons Cosmas sometimes calls also οἱ ἔξωθεν, those *without the pale of the Church*, an expression which we render mostly by *pagans*.

Cosmas had some skill in drawing, and seems to have taken as much delight in covering his MSS. with illustrative sketches as was taken, according to his showing, by the Israelites of old in covering the rocks of Mount Sinai with inscriptions when once they had been taught by Moses the art of writing. Montfaucon, having made a selection from these sketches, relegated them *en masse* to the end of

---

n. 4, p. 120; n. 1, p. 138; n. 1, p. 170; n. 2, p. 190; n. 1, p. 202; n. 1, p. 212; n. 1, p. 224; n. 2, p. 305; n. 4, p. 321; n. 1, p. 329; n. 3, p. 347; n. 1, p. 355; n. 7, p. 366; n. 2, p. 369; n. 2, p. 383.

[1] This point will be found further explained in n. 2, p. 3.

his work. His copies of them, which are not always quite exact, have been reproduced for the present work, by photographic processes, in a way which leaves nothing to be desired, and will be found, with explanatory notes, in the Appendix.

The passages of Scripture to which Cosmas refers are very numerous, and the words are cited at length both in the Greek text and in the Latin version. We have, however, given only the references, in cases where this could be done without inconvenience to the reader.

In conclusion we have to express our obligations to Mr. J. Coles, Map-Curator of the Royal Geographical Society, and to Dr. James Burgess of Edinburgh, for their kindness in writing for us those mathematical notes to Book vi, in which they show how egregiously Cosmas erred in his calculations of the size of the sun;[1] while to Mr. C. Robertson of Edinburgh, late of the Indian Civil Service, we stand greatly indebted for valuable suggestions and criticisms made while he had the goodness to hear us read over our translation to him. Mr. Foster, the Secretary of the Society, must permit us further to say how much the work has profited by his careful correction of the final proofs, and the suggestions which he was kind enough on occasion to offer.

J. W. McC.

32, LAURISTON PLACE, EDINBURGH,
November 1897.

---

[1] For the note with diagrams on pp. 247-8, we are indebted to Mr. Coles; and for n. 2, p. 249, n. 1, p. 250, and n. 1, p. 252, to Dr. Burgess.

INTRODUCTION.

Sources of the Text.

HE *Christian Topography* of Cosmas, surnamed Indicopleustes, or the Indian Navigator, has been preserved in two copies: one a parchment MS. of the tenth century belonging to the Laurentian library in Florence, and containing the whole work except only the last leaf; the other, a very fine uncial MS. of the eighth or ninth century, belonging to the Vatican library, and containing sketches drawn by Cosmas himself, but wanting entirely the twelfth book, which is the last. There is, besides, in the Imperial library in Vienna, a Cosmas MS., but this contains only a few leaves of the *Topography*.

The existence of the work, which had been for ages forgotten, and the importance and interest of its contents, were first made known in the latter half of the seventeenth century by Emeric Bigot. This learned French scholar, while visiting Italy, extracted from the Florentine Codex a copy of the

Adulitic Inscriptions,[1] and of passages relating to Ethiopia and India. These extracts were afterwards published in Thevenot's *Relation de divers Voyages*, accompanied with a translation into French. Twenty years later (1706), the work appeared in its complete form as exhibited in the Florentine Codex, collated with that of the Vatican. It was not, however, published separately, but was included in the second volume of the splendid work *Nova Collectio Patrum et Scriptorum Graecorum*, edited by Father Montfaucon, a Benedictine monk, celebrated for his profound knowledge of Patristic literature. The Greek text was illustrated by a learned introduction and a Latin translation of great elegance and accuracy. Notes were also added, chiefly to point out where discrepancies exist in the readings of the MSS. The present translation has been prepared from Montfaucon's text, as reprinted in the 88th volume of the *Patrologia Graeca*, printed at the Migne Press, Paris, 1864.

The Title of the Work.

In the Florentine Codex, the index of the work reads thus: Αὕτη ἡ Βίβλος Χριστιανικὴ Τοπογραφία περιεκτικὴ παντὸς τοῦ κόσμου παρ' ἡμῖν ὠνομασμένη. *This Book named by us Christian Topography comprehensive of the whole world.* Montfaucon entitles it: Cosmae Egyptii Monachi Christiana Topographia, sive Christianorum Opinio de Mundo: *The Christian*

---

[1] Pp. 57-66.

Topography of Cosmas, an Egyptian Monk, or the Opinion of Christians concerning the World. As Cosmas all through the work keeps harping, with the most provoking reiteration, on his doctrine that the universe consists of only two *places*, namely, the earth which is below the firmament, and heaven, which is above it, the term *Topography* designates the treatise properly enough; though on turning to peruse it for the first time, we should from its title expect its contents to be very different from what they are found to be.

Notice of the Work by Photius, Patriarch of Constantinople.

Montfaucon does not seem to have been aware that a brief notice of the *Topography* is to be found in the *Bibliotheka* of Photius, the Patriarch of Constantinople, who was elected to that dignity in A.D. 858. Photius states that the work had for its title Χριστιανῶν βίβλος, and was an exposition extending to the eighth book. He does not give the author's name, but states that he flourished in the reign of the Roman Emperor Justinus, and dedicated his work to a certain Pamphilus. He condemns it as being below mediocrity in style, and faulty in its syntax; and at the same time calls in question the author's veracity, saying that he makes up stories so incredible that he may fairly be regarded as a writer of fables rather than of facts. He then gives a very concise summary of the contents of the *Topography*, and concludes with a reference to the last four books, which had from time to time been added to defend the doctrines set forth in those which had preceded.

The Name of the Author of the "Topography."

A doubt long ago arose as to whether Cosmas was the proper or family name of the author of the *Topography*. Isaac Voss first started this doubt, and Fabricius subsequently gave currency to the opinion that Cosmas was so called because his work was devoted to a description of the Kosmos: just as the Abbot John of Sinai was called Climacius because he had published a work entitled *Climax*. In the absence of evidence, this must remain an open question.

Biography of Cosmas.

The *Topography* fortunately contains passages which throw light on the personal history of its author, and enable us also to fix with certainty the date at which he wrote. He was most probably a native of Alexandria, and may have been of Greek parentage. His education was confined to the more elementary branches of knowledge, such as would fit him for the career he pursued in the earlier part of his life—that of a merchant. But though he was not instructed, as he tells us himself,[1]

---

[1] P. 23.

in the "learning of the schools," yet so inquisitive was his turn of mind and so sharp his intellect that he eventually acquired such a knowledge of literature and science as raised him to the level of the culture of his time, and to his being accepted as a capable exponent and defender of the Christian faith.

The commercial pursuits of Cosmas carried him into seas and countries far remote from his home. Thus he tells us that he had sailed upon three of the great gulfs which run up into the earth from the ocean, namely, the Mediterranean Sea, the Red Sea, and Persian Gulf.[1] He sailed also upon that part of the Erythraean Sea which beyond Cape Guardafui stretches southward toward the outlying ocean, which in those days was regarded with terror and held to be unnavigable on account of the violent currents and dense and dismal fogs in which it was thought to be enveloped. When the ship which carried Cosmas was approaching this dread region of currents and fogs, a storm gathered overhead, and flocks of albatrosses, like birds of ill omen, hovered on the wing high above the mast. Dismay seized alike the passengers and the crew, and amidst outcries of "port the helm," the course of the vessel was reversed and she headed northwards.[2] Cosmas does not say whether in the course of this voyage he reached India, which was his destination when he embarked.

[1] P. 39.   [2] Pp. 39, 40.

If he did not, he must have made a second and more successful attempt; for no one, we think, who reads his eleventh book, in which he describes the island of Ceylon and the ports, commerce, and animals of India, can doubt that he writes about these places from personal knowledge of them.

One of the most interesting and instructive parts of the *Topography* is that in which Cosmas relates what he had heard and seen in the course of his travels in Ethiopia.[1] By the name of *Ethiopia* he designates in a general way the vast region which stretches southward from Egypt down towards the equator; and from an incidental remark which he drops when treating of the Adulitic inscription on the throne,[2] we learn that he had traversed it almost throughout its length and its breadth. Like Herodotus of old, he was ever athirst after knowledge, and when he was unable to visit places which lay in the vicinity of his route, he made inquiries about them from such persons as knew them and could be trusted to report things truly. The capital of Ethiopia at that time was Axum, an important centre of commerce, and also of religion and learning. It was one of the places which Cosmas, in pursuit of his calling, visited,[3] and from one or two of his statements we may infer that he was well received at Court, and was permitted by the King, who professed the Christian faith and could speak Greek, to travel freely through his dominions.

---

[1] Pp. 50-68.   [2] P. 67, line 9.   [3] P. 359.

The seaport of Axum was Adulê or Adulis,[1] the modern Zulá or Thulla, situated near Annesley Bay and distant from the capital about one hundred and twenty miles or an eight days' journey. Cosmas found himself here in the year 525 A.D., at which time Elesboas, the King of Axum, was preparing an expedition against the Homerites in Arabia.[2] Here, at the request of the Governor, Cosmas, along with his friend Menas, a monk of the monastery at Raithu, copied the famous Greek inscriptions on the marble tablet and the basanite throne, which lay together outside the town on the road which led to Axum.[3]

Among other parts of Ethiopia which our traveller visited we may include the Aromatic country— that great projection on the east of the African Continent which terminates in Cape Guardafui. His description of this district (which supplied the Egyptians of old with their spices for embalming the dead), and of its products and its foreign trade, shows that it must have come from the pen of an eye-witness.[4] He may also have proceeded to the north-west, and visited the kingdom of Meroë (now Khartum), for in that direction lay the seats of several tribes mentioned in the inscription on the throne. Montfaucon, in his Preface, credits him with the discovery, in the Abyssinian province called Agau, of the true source of the Nile. It was not, however, the source of the main stream

---

[1] P. 54. [2] Pp. 55, 56.
[3] Pp. 51-53. [4] P. 62.

which he discovered, but that of the Blue Nile,[1] which, a millennium afterwards, was rediscovered by the Portuguese, and more recently by the Scottish traveller Bruce. There was still another interesting locality which the traveller tells us he visited, and this lay on the other side of the Red Sea—the Desert, namely, of Sinai, where he found, strewn among the sands, fragments of rock covered with inscriptions which he took to have been carved by the Israelites when they were wandering in that wilderness.[2]

Cosmas, when all his travels were over, returned to Alexandria, perhaps after paying a visit to Jerusalem; and, abandoning the secular life, retired to the seclusion of the cloister, where he devoted his leisure to the composition of works on descriptive geography, cosmography, and Scriptural exegesis. Of these, the *Christian Topography* alone is extant. The loss of the geographical treatise, as Montfaucon well says, is to be deplored with tears. It has been conjectured that the geographical passages in the *Topography*, as, for instance, the description of Ceylon in the eleventh book, are extracts from that treatise.

THE CHRISTIAN SECT TO WHICH COSMAS BELONGED.

In the days of Cosmas ecclesiastical controversies were rife, and professing Christians were divided

---

[1] Pp. 52-54. [2] Pp. 159, 160.

into numerous sects. That to which Cosmas most probably belonged was the Nestorian. To this point Photius makes no reference, and it has been equally overlooked by Montfaucon. The first who called in question the orthodoxy of our Monk was De La Croze, who, in his *Histoire du Christianisme des Indes*, adduced the following arguments to prove his Nestorian proclivities :—1°, that Cosmas calls Patricius, who was the Archbishop of Persia when that country had been infected with Nestorianism, a divine man and an illustrious teacher ;[1] 2°, that Cosmas, in his list of heretical sects, names the Manichæans, the Marcionists, the Eutychians, the Arians and the Apollinarians, but not the Nestorians ;[2] 3°, that in his exposition of Scripture, and in his system of the world, he always follows Theodosius of Mopsuestia and Diodorus of Tarsus, who were the principal teachers of the Nestorians ; 4°, that concerning Christ and the Incarnation of the Word, he uses the same modes of expression as the Nestorians.[3] We may add as a fifth argument the glowing terms in which Cosmas speaks of the wide diffusion of Christianity among the heathen nations of the east, which was mainly the work of missionaries from Persia, where Nestorianism reigned supreme.[4] Only one passage occurs to throw some doubt on the certainty of this conclusion—that in which Cosmas addresses Mary as

---

[1] P. 24. [2] Pp. 212, 213.
[3] Pp. 187, 188. [4] Pp. 118-121.

the *Mother of God*, an expression abhorrent to the Nestorians. Had Cosmas in his monastery relapsed into what was there considered orthodoxy?

The Date at which the "Topography" was Written.

We have already mentioned that the *Topography* has data from which the time when Cosmas wrote can be certainly determined. In the second book (p. 55), where he mentions his visit to Adulê, he observes that it was made when Elesboas the Axumite King was preparing an expedition against the Homerites in Arabia, and that this was at the beginning of the reign of the Roman Emperor Justinus, since which time some five-and-twenty years more or less had elapsed. Now, as it is known that the expedition was made in A.D. 522, and that Justinus was at that date in the fifth year of his reign, Cosmas must have been writing about the year 547. It is true that an indication which apparently conflicts with this appears in the tenth book (p. 351), where he speaks of Theodosius, the heretical Bishop of Alexandria, as residing at the time in Constantinople, and then on p. 353 refers to the death of his predecessor in office, Timothy the younger,[1] as an event of recent occurrence. Now it is known that this Timothy died in 535, and was succeeded by Theodosius, who, after a brief

---

[1] So called to distinguish him from Timothy the Cat.

residence in his diocese went to Constantinople, whence he was banished in 536. The tenth book must therefore have been written in the year preceding. How, then, is this earlier date to be reconciled with the later? Montfaucon answers this question satisfactorily. Cosmas, he points out, in order to meet objections urged against his opinions, was in the habit of making additions from time to time to the number of its books. The earlier date thus probably indicates the time when he began to make such additions, and the later when he was making the last, or one of the last, recensions of his work.

Opinions of the Learned regarding the "Topography."

The condemnatory verdict of Photius upon the work of Cosmas has not been endorsed by modern opinion. The style of the *Topography* has no doubt the shortcomings which the Patriarch pointed out; but Cosmas, it is proper to remember, expressly disclaims all pretensions to the learning of the schools. He pleads that from his early years he had been so engrossed in business, and had been besides so much abroad, that he had found no spare time for studying rules of grammar and the art of composition; he could, therefore, only write in a homely style, without attempting any flights of rhetoric. Rhetoric, moreover would, he thought, be out of place in his books, since "he wrote for

Christians, who had more need of correct notions than of fine phrases." The style has, notwithstanding, some redeeming points. Cosmas, in spite of his loose grammar, seldom fails to make his meaning clear, or to put forward his arguments with sufficient point and force. Some passages, besides, which give us an insight into the depth and fervour of his faith, rise to an eloquence which suggests the belief that, had he cultivated the art, he might have shone in pulpit oratory.

It is, however, in relating his travelling experiences that Cosmas is found at his best. The language he uses is simple, and his descriptions are not only remarkably vivid, but are, above all things, truthful. In this respect modern opinion is entirely at variance with that of Photius. The greater knowledge now possessed of the remote regions which Cosmas visited goes all to show that the thought of tickling the fancy of his readers with tales of wonder had never entered his mind, but that on the contrary he was a man who had a supreme regard for truth, and who was at once an acute observer, and shrewd in judging the value of the information which he received from others.

As soon as the *Topography*, in its complete edition by Montfaucon, made its appearance, it excited great interest in the circles of learning, and at once took rank as a work which contained more accurate and more valuable information on geographical subjects than any other document that had come down from the early mediæval age.

At the same time, the extreme singularity of the views which it propounded on cosmology and on the interpretation of Scripture texts filled its readers with combined feelings of amazement and amusement.

Bibliographical Notices.

The *Topography* was republished at Venice in 1776 in Gallandi's *Bibliotheca veterum Patrum*, and its most valuable sections were printed, along with a French translation, at Paris in 1855, in Charton's *Voyageurs Anciens et Modernes*. Its contents were made use of by Robertson in his *Disquisition on Ancient India*, and by Gibbon in his *History of the Decline and Fall of the Roman Empire*. The latter, referring to the absurd theory of the world held by Cosmas, remarks that "the nonsense of the Monk was, nevertheless, mingled with the practical knowledge of the traveller".

Among the eminent geographers who have turned the *Topography* to account may be mentioned Mannert, Gosselin, Humboldt, Dodwell, Playfair, Bredow, Reinaud, Létronne, Sir Henry Yule,[1] and Mr. Raymond Beazley ;[2] while among

---

[1] This distinguished Orientalist, in the Introduction to his *Cathay and the Way Thither*, has given a translation of the geographical portions of the *Topography*. He also occasionally cites the work in his celebrated edition of *Marco Polo*.

[2] This writer, in his work *The Dawn of Modern Geography*, published this year,—a work remarkable for learning and research, and its happy combination of accuracy of detail with breadth of

ecclesiastical writers may be noted Allatius, Bandini, De La Croze, Assemanni, Cave and Milne Rae.[1] The Adulitic inscriptions again have exercised the pens of such scholars as: Fabricius, Chishull, Vincent, Salt, Boeckh, V. de Saint-Martin, Dr. H. Müller of Vienna, and Dr. Glaser of Munich.

The System of the World according to Cosmas.

The *Christian Topography* is a production of which it may be truly said τὸ πάρεργον κρεῖττον τοῦ ἔργου. It is essentially controversial, its professed design being to refute, from Scripture and common sense, the impious Pagan cosmography, according to which the earth is a sphere; and the centre around which the heaven, which is also a sphere, revolves with all its luminaries. The arguments with which Cosmas seeks to demolish this theory and to illustrate his own are absurd in the extreme; and were it not for the geographical, historical, and other kinds of notices which are here and there incidentally introduced into its pages, his work would chiefly serve for amusement. According to his view, the figure of

---

view, makes frequent reference to the *Topography*, and even devotes an entire chapter to a searching analysis and criticism of its several books.

[1] Author of *The Syrian Church in India*, a well-written, scholarly work (published in recent years), in which he comes to the conclusion that there is no evidence of the planting of a Christian Church in Southern India before the beginning of the sixth century, or less than half a century before Cosmas wrote.

the universe can best be learned from a study of the structure and furniture of the Tabernacle which Moses prepared in the wilderness.[1] This wonderful conception did not originate with himself. Some of the Christian Fathers who preceded him had entertained it in a vague and general way, believing it might be warranted by the expressions in *Hebrews*, ix, 23 and 24, where the Tabernacle and its contents are said to be *patterns* (ὑποδείγματα) and *antitypes* or *figures of the true* (ἀντίτυπα τῶν ἀληθινῶν). It was left to Cosmas to develop the conception and work it out into all its details. So he explains again and again that the division of the Tabernacle into two places, by means of the veil, typified the division of the universe into two worlds—an upper and a lower, by means of the firmament. The table of shew-bread, again, with its waved border, represented the earth surrounded by the ocean, while its other parts and the things upon it symbolized each some object or other in the natural world. Now, as the table was twice as long as it was broad, and was placed lengthwise from east to west, and breadthwise from north to south, from this we learn that the earth is a rectangular plane which extends in length from east to west, and in breadth from north to south, and is twice as long as it is broad. The ocean, he further gives us to know, is unnavigable, and, while encompassing this earth of ours, is itself encompassed by another earth, which had been the

---

[1] Pp. 42-4, 299, and *passim*.

seat of Paradise and the abode of man until the Ark, floating on the billows of the Flood, wafted Noah and his family over into this earth. The heavens come downward to us in four walls, which, at their lower sides, are welded to the four sides of the earth beyond ocean, each to each. The upper side of the northern wall, at the summit of heaven, curves round and over, till it unites with the upper side of the southern wall, and thus forms, in the shape of an oblong vault, the canopy of heaven, which Cosmas likens to the vaulted roof of a bathroom. This vast rectangular hall is divided at the middle into two stories by the firmament, which thus serves as a ceiling for the lower story and a floor for the upper. The lower story is this world, where men and angels have their abode until the Resurrection, and the story above is heaven—the place of the future state.

As to the position ($\theta \acute{\epsilon} \sigma \iota s$) of the earth in the scheme of things, Scripture left Cosmas in no doubt. The Psalmist had declared that the Creator had founded the earth upon its own stability ($\dot{\epsilon} \pi \iota \ \tau \grave{\eta} \nu \ \dot{a} \sigma \phi \acute{a} \lambda \epsilon \iota a \nu \ a \dot{v} \tau \hat{\eta} s$); Job, that He had hanged it upon nothing; and Isaiah, that, while heaven was His throne, the earth was His footstool. Clearly, therefore, the place of the earth was at the bottom of the universe—a position to which it must have naturally sunk (as he shows in a very curious passage) at the very instant of its creation.[1] What then can be more absurd than the Pagan doctrine that the earth is in the

---

[1] See p. 29.

middle of the universe? Were it in the middle, there must be something *below* it as well as *above* it; but there is nothing *below* it, since we learn from Genesis that God made heaven and earth, and nothing else beyond these. Here then the Pagans are at war with divine Scripture; but, not content with this, they are at war also with common sense itself and the very laws of nature, declaring, as they do, that the earth is a central sphere, and that there are Antipodes, who must be standing head-downward and on whom the rain must fall *up*.

Referring to the figure of the world as thus conceived by Cosmas, Sir Henry Yule with grim humour remarked that "one of the huge receptacles in which female travellers of our day carry their dresses, forms a perfect model of the Kosmos of Kosmas". The theory, again, by which Cosmas accounts for the vicissitudes of day and night is no less preposterous than his idea of the figure of the world. The Pagan theory that the earth is spherical and placed in the centre of the universe, with the heavenly bodies revolving round it, accounted satisfactorily for the disappearance of the sun during the night; but where could Cosmas, in whose philosophy there was neither a spherical earth nor any under-world, find a place for the great orb of light when no longer visible? The problem did not baffle his ingenuity. Calling to his aid the words of Solomon, which declared that the sun on rising turned first towards the south and then towards the north, where he went down, and thence hastened to the place in which he arose, he made them the basis of the following extraordinary theory. The earth, he tells us, gradually rising up from the south, extends westward, until it culminates at last in a huge conical mountain situated somewhere in the far-away frozen north. Behind this immense cone, the sun at the close of day disappears from view, and leaves the world which we inhabit in darkness, until, having circled round the cone, he reappears in the east to give birth to a new day. According, moreover, as he is high or low during his nocturnal revolution, the nights vary in their length; while, owing to a slight obliquity in his motion, eclipses are produced. On the question of the magnitude of the great luminary Cosmas differed widely from the Pagan philosophers, and wrote his sixth book mainly to prove that, instead of its being, as they thought, many times larger than the earth, it was no more than the size of two only of the earth's climates or zones, those between the latitudes of Alexandria and Rhodes, and Rhodes and Constantinople, an extent of about 635 geographical miles.[1] But the words of Solomon form by no means the only Scriptural warrant for taking this view of the order of nature, for the candlestick placed on the south of the table of shew-bread typified the sun shining upon the earth from the south towards the north, while the waved border

---

[1] See pp. 251-2.

which ran round the table typified the ocean surrounded by the outer earth, both of which were illuminated by the sun while circling round the gigantic mountain.[1]

The Pagan theory which Cosmas especially detested, and made most frequently the subject of his scornful and violent invective, was that which maintained that the heavens were spherical and in constant revolution. He heaps text upon text to confute the advocates of this most pestilent doctrine, which, if admitted, would, he contended, abolish the future state and make the resurrection of Christ of no account.

But while Cosmas regarded as impious the doctrine that the heavens revolve, he admitted the revolution of the celestial luminaries, which, he held, were propelled in their courses by the angels, who do not live in heaven but are restricted to the aërial spaces below the firmament, until the resurrection.

All these and other views no less absurd, though interesting, Cosmas states and re-states with the most wearisome pertinacity, and holding them to be most vital verities, sanctioned alike by common sense and the paramount authority of divine Scripture, denounces again and again those reprobate Christians who, instead of accepting them, prefer, through their perverse folly or downright wickedness, to adopt the miserable Pagan belief

---

[1] See pp. 40-43 and 322-4.

that earth and heaven are spherical, and that there are Antipodes on whom the rain must fall *up*.

Criticisms of his System.

Since the *Topography* had for its main design the exposition of these views, it has been compared by Yule to "a mere bank of mud, but remarkable on account of certain geographical fossils which are found imbedded in it". This comparison, however, we venture to think, does less than justice to the work, for besides the geographical there are many other "fossils" to be found in the mud, of different kinds and generally of more or less interest and value. A list of these—but not pretending to be complete—has been given by Montfaucon in his Introduction. Among others may be specified the indication of Clysma as the place of the passage of the Red Sea; the wares brought by merchants to the Israelites when they sojourned in the wilderness; the seat of the terrestrial Paradise; the worship of Mithras by the Persians; the rite of baptism; the date of the Nativity; the question of the canonicity of the Catholic Epistles; the exposition of the prayer of Hezekiah; the inscriptions on the rocks found in the desert of Sinai; the state of Christianity in Socotra, Ceylon and India; the extent to which Christianity had spread over the heathen world; the interpretation of the prophecies of Daniel; extracts from Pagan writers and Fathers of the Church preserved only by Cosmas; and his views on the destiny of children who die in the womb or in infancy. The portion, moreover, of the *Topography* which is the "mud bank" of the comparison is not without some value. It is a specimen of a once prevalent and not yet quite extinct mode of Scriptural exegesis; it reveals what were some of the main currents of thought which permeated the Christian world at the beginning of the Middle Ages; it discloses to what a lamentable degree, as Monotheistic Christianity rose to the ascendant, triumphant alike over the Persian Dualism of the Manichæans, and the Greek Pantheism of the Neo-Platonists, the light of Hellenic learning and science had faded from Christendom before as yet Islam, which was destined to receive and preserve that light, had appeared in the world; and while it exhibits the attitude in which Theology and Science in those days stood to each other, it illustrates the signal danger of regarding Scripture as a store-house of divine communications which may be turned to account in defending or in oppugning scientific speculations. To quote Yule once more: "The work is a memorable example of that mischievous process of loading Christian truth with a dead weight of false science."

Other Works besides the "Topography" written by Cosmas.

Besides the *Christian Topography* Cosmas wrote several other works, of which the most important was one addressed to Constantinus, in which he described the whole earth. Cosmas mentions it in Book I. A second was entitled *A Delineation or Image of the Universe and of the Stellar Motion, made in imitation of the artificial Sphere of the Pagans, and a Treatise thereon addressed to the most Pious Deacon Homologus.* A third book was *A Commentary on the Song of Songs;* and a fourth *An Exposition of the Psalms.*

GENERAL NATURE OF THE CONTENTS OF EACH BOOK OF THE "TOPOGRAPHY."

To the *Topography*, when first published, Cosmas prefixed two prologues, in the first of which he exhorts his readers to bestow upon his works a diligent and careful perusal; and in the second, which contained the dedication to Pamphilus and apologies for his own shortcomings as a writer, he points out the nature of the contents of each of the five books of which the work then consisted. In the first book he attacks, and to his own satisfaction demolishes, the pernicious anti-Christian doctrines of the Pagan philosophy, that the world is spherical and that there are Antipodes. In the second he propounds the true theory which all Christians are bound to accept, based as it is upon the inspired Word, and maintained, besides, even by some of the Pagan philosophers themselves. By the citation of measurements of the earth made from east to west and from north to south, he seeks to prove that the length of the earth is twice its breadth. In the third book he insists on the authority and harmony of Scripture, adducing many texts, which, as in the preceding book, he twists with audacious ingenuity to lend support to his own impossible theory. In the two following books he again demolishes the doctrine of the spheres, while he re-states and fortifies his own theory with a long array of additional texts.

The publication of these books, which gave definite and uncompromising expression to views of which the germs had long been vaguely floating about in the air of Christendom, produced, as might have been expected from their novelty when seen wrought together into a self-consistent system, a startling effect. Objections were urged — directed especially against his views regarding the figure of the world. How, he was asked, could the sun, which was many times larger than the earth, be hidden behind the mountain in the north, however great its altitude? The sixth book was written to show that the sun, so far from being many times larger than the earth, was in point of fact only the size of two of the earth's "climates".

The seventh book, addressed to Athanasius, sought to refute a work written by a professing Christian, who held that heaven was an ever-revolving sphere, but nevertheless dissoluble. Cosmas cites and expounds numerous texts to show that the heavens cannot be dissolved, and that neither men nor angels can enter into them until after the Resurrection. The eighth book is addressed by Cosmas to another of his friends, called Peter, who had asked him to expound the Prayer of Hezekiah. The exposition is given, and Cosmas then proceeds to show how the minds of the Babylonians had been impressed by the miraculous sign of the retrogression of the shadow upon the sun-dial and how Cyrus had been led to favour the Jews and dismiss them from their Babylonian captivity by his reading the prophecies of Isaiah which referred to himself even by name. The ninth book, treating of the heavenly bodies, ascribes their motions to the angels, who groan under this hard and incessant toil which they perform for the benefit of man, and not for their own. They would have sunk, therefore, into despair, had they not seen that, even after the Fall, God was merciful and kind to man, on whose destinies their own depended. They were further encouraged when they afterwards saw that the Apostle Paul was caught up into the third heaven, and was there entertained with a glimpse of its glories.

In the tenth book Cosmas cites a number of the Fathers to show that his doctrines were in closest harmony with the teachings of the Church. In the eleventh, which is entirely geographical, he describes some animals and plants which he had seen or heard of in the course of his travels, and gives an account also of the island of Ceylon, and of its extensive commerce with India, Persia, China, and the countries of the west. The twelfth and last book shows that several of the old Pagan writers bore testimony to the antiquity of the Old Testament scriptures.

The Maps and Sketches which Illustrate the Views of Cosmas.

"There is," says Mr. Raymond Beazley, in the admirable work we have already referred to, "another interest about the *Topography*. It contains in all probability the oldest Christian maps that have survived. There is little reason to doubt that the numerous sketches .... which are to be found in the Florentine manuscript of the tenth century were really drawn by Cosmas himself (or under his direction) in the sixth; and are thus at least two centuries earlier than the Map of Albi, or the original sketch of the Spanish monk Beatus" (p. 281). The Plates found in the Appendix have been reproduced by photography from those which accompany Montfaucon's edition of the *Topography*.

The Place of Cosmas in History.

With regard to the place which Cosmas holds in history, we cannot do better than cite the estimate expressed by the same writer, whose wide and accurate knowledge of mediæval literature enables him to speak *ex cathedrâ* on the subject. "Cosmas," he says, "is of interest to us as the last of the old Christian geographers, and in a sense, too, the first

d

of the mediæval. He closes one age of civilization which had slowly declined from the self-satisfied completeness of the classical world, and he prepares us to enter another that, in comparison, is literally dark. From the rise of Islam the geographical knowledge of Christendom is on a par with its practical contraction and apparent decline. Even more than actual exploration, theoretical knowledge seemed on its death-bed for the next five hundred years" (p. 33). In a subsequent passage dealing with the same topic, he says: "The place of Cosmas in history has been sometimes misconceived. His work is not, as it has been called (in the earlier years of this century), the chief authority of the Middle Ages in geography. For, on the whole, its influence is only slightly, and occasionally, traceable. Its author stated his position as an article of Christian faith, but even in those times there was anything but a general agreement with his positive conclusions. . . The subtleties of Cosmas were left to the Greeks, for the most part; the western geographers who pursued his line of thought were usually content to stop short at the merely negative dogmas of the Latin Fathers; and no great support was given to the constructive tabernacle system of the Indian merchant. . . . Yet, after all, the *Christian Topography* must always be remarkable. . . . It is one of the earliest important essays in scientific or strictly theoretic geography, within the Christian aera, written by a Christian thinker" (p. 283). Mr. Beazley concludes his long notice of the great Christian Cosmographer in these terms: "He felt himself to be the apostle of full supernatural theory in science. He knew that his work was unique. And such it has always been recognised by some with rapture, by others with consternation, by most with derision. At least it is a monument of infinite, because quite unconscious, humour. 'For neither before him was any like unto him, neither shall be after.'"

THE CHRISTIAN TOPOGRAPHY;

OR,

THE OPINION OF CHRISTIANS CONCERNING THE WORLD.

BY COSMAS, AN EGYPTIAN MONK.

This book, which embraces the whole world, I have designated "Christianike Topographia". [113]

N the name of the Father and of the Son and of the Holy Ghost—the one adorable Godhead in three Persons—the consubstantial and life-originating Trinity of the one God, from whom every good gift and every perfect gift comes down to us from above, I, a miserable sinner, open my slow and stammering lips, trusting that for my humility's sake in soliciting utterance, and for the advantage of my hearers, He will give me the spirit of wisdom and utterance in the opening of my lips: He who is the Lord of Grace and Dispenser of all good things; God over all and blessed for evermore, Amen!

---

[1] The numerals in the margin indicate the pages in Montfaucon's edition of Cosmas in the *Nova Collectio Patrum*.

PROLOGUE I.

First of all I exhort those who will read this book to peruse it with all attention and diligence, and not to run over it in a perfunctory manner, but with loving pains to study it and take into their minds impressions of the places, figures, and histories which it contains; and when the book has been read to the end, let them further look into the volume which we have composed for that lover of Christ, Constantinus: a volume wherein we have described more fully the whole earth, both the one beyond the ocean, and this one, and all its countries, together with the southern parts from Alexandria to the Southern Ocean, namely, the river Nile and the countries adjacent, and all the races of Egypt and Ethiopia; the Arabian Gulf besides, with the countries adjoining and their inhabitants as far as the same ocean, and likewise the middle country between the river and the gulf, with the cities, districts and tribes therein contained—a volume[1] to prove that what things are said by us are true, and those false which are said by our adversaries, for whose sake this book and the drawings[2] it contains have been prepared—those, I mean, concerning the size of the sun, and that sun-burnt, uninhabited part of the world about which they din our ears, and vomit out fictions and fables. Let me next exhort my readers to examine the sketch[3] of the universe and the stellar motions which we have prepared as a representation of

---

[1] This work on Cosmography is one of the lost treasures of antiquity. Its loss appeared to Montfaucon one to be deplored even with tears.

[2] Καταγραφαὶ. The Latin version erroneously renders this by *paragraphi*.

[3] Gr. σκάριφον. See Sketch No. 6 in the Appendix, and for the stars, Sketch No. 9.

the organic sphere of the pagans[1], and to study the account of it sent to the pious deacon Homologus, then they with God's help are quite competent, especially with this book and the volume mentioned, to overthrow from the foundation the error of the pagan[2] theories. For if any Christian possesses these three works, and is by divine grace carefully exercised in the divine scriptures, he will easily confute the foolish views of the fable-mongers, for, from the figure itself, the constitution of the world and the very nature of things, they prove that the divine scriptures and the doctrines preached by Christians are perfectly true. Be strong then, ye Christians, in the Lord.

PROLOGUE II.

The Christian Topography of the whole world demonstrated from divine scripture, about which Christians ought not to doubt.

IN days long gone by I hesitated, O God-beloved, God-loving and Christ-loving[3] Pamphilus, to take in hand the treatise descriptive of the constitution of the whole world which you enjoined me to draw up. For even had I so wished, it was out of my power, as you well know, on account of the lingering illness by which I was prostrated.

---

[1] Τῶν ἔξωθεν, *lit.* of those without *the Church.*

[2] Ἑλληνικῶν. The Greek-speaking Jews used Ἕλλην, *Græcus*, and some of its derivatives, in the sense of *pagan, gentile, idolater*, apparently because the Greeks were the most prominent Gentile people with which they were acquainted. This signification passed into the works of Christian authors, the Greeks, properly so-called, being designated by the term Ἑλλαδικοί or Γραικοί.

[3] Θεοφιλῆ, Θεόφιλέ τε καὶ Χριστόφιλε. These were official titles. The superlative of the first, θεοφιλέστατος, was applied to the Emperor, bishops, deacons and monks. In the Greek church it is now applied only to ἐπίσκοποι.

But since, in answer to your frequent prayers, I have recovered from that illness, accept at last the Preface to the books of the work which I submit, partly as fulfilling the obedience I owe you, and partly as dreading the condemnation of the sluggish servant which the discourse of our Saviour in the Gospels has pronounced. And let no one condemn me as overbold, because I conduct the exposition of my subject in a style homely and unmethodical, since it is not fine phrases the Christian requires but right notions. For while many be the darts and helmets and shields and wars set in motion against the Church, some supposed to be Christians, holding divine scripture of no account but despising and looking down upon it, assume like the Pagan philosophers, that the form of the heavens is spherical, being led into this error by the solar and lunar eclipses.[1] We have therefore conveniently divided the subject of the book into five parts. In the outset then the first part is directed against the persons referred to who have been misled, and argues that one who wishes to profess Christianity cannot be led away by the plausible errors of those outside the Church—errors which are opposed to divine scripture. For should any one choose to examine closely the Pagan theories he will find them to be entirely fictitious, fabulous sophistries, and to be utterly impossible. Then again, for the Christian who will naturally ask and say: these being refuted, what are the true theories that must be admitted in opposition to them? I have written the second book, which proceeds to explain from divine scripture the nature of the Christian theories—to describe the figure of the whole world, and to notice that some of the ancient Pagans have been of the same opinion. Then again, by way of replying to one

---

[1] Aristotle from the circularity of the earth's shadow in eclipses inferred the rotundity of the earth.

who should doubt and ask : how does it appear that Moses and the prophets in saying such things say what is true? the third book exhibits the credibility of Moses and the Prophets, showing that they spake not of themselves, but as inspired by divine revelation, and that the writers alike of the Old and New Testament, men approved both by word and deed, having foreseen these things, declared them accordingly. It further shows what is the utility of delineations of the world, and how the notion of the sphere had its origin and beginning. The fourth book, again, has been written for behoof of those who wish to run their eye over the figures, and is a brief recapitulation, along with delineations, of what has been said before—a refutation, in fact, of the theory of the sphere and of the Antipodes. Then again, the fifth book has been written for those enquiring what the Christian theories are, and it shows that in what we have said and have represented by drawings we have neither devised fictions of our own nor invented new fables ; but from revelation and from what God who created the world has ordained, have beheld the pattern of the whole world—namely the Tabernacle prepared by Moses, which the New Testament consistently with this view has pronounced to be an image of the whole world ; and which also by means of the vail Moses divided, and so made one tabernacle into two, just as God also in the beginning divided what was one region, extending from the earth to the highest heaven, into two regions, by means of the firmament ; and just as in the tabernacle there was an outer and an inner place, so here there was a lower and an upper. Now the lower is this world, and the upper is the world to come, into which also the Lord Christ, after having risen according to the flesh from the dead, ascended the first of all, and into which the righteous shall in their turn afterwards ascend. And since from Adam to Moses, and from Moses to John, and from John all the Apostles and Evangelists, have each and all in harmony, and both by words and types spoken of these two states; and since not one of them has uttered a discordant note, either saying that there was a state before the first, or supposing that there is a third after the second; but all of them, as if inspired by the Holy Ghost, have proclaimed that there are but two states only, we, therefore, putting our confidence in the scriptures, which are truly divine, have not only sketched the figures of the whole world, but also of those very places by which you will find the Israelites made their exodus, also the mountain on which they received the law in writing, and were instructed in the knowledge of writing; also the delineation of the Tabernacle and the settlement in the Land of Promise; until he who was expected to arise from among them, and who was predicted by all the men of old and by the Prophets, did actually appear, proclaiming the future second state, which on his coming he showed in himself to us all, having entered into the inner Tabernacle, into the upper celestial region, into which at his second coming he shall call the righteous, saying: *Come, ye blessed of my Father, inherit the Kingdom prepared for you from the foundation of the world.* To Him be glory for ever, Amen!

BOOK I OF COSMAS, A MONK.[1]

Against those who, while wishing to profess Christianity, think and imagine like the pagans that the heaven is spherical.

S many as ardently desire true knowledge and are lovers of the true light, and earnestly endeavour to become fellow-citizens of the saints in the age to come, who regard the Old and New Testament as in reality divine scripture, who are obedient to Moses and the Christ, who follow out to the end the principles they have adopted, who acknowledge

---

[1] To this title Cosmas has prefixed the following: "The notes (παραγραφαί) which occur in this work have been inserted for the clearer exposition of the text (τοῦ κειμένου). The reader should therefore read first the text and then the notes." As Cosmas in this book seeks to confute the system of astronomy called the Ptolemaic—because Ptolemy, though not its founder, was its chief exponent—it may be of service if we remind the reader of the main outlines of that system. It assumed that the earth was the centre of the universe, and that the heavenly bodies revolved round it in perfect circles and at a uniform rate of motion. Such phenomena as were found to be inconsistent with these assumptions were explained by means of subsidiary hypotheses. The belief that the earth was the centre of the universe seemed to accord with the relation in which the primary elements of which the material world was thought to be composed stood to each other. Thus *earth*, as being the stablest element, held the lowest place and supported *water*, above which was placed *air*, and above that

that the world was produced by God out of mere nothing, and who believe that there is a resurrection of men and a judgment, and that the righteous shall inherit the Kingdom of Heaven; all these carefully examine the divine scriptures all throughout, to see whether in Moses, who wrote the account of the Creation, and in the other Prophets, they

---

again, *fire*, while *ether* was supposed to extend indefinitely above the others. In or beyond the ether were certain heavens, each of which contained a crystalline sphere, whereto was attached a heavenly body, which by the revolution of its crystalline sphere was made to move round the earth. When it was discovered that the planets move sometimes from west to east, sometimes from east to west, and for some time remain stationary at the point where progression ends and retrogression begins, the ancient astronomers were greatly puzzled, and to account for these irregularities in the planetary movements invented the hypothesis of epicycles. This doctrine is explained as follows in the article on the Ptolemaic System of Astronomy in Chambers's *Encyclopædia:* "The acceleration of the sun on one side, and retardation on the other side of his orbit, is only apparent, and results from the earth not being in the centre of his sphere, C (see fig.), but at E, and consequently his motion appears to be slowest at P and quickest at R.

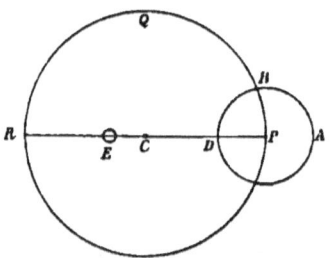

"The alternate progression and regression of the planets was accounted for by supposing them to move, not directly with their crystallines, but in a small circle whose centre was a fixed point in the crystalline, and which revolved on its axis as it was carried round with the latter; thus (fig.) the planet was carried round the small circle A B D, as that circle was carried round P Q R (now supposed to represent the planetary crystalline). The planet, while in the outer portion of its small circle, would thus have a forward and in the inner portion a backward motion. The larger circle was called an *eccentric* and the smaller an *epicycle*."

contain descriptions of the places and figures of the whole creation, among which is indicated also the position of the Kingdom of Heaven, which the Lord Christ promises God will give to righteous men. And when they find the Old and New Testaments to be in mutual harmony, they abide therein firmly grounded and immovable, in nothing confounded by their adversaries. But those on the other hand who prank themselves out in the wisdom of this world, and are self-confident that by scholastic reasonings they can comprehend its figure and position, scoff at all divine scripture as a mass of fables, stigmatising Moses and the prophets, the Lord Christ and the Apostles as idle babblers,[1] and given over to vain delusions ; while with supercilious airs, as if they far surpassed in wisdom the rest of mankind, they attribute to the heavens a spherical figure and a circular motion, and by geometrical methods and calculations applied to the heavenly bodies, as well as by the abuse of words and by worldly craft, endeavour to grasp the position and figure of the world by means of the solar and lunar eclipses, leading others into error while they are in error themselves in maintaining that such phenomena could not present themselves if the figure was other than spherical. But concerning these matters we shall not enter into any discussion just at present, since those persons sufficiently confute the one the other. But those who wish to profess Christianity, while wishing at the same time to

---

[1] Gr. σπερμολόγους. "The word", says Dr. Bloomfield in his annotated edition of the Greek New Testament, "was used properly of those small birds which live by picking up scattered seeds ; but metaphorically of those *paupers* who frequented the market-places, and lived by picking up any scattered or refuse produce ; and generally of *persons of abject condition,* without any certain means of support. Again, as the tribes of small birds which live by picking up seeds are especially garrulous, the word came to denote a *prater.*" Though Cosmas here uses the word in its metaphorical sense, he once or twice afterwards uses it in the literal sense of *a picker-up of seeds.*

bedeck themselves with the principles, the wisdom, and the diversity of the errors of this world, and contend that one thing and another should be accepted, seem to differ nothing from a shadow which exists while the intermediate body from which it is projected is in light, but which cannot exist when that body is not in light, nay, is even obliterated by the light when the body is illuminated all round.

It is against such men my words are directed, for divine scripture denounces them, as of old it denounced the strangers sojourning in Samaria, because they feared God and burned incense and offered worship on the high places.[1] Were one to call such men double-faced[2] he would not be wrong, for, look you, they wish both to be with us and with those that are against us, thus making void their renunciation of Satan whom they renounced in baptism, and again running back to him. Now, such men cannot be with us at all; but they occupy a middle position, like empty houses standing high up in the air, without having either foundations in the earth below, or anything from above to hold them fast.[3] For while they have as yet scarcely come by their principles they set about destroying them; and before they have yet destroyed them, they show that their end is unaccomplished, as they stand firm neither on the one side nor the other, but rather laugh at every one, and are themselves laughed at by all. In the first place, then, when arguing with them about the spherical figure, we showed that this figure was not possible, and was indeed quite inconsistent with the nature of things. Certain of them say that the heaven is a body consisting of four elements,[4] but some later on superciliously recon-

---

[1] See II Kings, xvii, 24-41.
[2] Gr. διμόρφους, lit. two-formed.
[3] An anticipation of the myth regarding Mahomet's coffin.
[4] The Platonists.

structed it with an additional fifth new element,[1] though formerly its essential constitution comprised only four elements, for they saw at a glance that the heaven could not revolve if it was composed of these. But herein again they are found to be blind even when they think that those who are sharp-sighted do not see. For since the heaven is seen to be of sundry and diverse colours, whence a power to produce heat and cold seems to be inherent in them, they say that the eyes of all are deceived by reason of their immense distance. Well, then, let any one of them who so wishes come forward and tell us: Why do the stars which, according to you are evidently fixed in an immovable sphere, not apparently differ in colour and size, though their distances from us are seen to be unequal, if the centre of the earth be the point from which our eyes are directed towards them? And how is it that many of the fixed stars are equal and like to the planet we call Mars, to which a lower sphere has been assigned, and how do we in like manner see not a few of them to be like the planet Jupiter? But

---

[1] Aristotle invented a term, ἐντελέχεια, to denote *actuality* of existence in contrast to its mere potentiality, δύναμις. His followers, however, eventually came to use the term in the sense of a *fifth element*, namely *mind*, which differed entirely in its nature from the four elements of common speech. To this effect I may quote the words of Cicero: "Dicæarchus .... quemdam Phthiotam senem .... disserentem inducit, nihil esse omnino animum et hoc esse nomen totum inane .... Aristoteles .... quum quattuor nota illa genera principiorum esset complexus, e quibus omnia orerentur, quintam quamdam naturam censet esse, e qua sit mens. Cogitare enim et providere et discere .... hæc et similia eorum in horum quattuor generum inesse nullo putat: quintum genus adhibet vacans nomine et sic ipsum animum ἐνδελέχειαν appellat novo nomine quasi quamdam continuatam motionem et perennem." (*Tusc. Disp.*, i, 21, 22). Cicero has here confounded ἐντελέχειαν with ἐνδελέχειαν, of which he has given the meaning correctly. Probably he had not seen the word in the written pages of Aristotle, but only heard it from the lips of Greek Peripatetics, who, like their countrymen of the present day, pronounced the letter ταῦ very like δέλτα.

further, we do not even see the heaven itself to be of one and the same colour, for, if it were asked from whence can we surmise that the cloud-like concretions which you have named the galaxy, and which you have so designated simply because of the difference of their colour, have derived their peculiar appearance, while the surface on which the ray of vision strikes is uniform? and if I replied that these were proofs of the composition and mixture of different elements, no one, I apprehend, would dare to contradict me, even though he were a lover of falsehood, and much less if one of those who always assign the foremost place to truth. Now if the heaven has been constituted not of one single element endowed with a circular motion of its own, but of the mixture of the four elements, then it cannot well revolve. For it has been said that it must either be moved downward if the heavy element preponderate, or be carried upward if the opposite light one prevail, or must be stationary when no element is preponderant. This is certainly obvious to everybody. For no one would admit that he has ever seen the heaven move either upwards or downwards.[1] It must be allowed therefore that it is firmly fixed. But should they ask : Whence are these motions that differ from the rest in an element that is simple and without qualities? since they say, and not untruly, that those bodies which they call planets revolve oppositely to the universe; and if in like manner they say that their revolution is accomplished in certain

---

[1] The Greek text, so far as I can see, must be wrongly punctuated. Οὐδὲ γὰρ ἄνω φερόμενον, οὐδὲ κάτω, τίς ὁμολογήσειεν ἑωρακέναι πώποτε ; I remove the mark of interrogation and construe the negative with τις, and not with φερόμενον. The Latin version, however, follows the punctuation : Quis autem dicat se vidisse coelum nec sursum nec deorsum ferri ? This rendering is inconsistent with the immediately subsequent context, where the author states his own view that the heaven is immoveable.

times which the Creator has fixed, it is evident that they do not even deny that the planets advance from the East.[1]

Then being mazed with perplexing doubts, as usually happens to those who shrink from the truth, they say, on finding no way of escape, that the stars make retrogressions and pauses. But tell me, ye souls that are so ingenious in tying and untying knots, if from their very nature they have motion, how comes it that they stand still? For nothing that can thwart them enters as an element into their natural constitution. And tell me this besides, what is the force or what the necessity which imposes on them the contrary motion? And here let no one tell me that it is an ocular deception; for it is no minute distance to which they advance, seeing that they are often observed to shift their place from a sign of the zodiac that is in the rear to one in front. But what must we say of our opponents when passing on to the operations of the stars themselves, they reach the very height of absurdity, all unconscious that they themselves stand still or move backward, and are but a sorry set of good-for-nothing rascals? Now anyone would say that the star previously seen in Aries, but at present appearing in Pisces, was not in the house of Mars, but in that of Jupiter, and that it makes *movements*, not such as they babble about when it is in Aries, but those which they ascribe to it in its transit through Pisces. But if they do not admit the retrograde motion *of the planets* which is apparent, whence then or wherefore is their course in both directions? They will perhaps in reply assign as the cause those invisible epicycles which they have assumed as vehicles on which, as they will insist, the planets are borne along. But they will

---

[1] This sentence ends with a clause which cannot be construed with it, but which might serve to begin the next paragraph. The clause is: 'Ουράνιον τε ποιούμενοι πορείαν = Then when making (*i.e.* tracing) the course *of the planets* through heaven.

be in no better case from this invention, for we shall ask: Why have they need of vehicles? Is it because they are incapable of motion? Then, if so, why should you assert them to be animated, and that too even with souls more than usually divine? Or is it that they are capable? The very idea is, methinks, ridiculous. And why have not the moon and the sun their epicycles? Is it that they are not worthy on account of their inferiority? But this could not be said by men in their sober senses. Was it then from the scarcity of suitable material the Creator could not construct vehicles for them? On your own head let the blasphemy of such a thought recoil.

Cease, O ye wiseacres! prating worthless nonsense, and learn at last though late to follow the divine oracles and not your own baseless fancies. For, tell us, how ye think that the fixed stars move in an opposite direction to the universe? Is such a motion theirs only or that of the sphere in which they are placed? Then, if it is theirs, how do they traverse unequal orbits in equal time? And how comes it that of the stars in the galaxy not one has ever gone outside of it, nor any of those outside is seen nearer it or within it? But if one should say that it is the sphere which moves in the opposite direction, then it will be found that at the same time it moves oppositely to itself. But who can imagine a greater absurdity than this? Thus they do their best to prevent any one surpassing them in their effrontery—or rather, let me say, in impiety, since they do not blush to affirm that there are people who live on the under surface of the earth. What then, should some one question them and say: Is the sun to no purpose carried under the earth? these absurd persons will, on the spur of the moment, without thinking, reply that the people of the Antipodes are there—men carrying their heads downwards, and rivers having a position opposite to the rivers here! thus taking in hand to turn every thing upside down rather than to follow the doctrines of the truth, in which there are no futile sophisms, but which are plain and easy and full of godliness, while they procure salvation for those who reverently consult them.

But you will most effectually rebuke them if you say: Why does that sphere of yours not revolve from the north to the south, or from some other quarter to its opposite? And do not tell me, in answer, that such seemed better to the Maker of the world, for my[1] .... But how can you deem that you speak consistently with the nature of things in supposing that the whole heaven is in motion and describes a circle, without also supposing that outside of it there is either some other space or body, even though it were imaginary. For it is impossible any thing can move apart from the four elements, but must move either in earth, or in water, or in air, or in fire, whether it is transferred from place to place into the infinite, or whether it always revolves in the same place. But if the heaven as it revolves passes into the infinity of space, we must suppose that beyond it there is an infinite earth into which it rolls, when noiselessly leaving what is behind it; but if one of the other three elements be supposed, in not one of them is the sphere adapted to roll and rotate; nay, were it to be shot into any of them, a whizzing noise would attend the transition. But if, again, it rolls and rotates always in the same spot without moving from place to place, then it must be upheld by supports like a turner's lathe, or an artificial globe, or on an axis like a machine or a waggon. And if so, then we must again inquire by what the supports and axles are themselves upheld, and so on *ad infinitum*. And tell me, pray, how are we to suppose the axis passes through the middle of the earth, and of what material it consists.

When these problems then concerning the nature of

---

[1] The hiatus has after it ἐσθαι φθεγγόμενος.

things are discussed, there remains the conclusion, as we said before, that the heaven is fixed and does not revolve. But even in supposing that the earth is in the middle of the universe, as its centre, you immediately give the death-blow to your own theory when you repeat that the middle is below, for it is impossible that the same thing can at once both be in the middle and below, for the middle is the middle between up and down, or between right and left, or between before and behind. Why do you then, when beleaguered with difficulties, utter absurdities contrary to nature, in opposition to scripture? For being in terror lest any one should pose you with this question: How can this unspeakable weight of the earth be held suspended by the air and not fall down? you have invented stories of things that are not true, but strange; and, reversing the order of things, give out that the middle is below; so that if any should suppose that instead of the earth, fire was the middle, you would then say that the middle was above instead of below, seeing that the tendency of fire is upward. To me, therefore, they seem to subvert the first by means of the second, and the second by means of the first. But if they say that the air because it surrounds the earth equally on all sides, is pushed on by the universe, and that the earth remains immovable, and swerves neither to the one side nor the other, why do men[1] and the irrational animals that live on land or fly in the air not move along with it, while all of them cleave the air in walking and in traversing it, and in going on high. And not only is it incapable of resisting these, but it cannot even sustain the weight of the lightest inanimate things, such as the shortest of feathers and the smallest of straws, but all of them cut it, it is so attenuated and so rare, and they outstrip it according to the force with which they are propelled. How then can we receive such false theories?

---

[1] The text has ἀνθρώπους, an evident mistake for ἄνθρωποι.

But should one wish to examine more elaborately the question of the Antipodes, he would easily find them to be old wives' fables. For if two men on opposite sides placed the soles of their feet each against each, whether they chose to stand on earth, or water, or air, or fire, or any other kind of body, how could both be found standing upright? The one would assuredly be found in the natural upright position, and the other, contrary to nature, head downward.[1] Such notions are opposed to reason, and alien to our nature and condition. And how, again, when it rains upon both of them, is it possible to say that the rain falls down upon the two, and not that it falls down to the one and falls up to the other, or falls against them, or towards them, or away from them. For to think that there are Antipodes compels us to think also that rain falls on them from an opposite direction to ours; and any one will, with good reason, deride these ludicrous theories, which set forth principles incongruous, ill-adjusted, and contrary to nature.

And if one should examine that other sophism of theirs, namely, that the earth is inflated with air, and that earthquakes occur when the pent-up air shakes the earth violently, he would be amazed at the imposture and the contradiction in their statements. For if the earth when equally pressed by the whole air stands unshaken and unswerving, then, when inflated it ought to be all the heavier in that quarter, and to swerve to a side, after the example of man which they adduce. For not only does a man shake and tremble when attacked with flatu-

---

[1] See Cicero, *Acad. Prior.*, 2, 39, and Plutarch, 2, 869 C., on Antipodes. Nearly all the Christian Fathers held the same opinion as Cosmas about the Antipodes: as, for instance, Lactantius, who asks: "Est quisqam tam ineptus qui credat esse homines, quorum vestigia sint superiora quam capita?" Augustin, Chrysostom, Severianus of Gabala, Beda, were likewise anti-Antipodeans.

lency, but he trembles when seized with terror, and when overcome with wine, and pinched with cold, and when his blood boils with anger, and when he is old and imbecile, but when he reels under the effects of flatulency death results. Why then does not the earth also, which according to them is inflated with air, not collapse and lose its proper place? And why, again, do they further say that Egypt, because its soil is porous and its furrows allow the air to escape without violent shocks, is not subject to earthquakes, while in point of fact earthquakes have been of frequent occurrence in that country, and so violent as to overthrow cities and level them with the ground: and not only so, but even in the times of the Greeks, when Alexander, and Seleucus, and Antiochus, and Ptolemy ruled and reigned, they had recourse to the assistance of philosophers—Aristotle and his like—and frequently gave practical effect to what they advised? And when Antioch was being founded by Seleucus[1] and Antiochus, how was it that the philosophers were not able to point out that the country there was not safe from earthquakes, but on the contrary exposed to their frequent visitations? And this we say from having seen that this city has been repeatedly overthrown by earthquakes; and not Antioch only but Corinth also, which has close at her hand the mob of the philosophers.

But if we should care to examine yet another of their opinions—that in which they say and try to prove by illustrations—that rain is produced from vapour drawn up

---

[1] Antioch on the Orontes was founded by Seleucus Nicator in 300 B.C. Its first recorded earthquake occurred in 148 B.C., and it has frequently suffered since from the same cause. The one to which Cosmas here refers occurred in 526 A.D., and almost entirely destroyed the city, which, however, Justinian had rebuilt with great splendour before it was captured by Chosroes in 540 A.D. Corinth also suffered severely from this memorable earthquake.

by heat into the atmosphere, in the same way, say they,
as the bath draws up vapour from the heat, and lets it fall
in drops; and just as a cupping-glass draws up moisture
by means of tow and fire, so too does the sun draw up
vapour, and in course of time lets it fall in drops, whence
rain is produced. One cannot but marvel at such wisdom
as this, imposing, as it does by its speciousness, upon the
multitude. For since the bath derives its heat not from
above but from below, how can it be said to draw up, and
not rather to push up? So too in the case of a caldron :
it receives its heat not from above but from below, and in
both instances the vapours are pushed up by the heat, and in
the rebound, due in the one case to the roof and in the
other to the lid, they fall in drops. Similar is the case of
the cupping-glass, which, did not this instrument itself
constrain nature and suck up moisture, would never have
sucked it up at all,[1] no, not even if fire and tow had been
applied ten thousand times over. But further, when one
thrusts a damp faggot into the fire, moisture is to such a
degree pushed by the heat that both moisture and smoke
are expelled from the other end of the faggot. And when
one has kindled a fire on the ground he sees the moisture
in the faggots conveyed upwards by the smoke, not drawn
up by what is above but pushed up by the heat of the fire.
Nay, more, if one washes a garment and spreads it on the
ground, and if, when it has been dried by the sun, he lifts
it up, he will find the moisture which has been expelled
from it by the heat impressed on the ground in the very

---

[1] Gr. σικύα, which means both a *cucumber* and a *cupping-glass*. Montfaucon renders the word by the Latin *cucumis*, which means a *cucumber* but not a *cupping-glass*. Can he have used it in mistake for *cucurbita*? Charton does not give this illustration, though he gives the two which precede it. The argument is that it is the instrument (ὄργανον, *i.e.*, the cupping-glass), which draws up the blood to the punctures, and not the heat from the wick burning inside the glass to produce a vacuum. There is an ambiguity in the statement of the argument.

shape of the garment. In like manner, if one places a hot piece of meat on a trencher he will see the moisture discharged in both directions, both upwards and downwards, the heat being intermediate, for above he sees the steam mounting upwards, and below he sees the trencher bathed in moisture on which the meat has impressed its own shape; whence it appears that heat does not draw up, as these sages tell us, but rather pushes up.

But when we propose a new question to them: Why is it that in the Thebaïd, where the ground is parched up by the heat, the moisture is not drawn up and turned into rain for that country? they defend themselves by saying that it is a moderate and not an excessive heat that causes the drawing up. To this we shall give a very summary reply: And how happens it, we shall ask, that beyond the Thebaïd, in Ethiopia, where the heat is far greater, there are frequent copious downfalls of rain? And how can they say, those many and tip-top wise men, that the sun has the power of drawing upwards, and assert also quite confidently that in the course of his revolution he becomes heated by friction, while they will not entertain the supposition that the heat is in him by nature. But more: when they allow that the air is moist and hot, what need have those wiseacres to resort to sophistry and say that the moisture is drawn up from elsewhere, when up above they have the heat and moisture at the same spot? But if one should ask them about one particular element as it is in itself, that is, should ask them to show its distinctive quality, they immediately find themselves at a loss, and attribute two qualities to one single element and say: Earth is *dry and cold ;* water, *cold and moist ;* air, *moist and warm ;* fire, *warm and dry ;* so that, being beleaguered with difficulties, they assign eight qualities to the four elements. But at times they say that all the qualities exist in each of the elements. Once more, therefore, they contradict their own words, by ascribing not four but only two qualities to each of the four elements. I marvel accordingly at those most excellent men when they attribute to water *coldness and humidity*, and to the air *humidity and heat*. How do they say that water, that is, the *cold and moist*, congeals and becomes ice in winter-time? Wherefrom comes that extreme cold which converts it into ice? For if they shall say that the departure of the sun naturally produces this effect, why does it not produce the same effect on the air, which is naturally *warm*, and at the same time *moist*, but makes it, on the contrary, extremely *cold?* And how does *the cold* itself—that is, water—not make the air—that is, *the moist*—freeze, but, on the contrary, it is the latter which makes the former freeze, as we actually see? Now though I have many things more to say about this question and the examples which they erroneously adduce in favour of their view of it, I curb myself, for I feel ashamed of the foolishness of what is said by them, and consider what has already been said on this subject sufficient.

There is, however, another sophism held by these wise men which I am especially anxious to deal with, and will forthwith proceed to discuss. They say that the heaven which they call a body contains the whole world, and stoutly maintain that outside of it nothing whatever exists; and yet they define angels and demons and souls, which are parts of the world as uncircumscribed, neither containing the heaven, nor contained by the heaven, not understanding what they say, since that which neither contains nor is contained is never by any possibility seen among things that are. If then these things be as they say, let them tell us with respect to their own soul whether it is, or is not. And if they say it is not, then to their own shame and disgrace they assume themselves to be soulless. But if they say that it exists, let them tell us whether it is in them or is not in them. If they reply that it is not in them, they answer not less shamelessly and foolishly than they did before. But if they reply that the soul is in them, we must ask them a further question: As the body is circumscribed by the heaven, why is not the soul also circumscribed? And if, as they say, it illuminates the body without being circumscribed along with it, the question arises, where is it when it illuminates the body? since it is impossible that, being a created thing, it should not exist with things created. And if they say it exists somewhere within the heaven, then it is again circumscribed by the body itself of the heaven, although it was represented by them as uncircumscribed. But if they make it exist outside the heaven, they, in the first place, confute themselves; in the next place, it will either be in a part of the heaven and occupy but a small part of it, or it will be in the whole of it, in which case it will circumscribe the heaven and will be found having form like a bodily substance; and this a spherical form embracing and limiting the sphere. But if, again, they say that as being uncircumscribed it pervades all things both within and without, let them not blind themselves to the fact that they are both introducing polytheism and imagining an equality with God. For this property pertains to none except the uncreated Deity who created and fashioned the universe. So then, professing themselves to be wise, they become fools, as says the blessed Paul the Apostle, having changed the glory of the uncircumscribed Deity to their own created souls, thus appropriating to themselves the glory due to God. They must therefore in every way be avoided. For, saith the Apostle, from those turn away who hold an outward form of godliness but deny the power thereof.

BOOK II.

The Christian theories regarding the form and position of the whole world, the proofs of which are taken from Divine Scripture.

OW long I put off the composition of my work regarding the figure of the world, even though other admirable men as well as thyself frequently urged me to undertake it, you know best of all, O dearest, God-loving and Christ-loving Pamphilus, a man worthy of that name, since all holy men love thee[1]—a sojourner in the earthly Jerusalem, but enrolled among the first-born and the prophets, with whom when of yore I knew thee only by report I was knit in the bonds of warmest friendship; but now I have had the satisfaction of having seen thee face to face, when by the will of God you came hither to us, to Alexander's great city, and never ceased to importune us about this work, enfeebled though we were in body, afflicted with ophthalmia and costiveness of the bowels, and as the result suffering afterwards from constant attacks of illness; while besides we were deficient in the school-learning of the Pagans,[2] without any knowledge of the rhetorical art,

---

[1] A play upon the name of Pamphilus, which means *beloved by all*.
[2] Gr. τῆς ἔξωθεν ἐγκυκλίου παιδείας. Ἐγκύκλιον παιδεία, the circle of the arts and sciences taught in Greek schools.

ignorant how to compose a discourse in a fluent and
embellished style, and were besides occupied with the com-
plicated affairs of everyday life. Nevertheless you ceased
not pressing us to compose a treatise about the Tabernacle
prepared by Moses in the wilderness, which was a type
and copy[1] of the whole world, as I explained to thee
personally by the living voice in a cursory way, not as
communicating opinions and conjectures of my own
framing, but what I had learned from the divine scriptures,
and from the living voice of that most divine man and
great teacher Patricius, who when fulfilling the vows of
the Abrahamic rule,[2] set out from Chaldæa with his
disciple Thomas of Edessa, a holy man who followed him
wherever he went, but by the will of God was removed
from this life at Byzantium. Patricius propagated the
doctrines of holy religion and true science, and has now
by the grace of God been elevated to the lofty episcopal
throne of all Persia, having been appointed to the office of
Bishop Catholic of that country.[3] So then being greatly
perplexed about this undertaking, on account more

---

[1] Gr. τύπος καὶ ὑπογραφή.

[2] Gr. ὡς τάξιν Ἀβραμιαίαν πληρῶν. Abram, or Abraham, of Cascar,
who flourished about the beginning of the sixth century of our aera,
retired into the desert of Scete and dwelt in a cave on Mount Izla,
near Nisibis. He founded a monastic order among the Nestorians.
The ὡς πληρῶν of the text is translated both by Montfaucon and De la
Croze: *quum implevisset*, but erroneously. The use of the present
participle indicates that Patricius set out to teach in fulfilment of
the vows of his order.

[3] According to the Latin version of Montfaucon, it was Patricius
who died at Byzantium, and Thomas who became Primate of Persia.
This rendering, however, conflicts with the rules of Greek syntax,
and states, besides, what is historically untrue. For from the
Catalogue of the Nestorian Patriarchs it has been clearly proved
that Patricius, who was a Magian and was called by the Syrians Abas
or Mar-Abas, became Bishop Catholic of the whole of Persia. This
passage has received much notice from writers on early ecclesiastical

especially of those who delight in censoriousness, whose tongues are glib at calumny, and who can always find abundance of material for their scoffs and jeers, I shrank with more than ordinary hesitation from addressing myself to the work. But you again pressed me to proceed with it, loading me with condemnation upon condemnation if I refused, and assuring me that the work would be useful for the guidance of life and for the study and understanding of the divine doctrines, as well as for a refutation of the Greek preconceptions; while showing that the whole scope of divine scripture has respect to the future state, as is most pointedly affirmed by the Apostle when he says: *For we know that if the earthly house of this our tabernacle were dissolved we have a building of God—a house not made with hands, eternal in the heavens.*[1] When in these and such like terms you appealed to me, and it was beyond my power to gainsay the injunctions laid upon me by your piety, I consented, trusting to receive the benefit of your prayers; while making supplication ourselves that the divine grace without which we can do nothing aright

---

history, and has been used to show that Cosmas was himself a Nestorian.

The real founder of Nestorianism was Theodorus of Mopsuestia. "In the Persian School of Edessa", says Gibbon, "the rising generations of the faithful imbibed their theological idiom; they studied in the Syriac version the ten thousand volumes of Theodore of Mopsuestia, and they revered the Apostolic faith and holy martyrdom of his disciple Nestorius, whose person and language were equally unknown to the nations beyond the Tigris"; vol. viii, c. 47. Nestorius, a presbyter of Antioch, was appointed Patriarch of Constantinople in 428, but having been deposed by the Council of Ephesus, was banished first to Antioch and afterwards to the Greater Oasis in Upper Egypt, where he died before the year 450. The Nestorians, or Chaldaean Christians as they call themselves, are still numerous in the East, and retain their tendency to distinguish carefully between the human and divine natures of Christ, and their objection to call the Virgin Mary the *Mother of God.* [1] II Cor. v, 1.

might be vouchsafed to us in the opening of the mouth, so that we might be able without polished and artistic modes of expression, but in the simple words of ordinary speech (while grace manifests her own peculiar powers), both to teach her foster-children the divine knowledge of the doctrines, the lives of pious men, and the figure of the world and its origin, without ambiguity; as well as to describe with all readiness, and to communicate ungrudgingly, what we ourselves have freely received from God.

Having finished, therefore, O God-beloved, the first book concerning pretended Christians, and having convicted them, to the best methinks of my power, of having attempted impossibilities, without our having sought to disparage the beauty of their language, which God forbid I should do, but to refute the fictitious and fabulous Greek theories; and having finished that book, we now in obedience to thy order proceed to discuss first in this second book the Christian theories regarding the figures and the position of the world. We shall then in the third book show that in describing and explaining the utility of the figures of the world, divine scripture alike in the Old and the New Testament is in itself sure and trustworthy. In the fourth book again we shall offer a recapitulation and a delineation of the figures of the world; and similarly shall in the fifth book present a description of the tabernacle prepared by Moses, and exhibit the harmony of what has been said by the Prophets and Apostles. Be this then the book which we have entitled *Christian Topography*, embracing the whole world and deriving its proofs from the truly divine scriptures, regarding which a Christian is not at liberty to doubt. Since then aid from above, as has been said, coöperates with us through your prayers, we proceed to state our theories. Moses, then, the Divine Cosmographer, says: *In the beginning God made the heaven and the earth.*[1] We assume, therefore, that heaven and earth comprise the universe as containing all things within themselves. And that this is so he himself again proclaims: *For in six days God made the heaven and the earth and all that in them is*[2]; and again in like manner he says: *And the heaven and the earth were finished and all the host of them.*[3] And again, when recapitulating and giving its name to the book, he speaks thus: *This is the book of the generation of heaven and earth,*[4] as if they contained all things, and as if all things that are in them ought to be signified along with them. For if, according to the counterfeit Christians, the heaven alone comprises the universe, he would not have mentioned the earth along with the heaven, but he would have said: This is the book of the generation of heaven. Evidently, however, he has not done so, nor any other of the prophets, and it is manifest that they knew that the two together comprised the universe, and indeed the whole company of the righteous and of the prophets always indicate the heaven along with the earth. Hear what each of them says. Melchisedech first when blessing Abraham thus speaks: *Blessed be Abraham of God most High who created the heaven and the earth.*[5] In the second place, Abraham says: *I will stretch out my hand to God most High who created the heaven and the earth.* And again: *Place thine hand under my thigh and I will make thee swear by the Lord the God of the heaven and the God of the earth.*[6] For when the most faithful Abraham wished to make his servant swear with more than usual solemnity by the circumcision as being a seal royal, *Place,* he said, *thine hand under my thigh,* instead of under the seal royal, that is, the circumcision. See also: Gen. xxiv, 7;

---

[1] Gen. i, 1. [2] Exod. xx, 11. [3] Gen. ii, 1. [4] Ibid., 4.
[5] Gen. xiv, 19. [6] Gen. xxiv, 2.

127 Psalm cxiv, 15; cxxxiv, 6, ci, 25; Isai. xlii, 5; Zech. xii, 1; Isai. li, 13, xliv, 24, xlviii, 13, xlvi, 1, xl, 22; Jerem. x, 11; Daniel iii, 59; Acts xvii, 24, xiv, 15; Math., xi 25.[1] Since then the divine scripture of both the Old and the New Testament shows by its customary declarations that all things are contained within heaven and earth, how is it possible that one can be a Christian who disbelieves all this, and says that all things are contained within the heaven only.

128 Since then the heaven and the earth comprise the universe, we assert that the earth has been founded on its own stability by the Creator, according once more to the divine scripture, and that it does not rest upon any body; for in the Book of Job it is written: *He hangeth the earth upon nothing;* and again (xxxviii, 4, 5, 6): *Where wast thou when I laid the foundations of the earth? etc.* And in like manner in David (Psalm cii, 5) it is said: *He who laid the foundations of the earth upon its own stability.* By the power, therefore, of the Deity who created the universe, we say that it was founded and is supported by him. *Upholding all things,* as the Apostle saith, *by the word of his power.*[2]

For if a body of any kind whatever were either underneath the earth or outside of it, that body could not keep its place, but would fall down according to what is seen always occurring in the natural world. For if we take air, for instance, or water or fire, we find that things which are heavier than these do invariably fall down in them. Since therefore the earth is heavier than any other body whatever, the Deity placed it as the foundation of the universe, and made it steadfast in virtue of its own inherent stability. To illustrate this, let us suppose a place to have a depth

---

[1] The passages are quoted in full both in the Latin and the Greek text.   [2] Heb. i, 3.

of a hundred cubits, and this place to be filled with a body denser say than water; then if one should lift a stone with his hand and drop it into the place, in what interval of time would it reach the bottom? One may reply, in four hours, let us say. But further, supposing the place to be filled with some rarer substance, air, for example, in what interval of time would the stone now reach the bottom? Evidently in a shorter time: in two hours, let us say. Supposing in the next place a still rarer substance, then the bottom will be reached in an hour, and with a yet rarer substance in half an hour. And again, if a rarer still be supposed, the stone will touch the bottom in a still shorter time; and so on until the body when attenuated to the last degree becomes incorporeal, and the time ceases of necessity to be any time at all. Thus then in the case supposed, where no body at all exists, but where there is only the incorporeal, the heavy body of necessity gains the bottom in no time at all and becomes stationary. The Deity, having thus in the order of nature, as the scripture declares, suspended the earth upon nothing, when it had reached the bottom of space laid its foundations upon its own stability so that it should not be moved for ever. But should one again, from a wanton love of contradiction, assume that outside of earth and heaven there exists a place made of another invisible and imaginary substance, even such a place must of necessity rest upon something else, and this again upon another, and so on *ad infinitum*. Nevertheless let us, with God's help, tackle this subject as more a question of physical science. If one should suppose that place to be chaos, then because . . . . .[1] as the heaven is light and tends upwards, and the

---

[1] Here some passage or passages must have fallen out, as there is no connection between the opening and the conclusion of the sentence. Cosmas, besides, does not here tackle, as he must have done in accord-

earth heavy and tends downwards, and extremes are bound together with extremes, that, namely, which tends upwards with that which tends downwards, they support the one the other by their pulling against each other, and so remain unmoved. The Deity accordingly having founded the earth, which is oblong, upon its own stability, bound together the extremities of the heaven with the extremities of the earth, making the nether extremities of the heaven rest upon the four extremities of the earth, while on high he formed it into a most lofty vault overspanning the length of the earth. Along the breadth again of the earth he built a wall from the nethermost extremities of the heaven upwards to the summit, and having enclosed the place, made a house, as one might call it, of enormous size, like an oblong vaulted vapour-bath. For, saith the Prophet Isaiah (xlix, 22): *He who established heaven as a vault.* With regard, moreover, to the glueing together of the heaven and the earth, we find this written in Job: *He has inclined heaven to earth, and it has been poured out as the dust of the earth. I have welded it as a square block of stone.*[1] Do not the expressions about inclining it to the earth and welding it thereto clearly show that the heaven standing as a vault has its extremities bound together with the extremities of the earth? The fact of its inclination to the earth, and its being welded with it, makes it totally inconceivable that it is a sphere.[2]

---

ance with what he says, the assumption that there was a place outside heaven and earth. I have indicated by marks, which, however, are found neither in the Greek text nor Latin version, that here there must be a hiatus.

[1] Gr. κεκόλληκα δὲ αὐτὸν ὥσπερ λίθον κύβον. Cosmas, in quoting the Old Testament, always uses the Septuagint. The reading in the Vatican copy of the Septuagint is λίθῳ κύβῳ. The English Revised Version reads: *When the dust runneth into a mass, and the clouds cleave fast together.*—Job, xxxviii, 38.

[2] Cosmas's idea of the figure of heaven and earth will be readily

Moses, likewise, in describing the table in the Tabernacle, which is an image of the earth, ordered its length to be of two cubits, and its breadth of one cubit. So then in the same way as Isaiah spoke, so do we also speak of the figure of the first heaven made on the first day, made along with the earth, and comprising along with the earth the universe, and say that its figure is vaultlike. And just as it is said in Job that the heaven has been welded to the earth, so do we again also say the same. Having learned, moreover, from Moses that the earth has been extended in length more than in breadth, we again admit this, knowing that the scriptures, which are truly divine, ought to be believed. But further, when God had produced the waters and angels and other things simultaneously with the earth and the highest heaven itself, he on the second day exposed to their vision this second heaven visible to our eyes, which, as if putting to use the creations of his own hands, he formed from the waters as his material. In appearance it is like the highest heaven, but not in figure, and it lies midway between that heaven and the earth; and God having then stretched it out extended it throughout the whole space in the direction of its breadth, like an intermediate roof, and bound together the firmament with the highest heaven, separating and disparting the remainder of the waters, leaving some above the firmament, and others on the earth below the firmament, as the divine Moses explains to us, and so makes the one area or house two houses—an upper and a lower story.

But again, the divine scripture speaks thus in Moses concerning the second heaven: *And God called the firmament heaven*[1]*;* and in the inspired David we find these words: *Stretching out the heaven as a covering*[2]*;* and he adds:

---

understood from his delineation of it, as shown in Fig. 7 at the end of this work.   [1] Gen. i, 8.   [2] Psalm cii, 3.

who covereth his upper chambers with the waters; saying this evidently with respect to the firmament. But scripture, when coupling the two heavens together, frequently speaks of them in the singular, as but one, saying through Isaiah: *He that established the heaven as a vaulted chamber, and stretched it out as a tent to dwell in*[1]; meaning here by the vaulted chamber the highest heaven, and by what is stretched out as a tent the firmament, and thus declaring them in the singular number to be bound together and to be of similar appearance. David again speaks to this effect: *The heavens declare the glory of God, and the firmament sheweth forth his handiwork*[2]; here beginning with a duality and ending with a unity. For since, agreeably to the idiom of the Hebrew language, the same word serves to express both *heavens* and *heaven*, and the two heavens are not only bound together as one, but are also like in appearance and aspect, the divine scripture speaks of heaven both in the plural and in the singular number indiscriminately. For the blessed David, using this idiom, exclaims: *Praise him, ye heavens of heavens*,[3] where you might say in the singular number a *heaven of heaven*, for he says elsewhere: *And the water which is above the heavens:* here distinctly employing the plural number, *heavens*, and indicating that the firmament has the waters above it. For following the idiom, instead of saying, *the heaven of the heaven*, he said *the heavens of the heavens*. For he again says also in another place: *the heaven of the heaven belongs to the Lord, but the earth hath he given to the sons of man*, here calling the highest heaven which is like a vault heaven of heaven, as it is the heaven of the firmament, being up above it and much loftier. And in Deuteronomy the great hierophant Moses thus speaks:

---

[1] Isai. xl, 42.   [2] Psalm viii, 1.   [3] Psalm cxlvii, 4.
[4] Psalm cxii, 16.

Behold unto the Lord thy God belongeth the heaven and the heaven of heaven, the earth with all that is therein. The great apostle Paul, moreover, uses this idiom, exclaiming: *For our citizenship is in the heavens, from which also we look for the Saviour;*[1] beginning here with the plural number and ending with the singular, for he uses *from which* in the singular number. David also frequently makes use of this mode of expression, exclaiming: *Praise the Lord from the heavens;*[2] and after he had said: *Praise the Lord from the earth,* he thus ends: *the praising of him in earth and heaven;*[3] and in another passage, *To him who made the heavens in wisdom;*[4] and on this subject he uses many such expressions.

We have said that the figure of the earth is lengthwise from east to west, and breadthwise from north to south, and that it is divided into two parts: this part which we, the men of the present day, inhabit, and which is all round encircled by the intermedial sea, called the ocean by the Pagans, and that part which encircles the ocean, and has its extremities bound together with those of the heaven, and which men at one time inhabited to eastward, before the flood in the days of Noah occurred, and in which also Paradise is situated.[5] Men, strange to say, having crossed the ocean in the Ark at the time of the Deluge, reached our part of the earth and settled in Persian territory, where also the Ark rested on the mountains of Ararat, having saved alive Noah and his sons, together with

---

[1] Philip. iii, 20.   [2] Psal. cxlvii, 1.   [3] *Ibid.*, 14.
[4] Psal. cxxxiv, 5.
[5] Montfaucon, in a note upon this passage, says: "The idea of Cosmas is that this earth which we inhabit is surrounded by the ocean, but that beyond the ocean there is another earth which on every side encompasses the ocean, and which had been formerly the seat of Paradise. It was this earth whose extremities were fastened together with the extremities of heaven."

their wives, so that there were four pairs, and all the brute animals, three pairs of clean, but of wild only one poor pair. Since Noah appears to have offered up to God in sacrifice the superfluous one pair of all the clean animals, there were four pairs of human beings, and of clean animals three pairs, but of wild beasts only one poor pair. Now when the Ark had crossed over into this part of the earth which we now from that time forth inhabit, the three sons of Noah divided the earth among them. Shem and his posterity obtained the regions extending from Asia as far as the eastern parts of the ocean[1]; Ham and his posterity the regions from Gadeira[2] in the west to the ocean of Ethiopia, called Barbaria, beyond the Arabian Gulf,[3] receiving besides the regions extending as far as our sea,

---

[1] By Asia here is meant the Roman province of Asia Minor. Shem, thus extending from the Mediterranean Sea to the Indian Ocean, intersected the portions of Japhet and Ham.

[2] Now Cadiz—the Gades of the Romans. The name is Phœnician, as we learn from Dionysius Periêgêtes and his copyist Avienus, who says:
    Gadir prima fretum solida supereminet arce,
    Attollitque caput geminis inserta columnis.
    Haec Cotinusa prius fuerat sub nomine prisco,
    Tartessumque dehinc Tyrii dixere coloni,
    Barbara quinetiam Gades hanc lingua frequentat :
    Poenus quippe locum Gadir vocat undique septum
    Aggere praeducto.—*Descriptio Orbis Terrae*, ll. 610-616.

Dionysius to the same effect says :
    Καὶ τὴν μὲν ναετῆρες, ἐπὶ προτέρων ἀνθρώπων
    Κληζομένην Κοτινοῦσαν, ἐφημίξαντο Γάδειρα. *Periêg.* ll. 455-6.

[3] Barbaria extended from the Straits of Bab-el-Mandeb to the Aromatic Cape, now called Cape Guardafui. Ptolemy, however, in his *Geography* (Books I, c. 17, and IV, vii, 28) applies it as a general designation to the coast regions of East Africa from the Aromatic Cape southward as far as Zanzibar, beyond which his knowledge did not extend. The author of the *Periplûs* again says that Barbaria, ἡ Βαρβαρικὴ χώρα, extended southward from Berenicê, a great seaport in the south of Egypt, not far from the Tropic.

that is to Palestine and Phœnicia, as well as the southern parts, together with all that part of Arabia which adjoins us, and that which is called the Happy; and Japhet and his posterity: the regions extending from Media and Scythia in the distant north, as far as the western ocean and the parts outside of Gadeira, according to what is written in Genesis by the inspired Moses, who, in describing the division of the earth, speaks thus concerning these three: *The sons of Japhet, Gamer (Gomer)*[1] *and Magog*[2] *and Madaï and Javan (Iouaun) and Elisa*,[3] whereby he indicates the hyperborean nations of the Scythians and Medes, and then similarly the Ionians[4] and the Greeks,[5] and likewise Thóbel[6] and Mosóch[7] and Théres (Θήρας) that he may show what nations lay near them. For he calls the Thracians *Théres*, and from these, he tells us, some

---

[1] Gomer is taken by Josephus to denote the Galatians of Northern Phrygia, by others the Gimmeri, or Cimmerii, who inhabited the Crimea and eastern shores of the Euxine; others, again, the Cappadocians.

[2] Magog is supposed by some to have been the ancestor of the Scythians and Tartars, and by others of the Persians.

[3] Gen. x, 2.

[4] Gr. Ἰωαύν. This is the reading of the Laurentian codex, while the Vatican has Ἰωωυάν. Javan was the ancestor of the Ionians and of the Greeks generally. The form of the name in the cuneiform inscriptions is *Yavnan* or *Yunan*, and this designates Cyprus, where the Assyrians first came into contact with the Greeks. Elisa is the Elishah of Ezekiel, xxvii, 7: "Blue and purple from the isles of Elishah". Josephus identified Elishah with Aeolis, but it is generally taken for Elis in the Peloponnesus, or for the Peloponnesus itself. The Tyrians found along the shores of Greece and her islands the shell-fish which yielded their famous purple dye.

[5] Gr. Ἑλλαδικούς. Ἕλληνες often means Pagans or Gentiles.

[6] Tubal, supposed to be the ancestor of the Tibareni, who were settled along the coast of Pontus. They are mentioned by Herodotus, and are thought to have been a Scythic people.

[7] Meshech, a remote nation, and one of the rudest in the world. "Woe is me", saith one of the Psalms of Ascents, "Woe is me, that I sojourn in Meshech!".

were removed and dispersed among the islands of the Gentiles[1] and adjacent localities, for this indicates Tharseis.[2] The inhabitants of Cyprus he calls Kétioi, and those of Rhodes, Rhodians.[3] *The sons of Ham* (Cham), *Cush* (Chous) *and Mesraim*, thereby designating the Ethiopians and Egyptians.[4] Finally, *Phut (Phouth) and Canaan*,[5]

---

[1] By the *islands of the Gentiles* are meant the sea-coasts and islands of the Mediterranean. The Thracians, I take it, were called Théres, i.e. *wild beasts*, on account of the barbarity and ferocity for which they were proverbial.

[2] The Tarshish of scripture and Tartessus of Greek writers, who designated thereby the district of Spain which lay beyond the pillars of Hercules, and also a city in the region, probably Gadeira.

[3] The Kétioi are mentioned by Homer, *Odys.*, xi, 521, and also by Strabo in several passages (B. XIII, i, 69, and iii, 2 ; B. XIV, v, 23 and 28). He makes them, however, a continental people, and places them between the Cilicians and the Pelasgi. They are the *Kittim* of *I. Chronicles* i, v. 7, as the Rhodians are the *Rodanim* of the same passage. For Κητίους the Florentine MS. has Σκυθίους.

[4] The word *Ham* means *adust*, and has reference to the dark sunburnt complexions of the Ethiopians and Egyptians, of whom Ham was the progenitor. *Mizraim* was the name of Egypt in Hebrew and *Mesr* that in Arabic. The Cushite settlements have proved a fertile theme of discussion among critics. Cush, as a country, is African in all passages of the Bible except Genesis, ii, 13, where the Revised Version has *Cush* instead of *Ethiopia*, as in the Authorised. It was supposed by the Greeks, after the conquests of Alexander had made them acquainted with India, that the Egyptians, Ethiopians or Nubians, and Indians, were derived from the same stock (Arrian, *Anab.*, vi, 9) ; while Diodorus Siculus held that the Egyptians and their civilisation were derived from Meroë. It has again been supposed that the early Babylonians came from Ethiopia ; but though in support of this view some striking evidence was advanced, it is now rejected along with that of Diodorus. It has been thought that there took place a later emigration of Cushites from the Nile to Western India, through Arabia, Babylon, and Persia.

[5] Phut is Libya. In the *Atlas Antiquus*, however, of Justus Perthes, Phut is placed along the south-western shores of the Red Sea, to the south of the Troglodytes. The tribes descended from Canaan are enumerated in Genesis, x, 15-19. They occupied Palestine and Phœnicia, and spread as far north as the valley of the Orontes.

whereby he designates the Libyans and adjoining nations. *The sons of Cush, Saba and Elisâ*, whereby he designates the Homerites and their neighbours[1]; similarly also the 132 nations one after another that occupy the southern parts. The Chananeans again, he says, were descended from Mesraim, that is the Egyptians and Sidonians and all the neighbouring nations. *The sons of Shem, Elam and Ashur*, that is the Elamites[2] and Assyrians and remaining nations, and as many of these as were spread far and wide over Asia and the East—the nations of the Persians, Huns, Baktrians,[3] Indians, onwards to the ocean.

The pagans even, availing themselves of what Moses has thus revealed, divide the whole earth into three parts: Asia, Libya and Europe, designating Asia the east, Libya the south, extending to the west; Europe the north, also extending to all the west; and in this our part of the earth there are four gulfs which penetrate into it from the ocean as the pagans also say, and say with truth when treating

---

[1] Saba denotes here that part of Arabia which is known as Yemen, or Arabia Felix, and which of old was thought to have been situated at the very ends of the earth. It was civilised in very early times. The climate was salubrious, the soil fertile, and its products varied and valuable. The inhabitants at the same time were noted for their great stature (Isaiah, xlv, 14), their commercial enterprise, and their opulence and luxury. The Homerites are the Himyari of Oriental history. Their alphabet is one of the oldest, and is thought to have been the source of the Indian. Saba denoted also the kingdom of Meroë, or at least that part of it which extended along the western shores of the Red Sea, from the Adulitic Gulf southward to the Aualitic. Elésâ probably denotes the Elisari (the El-Asyr tribe of Burchardt), who are mentioned in Ptolemy's *Geography* as situated between the Cassaniti and the Homerites at the Straits of the Red Sea. Cosmas may have called at Muza (one of their ports) on his way to India, and have there heard of this people.

[2] Elam is the name in scripture of Susiana, one of the provinces of which was Elymais.

[3] The Huns are again mentioned in Book XI, where see note regarding them (*Montf.* p. 338). Baktria is now the province of Balkh.

of this subject[1] namely, this gulf of ours, which entering from Gadeira in the west extends along the countries subject to Rome;[2] the Arabian Gulf called the Erythræan[3] and the Persian, both of which advance from Zingium to the southern and more eastern parts of the earth from the country called Barbaria, which begins where the land of the Ethiopians terminates.[4] Now Zingium, as those who navigate the Indian sea are aware, is situated beyond the country called Barbaria which produces frankincense,[5] and

---

[1] The Baltic is, however, omitted.

[2] Gr. (Κόλπος) ὁ κατὰ τὴν Ῥωμανίαν. Montfaucon has the following note upon this. "*Romania* hic intelligitur terra illa omnis, quae ad Romanam ditionem pertinebat. Quo item usu Athanasius, p. 361, et Epiphanius, p. 728, Ῥωμανίαν memorant." The numbers refer to the pages in his own editions of these two authors.

[3] The Erythræan, in its wider sense, includes both the Arabian and Persian Gulfs, beside the ocean between Africa and India.

[4] On Zingium Montfaucon has the following note: "Cosmas after the custom of his age designates by Zingium not only the strait of the Arabian Gulf (Straits of Bab-el-Mandeb), but also the sea-coast beyond the Straits, and likewise the adjacent sea: which name still subsists, since the Zanguebaric coast, from the strait of the Arabian Gulf almost to the very Cape of Good Hope, which is constantly visited by European ships, is by the inhabitants called *Zangui*, for Zanguebar signifies the sea of Zangui." Ptolemy in his *Geography*, IV. vii, 11, has a cape called Zingis or Zengisa on the coast of the Barbaric Gulf, which seems to be Ras Hafun in Lat. 10 25′ N. *Ethiopia* designated vaguely those parts of Africa which extended from the southern limits of Egypt and Libya southward to the Equator. It designated also the frankincense country of southern Arabia—as shown by the famous bilingual inscription of Axum. Dr. Glaser derives the name *Ethiopia* from *atyôb* (the plural of *taib*, frankincense), so that it thus denotes generally the frankincense countries. In its restricted application *Ethiopia* designated the Kingdom or Island of Meroë. This realm, which lay between the Abyssinian highlands on the east and the Libyan desert on the west, and which was watered by the Nile and some of its affluents, was wondrously opulent, and the seat of a civilization introduced in early times from Yemen, as shown by its place-names, many of which are Sabæan.

[5] Cosmas is here in agreement with the author of the *Periplûs*,

is girdled by the ocean which streams from thence into both the gulfs. The fourth gulf is that which flows from the north-eastern part of the earth, and is called the Caspian or Hyrcanian Sea.[1] These gulfs only admit of navigation, for the ocean cannot be navigated on account of the great number of its currents, and the dense fogs which it sends up, obscuring the rays of the sun, and because of the vastness of its extent. Having learned these facts from the Man of God, as has been said, I have pointed them out as coincident also with my own experience, for I myself have made voyages for commercial purposes in three of these gulfs—the Roman, the Arabian and the Persian, while from the natives or from seafaring men I have obtained accurate information regarding the different places.

Once on a time, when we sailed in these gulfs, bound for Further India[2] and had almost crossed over to Barbaria, beyond which there is situated Zingium, as they term the

---

who makes the Aromatic Cape (Guardafui) the end of Barbaria: τελευταῖον τῆς βαρβαρικῆς ἠπείρου. Ptolemy, however, makes it begin here, and extends it to Rhaptum in the Gulf of Zanguebar.

[1] Cosmas shared the error prevalent in ancient times, that the Caspian was not a land-locked sea but was a gulf of the great ocean. Herodotus, however, is not chargeable with having been under this delusion.

[2] Gr. ἐπὶ τὴν ἐσωτέραν Ἰνδίαν. Literally "Inner India". This generally means that part of India which lies on the further side of Cape Comorin or of the Straits between Ceylon and the mainland. But as the name of India was sometimes applied to Southern Arabia, and even to Eastern Africa, India as lying beyond these countries may be here meant. John Malela, or Malala, the Byzantine historian, who wrote not long after the time of Cosmas, calls both of them *India*: "At this time it happened that the *Indians* warred against each other, those called Auxumites with those called Homerites. . . . The Roman traders go through the Homerites into Auxumê, and to the interior Kingdoms of the Indians, for there are seven Kingdoms of the Indians and Ethiopians." Friar Jornandes calls Eastern Africa *India Tertia.*

mouth of the ocean, I saw there to the right of our course a great flight of the birds which they call Souspha, which are like kites, but somewhat more than twice their size.[1]

133 The weather was there so very unsettled that we were all in alarm; for all the men of experience on board, whether passengers or sailors, all began to say that we were near the ocean and called out to the pilot: "Steer the ship to port and make for the gulf, or we shall be swept along by the currents and be carried into the ocean and be lost." For the ocean rushing into the gulf was swelling into billows of portentous size, while the currents from the gulf were driving the ship into the ocean, and the outlook was altogether so dismal that we were kept in a state of great alarm. A great flock, all the time, of the birds called Souspha followed us, flying generally high over our heads, and the presence of these was a sign that we were near the ocean.

The northern and western parts of the earth which we inhabit are of very great elevation, while the southern parts are proportionately depressed.[2] For to what extent of its breadth the earth is imperceptibly depressed, it is found to have an elevation of like area in the northern and western parts, while the ocean beyond is of unusual depth. But in the southern and eastern parts the ocean beyond is not of unusual but of the medium depth. When these facts are considered, one can see why those who sail to the north and the west are called lingerers. It is because they are mounting up and in mounting up they sail more

---

[1] The size of these birds, and the fact afterwards mentioned that they kept flying aloft, might indicate them to be albatrosses.

[2] Virgil (*Georg.*, I, ll. 233 *seq.*) gives poetical expression to the same idea: "High as the globe rises towards Scythia and the pinnacles of Rhipaean hills, so deep is its downward slope to Libya and its southern clime. The one pole ever stands towering above our heads; the other is thrust down beneath the feet of murky Styx and her abyssmal spectres."—Conington's Transl.

slowly, while in returning they descend from high places to low, and thus sail fast, and in a few days bring their voyage to an end. Then the two rivers, the Tigris and Euphrates, flowing down from the northern parts, that is, from Persarmenia to the south, have far more rapid currents than our river the Nile—that is, the Gêôn. For this river Nile flowing from low-lying regions in the south towards the elevated northern regions, and running, as one may say, up,[1] pursues quietly the even tenor of its way. The eastern and southern parts again, as low-lying and overheated by the sun, are extremely hot, while the northern and western from their great elevation and distance from the sun are extremely cold, and in consequence the inhabitants have very pale complexions, and must keep themselves warm against the cold. But the whole of this portion of the earth is not inhabited, for the parts in the extreme north are to the last degree cold, and remain uninhabited, just as the parts in the extreme south remain also uninhabited on account of the excessive heat. For the blessed David thus speaks: *Neither from the goings forth nor from the goings down* (of the sun); *nor from the desert mountains*,[2] where he calls the east *exodous* and the west *dusmas*, and the other regions, namely the extreme north and extreme south *desert mountains*. The pagans when writing on these subjects say what is true concerning them.

These things being so we shall say, agreeably to what we find in divine scripture, that the sun issuing from the east traverses the sky in the south and ascends north-

---

[1] Gr. ἄνω που τρέχων. Cosmas here annihilates his own objection to the doctrine of Antipodes. Rain could as easily fall *up* to them as the Nile could run *up* to the sea.

[2] Gr. ἀπὸ ἐρήμων ὀρέων. Psalm LXXV. v. 6. The Revised Version translates the verse thus: "For neither from the east, nor from the west, nor yet from the south, *cometh* lifting up:" giving in the margin: "from the wilderness of mountains cometh judgement."

wards, and becomes visible to the whole of the inhabited world. But as the northern and western summit intervenes it produces night in the ocean beyond this earth of ours, and also in the earth beyond the ocean ;[1] then afterwards when the sun is in the west, where he is hidden by the highest portion of the earth, and runs his course over the ocean through the northern parts, his presence there makes it night for us, until in describing his orbit he comes again to the east, and again ascending the southern sky illumines the inhabited world, as the divine scripture says through the divine Solomon: *The sun riseth and the sun goeth down and hasteth to his own place. Rising there, he goeth to the south, and wheeleth his circuit, and the wind turneth round to his circuits.*[2] Here he calls the air *the wind*, for, as he says, the sun making a circuit in the air from east to south, from south to west, from west to north, from north to east, causes the vicissitudes of day and night and the solstices; for, by the expressions *wheeleth his circuit*, and *turneth round to his circuits*, he signified not only the revolution but also the solstices, for it is the plural number he uses. For he does not say that the wind describes a circuit, but that the sun does so through the wind, that is, through the air.[3] Yea, even the blessed Moses having been ordered on Mount Sinai to make the Tabernacle according to the pattern which he had seen, said under divine inspiration, that the outer Tabernacle was a pattern of this the visible world. Now the divine Apostle in the epistle to the

---

[1] Montfaucon has here this note: "Cosmas thought that in the northern parts of the earth there existed a very lofty mountain of a conical shape which the sun always went round; and that night was produced in this earth by the shadow of the mountain, while the sun was traversing that part of his orbit which is turned away from us." See, in the Appendix, the figure of the mountain as sketched by Cosmas. [2] Eccl. i, 5, 6.

[3] The Revised Version, however, attributes the making of a circuit to the wind as well as to the sun.

Hebrews, in explaining the inner Tabernacle, or that which was within the veil, declares that it was a pattern of the heavenly—that is, of the kingdom of the heavens or the future state, taking the veil which divides the one Tabernacle into two for the firmament; just as the firmament placed in the middle, between the heaven and the earth, has made two worlds—this world namely, and that which is to come, into which world to come the first who entered was the forerunner on our behalf, Christ, who thus prepared for us a new and living way. Now in his description of the first Tabernacle, Moses places in the south of it the candlestick, with seven lamps, after the number of days in the week—these lamps being typical of the celestial luminaries—and shining on the table placed in the north of the earth. On this table again he ordered to be daily placed twelve loaves of shewbread, according to the number of the twelve months of the year—three loaves at each corner of the table, to typify the three months between each of the four tropics.[1] He commanded also to be wreathed all around the rim of the table a waved moulding,[2] to represent a multitude of waters, that is, the ocean; and further, in the circuit of the waved work, a crown to be set of the circumference of the palm of the hand, to represent the land beyond the ocean, and encircling it, where in the east lies Paradise, and where also the extremities of the heaven are bound to the extremities of the earth. And from this description we not only learn concerning the luminaries and the stars that most of them, when they rise, run their course through the south, but from the same source we are taught that the earth is surrounded by the ocean, and further

---

[1] Cosmas extends the name of *tropics* to the points at which the sun turns northward from the Equator on the 21st of March, and southward from it on the 21st of September.

[2] Gr. Κυμάτιον στρεπτὸν κύκλῳ.

that beyond the ocean there is another earth by which the ocean is surrounded.

But again, from the prophecy of Lamech, the father of Noah, we learn that Noah, by means of the world-carrying Ark, was to convey men and the brute beasts into this earth of ours, for the prophecy runs somewhat to this effect: *This same shall give us rest concerning our work and toil of our hands, because of the ground which the Lord God hath cursed.*[1] For this reason also Lamech gave Noah his name, which means *rest*. For the first man having sinned, and having been cast by God out of the garden into the earth, which was foul with thorns and effete, those ten generations smarted under grievous chastisement, being forbidden according to the sacred scripture to eat any longer of fruit that grew upon a tree, because man had transgressed by eating the fruit of a tree. And meagre truly was the fare on which the generations from Adam to Noah subsisted, since they neither ate the olive, nor tasted either wine or flesh, but were commanded to eat only grain, and that too although there the earth was by no means productive, but required the very hardest toil for its cultivation; for thus saith the scripture: *Cursed is the ground in thy labours; in sorrow shalt thou eat of it all the days of thy life; thorns also and thistles shall it bring forth to thee, and thou shalt eat the herb of the field; in the sweat of thy face shalt thou eat thy bread.*[2]

Note.

With regard to wine, it is manifest from what is recorded in Scripture that, after the Deluge, Noah having planted and cultivated the vine and expressed the juice from the grapes, drank to excess of the sweet must of which he had no previous experience, and made himself drunk: and with regard to flesh the case is still more manifest, for God instructed him in these terms:

[1] Gen. v, 29.   [2] Gen. iii, 17.

Lo! I have given you all things as the green herb to eat, but flesh in the blood thereof shall ye not eat[1]*:* meaning this: Lately I interdicted you from eating many things, but now I permit you to eat of all things, and to eat even flesh. Sacrifice, therefore, and pour out the blood, and then eat the flesh as ye eat vegetables: and eat also of the olive, of which before the Flood it was not permitted to eat, because it also was the fruit of a tree. But perhaps someone will object and say: If it is true that before the Flood they did not eat flesh, why is it then written: *Abel was a keeper of sheep, and brought of the firstlings of his flock and of the fat thereof!*[2] If they did not eat flesh, why did they take upon them the care of sheep? And why did Abel, when he brought a lamb for sacrifice, not slay it? Now, one who so enquires, will be truly answered that, in making the oblation, he presented the holocausts alive; for one of the editions shows this, saying: Over Cain and over his sacrifice he did not apply fire, so that it is evident that the offerings were consumed with divine fire. They provided themselves with a flock to procure for themselves milk and wool. Another objection: If they did not eat flesh, how came it into their head to select the fat for the sacrifice to God? Answer— Because when anything is to be burned in the fire, fat is more readily set ablaze.

Text.

When God in his mercy wished that the human race should be no longer pinched with such scanty fare, and such hard toil, as they were less robust than the first men, who, being newly created, were better able to sustain their punishment, God taking occasion from the wickedness of men, of whom he found none righteous except Noah, brought in a flood for two or even for more reasons— that he might destroy the wicked, and save alive him that was righteous for the instruction of future generations— that, by the untimely end of the wicked, he might the better deter those who are liable to death, and will some

---

[1] Gen. ix, 3.   [2] Gen. iv, 3.

time or other die, from doing what is wicked—and that he might bring men, and the brutes that were created for the use of man, into this earth of ours, which is better than the other, and almost equal to Paradise; which also he hath done, having ordered Noah, who was left in this earth after the Flood, to taste of everything whether tree or grain, and having taught him also to eat flesh. But that he brought in the Flood not for the purpose merely of destroying the wicked, is evident from the fact that the water prevailed for a length of time, although one or two days were quite sufficient to have destroyed them all; but he brought it in also, that he might take the Ark across the ocean, and bring it to this earth of ours. For during one hundred and fifty days did the water prevail without diminishing, until, wonderful to relate, the Ark came to this earth of ours. The circumstance, moreover, that the water rose fifteen cubits above the tops of the highest mountains, makes it evident beyond all question that this was due to the depth to which the Ark was submerged in the waters, in order that it might rest upon the mountains. For a half of the height of the Ark was under water to the depth of fifteen cubits, for its entire height was thirty cubits. From this, then, as well as from the prophecy of Lamech, and the construction of the table in the Tabernacle, we can learn that beyond the ocean there is an earth which encompasses the ocean. Nay more; the hierophant Moses also in Deuteronomy saith thus: *And thou, Israel, hear the command which I give unto thee this day. Do not say in thine heart who shall go up into heaven to bring it down to us, or who shall go over the sea for us to bring it to us; but the word is nigh unto thee even in thy mouth.*[1] By this he means: Say not it is impossible to go up into heaven to bring down thence the divine precepts, or to

---

[1] Deut. xxx, 12.

cross over to the farther side of the sea to bring them thence, for lo! they are in thy mouth and in thy heart. In the same passage he teaches us two truths—that beyond the ocean there is land or a place, and that it is impossible to cross the ocean, just as we, while in this mortal state, cannot possibly go up into heaven. Even Baruch, the scribe of Jeremiah the Prophet, when giving counsels of prudence in his epistle, being a man well taught in the institutions of Moses, speaks in the same strain with Moses, and says: *Who hath gone up into heaven and taken it and brought it down from the clouds, who hath passed over the sea?*[1] Here he does not speak of our sea, for it admits of being crossed, but of the ocean itself.

Yet if Paradise did exist in this earth of ours, many a man among those who are keen to know and enquire into all kinds of subjects, would think he could not be too quick in getting there: for if there be some who to procure silk[2] for the miserable gains of commerce, hesitate not to travel to the uttermost ends of the earth, how should they hesitate to go where they would gain a sight of Paradise itself? Now this country of silk is situated in the remotest of all the Indies, and lies to the

---

[1] Baruch, iii. 29.
[2] Gr. μετάξιον—sometimes written ματάξιον—a foreign word, and only found in later Greek. In classical Greek the name for silk is βόμβυξ, and also σηρικὸν, from which our word *silk* is derived by the change, which is not uncommon, of *r* into *l*. The *Sêres* from whom it was procured inhabited Northern China, whence it was conveyed by various land routes to the nations of the west. Southern China, again, which Cosmas calls Tzinitza, was inhabited by the *Sinae*, who sent their products by sea to Ceylon and India, and other countries farther west. Full details as to the commodities which China in ancient times exported and imported, as well as to the trade routes by which they were conveyed, will be found in the late Dr. De Lacouperie's great work, *The Western Origin of Chinese Civilization.* It was in the days of Cosmas that the silk-worm was for the first time

left of those who enter the Indian sea, far beyond the
Persian Gulf, and the island called by the Indians Sielediba
and by the Greeks Trapobanê (*sic*).[1] It is called Tzinitza,
and is surrounded on the left by the ocean, just as Barbaria
is surrounded by it on the right. The Indian philosophers,
called the Brachmans, say that if you stretch a cord from
Tzinitza to pass through Persia, onward to the Roman
dominions, the middle of the earth would be quite correctly traced, and they are perhaps right. For the country
in question deflects considerably to the left, so that the
loads of silk passing by land through one nation after
another, reach Persia in a comparatively short time;[2] whilst
the route by sea to Persia is vastly greater. For just as

---

introduced into Europe. Gibbon, in the fortieth chapter of *The
Decline and Fall*, presents us with an admirable account of the silk
trade up till the time of the Emperor Justinian, and of the far-reaching
effects upon commerce which eventually resulted from the receipt by
that emperor of eggs of the silk-worm which had been surreptitiously
conveyed to him from China.

[1] Montfaucon has the following note here: "*Sielediba* is written
afterwards *Sielediba*. It is the island *Ceylan*, the name being so far
changed. For *diba*, or *diva*, means 'island'; hence *Maldive*, just
as Sielediva, signifies the island *Siele*. *Tzinitza*, immediately below,
in the Vatican copy is read Tzknê (Tzinê?) *Tsina*, or Sina, namely,
the country of the Sinae, which, as Cosmas himself attests, is bounded
by the ocean on the east." In Book XI Cosmas gives at some length
an account of this island, and in one of the notes to that book the
etymology of these names is examined.

[2] "A valuable merchandise of small bulk is capable of defraying the
expense of land carriage; and the caravans traversed the whole
latitude of Asia in two hundred and forty-three days, from the Chinese
Ocean to the sea-coast of Syria. Silk was immediately delivered to
the Romans by the Persian caravans, who frequented the fairs of
Armenia and Nisibis..... To escape the Tartar robbers and the
tyrants of Persia, the silk caravans explored a more southern road:
they traversed the mountains of Thibet, descended the streams of the
Ganges or the Indus, and patiently expected, in the ports of Guzerat
and Malabar, the annual fleets of the West."—Gibbons, *Decline and
Fall*, c. xl.

great a distance as the Persian Gulf runs up into Persia,[1] so great a distance and even a greater has one to run, who, being bound for Tzinitza, sails eastward from Taprobanê; while besides, the distances from the mouth of the Persian Gulf to Taprobanê and the parts beyond through the whole width of the Indian sea are very considerable.[2] He then who comes by land from Tzinitza to Persia shortens very considerably the length of the journey. This is why there is always to be found a great quantity of silk in Persia. Beyond Tzinitza there is neither navigation nor any land to inhabit.

If one measures in a straight cord line[3] the stages which make up the length of the earth from Tzinitza to the west, he will find that there are somewhere about four hundred stages,[4] each thirty miles in length. The measurement is to be made in this way: from Tzinitza to the borders of Persia, between which are included all Iouvia,[5] India, and the country of the Bactrians, there are about one hundred and fifty stages at least; the whole country of the Persians has eighty stations; and from Nisibis to Seleucia[6]

---

[1] The Persian Gulf has a length of 650 English miles, while the distance from Ceylon to the Malacca peninsula only is nearly twice that distance.

[2] Not very far short of 2,000 miles.

[3] Gr. ὡς ἀπὸ σπαρτίου ὀρθῶς ... τις μετρῶν. Eratosthenes estimated the breadth of the habitable world from the parallel of Thule (which he took to coincide with the Arctic Circle) to Sennaar, at 38,00 stadia, and its length, from the westernmost point of Gaul to furthest India, at 77,800, thus making its length about double its breadth.

[4] μοναί, mansions or halting-places.

[5] Gr. Ἰουνία. So the Florentine copy, while the Vatican has οὐννία in a second hand. This would mean the country of the Huns, concerning whom see note to Book XI.

[6] Nisibis, the capital of Mygdonia, was, after the time of Lucullus, considered the chief bulwark of the Roman power in the East. It was an ancient, large, and populous city, and was for long the great northern emporium of the commerce of the East and West. It was situated about two days' journey from the head waters of the Tigris

there are thirteen stages; and from Seleucia to Rome and the Gauls and Iberia, whose inhabitants are now called Spaniards, onward to Gadeira, which lies out towards the ocean, there are more than one hundred and fifty stages; thus making altogether the number of stages to be four hundred, more or less. With regard to breadth: from the hyperborean regions to Byzantium there are not more than fifty stages. For we can form a conjecture as to the extent of the uninhabited and the inhabited parts of those northern regions from the Caspian Sea, which is a gulf of the ocean. From Byzantium, again, to Alexandria there are fifty stages, and from Alexandria to the Cataracts thirty stages;[1] from the Cataracts to Axômis, thirty stages;[2] from Axômis

in the midst of a pleasant and fertile plain at the foot of Mount Masius. The Seleucia here referred to was situated on the Tigris about 40 miles to the north-east of Babylon, from the ruins of which it was mainly constructed: just as, afterwards, its own ruins served to build Ctesiphon. Next to Alexandria, it was the greatest emporium of commerce in the East.

[1] Gr. μοναὶ λ'. Here the numeral $\lambda' = 30$ must be an error for $\kappa' = 20$, because the distance from Alexandria to Syênê, in the neighbourhood of the Great Cataract, is about 600 Roman miles; and because, moreover, in the summing-up of the figures as in the text there is an excess of ten over the given total. Montfaucon has not noticed this discrepancy.

[2] Axômis (Auxumé in Ptolemy) is the modern Axum, the capital of Tigré. In the early centuries of our era it was a powerful State, possessing nearly the whole of Abyssinia, a portion of the south-west Red Sea coast and north-western Arabia. It was distant from its seaport, Adulé, which was situated near Annesley Bay, about 120 miles, or an eight days' caravan journey. It was the chief centre of the trade with the interior of Africa. The Greek language was understood and spoken, both by the court and the numerous foreigners who had either settled in it or who resorted to it for trading purposes. In this connection I may quote the following remarks from the pen of M. Vivien de Saint-Martin: "Plusieurs faits bien connus prouvent d'ailleurs l'action direct de l'hellénisme égyptien sur le developpement de la civilisation Axoumite. Ainsi l'auteur du *Périple* rapporte que le roi d'Axoum qu'il nomme Zoskalès, était familiarisé avec les lettres Grecques; et ce qui montre que cette influence eut un longue durée

to the projecting part of Ethiopia, which is the frankincense country called Barbaria, lying along the ocean, and not near but at a great distance from the land of Sasu which is the remotest part of Ethiopia, fifty stages more or less; so that we may reckon the whole number of stages at two hundred more or less; and thus we see that even here the divine scripture speaks the truth in representing the length of the earth to be double its breadth; *For thou shalt make the table in length two cubits and in breadth one cubit*, a pattern, as it were, of the earth."[1]

The region which produces frankincense is situated at the projecting parts of Ethiopia, and lies inland, but is washed by the ocean on the other side. Hence the inhabitants of Barbaria, being near at hand, go up into the interior and, engaging in traffic with the natives, bring back from them many kinds of spices, frankincense, cassia, calamus,[2] and many other articles of merchandise, which they afterwards send by sea to Adulè, to the country of the Homerites, to Further India, and to Persia. This very fact you will find mentioned in the Book of Kings, where it is recorded that the Queen of Sheba, that is, of the Homerite country, whom afterwards our Lord in the Gospels calls the Queen of the South, brought to Solomon spices from this very Barbaria, which lay near Sheba on

---

c'est que deux siècles et demi plus tard on voit la langue Grecque employée à Axoum dans les inscriptions concurremment avec la langue éthiopienne. Ce qui existe encore de l'ancienne Axoum, particulièrement ses obélisques, est d'un style grec, bien qu'on y sente une réminiscence égyptienne. Enfin, la religion des Grecs d'Egypte avait pénétré dans le royaume d'Axoum, en même temps que leur langue et leurs artistes, car dans les inscriptions le roi éthiopien se dit 'fils d' l'invincible Arès'" (*Journal Asiatique*, sixth series, vol. ii, pp. 333-4). Christianity was introduced into Axum in the fourth century by Œdisius and Frumentius, the latter of whom was afterwards appointed its first bishop. Sasu, which is next mentioned, is near th coast, and only 5° to the north of the equator.   [1] Ex. xxxvii, 10.

[2] The sweet calamus mentioned in Exodus, xxx, 23.

the other side of the sea, together with bars of ebony, and apes and gold from Ethiopia which, though separated from Sheba by the Arabian Gulf, lay in its vicinity. We can see again from the words of the Lord that he calls these places the ends of the earth, saying: *The Queen of the South shall rise up in judgment with this generation and shall condemn it, for she came from the ends of the earth to hear the wisdom of Solomon.*—Matt. xii, 42. For the Homerites are not far distant from Barbaria, as the sea which lies between them can be crossed in a couple of days, and then beyond Barbaria is the ocean, which is there called Zingion. The country known as that of Sasu is itself near the ocean, just as the ocean is near the frankincense country, in which there are many gold mines. The King of the Axômites accordingly, every other year, through the governor of Agau,[1] sends thither special agents to bargain for the gold, and these are accompanied by many other traders—upwards, say, of five hundred—bound on the same errand as themselves. They take along with them to the mining district oxen, lumps of salt, and iron, and when they reach its neighbourhood they make a halt at a certain spot and form an encampment, which they fence round with a great hedge of thorns. Within this they live, and having slaughtered the oxen, cut them in

---

[1] The Agau people is the native race spread over the Abyssinian plateau both to east and west of Lake Tana. Montfaucon has the following note: "There is at this day in those parts, namely in the kingdom of the Abyssinian Ethiopians, a region called Auge, where those celebrated fountains of the Nile are, as is related farther on. But what Cosmas here tells us about that singular method of trading practised by the Ethiopians and the Barbarians who speak a different language . . . . is still in vogue in many parts of Africa, as one may see in books of travel in Africa, and the descriptions given in them of the country." This "dumb commerce", as it was carried on along the Atlantic coast of Africa, is described by Herodotus in his Fourth Book, c. 196. It was practised elsewhere than in Africa, as, for instance, in China (see *Periplûs of the Erythræan Sea*, chap. lxv).

pieces, and lay the pieces on the top of the thorns, along with the lumps of salt and the iron. Then come the natives bringing gold in nuggets like peas,[1] called *tancharas*, and lay one or two or more of these upon what pleases them—the pieces of flesh or the salt or the iron, and then they retire to some distance off. Then the owner of the meat approaches, and if he is satisfied he takes the gold away, and upon seeing this its owner comes and takes the flesh or the salt or the iron. If, however, he is not satisfied, he leaves the gold, when the native seeing that he has not taken it, comes and either puts down more gold, or takes up what he had laid down, and goes away. Such is the mode in which business is transacted with the people of that country, because their language is different and interpreters are hardly to be found. The time they stay in that country is five days more or less, according as the natives more or less readily coming forward buy up all their wares. On the journey homeward they all agree to travel well-armed, since some of the tribes through whose country they must pass might threaten to attack them from a desire to rob them of their gold. The space of six months is taken up with this trading expedition, including both the going and the returning. In going they march very slowly, chiefly because of the cattle, but in returning they quicken their pace lest on the way they should be overtaken by winter and its rains. For the sources of the river Nile lie somewhere in these parts, and in winter, on account of the heavy rains, the numerous rivers which they generate obstruct the path of the traveller. The people there have their winter at the time we have our summer. It begins in the month Epiphi of the Egyptians and continues till Thôth,[2] and during the

---

[1] Gr. Θέρμια. Dimin. form of Θέρμος, a lupine.
[2] From July to September.

three months the rain falls in torrents, and makes a multitude of rivers all of which flow into the Nile.

The facts which I have just recorded fell partly under my own observation and partly were told me by traders who had been to those parts. And I now wish to give an account to your Piety of a matter quite pertinent to our subject. On the coast of Ethiopia, two miles off from the shore, is a town called Adulê, which forms the port of the Axômites and is much frequented by traders who come from Alexandria and the Elanitic Gulf.[1] Here is to be seen a marble chair, just as you enter the town on the western side by the road which leads to Axômis. This chair appertained to one of the Ptolemies, who had subjected this country to his authority.[2] It is made of costly white marble such as we employ for marble tables, but not of the sort which comes from Proconnesus.[3] Its base is

---

[1] In the *Periplus* (c. 6), which is perhaps the earliest work in which the name of Adulê occurs, a list is given of its imports and exports. Pliny says it was the greatest emporium of the Troglodytes—or, as we must now write their name—*Trogodytes*. It is represented by the modern Thulla or Zula, of which the latitude is 15° 13' north. With regard to the Elanitic Gulf, Ela, the Vatican copy has 'Ελᾶ, the Laurentian, i.e., the Florentine, 'Αηλά. It is the Elath of scripture, the Ailanê of Josephus, and the Elána of Ptolemy.

[2] Cosmas was mistaken in thinking that the inscription on this celebrated chair was a continuation of the inscription on the basanite tablet afterwards mentioned, in which Ptolemy Euergetês recorded a series of conquests which he had made in Asia in the earlier years of his reign. Mr. Salt showed that the two inscriptions had nothing in common except their juxtaposition, and that the one on the chair related to conquests made in Ethiopia and Arabia by an Axomite king who lived several centuries after King Ptolemy. Attempts have been made to discover these precious monuments of antiquity, but hitherto without success.

[3] Proconnesus is the island now called *Marmora*, a name which it has given to the sea in which it lies, and for which it is indebted to the celebrity of its rich marble quarries. The marble, which is of a white colour with streaks of black, was used in building the palace of

quadrangular, and it rests at the four corners on four slender and elegant pillars, with one in the middle of greater girth and grooved in spiral form. The pillars support the seat of the chair as well as its back against which one leans, and there are also sides to right and left. The whole chair with its base, five pillars, seat and back and sides to right and left, has been sculptured from a single block into this form. It measures about two cubits and a half, and is in shape like the chair we call the Bishop's throne.[1] Behind the Chair is another marble of basanite stone, three cubits in height and of quadrangular form, like a tablet, which at the centre of its upper portion rises to a sharp point whence the sides slope gently down in the form of the letter *lambda* (λ), but the main body of the slab is rectangular. This tablet has now fallen down behind the Chair, and the lower part has been broken and destroyed. Both the marble and the chair itself are covered over with Greek characters. Now when I was in this part of the country some five and twenty years ago, more or less, at the beginning of the reign of the Roman Emperor Justinus,[2] Elesbaan, who was then King of the Axômites, and was preparing to start on an expedition against the Homerites on the opposite side of the Gulf[3] wrote to the

---

Mausolus, and in paving the floor of the famous church of St. Sophia, erected in Constantinople by the Emperor Justinian.

[1] Gr. καθέδρα. A drawing to show the shape of the chair is given in the Appendix.

[2] Justinus I, or the Elder, was Emperor of the East from the year 518 to 527 A.D. He was succeeded by the great Justinian, whom he had adopted, and who reigned till 565.

[3] John Malala, whom we cited in a previous note, gives an account of an embassy sent by Justinian to the Emperor of the Axômites, whom he calls Elesbóas: thus fortunately, says Salt in his work descriptive of his Voyage to Abyssinia (p. 468), identifying Anda, Ameda and Elesbóas, as titles of the same sovereign. This author points out that what gave occasion to the expedition of Elesbóas was the murder of St. Aretas by the Homerites. He fixes the death of

Governor of Adulé directing him to take copies of the inscriptions on the Chair of Ptolemy and on the tablet,[1] and to send them to him. Then the Governor, whose name was Abbas, applied to myself and another merchant called Ménas, who afterwards became a monk at Rhaithû,[2] and not long ago departed this life—and at his request we went and copied the inscriptions. One set of the copies was made over to the Governor ; but we kept also like copies for ourselves which I shall here embody in this work, since their contents contribute to our knowledge of the country, its inhabitants, and the distances of the several places. We found also sculptured on the back of the Chair figures of Hercules and Mercury; and my companion, Ménas, of happy memory, alluding to these would have it that Hercules was the symbol of strength and Mercury of wealth. I remembered, however, the Acts of the Apostles, and would on this one point differ from him, upholding

---

Aretas in the year 522, which was the fifth year of the Emperor Justinus; the visit of Cosmas to Adulé to about 525, and the expedition against the Homerites to about 530. Montfaucon has here the following note : " In the Vatican copy in the first hand the reading is Ἑλλατζαβδάα. This Elesbaan, King of the Axômites, in that expedition which Cosmas mentions, destroyed the kingdom of the Homerites, having defeated Dunaanus, a king of the Jewish religion, who inflicted horrible tortures on the Christians. This Elesbaan was known by another name, Caleb, and was celebrated alike by Greeks and Arabians and Ethiopians, and was enrolled in the number of the saints. He is mentioned by Nonnosus in *Photius*, by Metaphrastus, by Callistus, and by Abulpharagius. All this you will find recorded at great length in Job Ludolph, a most accurate expounder and investigator of Ethiopian affairs."

[1] Gr. εἰκών. The word εἰκών denotes both an image or a figure, and also a picture. In the Greek church the word has only the latter signification.

[2] Rhaitô was a place on the Red Sea near Mount Sinai. It is now called *Tor*. Cosmas, in Book V., says that it was formerly Elim, where the Israelites found twelve springs of water which still existed in his time.

that we should take Hermes rather as the symbol of speech, for it is recorded in the Acts that they called Barnabas, Jupiter, and Paul, Mercury, because he was the chief speaker. Here is the form of the Chair and of the marble, and Ptolemy himself.[1]

Inscription on the Tablet.

The great king, Ptolemy, son of King Ptolemy and Queen Arsinoê, twin gods, grandson of the two sovereigns King Ptolemy and Queen Berenicê[2]—gods sôtêres—sprung from Hercules the son of Jupiter on the father's side, and on the mother's side from Dionysus the son of Jupiter—having received from his father the Kingdom of Egypt and Libya and Syria and Phoenicia and Cyprus, and Lycia and Caria, and the Islands of the Cyclades, made an expedition into Asia with forces of infantry and cavalry, and a fleet and elephants from the Troglodytes and Ethiopia—animals which his father and himself were the

---

[1] He here refers to his drawing of the chair and the tablet, the latter of which is surmounted by the figure of Ptolemy armed with buckler, helmet and spear, and standing in a very warlike attitude. The inscription on the tablet is of great historical value, as it is the only record now extant of the expedition which was made into Asia by Ptolemy Euergetês soon after his succession to the throne in 247 B.C.

[2] Ptolemy I., surnamed Sôtêr, was reputed to be the son of Lagus by Arsinoê, while Berenicê was the daughter of the same Lagus by Antigonê, the niece of Antipater. Ptolemy Sôtêr was regarded by the Macedonians as the son of Philip, the father of Alexander the Great, since his mother had been Philip's concubine, and was pregnant with Ptolemy when she married Lagus. This story seems, however, to have been invented to flatter Ptolemy when he had become a great King. The second Ptolemy, surnamed Philadelphus, married Arsinoê, the daughter of Lysimachus, the King of Thrace, and his wife Nicaea, and by her became the father of Euergetês. He banished her, however, and afterwards, to the great scandal of the Grecian world, married his own sister Arsinoê, who had been the wife of the same Thracian King. By her he had no children.

first to capture by hunting in those countries, and which they took down to Egypt, where they had them trained for employment in war.¹ And when he had made himself master of all the country on this side of the Euphrates, and of Cilicia and Pamphylia and Ionia, and the Hellespont and Thrace, and of all the forces in the provinces, and of the Indian elephants,² and had also made subject to his authority all the monarchs who ruled in these parts, he crossed the Euphrates river, and when he had subdued Mesopotamia and Babylonia and Susiana and Persis and Media, and all the rest of the country as far as Bactriana, and had collected all the spoils of the temples which had been taken away from Egypt by the Persians, he conveyed them to that country³ along with the other

---

¹ Conf. *Periplûs*, c. 3. "To the south of the Moschophagi, near the sea, lies a small emporium about 4,000 stadia distant from Berenicê, and called Ptolemaïs Therôn, from which, in the days of the Ptolemies, the hunters whom they employed used to go up into the interior to catch elephants. This place was very suitable for the purpose, as it lay on the skirts of the great Nubian forest in which elephants abounded. Before it was made a depôt for the elephant trade, the Egyptian Kings had to import these animals from Asia; but as the supply was precarious and the cost of their importation very great, Philadelphus made most tempting offers to the Ethiopian elephant hunters to induce them to abstain from eating the animal, or at least to reserve a portion of them for the royal stables. They rejected, however, all his offers, declaring that even for all Egypt they would not forego their favourite luxury."

² Probably among them some of the 500 which Seleucus Nicator had received from Sandrocottus, the King of Palibothra (now Pâtnâ).

³ Ptolemy Euergetês added greatly to his popularity with his Egyptian subjects by restoring to them the statues of their gods, which had been carried away to Persia by Cambyses and some of his successors. For this and other benefits, a synod of priests which assembled at Canopus in the ninth year of his reign passed a decree which conferred upon him and his queen the title of Benefactors. This queen was Berenicê, the daughter of Magas, King of Cyrene. She vowed to sacrifice her hair to the gods if her husband returned safe from the expedition recorded in the inscription. The hair was stolen, but according to the great astronomer Conon, the winds wafted

treasures, and sent back his troops by canals which had been dug.[1]

Such was the inscription on the tablet so far as we could copy it out, and, but for a few words, it would have been the whole, for it was only a small part of the tablet that had been fractured. The inscription again on the Chair was a continuation of the other,[2] and ran thus:—

Having after this with a strong hand compelled the nations bordering on my kingdom to live in peace, I made war upon the following nations, and by force of arms reduced them to subjection.[3] I warred first with the nation

---

it to heaven, and there it forms the constellation *Coma Berenices*. The inscription was not written by Euergetes himself, but that it is a truthful record is confirmed by a passage in St. Jerome's commentary on Daniel (xi, 8): "in tantum ut Syriam caperet et Ciliciam, superioresque partes trans Euphratem, et propemodum universam Asiam." See Mahaffy's *Empire of the Ptolemies*, p. 200.

[1] Gr. δυνάμεις ἀπέστειλε διὰ τῶν ὀρυχθέντων ποταμῶν. Dr. Vincent was of opinion that the canals mentioned here were those near Susa, in which Cambyses had deposited the gods and the other spoils which he had carried away from Egypt. He remarks that Susiana was, like Babylonia, intersected with numerous canals. Bigot, however, to judge from his translation of the clause, supposed that the canals were dug by order of Ptolemy: *Et faisant des canaux où il était nécessaire pour rendre à ses troupes le passage plus aisé*. Boeckh, again, believed that the words were badly transcribed, and referred to a new expedition, and therefore to Nile canals.

[2] In note 2, p. 54, it has been pointed out that the inscription on the chair had no connection with that on the tablet.

[3] "If we had the precise date of this inscription," says V. de Saint-Martin, "the chronological question of the origin of the kingdom of Axum would be resolved, for it enables us to accompany, in a sort of way, step by step the formation and development of the Axumite empire. *The first and only one of the kings of my race I have brought all these peoples under subjection*, says the Prince; and the identification which we are able still to make of one part at least of the districts and tribes mentioned in the inscription shows us his first conquests in the neighbourhood itself of Axum, and at a little distance from that city, which was evidently the seat of his native principality. Then we see his arms carried successively into one

of Gazé,[1] then with Agamé[2] and Sigyé,[3] and having
conquered them I exacted the half of all that they

---

after another of the surrounding countries—to the west, between the
Takazzé and the great lake Tzana (Tana); to the north, into the low
plains watered by the Atbara and the Mareb, and thence still farther
into the deserts of Nubia, where the caravans will henceforth have
an assured communication from Axum to Egypt; to the south into
the hot region which we designate by the very improper name of the
kingdom of Adel, into the country of Harrar and of the Somâlis,
which produces aromatics, and on to the coast region which is washed
by the sea of Aden, and which terminates at Cape Guardafui. Finally,
crossing over the narrow basin of the Arabian Gulf, the Ethiopian
conqueror sends a naval expedition to the opposite coast, and makes
his authority to be recognised, if not over Yémen or the country of
the Sabaeans (this the text leaves doubtful), at least over a great part
of the coast of Hedjaz, in his progress northward to the latitude of
Berenicé of Egypt, that is to say, over an extent of coast of 6 degrees
at least, even towards the 25th parallel." *From a memoir read to the
Academy of Inscriptions and Belles Lettres, and published in the
Journal Asiatique*, 1863, 6th series, vol. ii, pp. 347-8. For the identifi-
cations which follow I am chiefly indebted to this memoir. Dr.
Glaser has quite recently been able to determine approximately the
date of this inscription, as towards the end of the third century of our
aera.

[1] Salt sees in this word the town of Adé-Gada in the north of Tigré,
but Saint-Martin believes that it has a much wider signification. "It
is certain", he says, "that *Agazi* or *Agoazi* has been at another time
the name of the portion of the Abyssinian plateau, the declivity of
which commands the Red Sea above Massâwa. The name appears
to have now fallen into disuse, but the passages which Ludolf (in his
Hist. Aeth., I, i, iv, and *Commentar.*, p. 56) has collected prove that
even till the seventeenth century it was employed, at least by the
learned, as a synonym of Abyssinia. The word remains in use for a
different purpose to designate the ancient language of northern
Abyssinia (the ghiz or ghez, at present the learned language)."
—pp. 349, 350. Pliny (vi, 29) mentions a place called Gaza, which lay
farther south than the Abalitic Gulf and the Island of Diodorus.

[2] *Agamé* still designates an important province of the plateau of
Tigré, directly to the east of the position of Axum. Salt describes it
as a rich and fertile territory, owing to its great elevation in a torrid
climate.

[3] Saint-Martin thinks that the name *Sigyé* is connected with
Tzigam, the name of a large Agau tribe now seated to the west of

possessed. I next reduced Aua[1] and Tiamò, called Tziamò, and the Gambéla,[2] and the tribes near them [he means the nations beyond the Nile],[3] and Zingabênê and Angabe and Tiama and Athagaûs and Kalaa,[4] and the Seménoi—a people who lived beyond the Nile on mountains difficult of

Lake Tzana, but which its own traditions connect with the Agaus of the Takazzé. The Agaou people, which is the aboriginal race of the Abyssinian plateau, has been in conflict at all the epochs of history with the lords of the country of Axum, now Tigré.—pp. 350-1.

[1] The position of Aua is fixed by the itinerary of Nonnosus, the envoy of Justinian to the King of Axum in 531, only eleven or twelve years after the time when Cosmas visited those shores. In this itinerary Auê is a district situated half-way between Adule and Axum. The name still exists in that of the city of Adoua (Ad'Oua = city of Oua) the present capital of Tigré (p. 351). Nonnosus on his return from Axum wrote a history of his embassy, which has perished, but of which we have an abridgement by Photius, reprinted in the Bonn Collection of the Byzantine writers. Bent thinks Aua is perhaps in Yeha.

[2] Montfaucon here notes that *Tiamò* is read *Tiama* in the Vatican copy, and that *Tziamò* was called also *Tziama*. He says that *Tzama* is the name by which a certain prefecture of the kingdom of Tigré, immediately adjacent to Agame, is to this day designated. Both Salt and Saint-Martin confirm this identification, and the latter recognises Gambéla in the valley of Iambéla in the province of Enderta. The name of Tiamò, he adds, recurs elsewhere several times in Abyssinian geographical inscriptions.

[3] The words within brackets appear, says Montfaucon, to have formed a marginal note which has crept into the text of Cosmas. By the Nile here is not meant the Nile proper, but its great eastern tributary the Takazzé, which, however, before joining the Nile unites with the Atbara (the *Astaboras* of the ancients) in Nubia.

[4] Zingabênê, Angabê, and Tiama cannot now be identified, but Athagaûs and Kalaa seem to correspond respectively to Addago and Kalawé, two districts which lie to the left of the Takazzé below the mountains of Semen. Dillmann conjectures that Zingabênê was written for Zingarênê, and so identical with Zangarên in Hamásén. Dr. Glaser suggests that Kalaa may be the Koloê of the *Periplus*, which describes it as a town three days' journey inland from Adulè, and a five days' journey from Axum. With regard to the Athagaûs, Dillmann agrees with Montfaucon in taking them to be a part of the very ancient Agaû people, perhaps those in Lasta.

access and covered with snow, where the year is all winter with hailstorms, frosts and snows into which a man sinks knee-deep.[1] I passed the river to attack these nations, and reduced them. I next subdued Laziné and Zaa and Gabala, tribes[2] which inhabit mountains with steep declivities abounding with hot springs, the Atalmô and Bega,[3] and all the tribes in the same quarter along with them. I proceeded next against the Tangaïtae,[4] who adjoin the borders of Egypt; and having reduced them I made a footpath giving access by land into Egypt from that part of my dominions. Next I reduced Annine and Metine—tribes inhabiting precipitous mountains.[5] My arms

---

[1] For *Seménai* the Vatican copy reads *Saminé*. The inscription gives this name in exact accordance with its present orthography. Samen, or Semen, with its lofty mountains which rise to the height of 15,000 ft. above the sea-level, is the most remarkable region in all Abyssinia.

[2] A little below, Cosmas tells us that in his time these three provinces still bore the same names as in the inscription, from which it would appear that these were well-known districts. Their names have now disappeared, or are too much changed to be recognisable. Saint-Martin, however, conjectures that Laziné may be the land of Baséna on the northern frontier of Tigré, at the foot of the last declivities of the plateau. Baséna, he adds, is in the direction of the Taka, the great oasis of eastern Nubia, whereto the inscription proceeds to lead us.

[3] "Bega refers to the ancient race of the Bedjas or Bodjas (which the Arab authors call also Boga), who, under the actual name of Bicharieh cover with their nomadic tribes a great part of the sandy regions of Nubia between the Nile and the Red Sea" (*l. c.* p. 354). In a note it is pointed out that *Bicharieh* and *Bedja* are but two forms of the same name. Dr. D. H. Müller, of Vienna, identifies the Bega with the *Bougaïtai* of the Greek inscription of Axum.

[4] "The Tangaïtes, at the time to which the inscription takes us back, were the most powerful of the Bedja tribes; this tribe has given its name to the country of Taka, which is watered and fertilised by the united waters of the Takazzé and Atbara. Tangaïtes, for Tanga or Taka, is a form purely Greek" (*l. c.* p. 354).

[5] The fact that these two tribes lived in a mountainous region

were next directed against the Sesea nation. These had retired to a high mountain difficult of access; but I blockaded the mountain on every side, and compelled them to come down and surrender. I then selected for myself the best of their young men and their women, with their sons and daughters and all besides that they possessed. The tribes of Rhausi I next brought to submission: a barbarous race spread over wide waterless plains in the interior of the frankincense country. [Advancing thence towards the sea] I encountered the Sôlate, whom I subdued, and left with instructions to guard the coast.[1] All these

143

---

showed that their position was eastward toward the coast of the Red Sea.

[1] "The rest of the inscription is concerned with expeditions all different. Here the Axumite conqueror conducts us towards the country of Barbara, where incense grows, that is to say, into the cinnamon-bearing country of the Greeks and Romans. He then subdues the peoples of Sesea, the Rhausi, and the Sôlate, and obliges the last to watch over the security of the coast. With the exception of the Sôlate, of whom the identification is uncertain, the other names mentioned in this part of the inscription are recognisable without difficulty. Barbara, or Berbera, has been at all times the appellation of a part of this country stretching towards the Indian Ocean. It is on this side the last extension of a name of aboriginal race and of primordial origin of which we find the traces disseminated through a great portion of the valley of the Nile, and through all the north of Africa, and we know that Berbera remains the name of the principal part of the coast of Somâl, right opposite Aden. Sesea ought to designate a part at least of the Somali people, of which one of the principal tribes bears still the name of Issa, which even appears to have been the patronymic appellation of the race. Cosmas, who beyond question employs the name as it was pronounced by the Greek sailors in these seas, departs still further from the proper Ethnic name in writing *Sasu*. It was, he says, the last country of Ethiopia towards the Erythraean Sea, and he informs us that in his time the kings of Axum sent thither annual caravans which brought back much gold. Lastly, the name of the *Rhausi* (who very probably are no others than the Rhapsii of Ptolemy, IV, viii) exists with but little alteration in that of the *Arousi*, a large tribe in the interior to the south of Abyssinia, one of those which carry on a regular traffic with the coast" *l. c.* pp. 354-5).

nations, protected though they were by mountains all but impregnable, I conquered, after engagements in which I was myself present. Upon their submission I restored their territories to them, subject to the payment of tribute. Many other tribes besides these submitted of their own accord, and became likewise tributary. And I sent a fleet and land forces against the Arabitae and Cinaedocolpitae[1] who dwelt on the other side of the Red Sea, and having reduced the sovereigns of both, I imposed on them a land tribute and charged them to make travelling safe both by sea and by land. I thus subdued the whole coast from Leucè Còmè[2] to the country of the Sabaeans. I first and

---

Sasu, as Dr. Glaser tells us, lay in the south-east part of the Somali peninsula, not far from the Italian colony Hobia (Oppia, Obbia), and consequently quite in the *eastern* portion of the conquests made by the king who was the author of the inscription. This decision as to the position of Sasu was indubitably correct, but was utterly inconsistent with the statement in the inscription that Ethiopia and Sasu formed the *western* boundary of his dominions. Here was indeed a Gordian knot to untie, and Dr. Glaser's peace of mind was quite taken away until he found a solution, namely, that not Sasu at all, but Kasu is to be read. Kasu, he explains, was shown by Dillmann to be a far westward territory, since in the Axumite inscription in which it occurs, it admits of being located only in or near Meroë. "Now", he exclaims, "did all at a stroke become clear. The king penetrated westward to Ethiopia and Kasu, that is, into the region of Khartûm."

[1] The name of this people is found in Ptolemy, and written exactly as here. Saint-Martin takes them to have been a branch of the great tribe of Kinda, to which the tribe of Kelb united itself. They occupied Hedjaz, which is now the Holy Land of Arabia, containing as it does the sacred cities of Mecca and Medina.

[2] Towards the northern frontier of the Cinaedocolpitae was situated the port and trading mart of Leucè Còmè, from which at one time the costly wares received from India and Arabia were transmitted to Petra of the Nabathaeans. It has been identified with the port called Hauara [lat. 24° 59′ N., long. 37° 16′ E.]. Cosmas in a note says, that in the country of the Blemmyes there is a village (Κώμη) called Leucogè, which he erroneously takes to be Leucè Còmè, since the Blemmyes lived not in Arabia but Nubia, on the other side of the Red Sea.

alone of the kings of my race made these conquests. For this success I now offer my thanks to my mighty God, Arès, who begat me, and by whose aid I reduced all the nations bordering on my own country, on the East to the country of frankincense, and on the West to Ethiopia and Sasu.[1] Of these expeditions, some were conducted by

---

[1] Saint-Martin, commenting on the geography of this passage, says: "This shows, first, that the Axumites properly called (that is to say, the inhabitants of our actual Tigré, which is the north-east part of the Abyssinian plateau) had not yet adopted for themselves the Greek appellation of *Ethiopians*, as they have since done. The name of *Saso*, which appears there for the first time, carries us to the unknown countries of the West; it is then by a manifest confusion that Cosmas, deceived by an apparent relation, has confounded it with the maritime country of Sesea. Mr. Harris, who was sent to the Ras du Choa in 1842 by the East India Company, with a view to form commercial relations with this powerful chief of southern Abyssinia, among the items of information that he collected during his stay about the countries of the Nile basin still more southern, heard mention of a great kingdom of *Sousa*, the most powerful, he was told, of the native states towards the south and south-west of the Choa."—(*l. c.* pp. 357-8). Saint-Martin takes this country, of which Mr. Harris had heard, to be *Kâfa*, which he thinks is the name given to it by the Galla, while *Sousa* is its ancient and indigenous name. Dr. Glaser's solution of the difficulty regarding Sasu, given in note 1. p. 63, is, however, preferable. Saint-Martin follows up his examination of the geography of the inscription with an attempt to ascertain its date, and this he is led to assign either to the earlier or to the later half of the second century of our aera. Professor Dillmann, on the other hand, assigned to the inscription a much earlier date, being of opinion that the king whose conquests it records reigned in Axum before Zôskales (called Zahakale in the list of Axumite kings), who filled the throne at the time when the author of the *Periplûs*, from whom we learn the fact, was making trading voyages in the Erythraean Sea. As these voyages appear to have been made between A.D. 56 and A.D. 71, the inscription would thus date as far back as about the beginning of the Christian aera. Professor D. H. Müller, of Vienna, again, thinks that the author of the inscription was no other than this Zôskales himself, who is described in the *Periplûs* as an ambitious man, and well versed in Greek literature (τοῦ πλείονος ἐξεχόμενος . . . καὶ γραμμάτων Ἑλληνικῶν ἔμπειρος). Dr. Glaser, however, who is one of the greatest living authorities on questions of Arabian history, which he has

myself in person, and ended in victory, and the others I entrusted to my officers. Having thus brought all the world under my authority to peace, I came down to Aduli and offered sacrifice to Zeus, and to Arês and to Poseidôn, whom I entreated to befriend all who go down to the sea in ships. Here also I reunited all my forces, and setting down this Chair in this place, I consecrated it to Arês in the twenty-seventh year of my reign.

Scholia of Cosmas on the Inscription of Ptolemy.
From the Vatican codex.

Then Lazine and Zaa and Gabala. These nations are called by these names up to the present time.

I conquered the Sesea nation. Here he indicates the nations of Barbaria.

The Arabitae and Cinaedocolpitae. Note—He refers to the people of the Hômerite country, that is, the inhabitants of Arabia Felix.

From Leucê Cômê. Note—In the territories of the Blemmyes there is a village (κώμη) called Leucogê.

As far as the country of the Sabaeans. Note—The land of the Sabaeans is also in the Hômerite country.

And to the places of Sasu. Note—The land of Sasu, where there is much gold—that which is known as Tancharas, is the remotest in Ethiopia. Beyond this, and also beyond the country of the Barbarcôtes, the people who trade in frankincense, lies the Ocean.

---

assiduously studied, by the light of numerous inscriptions found in various parts of Arabia, refers the inscription in question to the closing years of the third Christian century. Some of the conquests of the Axumite king lay in Arabia, and Dr. Glaser finds that the date he has fixed is that which is most compatible with ascertained facts, both of Arabian and Axumite history. To this conclusion he has also been guided by statements advanced in the *Periplûs*, and the famous bilingual Axumite inscription.

Such is the inscription on the Chair, and at this very day in the very place where that Chair stands they execute in front of it condemned criminals; but whether this custom has prevailed from the time of Ptolemy I cannot say. I have set all this down from a desire to show that he is quite correct in taking the land of Sasu and Barbaria to lie at the extremity of Ethiopia, since he had subjugated all these regions and the tribes by which they were inhabited, most of which we ourselves have seen, while about the rest we obtained accurate information when we were in their neighbourhood. For most of the slaves which are now found in the hands of merchants who resort to these parts are taken from the tribes of which we speak. As for the Seménai,[1] where he says there are snows and ice, it is to that country the King of the Axômites expatriates any one whom he has sentenced to be banished. The nation again which has its seats beyond the Arabitae and the Cinaedocolpitae and the country of the Sabaeans he calls the Homerites. We can accordingly, from what has been above recorded, correctly estimate the breadth of the earth from the hyperborean regions down to Sasu and Barbaria, the frankincense country, to be not more than two hundred stages (*of thirty miles each*). I have written thus with the advantage of possessing exact knowledge, and I cannot therefore have fallen much short of the truth. For the facts I am indebted partly to what I observed in the course of my voyages and travels, and partly to what I learned from others on whose accuracy I could depend. Thus even in this matter divine scripture is proved to be right and the pagans to be wrong, who, in preference to the truth and in support of their vanity, advance conjectures, sophistries, and old wives' fables no matter how false, inventing forsooth another zone farther

---

[1] The Vatican copy has Salméné.

south than the torrid, and like the earth which we inhabit;
and although no one has either seen or heard of such. For
how could that be seen or heard of, that has never come
within the ken of our senses? Hence the nonsense they
babble cannot be accepted; for it is the jargon of mere
novices in quibbling, and not of old adepts in that art.
These youngsters supposed that by their plausible
sophisms they could refute the opinions of those who
were born before them, thus attempting the impossible, as
we have proved in brief in the preceding book.

Note on Ptolemy.

This Ptolemy is one of those Ptolemies who reigned after
Alexander the Macedonian, concerning whom the prophet Daniel
prophesied in different passages, and especially in the dream of
Nabuchodonosor and in the vision of the four beasts that rose
up from the sea which Daniel himself saw; namely in the image,
a head of gold, but in the vision a lioness, by which he signified
the kingdom of the Babylonians, that is Nabuchodonosor. Then,
145 in the image, the breast and the arms of silver, but in the vision, a
bear—namely, the empire of the Medes, which was inferior to
that of the Babylonians, whereby he means Darius the Mede.
Next again in the image—the belly and the thighs of brass, but
in the vision a leopard, the kingdom namely of the Persians, by
which he signifies Cyrus, whose empire was no less splendid and
renowned than that of the Babylonians. Then again in the
image, the legs of iron, and in the vision, a beast terrible and
dreadful, with claws of brass and teeth of iron, by which he
indicates the Macedonian empire—that is Alexander—breaking
kingdoms in pieces and subduing them. Then again in the
image, the feet and toes partly of iron and partly of clay; and in
the vision, ten horns corresponding in number with the toes, by
which he means the empire of Alexander broken up after his
death, which, in the vision also of the ram and the he-goat was,
he says, broken up towards the four winds of heaven. For,
when Alexander was approaching his end, he divided his empire
among his four friends, of whom one reigned in Europe, that is,
in Greece, another in Asia, another in Syria and Babylonia, and

the fourth in Egypt, Libya and the southern parts.[1] Unto these four were many sons born, who filled their thrones after them and brought manifold evils upon the world, as has been recorded in the book of the Maccabees. Now the little horn speaking great things, that was in the midst of the ten horns, signifies Antiochus Epiphanes, who warred against the Jews in the days of the Maccabees. He speaks therefore of all these things as partly of iron and partly of clay, to show them as conquering each other and being conquered in turn, and not mixed together, just as iron and clay do not commingle.

Then again, in the image, he speaks of a stone cut out of the mountains without hands, and, in the vision, of the Son of Man coming on the clouds of heaven, whereby he indicates the Lord Christ on both sides of his descent—from Abraham and from the Virgin without human seed, for here the words *without hands* mean *without human seed;* while the words *on the clouds of heaven* are employed because the clouds without human hands carry as it were in their womb the rains to which they give birth. Then again, in the image, the words: *And he smote the clay, the iron, the brass, the silver and the gold, and they became like the chaff of the summer threshing-floors, and the wind with its gusts swept them away and there was no more place found for them* (Dan. ii, 35); and in the vision the words: *I beheld till the beast was slain and his body destroyed, and given to be burned with fire; and as for the rest of the beasts their dominion was taken away, yet their lives were prolonged for a season* (Dan. vii, 11), signify respectively the same thing—namely, that at the coming of the Lord Christ all these empires would be taken away—the Babylonian, the Median, the Persian and the Macedonian, while all the kingdoms that arose from the partition of the last would become of no account. And such was the very condition of things in the time of Christ, for neither did the Babylonian, Median, Persian nor Macedonian empires then exist, but they had all been destroyed.

Then again, in the image, he says: *And in the days of those kings shall the God of Heaven set up a Kingdom which shall never be destroyed, nor shall the sovereignty thereof be left to another people, and it shall stand for ever* (Dan. ii, 44). And in the

---

[1] Antigonus, Perdiccas, Seleucus Nicator, and Ptolemy.

vision he says : *And he came even to the Ancient of days and they brought him near before him—and there was given him dominion and glory and a kingdom, that all people, nations and languages should serve him; his dominion is an everlasting dominion, and his kingdom that which shall not be destroyed* (Dan. vii, 13, 14). This is one instance more of his saying the same thing both in the image and the vision, namely, that at the coming of the Lord Christ those kingdoms shall pass away and be destroyed, but his kingdom shall be indissoluble and eternal. This Ptolemy is therefore one of those who reigned, either Philomêtor or Euergetes the Second, or the king called Dionysus, who preceded the last Cleopatra.[1] For these reigned more than seven and twenty years, and were descended from the first Ptolemies who were the sovereigns of Egypt, in accordance with the inscription on the marble tablet of which we have given a copy. For concerning the kings that now are, nothing has been written in the Prophet (*Daniel*), as the Lord himself says that the Law and the Prophets prophesied until John. For when Nebuchodonosor was cogitating whether his kingdom would endure, and Daniel whether the Judaic rites would be perpetually observed, the same revelation was made to both alike. At one and the same time shall thy kingdom come to an end, and the Judaic and ritual observances be abolished, and a new and better dispensation shall supersede the old—and be eternal and indissoluble—and this shall have its beginning when the first kingdoms and legal rites shall cease, and be openly exhibited when its supreme head makes his appearance. For concerning the Roman empire nothing is expressly written in the Prophet, for it did not rise by succession from Nabuchodonosor, nor has it congruity with the polity of the Jews, or, to speak more correctly, with the laws which they obey; but is rather calculated to destroy them. Nor did it succeed the empire of the Macedonians, for he says : *The God of Heaven shall set up a kingdom which shall never be destroyed.* Here he speaks of the Lord Christ, and within the scope of his words includes, though but darkly, the Roman empire, which made its appearance contemporaneously with the Lord Christ. For while Christ was yet

---

[1] Philometor was the sixth of the Ptolemies, and Dionysus, the brother of the celebrated Cleopatra, was the twelfth.

in the womb, the Roman empire received its power from God as the servant of the dispensation which Christ introduced, since at that very time the accession was proclaimed of the unending line of the Augusti by whose command a census was made which embraced the whole world. The evangelist certainly indicates that *this enrolment*[1] *was first made in the days of Augustus Cæsar*, when the Lord Christ was born, and deigned to be enrolled in a country subject to Roman dominion, and to pay tribute thereto.

The empire of the Romans thus participates in the dignity of the Kingdom of the Lord Christ, seeing that it transcends, as far as can be in this state of existence, every other power, and will remain unconquered until the final consummation, for he says that *it shall not be destroyed for ever*. Now, if that expression *for ever* be taken as applying to the Lord Christ, it signifies *endless duration*, in accordance with what Gabriel also says to the Virgin: *And he shall reign over the house of Jacob for ever, and of his Kingdom there shall be no end.*[2] If again the expression be taken as applying to the Roman empire which made its appearance in the world along with Christ, this shall not be destroyed while this world continues. For I assert with confidence, that though, by way of chastisement for our sins, hostile barbarians rise up for a short while against the Roman dominion, yet that by the valour of him who governs us the empire will continue to be invincible, provided it does not restrict but widens the influence of Christianity. I say so because this imperial family[3] believed in Christ before the others, and this empire is the servant of the dispensation established by Christ, on which account he, who is the Lord of all, preserves it unconquered till the final consummation. The royal family of the Persians on the other hand is not of Persian lineage, nor in the line of the succession of its former kings, but it sprang from an

---

[1] Gr. ἀπογραφή – the term used in Luke ii, 2.

[2] Luke i, 32.

[3] Gr. βασίλειον—Montfaucon here translates this word by *imperium* (and in the next sentence by *regnum*), leaving βασιλεία, which almost immediately follows, unrendered. It is evident, however, that in each sentence βασίλειον means *the reigning dynasty*, γένος being understood.

alien power, that is, from the Magi.¹ For by the time of Christ the empire of the Persians had been destroyed by Alexander in accordance with the prophecy, and the successors to his empire ruled that part of the world until the time of Antiochus, after which the Parthians gradually made themselves masters of the country.² In point of fact, they marched in arms against Jerusalem, and took prisoner Hyrcanus, the Ruler of the Jews, not long before the advent of the Lord Christ.³ As regards this empire of the Magi, it is now about four hundred years since it was founded, and in my opinion it ranks next to that of the Romans, because the Magi, in virtue of their having come to offer homage and adoration to the Lord Christ, obtained a certain distinction. For it was in the Roman dominions that the preaching of Christianity first became current in the days of the Apostles, and it was immediately afterwards extended to Persia by the Apostle Thaddaeus.⁴ And, to be sure we find this written in the Catholic Epistles: *The Church that is in Babylon elect together with you, saluteth you.*⁵ The Roman empire,

---

¹ The monarch of Persia when Cosmas wrote was the great Khosru, or Chosroes I, as he is called by the Greeks. His reign extended from A.D. 531 till A.D. 579. He belonged to the dynasty of the Sassanidae, which was founded by Ardishir, the Artaxerxes of the Greeks and Romans, in A.D. 226. The family to which he belonged was Persian, and professed the faith of Zoroaster and his priests the Magi.

² Arsaces, the founder of the Parthian power, revolted from the Syrian yoke in the reign of Antiochus II, in the year B.C. 250. One of his successors, Mithridates I, who reigned from B.C. 174 to B.C. 136, made extensive conquests, and exalted the Parthian name to great glory. Before the Christian aera his successors had extended their rule along the east coast of Arabia, and also along the southern, so that they possessed the frankincense country.

³ In the year B.C. 40, under Pacorus, the son of the Parthian King Orodes I.

⁴ Eusebius, in his *Ecclesiastical History*, informs us that Thomas, one of the twelve Apostles, sent Thaddeus, who was reckoned among the seventy disciples of Christ, to Edessa, as a preacher and evangelist of the doctrine of Christ.— Book I, c. 13. Edessa, which was a town of great importance, situated in the northern extremity of Mesopotamia, in the province of Osrhoëné, played a very prominent part in the early history of the Christian Church. ⁵ I Pet. v, 13.

moreover, has many bulwarks of its safety in that it is the foremost power in the world, in that it was the first to believe in Christ, and in that it renders services to every department of the Christian economy. There is yet another sign of the power which God has accorded to the Romans. I refer to the fact that it is with their coinage all the nations carry on trade from one extremity of the earth to the other. This money is regarded with admiration by all men to whatever kingdom they belong, since there is no other country in which the like of it exists.[1] Let us now return to our proper subject.

Text.

For some of the old philosophers, who in the course of their travels visited almost every part of the inhabited world and wrote accounts of what they learned, have explained the position of the earth[2] and the revolution of the heavenly bodies in close agreement with divine scripture. Let one of them now come forward and give this evidence.

Extract from the fourth Book of the History of Ephorus.[3] The Indians inhabit a country in the east near sunrise, while the Ethiopians dwell in the south near the Meridian, the Kelts in the west near sunset, and the

---

[1] See below (Book XI, text and notes).

[2] This expression seems to mean here the relative position of the our great divisions of the inhabited world.

[3] Ephorus was a native of the Æolian city of Cymê, in Asia Minor, and flourished in the fourth century B.C. Like the historian Theopompus, he studied oratory under Isocrates, who advised him to devote his powers to the study and composition of history. The most celebrated of his works was a history consisting of thirty books, which began with the Return of the Heracleidæ, and brought down the narrative of events to the siege of Perinthus by Philip of Macedon, in 431 B.C. The work treated not only of the history of the Greeks but also of the barbarians, and was thus the first attempt made in Greece to write a universal history. The work is unfortunately lost, with the exception of some detached fragments. Ephorus attempted to give a faithful record of events, but was deficient in critical acumen.

Scythians in the north towards the Pole. These divisions are not of equal size, Scythia and Ethiopia being larger and India and the Keltic divisions smaller. The two larger, however, are of similar size, and so are the two smaller. For the Indians are situated between the summer and the winter sunrise, while the Kelts occupy the regions from the summer to the winter sunset. The two distances are equal as well as nearly opposite each other. The Scythians again inhabit those regions which the sun leaves unvisited in the course of his revolution. They are situated opposite the nation of the Ethiopians, which seems to extend from the winter sunrise to the shortest sunset.

Note.

149 This Ephorus is an old writer, philosopher, and historian.

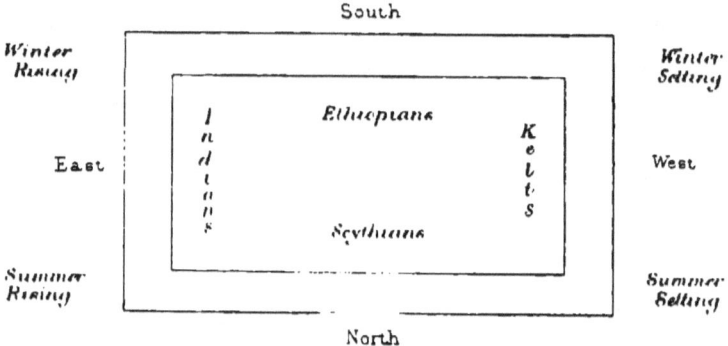

Ephorus, both in his text and by means of his sketch, explains accurately, like the divine scripture, the position of the earth and the revolution of the heavenly bodies. For this Ephorus was an historical writer who, in the fourth book of his *History*, has inserted the exposition which we have cited. Pytheas of Marseilles,[1] again, in his work concerning the ocean, informs us

---

[1] The date of this navigator cannot be fixed with certainty, but he probably lived in the time of Alexander the Great, or somewhat later. Besides the work *Concerning the Ocean*, which Cosmas here mentions, he wrote another called a *Periplus*, in which he described a voyage

that when he had reached the remotest parts of the north the barbarous people found there showed him the cradle of the sun, for, in the parts where they live, the nights always have their source. Xenophanes also, the Colophonian,[1] is clearly no believer in the sphere, for he supposed that the earth had no limits. Thus, then, the pagans are found, in what they have said, chiming in with sacred scripture.

But, to pursue our argument, we again assume that the four rivers which divine scripture says emanate from Paradise cleave a passage through the ocean and spring up in this earth. Of these, the Pheisôn is the river of India, which some call Indus or Ganges. It flows down from regions in the interior, and falls by many mouths into the Indian Sea. It produces beans of the Egyptian sort, and the fruit called Neilagathia; savoury herbs, also, and lotus plants, and crocodiles, and everything the Nile produces.[2] The Gêon, again, which rises somewhere in Ethiopia, passes through the whole of Ethiopia and Egypt, and discharges its water into our Gulf by several mouths, while the Tigres and

---

from Cadiz to the Tanaïs, or Don, a name which he probably applied in error to the river Elbe. He is frequently cited by the ancient writers, who inclined, however, to disparage his authority—Strabo especially, who denounces him again and again as a charlatan and a liar; although even he is constrained to admit that, as far as astronomy and the mathematics are concerned, he reasoned correctly. Pytheas is better appreciated by modern writers. For Μασσαλιώτης the Vatican codex has Μεταλεώτης.

[1] Xenophanes flourished between 540 and 500 B.C. He was a poet, and the founder also of the Eleatic school of philosophy. With him the Eleatic doctrine of the oneness of the universe is supposed to have originated.

[2] Strabo informs us that Alexander the Great, upon seeing crocodiles in the Hydaspes (Jhilam), and Egyptian beans in the Acesines (Chenâb), thought that he had discovered the source of the Nile.—Book XV, i, 25. Diodorus Siculus has a passage similar to this of Cosmas. He says (Book I, c. 34): "The lotus grows in great plenty here, of which the Egyptians make bread for the nourishment of their bodies. Here is likewise produced in plenty *Ciborium*, called the Egyptian bean." Κιβώριον, the name under which Cosmas mentions this bean, designates the seed-vessels of the κολοκασία in which it is contained. Cosmas appears to be the only writer in whom the word *Neilagathia* occurs.

Euphrates, which have their sources in the regions of Persarmenia, flow down to to the Persian Gulf. Such, then, are our opinions on these points. Divine scripture, with a view to show the diameter of Paradise, how great it is, and how far extended eastward, mentions the four rivers only, and thence we learn that the fountain which springs up in Eden and waters the garden, distributes the residue of its waters among the four great rivers which cross over into this earth and water a large part of its surface.

Text.

Since then, the luminaries of heaven in this manner pursue their course, making day and night, seasons and years, serving also for signs for those sailing upon the seas or travelling through deserts, while they also supply the earth with light, we shall not say that they are moved by the revolution of the heavens, but rather by powers that are rational, as if they were so many torch-bearers, as we shall prove once more by the declaration of divine scripture. For the divine Apostle, speaking of the Adversary, teaches what was his work from the beginning in these words: *According to the prince of the power of the air, of the spirit that now worketh in the sons of disobedience*[1] —words which clearly show him to have been formerly a prince endowed with the power of moving the air and changing its place, but one now cast out for ever from this dignity; yea, rather, one who from sheer depravity works upon sinners, as is evident from the fact that he stood not alone in having the power to do this, but shared it in common with many others. For some of the angels were commissioned to move the air, some the sun, some the moon, some the stars, while others prepared the clouds and the rains, and rendered many other services—for this is the work, the appointed duty, of the angelic orders and powers—to minister to the well-being and honour of the

---

[1] Ephes. ii, 2.

image of God, that is, of man, and to move all things like soldiers obeying the commands of the king. This work they were commanded to do on the fourth day, when God adorned the heaven with its stars. The work of the adverse demons, as rebels against God, is to do what will mar his image, for on the fourth day they transgressed the command and were cast out of heaven, as elsewhere he says: *Are they not all ministering spirits sent forth to minister to those who shall be the heirs of Salvation?*[1] thus expressly declaring that they were ordained for the service of man. He further says: *For the earnest expectation of the creature waiteth for the revealing of the sons of God. For the creation was subjected to vanity not of its own will, but by reason of him who subjected it, in hope because the creation itself also shall be delivered from the bondage of corruption into the liberty of the glory of the children of God.*[2] By *the creature* he here designates the angels, and by the *sons of God* the human race. By the term ἀποκαραδοκία (earnest expectation), he represents the creature as straining its neck to scan the distant horizon in hope of descrying some help coming to man. For if the angels had not been subjected to servile ministrations they would not have longed for liberty; for when man had sinned and received sentence of death, they were smitten with sore grief, concluding that all was hopelessly lost; for since man was the bond uniting the whole creation, as well as the image of God, they abandoned after his sentence all hope both of themselves and of the universe, and were unwilling to be his servants and subordinates without resulting advantage. By the words, however, in the passage cited, *by reason of him who hath subjected it in hope*, the Apostle would have us understand that God did not permit the wish of the angels to prevail, but gave them some hope that they

---

[1] Heb. i, 15.   [2] Rom. viii, 19.

might not despair, but be cheered with the prospect that in the course of time some good would accrue to man.

Note.

On the sixth day the demon who hates good, seeing man honoured and thought worthy to have great care bestowed on him, became envious, and formed a design to drag him down to ruin with himself. But when he was at a loss how to assail him, he happened to perceive the beasts running straightway to their food, while the object of his envy, looking around him at such of the trees as were pleasant to the eye, remained quite unmoved the while by the calls of appetite; whence he concluded he had received some command from God about them. Having then approached nearer in the form of the serpent, he sought to learn the nature of the command, and craftily says: *What! hath God said ye shall not eat of every tree in the Garden?*[1] Then the woman who had just been brought into the world, and was far inferior to the other in quickness of intelligence, answered his enquiry. Then, pretending he had already known the command (which he had only that moment learned), he began to accuse God of giving grudgingly, and to entice man to eat of the fruit, advising him at the same time to transfer his allegiance to himself; and thus, forsooth, become as God, infecting him in this way with his own disease. The man was, in fact, persuaded in the afternoon, and was that same day cast out of the garden, just as his tempter had himself, as soon as he sinned, been cast out of Heaven. Then the man heard the sentence of death pronounced upon him: *Dust thou art, and unto dust shalt thou return.*[2] This filled the angels with sore grief, and all the more as they were also disheartened at some of their own number having transgressed; although they were more especially distressed about man, as on him depended what lot should befall the whole creation and he was also the pledge that secured the amity of all the world. For should this bond be in reality dissolved, the universe would of necessity be also dissolved. They bewailed, therefore, their own dissolution along with that of the universe, and could no longer endure to minister to man without any good resulting. But when

[1] Gen. iii, 1. [2] Gen. iii, 19.

God, who is full of compassion, had, through his renewed care for man and the postponement of his punishment, inspired them with good hope, they began under its influence to render their services with alacrity. In each generation, moreover, God, by exalting the righteous to great renown, still further stimulated their alacrity, and implanted in them hopes of renovation, of restoration, and of resurrection. At the birth, particularly, of the Lord Christ according to the flesh, the whole multitude of the invisible powers, having seen him born through whom comes the destruction of death, the beginning of the renovation and the resurrection, and their own freedom, lifted up their voices in hymns of praise to God, the cause of all, exclaiming: *Glory to God in the highest, and on earth peace, good will towards men.*[1] Then away were thrown at last all the sorrow and dejection which at one time they had suffered on account of man, and they gave expression to their joy at the birth of the second Adam. Wherefore they also, at the time of his temptations, remembering how in the days of old they had witnessed the discomfiture of the first Adam, which had filled them with dismay, but seeing now the victory of the second Adam, and how fairly not once but thrice in close grip with his tempter he had flung him out of the lists—they, I say, rejoiced with a great joy, and were eager in bestowing their services, as scripture has recorded, not now as if prompted by some hope, but because, having seen with their own eyes the victory of the second Adam, they came to minister to him with joyful alacrity.

But the host of his adversaries in their turn now mourned and lamented, being confounded with shame at the victory of the second Adam. Their chief accordingly finding himself unable to throw him down began to plot against him, with the Jews as his instruments, and having stirred up the Jewish mob against him and crucified and put him to death, imagined that he was at once and for ever rid of him. But when, not long afterwards, the resurrection—that wondrous, glorious, unexpected and mighty event—had taken place, and he had no longer to experience death or any other form of suffering whatever, but along with incorruption and immortality had obtained also immutability of soul; and when again he afterwards ascended heavenward in a chariot of cloud,

---

[1] Luke ii, 14.

borne up like a conqueror who celebrates his triumph; then did he enter within the firmament, and was the first of all who opened up for us a new and living way. The angels therefore, clad in white raiment, rejoiced along with men, and brought the good tidings to the disciples and the women. But their adversaries, seeing the superiority to themselves and to the whole creation of the human nature, which they had at one time tripped up by the heels, but by which they were now thrown down, remained dumb with madness and overwhelmed with uttermost shame. Wherefore the Lord exclaimed to the disciples: *Let not your hearts be troubled. I have overcome the world.*[1] And again: *Lo! I have given you power to tread upon serpents and scorpions and all the power of the enemy*[2]—as much as to say: Man of old having sinned when the serpent in Paradise assailed him, it was said to him: *He shall lie in wait for*[3] *thy heel, but thou for his head*; that is, Ye shall be divided and at enmity against each other, that man may not be under obedience to him. So the warfare was then waged on equal terms, each having the power to hurt the other; for the serpent watching for the heel of man, that is, besetting his path in order to hurt him on finding him out of the path, as he could do by creeping about his heel: while man being of upward stature and on his guard, and not straying from his path, was able to bruise[4] the head of the serpent. And now having conquered the serpent and brought him finally to shame, and having through his agency unjustly endured death for the whole race, and nailed the bond against it to the cross and blotted it out, I rose again on the third day victorious over death, and became the champion[5] who has achieved victory for all the human race, for through me the victory has been extended to all humanity. Be ye therefore of good courage. Behold, I have given you power to tread upon serpents and scorpions and on all the power of the enemy. He says in effect the serpent is no longer able to hurt your heel, being himself trampled down under your feet. So then, just as Adam

---

[1] John xvi, 33.   [2] Luke x, 19.   [3] Gr. τηρήσει. Gen. iii, 15.
[4] Gr. θλάσαι.
[5] Gr. πρόξενος. This name was given to a citizen of a state who undertook or was appointed to protect and act hospitably towards visitors to that state who belonged to a friendly state. His functions resembled those of our modern consuls.

had on the sixth day sinned by eating about mid-day of the fruit of the tree, and was cast out of the garden in the afternoon, so also on the sixth day and at the sixth hour, the Lord Christ for his sake endured in the flesh the Cross, by which we are saved. And just as again from the time of the transgression to the expulsion from the garden, all the angels were filled with great dismay, expecting nothing else than the destruction of man and of themselves and of the universe, so also during the Passion from the sixth hour until the ninth the whole creation was shrouded in darkness at the wickedness that was being perpetrated. And just as the two, Adam and Eve, were at the ninth hour cast out of Paradise, so also at the ninth hour the Lord Christ in the spirit and the thief entered into Paradise. On the same day, therefore, in which Adam was made, that is, on the sixth, there occurred both the Fall and the grief of the angels, the sentence of death and the expulsion from Paradise, so also at the time of the Passion, on the same day, there occurred the death of the Saviour by the tree of the Cross, the mourning of the creation, and in the afternoon the putting away of the mourning and the entrance into Paradise. *Verily I say unto you*, saith the Saviour to the thief, *to-day shall thou be with me in Paradise.*[1] Glory to God for ever and ever, Amen! But we must now return to our text.

Text.

Wherefore the angels did not desist from the ministrations which they rendered to men liable to death and corruption, for the Apostle speaks thus: *For the creation was subjected to vanity, not of its own will*, that is, they were unwilling to labour and serve to no purpose; *but*, he goes on to say, *by reason of him who subjected it in hope.*[2] In what hope? Because, as is quite evident, after the transgression the angels, when they saw that God was not carrying into effect the sentence upon man, but treating him with loving care and providing him with clothing, came to entertain better hopes of man, so that they did not despair of him but ministered in his behalf. Then after-

---

[1] Luke xxviii, 43. [2] Rom. viii, 20.

wards he says: *And the creature itself shall be delivered from the bondage of corruption into the glory of the liberty of the sons of God;*[1] that is, the angels themselves shall be delivered and with them the whole creation, when men shall be delivered from corruption and be glorified, and be made immortal, and the sons of God at the world's final consummation, when the form of this world shall pass away, and the resurrection of the dead shall take place, and the existing order of things shall be changed. For when it shall come to pass in accordance with divine scripture that the stars shall fall, and the course of night and day cease, and the angels who move them be liberated through the exemption of men from corruption, who shall thus not at all need them, what then can these new law-givers say who think that the heaven is spherical, and assert that the stars are moved and yet move of themselves? For what useful purpose, let them tell us, if at least they define themselves to be Christians, will the heaven then perform revolutions? But away with these inept, these unstable men, for the Apostle yet again exclaims that *the whole creation groaneth and travaileth together in pain until now,*[2] thereby again showing that the whole creation, and especially the angels themselves, are burdened in this state of existence from being subservient to corruption and mutation. For since they are themselves mutable they are constantly absorbed in reflections about mutation, thinking over and hoping for liberty and longing to obtain it; and obtain it they shall, as has been stated, when men rise from the dead. For unless they had themselves received a law prescribing what they should and should not do, they could not have fallen into sin, for some of them could not have transgressed (*as they did*) unless they had received this law from God. Those consequently who transgressed were cast

---

[1] Rom. viii. 21. [2] Rom. viii. 22.

down from on high to the earth, for *I saw*—it is the Lord who speaks—*Satan like lightning fall from heaven.*[1] But without law it is impossible there should be transgression, as saith the Apostle: *For where there is no law there is no transgression,*[2] and *Without the law sin is dead.*[3] So that the angels themselves in every way want to obtain freedom from the law and from mutation. Now, of this liberty, the cause has been and will be the advent of our Lord Jesus Christ. *For all things,* the Apostle saith, *both those which are in heaven and those which are on the earth are summed up in Christ*; and, *If any one is in Christ he is a new creature; old things are passed away, behold all things are become new.*[4]

Note.

On the first day, that is the Lord's day, the foundation of the world and the beginning of the creation took place. God having begun in the evening to create those things which comprise the whole world, that is to say, heaven and earth, creating along with them the darkness and the water and the air and the fire which has been commingled with the earth, and the angels—producing all these at one time. Wherefore on the same day and the same night a new creation of the whole world again took place, for the whole world has its circumscription in man,[5] because man, as has been frequently stated, is the bond which holds all the world together. When man, therefore, rose again on the same night of the Lord's day, incorruptible and immortal and unchangeable, he gave a pledge to the whole creation visible and invisible that it would obtain like benefits. Wherefore the Apostle saith: *To sum up all things in the Christ, both the things that are in heaven and that are in the earth;*[6] and: *If any one be in Christ he is a new creature. Old things are passed away, behold all things have become new.*[4] He says *all things,* because in man are contemplated things visible and invisible. He then who denies

155

---

[1] Luke x. 18.   [2] Rom. iv. 15.
[3] Rom. vii. 8.   [4] II Cor. v. 17.
[5] Gr. ὁ πᾶς γὰρ κόσμος ἐν τῷ ἀνθρώπῳ περιγράφεται.
[6] Ephes. i, 10.

to the Lord Christ the possession of perfect manhood[1] is deceived by failing to understand the great dispensation which God has planned, as well as to conceive aright the Christian doctrine. In like manner again he who denies his perfect godhead[2] is chargeable with guilt and is utterly misled. Since then this hope is placed before Christians, that the angels and the whole creation shall be renovated into a better and a blessed state of existence, who is so malignant and so impious as to abandon this hope and lean for support on the new and beguiling folly of the pagans? For he shall hear in that day from the Judge these words: *Verily I say unto you I know you not ; depart from me, all ye that work iniquity.*[3] For it is in sooth a great iniquity to reject the declarations of God, and in opposition to them to ascribe a spherical form to the heaven. For such men are incapable of receiving the blessed hope and manifestation of the glory of the great God, our Saviour Jesus Christ, who gave himself for us: nor do they wish along with the faithful to hear the Lord Christ exclaiming from on high: *Come, ye blessed of my Father, inherit the Kingdom prepared for you from the foundation of the world;*[4] but always erring in their opinions they are whirled round in ceaseless revolution along with their sphere, without any hope that there will ever be a pause.

Text.

Since the heavenly bodies then, according to divine scripture, are moved in their orbits by invisible powers, and run their course through the north, and pass below the elevated part of the earth, it is possible, with such a configuration, for eclipses of the moon and the sun to be

---

[1] Cosmas, who was most probably a Nestorian, here hits at the Docetæ and Gnostics, who held that the human nature of Jesus Christ was a semblance and not a reality; and hits also at the Monophysites, who maintained that Jesus Christ had but one nature, or that the human and divine were so intimately united as to form one nature only.

[2] Cosmas refers here to the Arian heretics, who held that the Son was not co-equal or co-eternal with the Father, but was created by an act of the divine will. The Nestorians have always maintained that Christ was perfect God and perfect man, and that these natures were distinct.   [3] Matt. vii, 23.   [4] Matt. xxv, 34.

produced. For the angelic powers, by moving the figures on rational principles and in regular order, and with greater speed than lies in us to apprehend, produce these phenomena, plying their labours by night and by day without ever pausing. For as on the one hand the pagans assert that underneath the earth these bodies revolve far out of sight, thus, as was before shown, advancing views not only out of harmony with the nature of things, but opposed to the divine testimony, so we on the other hand following divine scripture, conceive that the revolution and the course of the heavenly bodies have some slight obliquity, and affirm that they are accomplished in this manner. For this being so, eclipses of necessity follow, and we are thus opposed neither to the Deity nor to the nature of things. For God must be believed in preference to all the notions and all the teaching of men. And with reference again to the four elements, we say that God having first established the earth as being dry, made it the foundation of the universe because of its heaviness. Water again, which is the moist element, he set above the earth on account of its fluidity; and the two as being opposite in their qualities he thought good to place together on account of their good temperature.[1] Next he placed above these the air, which is the cold element, and above the air again fire, which is the warm element, because these are both lighter than the other elements. They are, however, mutually opposed, and therefore the two elements which are placed together in the middle—water which is moist and air which is cold—having many mutual affinities, the one being of a fluid and the other of a porous nature, while both are soft to the touch, and

156

---

[1] Montfaucon, following the punctuation, construes the words διὰ τὴν εὐκρασίαν with the clause which follows, but they seem to belong to that which precedes.

readily receiving into themselves the qualities of each other and of their opposites, impart them in return to each other and blend the whole together; these two elements, I say, he thought good to place in the middle between the other two, the dry and the warm, that all nature might not be destroyed and reduced to a cinder. For from the readiness with which these two middle elements pervade each other, the pagans have fallen into error, and turning things the opposite way call air moist and water cold; consequent upon this they bestow two qualities upon a single element, and frequently even four.

God again provided rains for the good of the earth through the angelic powers, who with the utmost exertion bring them up from the sea into the clouds, and in obedience to the divine command discharge them wherever the divine command directs, for saith scripture by the prophet Amos: *He that calleth forth the water of the sea, and poureth it out over the face of the earth* (Amos ix, 6; see also Zech. x, 1; I Kings xviii, 41). With regard to earthquakes we affirm that they are not produced by wind, for we do not, like our opponents, have recourse to fables, but simply say that they occur by divine appointment, for saith scripture through David: *He looketh upon the earth and maketh it tremble* (Psalm civ, 32; see also Acts ii, 2; Amos ix, 5; Haggai ii, 20; Isaiah, in sundry passages).

With regard again to the Antipodes, divine scripture does not suffer me either to say or hear anything about these fables: *For he made*, saith the Apostle, *of one the whole race of men to dwell upon the whole face of the earth.* He does not mean upon every face of the earth, but upon its face.[1] The dead, again, that are buried in the earth,

---

[1] Acts xvii, 26. Cosmas argues that as scripture speaks only of two classes of men, the terrestrial and the subterranean, and by the latter means those buried *in* the earth, there can be none *under* the earth.

he calls the subterraneans, as in the passage: *That in the name of Jesus every knee shall bow, of beings celestial and terrestrial and subterranean*[1]; where by *beings celestial* are meant the angels, by the *terrestrial* men, and by the *subterranean* those that are buried in the earth. For the Apostle says that this is to take place at the resurrection, when all, alike angels that are in heaven, men that are upon the earth, and the dead that are buried in the earth, shall all rise and bow the knee in the name of Jesus the Son of God. For we are said to tread upon the earth, in the sense of the expression as used in the passage: *I have given you power to tread upon serpents and scorpions.*[2] To tread therefore implies treading above some one, but if we tread above any one he who treads in the opposite direction must be below him who treads above him; but according to those wiseacres, a spherical body has neither an above nor a below, and hence we neither tread nor are trodden on in return, nor do we at all walk on the earth. Consequently, all their theories are but inventions and fables.

With regard again to angels and demons and souls, divine scripture represents them as completely circumscribed, and as living in this world, as when the Apostle says: *We are made a spectacle unto the world and to angels and to men,*[3] as if they all lived in one and the same world. In Daniel also it speaks thus on the same point: *And the prince of the Kingdom of Persia withstood me one and twenty days, but lo! Michael one of the chief princes came to help me, and I left him there with the King of the Persians. Now I am come to make thee understand what shall befall thy people in the latter days.*[4] The expression *he withstood me*, and that other, *he came and went away and I left him there*, and others of like import, refer to beings whose

---

[1] Philipp. ii, 10. [2] Luke x, 19.
[3] I Cor. iv, 9. [4] Dan. x, 13 *seqq*.

natures are circumscribed. It is, moreover, to be observed that archangels are entrusted with the administration and guardianship of particular nations and kingdoms: Yea, even that an angel attends each man as his guardian; as when the church says concerning Peter in Acts: *It is his angel.*[1] The Lord likewise in the Gospels exclaims: *For their angels always behold the face of my Father who is in heaven;*[2] thus plainly showing that each one of us has his angel, evidently as his guide and his guardian. For Deity alone is uncircumscribed, existing everywhere, and as the same and in the same manner. *For if I ascend*, saith David, *into heaven, thou art there; if I descend into Hades thou art present there; if I should take to myself wings at morning*—that is, in the east—*and dwell in the uttermost parts of the sea*—that is, in the west—*even there shall thy hand lead me:*[3] evidently indicating here the uncircumscribed nature of the Deity. But this cannot be supposed to hold good of the angels, who in the passage above cited are said to have been left in a certain place. With respect to souls, divine scripture declares them to be circumscribed, and indicates them to be circumscribed by the body itself, as in the passage: *Bless the Lord, O my soul, and all that is within me;*[4] thus speaking of the soul as being within. And again: *My heart and my flesh.*[5] Here it uses *the heart* instead of *soul*, as if the soul had its seat in the heart, and was within the body, as when it again says: *In my heart have I hid thy words that I might not sin against thee;*[6] that is, I have hid them in my soul. And again: *Create in me a clean heart, O God!*[7] meaning a clean soul. The Lord too speaks thus: *Not that which goeth into a man defileth him, for it goes into the belly and is cast out into the draught,*

---

[1] Acts vi, 13. [2] Matt. xviii, 10.
[3] Psalm cxxxix, 8. [4] Psalm ciii, 1.
[5] Psalm lxxxiv, 2. [6] Psalm cxix, 11
[7] Psalm li, 10.

but the things which proceed out of the heart—that is, the soul—*these defile the man: such as evil thoughts*[1] and other things peculiar to the soul which he enumerates. Elsewhere again he says what is more adapted to put the Jews to shame: *The Kingdom of God is within you*,[2] instead of saying: Ye ought always to have the Kingdom of God within the soul. And again, to the thief who believed in him he gave this promise: *Verily I say unto you, to-day shalt thou be with me in Paradise.*[3] Here as evidently as possible he speaks of the soul as in a place. And that he speaks with reference to the soul and not to the body, is evident from the fact that the body of the Lord was buried by Joseph of Arimathea in Jerusalem, and that of the thief was buried there also. Most manifestly therefore he speaks of the soul when saying: *To-day shalt thou be with me in Paradise.* Besides, most of the evangelists when speaking of the death of the Lord say: *He gave up the spirit*—that is, the spirit within—namely, the soul, which went out of the body. Another of the evangelists says: *Having bowed his head, he gave up the spirit.*[4]

We have advanced the foregoing conclusions as expressive of the true Christian theory, having been moved to accept them by divine scripture, for they are not inventions or conjectures of our own, but we have strictly followed what God has spoken to us through the prophets and the Apostles and his own Son. Now, as all those who undertake to deal with such topics in dependence on their own reasonings and conjectures fall into endless perplexities and errors, and can say nothing with certainty, it behoves every true Christian to take refuge in God, the Maker of all, who knows the how and the why of everything, in order that we may not wander and be blown about by

---

[1] Matt. xv, 17.
[2] Luke xvii, 21.
[3] Luke xxiii, 43.
[4] Matt. xxvii, 50.

every wind of the doctrine of men, according to what the Apostle says: *In craftiness of speech and after the wiles of error*,[1] and thus even ourselves be condemned along with the world. Moses also in the Old Testament, in the Book of Numbers, gives expression to the same thoughts: *And the Lord said unto Moses, Speak unto the children of Israel and bid them that they make them fringes in the borders of their garments throughout their generations, and that they put upon the fringe of each border a cord of blue: and it shall be unto you for a fringe, that ye may look upon it and remember all the commandments of the Lord and do them: and that ye go not about after your own follies and after your own eyes, after which ye used to go a whoring, that ye may remember and do all my commandments and be holy unto your God. I am the Lord your God who brought you out of the Land of Egypt to be your God: I am the Lord your God* (Num. xv, 38). God himself in that passage teaches more clearly what the Apostle also has taught us, that we should not follow our own imaginations, but rather the divine precepts. God grant, O honoured Head, that we may abstain from these things, and cling instead to those that are divine, through the prayers of your Holiness,[2] O most Christian Father, so that we may find mercy and grace before the throne of grace for evermore, Amen!

---

[1] Ephes. iv, 14. [2] Gr. Ἁγιωσύνης.

BOOK III.

That the divine scripture is firm, sure and trustworthy, both in the Old and the New Testament, and in accordance with itself in the details which it gives, while it also shows the utility of the figures representing the whole world.

HEN men at first after the Deluge were high up in the air, building the tower in their warfare with God, they suspected from their constantly observing the heavenly bodies, but erroneously, that the heaven was spherical; for since the city where they were building the tower belonged to the Babylonians, an invention such as this must have originated with the Chaldaeans; whence also the descendants of Abraham who were Chaldaeans elaborated a barbaric sphere, and when they went down to Egypt communicated this notion to the Egyptians. The Egyptians in turn having grasped it as a basis for much active investigation developed it still further, until the Greek philosophers who visited Egypt—Pythagoras, Plato and Eudoxus the Cnidian—became acquainted with it, and basing their study of it on what they had learned from preceding enquirers elaborated it still further.

Note.

After the Deluge, when men had multiplied in the interior parts of the East, where, as has been recorded, the Ark rested, they removed a little way from their first seats and found a plain in the land of Sennaar (Shinar). Now, as they were all of one speech, they talked together with one accord, saying: The men who were before us God has destroyed with a deluge; if he shall again think fit to be wroth with us and seek to destroy us even with a deluge, we shall *all* perish to a man. But come, let us prepare bricks and burn them with fire, that they may withstand the waters, and building them together with asphalt, let us make a high tower the top of which shall reach to heaven, in order that being delivered from the deluge we may find safety in the tower. And we shall readily be able to array ourselves against him in battle, being very near him, as long as we are all of us together, before being scattered in different directions, for this is shown by their saying: *And let us make unto ourselves a name before we are dispersed over the face of the earth.*[1] When they had therefore begun to build, and in their rebellious mood[2] wanted to mount up into heaven, God, who is full of kindness and compassion, knowing and foreknowing man whom he had created with freedom both of will and action—knowing, I say, the strength of reason which he possessed, but at the same time the weakness of his flesh, was moved with compassion rather than with anger towards him, and made again a grand dispensation, and suffered them not to labour and toil in vain. For, besides being crushed with hard labour, they were dashed to pieces, if when high up in the tower they were hurled down from the top by the violence of the winds, or tumbled down if scorched by heat through their nearness to the sun, and blinded by terror at the dizzy height. He therefore confounded their language and divided it into many kinds, and put an end to their impious madness. He scattered them besides, and settled them over the whole earth. This was the cause of the dispersion of the nations, and of every country becoming inhabited. In the last days therefore God being well pleased with men, according to what is written: *Good pleasure towards men,*[3] of his own counsel and goodness resolved to lead them up into heaven, and after forty days from his resurrection led (Christ) our first-fruits up into heaven. And further, in order that

---

[1] Gen. xi, 4.

[2] Gr. τυραννικῷ τρόπῳ. In later Greek the adjective was used in this sense. Montfaucon, however, translates: *tyrannico more.*

[3] Luke ii, 14.

he might indicate beforehand the ascension of the rest of mankind, he on the day of Pentecost, having through the Holy Spirit joined together the tongues which he had formerly divided, gave them from heaven to the Apostles, and they spake with tongues the mighty works of God, as the Spirit gave them utterance, so that all who stood around gathered together from all the nations heard, each of them in his own speech, the mighty works of God, and knew the good-will he was pleased to show to men, because when of old men had rebelliously sought to go up into heaven, their design proved abortive; whereas now by the good pleasure of God, the faithful are carried up into heaven. Glory to the wise and compassionate God who has granted these favours to men. Amen!

Further Note.

When the first men were there at a great height engaged in building the tower, and frequently turned their eyes upward to the heavenly bodies and saw some of the stars ascending and others descending, they suspected that the heaven was somehow made to revolve on some kind of mechanical contrivance, so that it was spherical. For they were ignorant of the figure of the earth, and were not aware that the heavenly bodies are moved in the air by angels. Under the influence of this suspicion they made those gates which gave passage through the tower in all directions, contriving that the tower might not be of course thrown down by the waters of the deluge. In like manner also they built it with bricks that it might withstand the waters; for it was thus the tower was constructed. They say, moreover, that its foundations occupy a breadth in every direction of three miles, and also affirm that the steps by which it is ascended are arranged circle-wise in the exterior walls, in order that they may receive light through the windows made in them.

Text.

While the Israelites were still sojourning in Egypt Moses was born, and being reared in the palace of the Egyptian king was instructed in all the wisdom of the Egyptians. Having also from his own observations accepted the sphere and made himself acquainted with astronomy, or even with magic and hieroglyphic letters—or as I should rather say, the symbols of letters, for as yet letters were unknown; and, to speak briefly, having become a participant of all this wisdom, as the divine scripture informs us, when he reached manhood he preferred to side warmly with his own ancestral race, and he slew the Egyptian; and being afraid fled into the land of Midian, where he married and became the father of two sons. And when he was feeding the flocks of his father-in-law and led them up to Mount Sinaï, he saw that wonderful vision of the bush—the bush which burned with fire and yet was not consumed. Then, when he was making haste to see the great marvel, the angel of God called to him in the name of God, and commanded him to go to King Pharoah in Egypt for the purpose of leading the children of Israel out of their bondage to the Egyptians. And when he begged to be let off on account of the impossibility of the thing (for he saw that as he was a mere man he could not fight against such a mighty king), God through the angel filled him with confidence, reminding him of his forefathers: how that through a barren woman and aged parents he had raised up a great and numerous people. At the same time he prepared him beforehand for working wonders by means of the rod which Moses held in his hand. By these wonders Moses was quite astounded, and was persuaded to go away into Egypt. When he had gone thither, and had several times conversed with Pharoah, since he was going to show him how God had produced the whole creation— what creatures first and what second, and so on in proper order[1] . . . And these things were incredible to men, even as they are also now to those very clever men—yea, they

---

[1] There is evidently here a hiatus. Montfaucon has passed without notice.

were even incredible to Moses himself, for he had not as yet acquired experience of these matters; but in agreement with the Egyptians, he also conjectured that the heaven was of a spherical figure.

God therefore prepared him to work wonders, and in the name of God to change the elements, and to show to all the Egyptians and to the Israelites, and through them to the whole of mankind, that he was faithful to God in all that he said and did, disposing them and preparing them beforehand to accept him with readiness. The enchanters also by whom he had been educated combined to contend with him, and in the divine power he enters the lists against them, instructed to hold such opponents in contempt, so that they cry off and say: *This is the finger of God.*[1] When he had changed accordingly the constitution of the waters into blood and killed the fish, and changed the blood back into water living and productive, and had divided the Red Sea and made it stand as a wall on this side and that side in presence of the Israelites and the Egyptians, he was fully believed by them when he afterwards said:—*God said let there be a firmament in the middle of the water, and it shall divide in the middle water from water, and it was so.*[2] In like manner again, when he had made darkness for three days successively among the Egyptians, while the Israelites had light, he was again fully believed when he said:—*And there was darkness over the abyss, and God said let there be light, and God divided the light from the darkness*; and he assumed that the first and second and third day had passed without the sun, moon and stars running their course, saying:—*God divided the light from the darkness.*[3] Then again he brought frogs out of the river and fleas out of the earth, and therefore he was trusted when saying:—*God said let the waters bring*

---

[1] Exod. viii, 19.   [2] Gen. i, 6.   [3] Gen. i, 2.

forth living creatures, and it was so; and again he said :— *Let the earth bring forth this and that, and it was so*; and other things in like manner marvellous. Last of all, when he had slain all the first-born he was entitled to belief when saying last of all :—*God made man.*[1] And, as we have said above, he so prepared him beforehand that the Israelites could readily believe what he said and did, since they saw with their own eyes what he performed.

When again he had led them out of Egypt and had brought them through the Red Sea on dry land, and conducted the people to Mount Sinaï, in which he had seen the divine vision, God still working wonders before the people filled the mountain with flames of fire and with smoke, while there were heard the notes of trumpets resounding from heaven and waxing louder and louder; and when with gloom and darkness and tempest he had made them tremble with exceeding great fear, he began to speak to Moses in sight of the people out of the cloud. Then, having taken him up into the mountain to remain for forty days without food, he hid him in a cloud and in a manner abstracted him from all earthly things, and made him oblivious of all, including even what he had learned from the Egyptians, giving him birth anew as if he were a child in the womb. But at the end of the forty days he gave him a new form and a new soul, and revealed to him all that he had done in the making of the world in six days, and showing him in other six days by means of visions the making of the world, performing in his presence the work of each day, namely, on the first day the first heaven, and the earth a most spacious house, and within it water, air, fire commingled with the earth, darkness and angels, having produced everything singly and collectively from nothing whatever; employing,

---

[1] Gen. i, 20.

moreover, his voice alone for the instruction of the angels,
he created the light for the house itself, thus giving light to
everything as by a lamp. Then on the second day he
constructed out of the water the firmament, which in the
middle of the height of heaven binds all firmly together,
dividing the waters above from the waters below, as it is
placed in the middle between them. There are therefore
two places—an upper and a lower story, so to speak; the
lower he made fit to be a dwelling-place for this mortal
and changeful life; the upper he has made ready beforehand for the coming deathless and unchanging life.

Note.

The great Moses, after relating that on the second day God had
created the firmament, and by dividing it had made one place
into two, explained nothing further about the future state—that is,
the upper place—but turned his discourse entirely upon this
state—that is, upon the lower place—relating that God gathered
together the waters, and brought forth out of the earth the green
herbs and the trees, and in like manner adorned the heaven with
stars, and again from the waters produced the winged fowl and
aquatic animals, and in like manner again made from the earth
brute animals and man. Then again, when he had been commanded to make the Tabernacle in imitation of the form of the
world, he divided the one tabernacle by means of the veil, and
made it into two—an inner and an outer—within the outer of
which the priests continually discharged their sacred offices as
being in this world, while into the inner the high priest alone once
a year entered, as if into the upper place, that is, into heaven. 164
On this account the inner Tabernacle was entirely inaccessible to
them, being a type of the things in heaven. He was, moreover,
believed when with the same authority he suitably prescribed the
laws, and burdens, and punishments, and the correction of trans-
gressors, having prepared himself for prescribing what was con-
ducive to discipline and the working of wonders, as when he
involved the Egyptians in plagues and chastisements of various
kinds, and likewise made the Israelites suffer so sorely in the
wilderness for their repeated sins and transgressions, that he

destroyed all the men of that generation except two only that were left alive, while even he himself came to his end with that generation.

But when the Lord Christ for the salvation of the whole world had appeared among us to bring to a close the present state and proclaim the one to come, and announced expressly that the kingdom of heaven was at hand, he also, appropriately to his proclamation, wrought wonders for the benefit of men, and not in a single instance for the punishment of any man. He freed those that were possessed with devils, healed the sick, strengthened the weak, made the lame walk erect, restored sight to the eyes of the blind, opened the ears of the deaf, loosened the tongues of the dumb, cleansed lepers, restored the withered to a well-tempered life, cured withered hands, stanched by his power issues of blood, reanimated the dead even when corrupt and stinking, prepared the living for finishing their course, brought good tidings to the poor of treasures of which they could not be robbed, stilled by his rebuke the rage of the winds and the fury of the sea, and did all things else which are in harmony with the proclamation of the Gospel and with the future state; for in that state no devil gives trouble, no debility exists, all sickness has been banished, with disease of limbs and distempers, and penury, and issues of blood and commotions of the elements, and the last enemy—death—is destroyed. When the Jews considered all this—when they saw that he had not wrought a single miracle for the punishment of men, except only two, and these not inflicted on man, but upon the swine and the fig tree, upon brutes and an inanimate object, in order to show that these also were subject to his power —they attempted to bring a charge against him, saying to him in turn: *We wish to see a sign from thee*, that is, a sign such as that of Moses, which was for the punishment of men. But the Lord, knowing the thoughts of their hearts answered, saying: *An evil and adulterous generation seeketh after a sign, and no sign shall be given it except the sign of the prophet Jonas.*[1] *For as Jonas remained shut up in the belly of the whale for three days, and afterwards came out therefrom alive and uncorrupted, so I also being dead, after remaining in the earth three days shall rise up from the dead living and incorruptible.* At another time, again, when he had made a

---

[1] Matt. xi, 38.

scourge of small cords and cast out all from the temple, they said to him: *What sign shewest thou that thou dost these things?*[1] and this although many signs had been given by him. But he in turn said to them: *Destroy this temple, and in three days I will raise it up again*[2]—thus giving the same answer both times and speaking of the resurrection of his body as if he should say: When ye see me risen from the dead and see miracles wrought in my name, then shall ye know our power and our proclamation of good tidings; that my coming is not for the punishment of men, but for conferring upon them the resurrection, and immortality, and incorruption, and immutability, and blessedness. Accordingly, in consistency with his teaching, he wrought also his miracles. And this very thing Matthew also shows when speaking thus: *And Jesus went about their cities and villages teaching in their synagogues, and preaching the Gospel of the Kingdom, and healing all manner of disease and all manner of sickness*,[3] thus implying that he wrought miracles of a nature consistent with what he preached. But John the Evangelist thus speaks: *Many of his disciples went back, and walked no more with him.* Jesus said, therefore, unto the twelve: *Would ye also go away?* But Peter immediately answering on behalf of all said: *Lord, to whom shall we go away? Thou hast the words of eternal life, and we have believed that thou art the Holy One of God;*[4] meaning this: What thou teachest us we see even by the works which are done by thee, for thou promisest us life and a heavenly kingdom, and we see all things that are done by thee to have regard to the life of men. How then can we leave thee and attach ourselves to another? Our portion is therefore with thee, Lord Jesus Christ. Amen!

But some one may raise a difficulty and ask: Since he had given not even one sign with a view to the punishment of men, how then did he, taking, as has been said, a scourge, beat those that were selling in the temple and cast them out of the temple? Answer: What is alleged is false, for it was not at all to the human being he applied the scourge, but he adopted an admirable and becoming and appropriate course, for he scourged the brute beasts only, as it is written: *And having made a scourge of small cords he drove all out of the temple, both the sheep and the oxen*,[5] as

---

[1] John ii, 18. [2] John ii, 19. [3] Matt. ix, 35.
[4] John vi, 67. [5] John ii, 15.

much as to say: He scourged animals, but only the irrational, driving also out of the temple even those that were brought for sacrifice according to the law, showing by this means that the Judaic dispensation was coming to an end. Things, again, that had neither life nor sensation he pushed away and overthrew, as it is written: *And he poured out the money-changers' money and overthrew their tables.* The rational beings, however, he neither scourged nor drove away, but he chastised the irrational, as it is written: *And to those that sold doves he said: Take these things hence, and make not my Father's house a house of merchandise*[1]—showing by all these words and acts that the things offered for sacrifice in the first tabernacle according to the law were to cease, and that another dispensation would be introduced in its place, harmonising with the inner tabernacle, which was a type of the things in heaven—that is, of the future dispensation. But the Jews having perceived how he was shadowing forth to them the cessation of the Jewish dispensation, questioned him, saying: *What sign showest thou that thou dost these things?*[2] But taking appropriate advantage of the question, he promised them that he would do something darkly to foreshadow the answer. I refer to the destruction of the temple and to its renovation, because the destruction of the temple—that is, of his body—is the destruction of this world, while the renovation and change made upon the temple—that is, upon his body—is a manifestation of the future state. My argument, accordingly, good reader, holds sure that he never wrought for the punishment of man but for his benefit, and he himself elsewhere exclaims: *For the Father hath not sent the Son to condemn the world, but that the world through him might be saved.*[3]

Text.

Then he collected the water into one mass and exposed to view the dry land, which he called earth and which was before hidden by the waters; and he made the seas, that is, the ocean, as it is called, which encircles this earth, and is itself encircled by the earth beyond it, and also made

---

[1] John ii, 16.   [2] John ii, 18.   [3] John iii, 17.

the four gulfs which run up into this earth of ours—
in order that he might render the air of the ocean which
is interposed between the earth here and the earth beyond
salubrious to those at any time inhabiting either the one
or the other. He also so prepared the gulfs that they
could be navigated and afford a means of transit to
different parts of the world, thus always uniting the
dispersed nations in the bonds of amity through the facility
with which commodities might be transported from nation
to nation. And he commanded all kinds of fruits and trees
and green herbs to spring up out of the earth. And
again on the fourth day he divided the light, and with
its purer portion made the sun, and with the remainder
the moon and the stars, embellishing these heavenly bodies
with the harmonious beauty which adorns all nature,
giving order and harmony to the universe, while assigning
to the invisible powers as their function and their law to
administer, rule, and adjust these bodies to the service of
God, that is, of man, and of all that exists on his account;
thereby accustoming and training even these exalted
powers to be under law, and calling into play the good or
evil qualities of their rational powers, whence some of them
having transgressed were hurled down from heaven and
deprived of their dignity. For, *I saw*, saith the Lord,
Satan like lightning fall from heaven;[1] for being puffed
up because of the service entrusted to him by God for
the good of men, and because it was his office to move
the air for man and regulate its motion for his uses, and
deeming that he had of himself advanced of his own will
to this height, he usurped to himself the worship due to
God, and was forthwith hurled down. For the Apostle
again when instructing Timothy not to be hasty in conferring office on a neophyte—one, that is, who has but

---

[1] Luke x, 18.

recently been converted to the faith, thus addressed him: *Not a neophyte, lest being puffed up he fall into the condemnation of the devil*[1]; which, says the Apostle, the devil suffered through being puffed up, and has hereby clearly shown why he was hurled down, namely, by his being puffed up, deeming himself to be God, whence also he had the wish to communicate his own disease to man, saying: *Ye shall be as Gods.*

Note.

When God Almighty had along with the heaven and the earth produced all the angels, who had not hitherto existed, they stood all of them mute with surprise, being distinguished by the possession of reason from all around them, and were at once filled with amazement, and bent on considering who he was, the Creator who had called themselves and everything with them into existence. For they saw themselves existing in the midst of these things, and that they did not exist before them, and further reflected: The Creator of these and those things is surely one, or each must have had a different creator—or again: Were all things produced spontaneously of themselves, or who then is greater than the other? But when they were revolving such thoughts in their minds for the space of that night (for, as it is written, *God called that darkness, night*) God entering into their thoughts, all at once without being visible, said in clear tones: *Let there be light*; and the production of the light from nothing, following instantaneously with the word, struck them all with astonishment, and at the same time taught them that he who had produced this light out of nothing had produced also themselves and the things existing with them out of nothing. Then all bending down worshipped the invisible God, who had produced themselves and all things out of nothing. This, moreover, divine scripture declares in Job speaking in the person of God: *When I made the stars all my angels praised me with a loud voice and celebrated me with hymns,*[2] from one indicating all successively. It must, however, be observed that in the sight of the angels he called into existence out of non-existence two substances the one first

---

[1] 1 Tim. iii, 6.   [2] Job xxxviii, 7.

of all and the other last of all—the one first created being the light, and the other our soul; the one visible, perceptible and devoid of reason, the other invisible, intelligent and rational. All other things, however, he produced from things that are; intending thereby to teach them in turn that he was the maker of all creatures, both rational and non-rational, both those discernible by sense and those by intelligence, both those visible and those invisible—having called them into existence from the state of non-existence. Nor is it unlikely that they on that day and night, since they possessed reason, considered with themselves whether he who had produced this light had also produced the heaven. Then by a further word of command, he made before their eyes the second heaven, forming it from waters and like in its appearance to the first heaven. And by this they were once more taught that he is the maker both of this and of the first heaven —and so he brought to an end the work of the second day. Then when they were again engaged in thinking and looking to the things of the earth, he, in like manner [as when making the second heaven] gathered the water together, and having exposed the dry land itself to view named it the earth, for, being its lord, he gave it its name just as he also named the firmament heaven. Then he produces from the earth seeds and plants and green herbs and trees, teaching them that he uses each of his creatures to effect his purposes, since they were created by him. Then, when on the third day he had produced plants and seeds, thereafter on the next—that is, on the fourth day, inasmuch as such productions had need of temperature and arrangement, he makes out of the light, which he had before produced, the great luminaries and the stars—and having placed in the firmament of heaven the host of the invisible powers he directed them to move these bodies in order, on rational principles, and to make them revolve for the supply of temperature to the plants and all that would use them, in order that after their setting the plants might be refreshed by the coolness and motion of the air, and be again warmed by the presence of the luminaries. Accordingly some of the invisible powers, having from the beginning remained till now wavering in their mind, and ungrateful to their maker, entered on the office with which he had entrusted them in forgetfulness of his goodness, and being inflated with pride in their natural acumen, and in the power and the reason bestowed on them, and valuing nothing, but even despising the voice and the command which had come forth from God—yea, not so much as understanding that they had been, like the other creatures, produced along with the darkness, they were overcome by the delirium of their folly, and fancied they had of themselves by their own free act advanced to their high estate. I refer, of course, to the devil, who had been entrusted with the power of the air, and his associates, who had been entrusted some with this and others with that office, who having usurped for themselves the worship and glory due to God, and having been puffed up with pride and become insubordinate, were promptly—to prevent them misleading the others—hurled down from on high and from their dignities to go wandering about the earth. Whence also on the sixth day and after man had been formed, Satan, who was going about in the earth and envying the great care shown by God towards man, wished by affecting him with his own disease to drag down man along with him.

Text.

On the fifth day again he ordered animals after their kind to issue forth from the waters—the monsters of the deep and the other sorts of fish, and along with them the winged fowl of every species that pass through the air. Then again on the sixth day he made out of the earth all cattle and wild beasts and creeping things after their kind. And after he had prepared the whole house and fully furnished and adorned it, then, just as a king, when he has founded a city and completed it, places there his own image, tinting and embellishing it with various colours, so also the all-wise God, when he had as it were gathered together the manifold and diversified works of his hands—the rational and non-rational—the mortal and the immortal—the corruptible and the incorruptible—the sensible and the intelligible—he completed and adorned one particular animal constituted with every natural quality, namely, Man, and in the house which had been prepared he installed him in the rank of his own image which makes known that he who is the Creator of all is one. Hence those angels, who are well-affected towards God, admire his image, and hover as guardians around it, and minister thereunto. In like manner also the whole creation—the sun on high shining and making day for man, the moon and stars which impart some light amid the deepest gloom, accomplish their course by night for man; while all the months and seasons and tropics and years furnish signs to those who traverse the open seas or pursue their way through the desert; the air again serves the image for respiration, coolness and warmth; fire, for baking bread, heating water, giving light by night, cooking food and for other purposes; water, for drinking, washing, fermentation, irrigation and many other useful purposes; the earth, for habitation and the production of all kinds of fruit and for ministering to many other wants. Then the clean quadrupeds minister to his pleasure and supply him with clothing, the cattle labour for him and afford him leisure, the wild beasts contribute the delight and terror of the chase, and so also do the reptiles; while all things serve for the exercise of his rational powers and supplying what is useful for man, who is the bond uniting all the creation in friendship—who walks upon the earth, and yet flies on the wings of thought and surveys the universe, who is upright of stature and with ease confronts face to face the heavens as his dwelling-place, who is the king of all things on earth and reigns along with the Lord Christ in the heavens, and becomes a fellow-citizen of heavenly beings, and unto whom as the image of God all creation ministers while it is under subjection to God, and preserves its affection and gratitude towards its Creator.

Note.

When on the fifth day again animals were produced from the waters, the angels were taught that God is the Maker of this water, which was produced simultaneously with themselves. In like manner again when on the sixth day animals were produced from the earth, they were still more effectively taught that God is the Maker both of animate and of inanimate creatures. Accordingly all the angels again looked around them, gazing at all the things made by God which had sprung into existence before their eyes in the six days, and concluded that all things were varied, and wonderful, and fitted to excite astonishment, but among them they did not see anything like themselves—rational and invisible and intelligent. There was here ground for suspecting whether after all the Creator of the rational, invisible and intelligent beings is one person, and the Creator of the objects that are irrational, perceptible and visible, a different person. God, however, wishing to remove this supposition of theirs, produced last of all one living being constituted with all the natural qualities, namely, man—constituted with reason and sensation and intelligence, and with visibility and invisibility, and appoints him to serve as his image, which makes known that the Creator of the universe is one. Whence the angels being lost in wonder were taught by their own eyes through man the glory and the power and the greatness and the wisdom and the goodness of the one and only God, and that all the elements and what had been brought into existence after themselves had been prepared before on account of man. With alacrity therefore did they obediently serve and minister in moving everything that conduced to assist the image of God as being themselves members thereof, whence again they greatly rejoice over the well-doing and the righteousness of men, but are on the other hand greatly distressed by his evil-doing and by his sinning, as saith also the Lord himself: *For there is great joy in heaven over one sinner that repenteth*.[1]

It must, however, be here observed that just as God produced first in the sight of the angels out of non-existence the sensible, visible and non-rational light, and afterwards that which is rational and intelligible[2] and invisible, so also in the case of man he

---

[1] Luke xv, 7.

[2] Gr. τὸ νοητόν.—Montfaucon translates this by *intelligentem*, but what Cosmas means is that the soul is discerned by the intellect and not by the senses.

made first, according to Moses, his body, and afterwards his soul. Hence it was possible for some to fancy that if there had been another day after the six days, God would have made some other things, but since there is not another day after the six, he would not have been able to produce more. But God to remove this supposition of theirs, makes also a seventh day over and above, and does no work therein, thus showing that the world is quite finished and without any defect left in its structure to be afterwards supplied, for if he had left such he would have completed on the seventh day what was defective. But since nothing had been left defective in it, he rested on the seventh day from all his works which he had undertaken to make. Perhaps again some one will ask: Why did he make the whole creation not in one, or two, or three, or four, or five, but in six days? Such an one will learn this to be the truth of the matter—that, inasmuch as the angels are rational and mutable, one day would not have sufficed for their instruction if the whole had been produced in one day, for they would certainly have thought that things had been confusedly brought into existence like so many phantasms and been produced in disorder. But God Almighty having set apart one day for each single work, in due order formed the universe in parts, that it might be discriminated and thus better understood by the angels. First of all on the first day after they had been produced along with the heaven and the earth and the elements, he made the light before their eyes. On the second day he made the firmament: on the third day he gathered together the waters and produced from the earth trees and green herbs. On the fourth day he adorned the heaven with the luminaries: on the fifth he produced fish and fowl from the waters; and on the sixth he made from the earth animals and man, and accomplished the whole of those works in the six days. On this account therefore he made the whole world by parts in the six days for the discrimination and instruction of the angels, who from their acute intelligence were able each day to discriminate each separate part of the work and the Maker thereof. Whoso wishes can hence learn that along with the heaven and the earth the angels were also produced, because as they were present at all his works, God uttered his voice in their presence for their instruction, saying: Let this and let that be; but when he created the heaven and the earth he did not utter his voice nor say : Let heaven and earth and the things in them be ; for there were none to hear and be instructed. But since in the case of all the other works, there were present those who could be instructed, the voice was opportunely uttered.

Since the angels therefore were produced along with the heaven and the earth, the historian Moses, inspired by the Holy Spirit began his narrative with them, as they contained the angels, saying : *In the beginning God made the heaven and the earth.*[1] And further the Apostle, knowing well what pertains to man and how he is figured, in his Epistle to the Romans has placed man, as destined in the future for heaven, superior to all, for he says : *And they changed the glory of the incorruptible God for the likeness of an image of corruptible man, and of birds, and of four-footed beasts and creeping things ;*[2] mentioning man as superior to all, then the birds as inferior to him, then again the four-footed beasts as inferior to the birds, and as inferior to these again the creeping things which lurk underneath the earth, mentioning them according to their rank in the scale of being. But further, of all the quadruped brutes which walk upon all fours and turn their looks earthward, not one is capable of observing the heaven with ease. In like manner with regard to creeping things which with their whole body wriggle along the earth, not one of these is able to observe the heaven. All birds again, being bipeds, and in consonance with this having their legs in the middle of their body, direct their eyes towards the earth when they are high up on the wing ; but when they are standing they find it difficult to turn their eyes upwards unto the heaven. Man alone, of all the animals on the earth, being rational and destined for heaven, received from the Creator a figure in congruity with such a destiny. For he is a biped, being destined to fly away and walk in heaven. In figure he is erect, as if he were ready and destined to ascend on high.[3] And it is easy for him to behold with his eyes both the earth and the heaven as if he were hastening to ascend from the earth into heaven, conscious that

---

[1] Gen. i, 1.   [2] Rom. i, 23.
[3] Compare Ovid, *Metamorph.*, Book 1, ll. 84-86 :
    Pronaque cum spectent animalia caetera terram,
    Os homini sublime dedit, coelumque tueri
    Jussit, et erectos ad sidera tollere vultus.

earthly and heavenly things were bound together through him. Moreover, all the brute animals copulate without seeing each other face to face, and have commerce in a brutal and shameless manner. But man alone as rational proceeds to the act face to face, so that the pair seeing each other may embrace with reason, modesty, and reverence, and may thankfully sing the praises of their Maker for his goodness in giving to their nature help and mutual impulse for the propagation and multiplication of our race. God moreover made the woman from the man's side, because the two sides bind the whole body close together; for he neither made her from the front of man lest the woman should exalt herself above him, nor from his back parts that he might not exalt himself above the woman; but from his side, as being in her nature his equal, although the man, as the cause, is first in point of time, but not, however, in his nature itself. And still further—since the hand always protects and guards the side to which it belongs, so when he had made the female from the male, and the male from the earth, God pronounced the two to be one flesh, both from the constitution of the two sides, and from the fruit that springs from their connection. Wherefore the fornicator sins by estranging his own flesh and sowing illegitimate progeny; nay, he that commits adultery is ranked with the homicide, since he divides what is one flesh, and thus perpetrates murder.

Some one again may perhaps propose a question and say: Why was it that, while all the irrational animals were created by God, male and female at the same time, man alone was not created with the female, but remained quite solitary until the female was made later on? To this enquirer I shall reply that since all the animals were created by God without either the gift of reason, or the capacity of knowing anything, while all the angels, the instant they were created, were rational and knew the Maker of all things from those things which had been produced, one by one, that is, in the six days, it was necessary that man who had been created by God possessed of reason, and as the bond uniting all the creation, should himself be taught to know the Creator of all; but since, as he was not the first but the last of all to be produced, he could neither from the things made before him, nor from himself know God, it was God's pleasure to produce the female not along with him, but afterwards out of him, that he might thereby know that he who had taken out from him a being like himself was his Creator. Wherefore also he threw him into a trance[1] and a deep sleep, in order that by taking his rib from him without trouble and pain as in sleep, he might by the grace of God gain a perception of what had occurred, and celebrate the praises of his Maker, confessing and saying: *This is now bone of my bones and flesh of my flesh—she shall be called woman, because she was taken out of man.*[2] As then the angels had been created rational, and from the works produced in the six days had been taught to know him who was the cause of them, so of necessity man also was taught through the female, and learned that God was the Maker both of himself and of the universe; but especially as he had beforehand heard God say: *Let us make a helpmeet for him.*[3]

Text.

Then again on the seventh day, after he had revealed to Moses how the whole world had been made, and had honoured him with such mystic visions, he then held converse with him, and having given him the law written with the finger of God on tables of stone, and instructed him in the knowledge of letters and made his countenance shine with glory, he let him descend from the mountain.

Note.

Here men, having first received the Law from God in writing, were taught letters and communicated them to all the nations.

Text.

He then afterwards directed him to construct the Tabernacle according to the pattern which he had seen in the mountain—being a pattern, so to say, of the whole world. He therefore made the Tabernacle, designing that as far as possible it should be a copy of the figure of the world, and thus he gave it a length of thirty cubits and a breadth of

---

[1] Gr. ἔκστασιν.   [2] Gen. ii, 23.   [3] Gen. ii, 18.

ten. Then, by interposing inside a veil in the middle of the Tabernacle, he divided it into two compartments, of which the first was called the Holy Place, and the second behind the veil the Holy of Holies. Now the outer was a pattern of this visible world which, according to the divine Apostle, extends from the earth to the firmament, and in which at its northern side was a table, on which were twelve loaves, the table thus presenting a symbol of the earth which supplies all manner of fruits, twelve namely, one as it were for each month of the year. The table was all round wreathed with a waved moulding symbolic of the sea which is called the ocean, and all round this again was a border of a palm's breadth emblematic of the earth beyond the ocean, where lies Paradise away in the East, and where also the extremities of the first heaven, which is like a vaulted chamber, are everywhere supported on the extremities of the earth. Then at the south side he placed the candlestick which shines upon the earth from the south to the north. In this candlestick, symbolic of the week of seven days, he set seven lamps, and these lamps are symbolic of all the luminaries. And the second Tabernacle which is behind the veil and called the Holy of Holies, as well as the Ark of Testimony, and the Mercy-seat, and above it the Cherubim of glory shadowing the Mercy-seat, are, according to the Apostle, a type of the things in heaven from the firmament to the upper heaven, just as the space from the veil to the wall of the inner Tabernacle constitutes the inner place.

Note.

That the first historian in the world was Moses, both Eusebius, *the son of* Pamphilus,[1] and Josephus in their writings testify; for

---

[1] This is Eusebius, the father of ecclesiastical history, who succeeded Agapius as Bishop of Cæsareia in 315. He was a native of Palestine, and took the surname *Pamphili* as a token of his great affection for

they have clearly shown that of all writers Moses was the most ancient.

Text.

When Moses had accordingly been instructed in letters by God, having with his very eyes perceived the beginning of all things revealed to him, and when his countenance had been glorified so that he could not be beheld by his people without a veil, then as one who could claim belief and who had been glorified by God, he, the first among men, wrote the Book of Genesis in these words: *In the beginning God made the heaven and the earth,*[1] showing that when the world was created by God heaven and earth were produced at the very beginning, comprising as they did all existing things, while all the other creatures which he made either along with them or after them one by one, were contained within them. Then having ended his account how all things existing within heaven and earth had been successively created from the first day onwards to the sixth, and having then spoken of God as having rested on the seventh day and made nothing more, because the whole creation had been completed, and nothing been left defective in the harmony of the world to mar its supreme beauty, he again adds: *This is the book of heaven and earth;* thinking these words sufficient to indicate collectively all things within heaven and earth. And again in another place he says: *For in six days he finished and rested from all his works which God had begun to make;*[2] always speaking to the same effect, namely, that all things are contained within heaven and earth, and that before these seven days he had made nothing whatever, but began on the first day

---

the martyr Pamphilus, who had been the bishop of the same See, and of whom he wrote a life, now lost.

[1] Gen. i, 1. [2] Gen. ii, 3.

and finished on the sixth, and rested on the seventh without making anything else, and that he made only two heavens, the first along with the earth, while placing the second in the middle and preparing two states—the present and the future—just as in the Tabernacle he had ordered two places to be formed in imitation of the world, for he says : *According to the pattern shown to thee in the mount;*[1] for the Apostle in his Epistle to the Hebrews explains with regard to this Tabernacle that the outer was a pattern of this world, and the inner of the heavens.

When therefore a describer of the world so great and so divine as Moses had been attested and glorified, in the Old Testament by God and in the New by the Christ, while other divinely inspired prophets and apostles along with him bear witness about all things and about the figure of the whole creation as we have set forth in the preceding book, and they agree with him in every particular concerning the creation itself, who can be so obtuse, so foolish, and so far led astray, especially if he calls himself a Christian, as to disbelieve such truth as this, confirmed by such sacred testimony, and would not rather, bending lowly to earth, reverence the crowd of testimonies, the selection, the revelations, the wisdom, the glory, the predictions, the astonishing signs, the great wonders, the fulfilments of prophecies, the testimony of God himself, who spake with Moses face to face as a friend with a friend, while in the New Testament the Lord Christ frequently bears witness to him ? In very truth, to express myself more warmly, I assert that, unless one fights against God, he shall not find it in his power to gainsay these things. For afterwards repenting he shall say : the finger of God is in it ; and he will confess his defeat, just as the Egpytian enchanters and sorcerers Jannes and Jambres spoke concerning him.

---

[1] Exod. xxv, 40.

Since therefore according to the great cosmographer Moses, and according to Paul, that most divine teacher of the Church, in whom the Lord Christ speaks, two heavens, and two only, were created by God, and not seven or eight, or nine, how is it possible to listen to the pagans advocating views based on conjecture, sophistries, and arrogant assumptions, and inventing fables, not from the old but chiefly from certain recent writers, who, to meet the difficulties of their own doctrines, have devised apologies more foolish even than the doctrines themselves. And how can those who listen to these pagans maintain and yet be in accordance with scripture, that there are waters above the heaven, or that the first, the second, and the third day passed without the sun, moon and stars running their course? Or how in the deluge of Noah did the waters cover the whole earth and again retire? Or how can they say that there will be a final consummation of the world—that the heavenly bodies falling will cease to run their courses, and no longer cause the succession of day and night; and that the present state will altogether end, and that another state will be exhibited quite strange and far superior to this; and that the righteous will enter into the upper heaven beyond this the visible heaven, where is the kingdom of the heavens—the second Tabernacle called the Holy of Holies, of which the inner place in the Tabernacle was a pattern, into which also the Lord Christ entered, having been taken up into the heaven above the firmament, having become the forerunner on our behalf, and having prepared for us a new and living way? Or how can they say that, after the consummation, the seven or eight or nine heavens, or the heaven again which is by them called the sphere, will revolve? For what useful purpose will this revolution be? let them tell us and not grudge us this information; or how can such persons believe the stupendous miracles of which we have often spoken, that were wrought in the time of the great Moses? And likewise that miracle wrought in the time of Joshua, the son of Nun, when he made the sun and moon stand still, and added greatly to the length of the day, until he put the enemy to rout? And that other miracle performed in the time of Hezekiah, the going back of the sun ten degrees, which struck the Babylonian with consternation and induced him to send an embassy to Hezekiah?

Note.

Some have said that up to the present day a feast is celebrated by the Persians to Mithras, that is, the sun,[1] in commemoration of the sign in the time of Hezekiah.

Text.

Why need I speak of the all-devouring fire in the time of Nebuchodonosor, which burnt the bonds of the three children, but did not consume so much as a hair of their head, or any of their garments? Or of the renowned Elijah, who in a chariot of fire sped his way through heaven, who raised the dead, and who by his word withheld rain for two and forty months? Or of his disciple Elisha, who threw the wood into the water and brought back iron, and whose dust raised up the dead? In like manner why should I speak of the miracles wrought under the Lord Christ: his marvellous birth from a virgin; the attestation of the Star that then appeared; the adoration of the Magi; the good tidings brought with joy to the shepherds by the angels; the doxology of the whole angelic host; the prayer of Simeon conjoined with the giving of thanks; the confession of Anna; the first miracle of Christ himself in Cana of Galilee, who at a marriage miraculously provided a liberal supply of wine for drinking; the giving of sight to the eyes of the man born blind, by clay wrought with spittle; 177

---

[1] See Strabo, XV, iii, 13.

the restoration to life of Lazarus after he had been four days dead and his intestines were stinking; the host of opposing demons trembling at his power and exclaiming: *Thou hast come before the time to torment us*[1]; the command and the bridle imposed on the raging sea; the walking upon the surface of the waves, when he invited Peter to walk with him upon them; and when Peter was seized with distrust and began to sink and cried out: *Lord, save me!*[2] his drawing him up from the deep, and his again going with him and placing him safe and sound in the boat; the eclipse of the sun at the time of the Passion which continued for three hours, and that too in the fourteenth day of the moon: an occurrence quite contrary to worldly philosophy, for according to the adepts therein an eclipse cannot result except at the time of new moon; the quaking of the earth, the rending of the rocks and of the veil of the temple? But passing over all the other miracles which cannot now conveniently be enumerated, I hasten to speak of the resurrection itself, which is the renovation of men and of all the world; the gift of incorruption, immortality and immutability bestowed by God upon the whole world; of the ascent again of men into heaven, into which the first who entered in flesh was the Lord Christ; of the shadows of the Apostles which gave strength to the weak; of the rapture of the Apostle Paul even into the third heaven,[3] that is, to a third of the distance of the height of heaven from the earth—namely, as far as the firmament; then his rapture into Paradise where he was privileged to be the

---

[1] Matt. viii, 29. [2] Matt. xiv, 30.

[3] "The expression ἕως τρίτου οὐρανοῦ is founded on *Jewish* phraseology, by which heaven was considered as threefold, consisting of: 1. the *aerial* (or skyey); 2. the *sidereal* (or starry); and 3. *heaven itself*, the abode of God and the angels."—Bloomfield, Note on II Corinthians xii, 2. The interpretation put upon the expression by Cosmas is manifestly disingenuous.

hearer of the unspeakable words which it is not lawful for a man to utter. All which things are marvellous and transcend our nature or our state.

Another Note.

In the days of Joshua, the son of Nun, the sun stood still. In the days of Hezekiah, through the agency of Isaiah, it went back. At the Passion of the Christ, contrary to the law of the pagan philosophers, it was altogether eclipsed. The credentials of the prophets and Apostles and of Christ himself are great and amazing miracles, and the prophecies: while Plato and Aristotle, Ptolemy and the others, challenge our belief on the ground of their knowledge of eclipses of the sun and moon derived from calculations—if even thus they speak what is true.

Text.

The occurrence of these marvels prepared the men of those days to place belief in the prophecies also, while the fulfilments of the prophecies prepare ourselves to believe in the signs and in all things of which the prophets spake, as was the case also in the time of the Lord Christ, who in those days when he had come down from the Mount of Olives, and beheld Jerusalem and wept over it as it lay opposite, said: *How often would I have gathered thy children even as a hen gathereth her chickens under her wing, and ye would not. Behold, your house is left unto you desolate.*[1] Then when he had passed sentence on the temple, his disciples who were still under the influence of Judaic sentiment were sorrow-struck; and scripture afterwards says: *When descending from the Mount they showed him the building of the temple,*[2] in order no doubt that they might move him to pity, and that he might recall what he had said with regard to the temple, for they knew and believed that everything spoken by him would come to pass. But he knowing [what would be] said to them: *Do you see all these things? Verily, I*

---

[1] Matt. xxiii, 37, 38. [2] Matt. xxiv, 1.

say unto you, there shall not be left here one stone upon another that shall not be thrown down.[1] Then were they possessed with fear, and remained silent, and said nothing further on this matter. Accordingly thereafter came the Romans, and levelled with the ground the temple and the city, and made it an utter desolation, executing as if by compact what had been commanded by the Lord. And up to this day we see with our very eyes that lo! for more than five hundred years it has lain so desolate that it cannot be renovated. Moreover he said to his disciples: *Be of good cheer, I have overcome the world.*[2] And again: *The gates of hell shall not prevail against the church;*[3] and again he declares that all the world shall be filled with his doctrine, even as the three measures of meal, in which the woman hid the leaven, were all leavened throughout and made one by that leaven. And again: *The Gospel shall be preached throughout the whole world:*[4] and along with it shall the woman too be told of who did him a kindness— and we see that all these predictions have been fulfilled. For the Christians who were at one time persecuted by the Greeks and Jews have conquered, and drawn their persecutors over to their own side. In like manner we see that the Church has never been destroyed, but that its adherents have been greatly multiplied, and that similarly the whole earth has been filled with the doctrine of the Lord Christ, and is still being filled, and that the gospel is preached throughout all the world. This I avouch to be the veritable fact, from what I have seen and heard in the many places which I have visited.

Even in Taprobanê,[5] an island in Further India, where the Indian sea is, there is a Church of Christians, with clergy

---

[1] Matt. xxiv, 2.   [2] John xvi, 33.
[3] Matt. xvi, 18.   [4] Matt. xxiv, 14.
[5] For a description of Taprobanê (Ceylon) see Book XI.

and a body of believers, but I know not whether there be any Christians in the parts beyond it. In the country called Malé,[1] where the pepper grows, there is also a church, and at another place called Calliana[2] there is moreover a bishop, who is appointed from Persia.[3] In the island, again, called the Island of Dioscoridês,[4] which is situated in the same Indian sea, and where the inhabitants speak Greek, having been originally colonists sent thither by the Ptolemies who succeeded Alexander the Macedonian, there are clergy who receive their ordination in Persia, and are sent on to the island, and there is also a multitude of Christians. I sailed along the coast of this island, but did not land upon it. I met, however, with some of its Greek-speaking people who had come over into Ethiopia.[5] And

---

[1] Malabar, see below, Book XI.   [2] *Ibid.*

[3] Gr. ἀπὸ περσίδος χειροτονούμενος. This is the verb used in the Acts of the Apostles, xiv, 23 : *ordained by the laying on of hands.*

[4] Dioscoridês is the island now called Socotra. The name, though in appearance Greek, is in reality Sanscrit, from Dvipa Sukhâdâra, that is, *Island Abode of Bliss.* A description is given of it in c. 30 of the *Periplûs* of the Erythraean Sea, which was writtten about the middle of the first century. It is described as "of great extent but desert, and very moist, and as having but a scanty population, which was settled on its north side, and consisted of an intermixture of foreigners—Arabs, Indians, and even Greeks—engaged in commerce." The people of the interior are still of distinct race, with curly hair, Indian complexion, and regular features, while the coast people are of mixed descent. Abulfeda says the people were Nestorian Christians and pirates, but the late Sir H. Yule says that " some indications point rather to a connection of the island's Christianity with the Jacobite or Abyssinian church. Thus they practised circumcision . . . . and De Barros calls them Jacobite Christians of the Abyssinian stock. Barbosa speaks of them . . . . as Christian only in name, having neither baptism nor Christian knowledge . . . . Now not a trace of former Christianity can be discovered, and the social state of the people could scarcely be lower." See his edition of *The Book of Ser Marco Polo*, vol. ii, pp. 401-2.

[5] Gr. ἀνδράσιν τῶν ἐκεῖ . . . . ἐλθοῦσιν ἐν τῇ Ἀιθωπίᾳ.—Montfaucon translates : qui in Aethiopian *proficiscebantur.* Cosmas had probably met them at Adule or at Axum.

so likewise among the Bactrians and Huns and Persians, and the rest of the Indians, Persarmenians, and Medes and Elamites, and throughout the whole land of Persia there is no limit to the number of churches with bishops and very large communities of Christian people, as well as many martyrs, and monks also living as hermits. So too in Ethiopia and Axôm, and in all the country about it; among the people of Happy Arabia—who are now called Homerites—through all Arabia and Palestine, Phœnicia, and all Syria and Antioch as far as Mesopotamia; among the Nubians and the Garamantes,[1] in Egypt, Libya, Pentapolis,[2] Africa[3] and Mauretania, as far as southern Gadeira,[4] there are everywhere churches of the Christians, and bishops, martyrs, monks and recluses, where the Gospel of Christ is proclaimed. So likewise again in Cilicia, Asia, Cappadocia, Lazica[5] and Pontus, and in the northern

---

[1] The Garamantes were the inhabitants of the great oasis in the Libyan desert called Phazania, and now Fezzan, but the name was often used in a wider sense to denote the people of northern Africa who lived to the south of the Syrtis.

[2] Pentapolis, the name for any association of five cities, denotes here the five chief cities of the province of Cyrenaïca in north Africa. These were Cyrênê, Berenicê, Arsinoê, Ptolemaïs, and Apollonia, the port of Cyrênê.

[3] Africa, in its narrow sense, meant the regions between Mauretania and Cyrênê.

[4] Gr. Γαδείρων, τὰ πρὸς νότον. Cosmas slips here in his grammar, using τὰ for τῶν. A little below he speaks of another Gades—Γάδειρα τοῦ Ὠκεανοῦ, that is, Gades in Spain. Southern Gades, Yule thinks, may be Tingis, or Cape Spartel, called by Strabo Kôteis.

[5] "In the time of Pliny, Arrian, and Ptolemy", says Gibbon, "the Lazi were a particular tribe on the northern skirts of Colchos. When the Romans stationed on the Phasis were either withdrawn or expelled, the tribe of the Lazi, whose posterity speak a foreign dialect, and inhabit the sea-coast of Trebizond, imposed their name and dominion on the ancient kingdom of Colchos. Their independence was soon invaded by a formidable neighbour .... In the beginning of the sixth century their influence was restored by the introduction of Christianity, which the Mingrelians still profess with becoming zeal,

countries occupied by the Scythians, Hyrcanians, Heruli,[1] Bulgarians, Greeks[2] and Illyrians, Dalmatians, Goths, Spaniards, Romans, Franks, and other nations, as far as Gadeira on the ocean towards the northern parts, there are believers and preachers of the Gospel confessing the resurrection from the dead; and so we see the prophecies being fulfilled over the whole world.[3]

Among the famous philosophers who flourished among the pagans, which of them, Socrates, or Pythagoras, or Plato, or Aristotle, or any other, was held worthy to foretell or announce any thing of such advantage to the world as the resurrection of the dead, and the free gift to men of the Kingdom of Heaven, which cannot be shaken? For they can announce nothing except only that, by means of calculations and secular learning, they declare when eclipses of the sun and the moon will occur, whereby, even if they predict them truly—as in fact they do—no benefit will accrue to the world, but rather the evil of pride; while should they say nothing about them they will do no manner of harm. For what boy who learns arithmetic will be found ignorant of this knowledge? or what old woman or country-bred yokel has not an acquaintance with some of the works and ways of nature? or what nation or what barbarian knows not these things—astronomy I mean, and geometry and the various practical arts, medicine, carpentry, stone-cutting, weaving, smithwork, agriculture, and others of which the Greeks have no conception? or what nation

without understanding the doctrines or observing the precepts of their religion."—*Decline and Fall*, Chap. xlii.

[1] The Heruli under Odoacer, who is styled their king, in A.D. 476 overthrew the western empire. Their seats lay to the north of the Euxine.

[2] Gr. Ἑλλαδικῶν.

[3] Towards the end of the seventeenth chapter of the *Decline and Fall*, Gibbon has summarised what Cosmas here says regarding the wide spread of Christianity.

between east and west, between north and south, that believes in Christ, does not by various methodical calculations fix for many years beforehand when the Easter festivals are to be celebrated? In fact, they correctly determine the dates in advance, since they all with one consent, from one end of the earth to the other, on one and the same day, celebrate Easter according to their different calculations and methods of computing the time.

For since God has endowed man with wisdom and reason he has rendered him capable of finding out whatever mind can attain to, and whatever he can acquire from education; for such is the nature of that rational animal—man. For when the men of early times had invented an art, they made many mistakes; but afterwards either they or their successors rectified these mistakes under the teaching of experience, time and practice. In like manner those who received the art from them firmly retained what had been transmitted to them. On the other hand the divine teachings, be they doctrines or be they arts, are not in this manner brought to perfection by human intelligence; but being at first given by God, one receives them with full assurance, even as did those whom God inspired with wisdom for the preparation of the Tabernacle in the time of Moses, namely, Beseleél himself the son of Urias, the son of Ôr, of the tribe of Judah, and Eliab, the son of Achisamach of the tribe of Dan, and all to whom he gave understanding, and filled with the Spirit of God and knowledge to devise all manner of workmanship, both of carpentry and of working in gold and silver and brass— and blue and purple and scarlet thread, and fine twined linen—and stonework and woodwork, according to all the works which the Lord commanded them to make for the Tabernacle of testimony, both the Ark of the Covenant and the Mercy-seat over it, and the furniture of the Tabernacle, its altar and its table and all its vessels, and the laver and its base, and the official robes of Aaron and his sons when ministering as priests before God, and the anointing oil and the sacred incense composed of sweet aromatics, according to all things which God commanded him to make. And beyond question you will find that up to this very day the most of these arts are most zealously cultivated among the Jews.

Note.

When the first man had sinned and had come to a sense of his transgression, and was fittingly convicted thereof by God and filled with confusion and shame, he began to consider next by what contrivance he could cover his nakedness, and being stimulated by God to exert his faculty of reason, he invented the art of sewing, and with the thorns of shrubs stitched together for himself leaves of the fig tree. And being at the same time instructed by God as to the preparation of tunics, he learned to make them from the bark of trees.[1] It is attested by scripture that Cain discovered the art or science of agriculture, and Abel that of the keeping of sheep. Then again, when Cain after the murder of his brother had been cast out by God, as it is written: *Cain went out from the presence of God and dwelt in the land of Nain*,[2] as much as to say, that Cain was cast out by God and banished from his home to a wretched country, for they thought that Paradise was God's dwelling-place, as he was wont to go forth therefrom and ofttimes showed himself there. The sons therefore of Seth who lived near Paradise, and were so to speak under God's care, and ofttimes conversed with him, were always called the sons of God, while the sons of Cain who were settled somewhere far away from Paradise, and were not constantly under the care of God, but lived in a wild and wretched country, and were under their own care rather than God's, were called the sons of men. Since Cain therefore and his offspring lived in fear, they invented other arts for their security, as, for instance, carpentry,

---

[1] Gr. ἐκ δερμάτων ξύλων—Montfaucon translates *ex pellibus ovium*, taking ξύλων to be a mis-reading of the MS. ξύλον, however, has sometimes, especially in Alexandrian Greek, the meaning of *live-wood*, or a *tree*.   [2] Gen. iv, 16.

stone-cutting, metallurgy and music. Carpentry—for making tents and doors and roofs for the protection of themselves and their cattle; masonry—for building houses and cities by way of providing for their safety and defence; metallurgy—for the tilling of the soil, and breaking it up with the ploughshare, and reaping the crops with hooks, and for making flutes and many other articles; lastly—music to keep them awake by night with the flute and the lyre and the singing of songs, and to protect themselves and their cattle from the attacks of wild beasts. So then they lived on in fear, and in exile they devised all kinds of expedients to ensure their safety, for scripture thus speaks of them, saying of Cain: *And he built a city and named it Enoch after the name of his son;*[1] then of Thobel (Tubal), the son of Lamech by Ada, it says: *He was the father of such as dwell in the tents of shepherds;*[2] and of Jubal, the brother of Thobel, it says: *It was he who taught the use of the psaltery and harp.*[3] Scripture speaks also of metallurgy when it says concerning Thobel whom Sella (Zillah) bare: *He was the forger of cutting instruments of brass and iron.*[4]

182 God having thus from the first given man ingenuity, fitted him to invent arts, and while the first men at the outset invented them, their successors, starting from where they left off, by dint of assiduous practice, brought them to greater perfection. It will be well therefore if we here take up an argument against those sophists who say that the world is eternal and without beginning, and remind them how far they are in error, understanding neither from the things themselves —namely, from the arts, that it is not eternal and without beginning, but of recent production. For if the arts were discovered gradually, and all human society subsists through art and rational science, how is it possible for the world to subsist without art and rational science? For without the art of stone-cutting, how can houses, fortifications and cities be reared for the protection of men and civic communities? In like manner, without the art of weaving, whence could men obtain coverings sufficient to protect them from cold and from frost. In like manner, were there not an art of working in metals, how would

---

[1] Gen. iv, 17.
[2] Gen. iv, 20.
[3] Gen. iv, 21.
[4] Gen. iv, 22.

it be possible for men to till the soil, and break up the earth with ploughs, or reap the crops with sickles, in order to provide themselves with food? If again there was no art of medicine, how could the sufferings to which men are liable be cured and their illnesses be mitigated?

From all this it is quite manifest that the world is not eternal, but a recent production, just like the inventions and the arts and the sciences of men. For where will they find among astronomers one equal to or greater than Ptolemy; or among philosophers, than Plato and Aristotle: or what greater geometricians and arithmeticians will they find than Euclid and Archimedes, who alone discovered the quadrature of the circle?[1] But if these learned men were more exact than their predecessors, is it not most manifest that the arts were gradually discovered through the ingenuity which was bestowed by God upon men? Wherefore also the scripture, referring everything to God, exclaims: *All wisdom is from God*.[2] They are therefore either liars or consummate fools in supposing the world to be eternal, when they are convicted of being in error by actual facts. But sacred scripture speaks more truly when it says: *In the beginning God made the heaven and the earth*.[3] I should like again to put to those wise men this question: since the hammer, the anvil and the forceps precede the entire art of metallurgy, who was it prepared these instruments? Let them tell us and not begrudge us a reply. They, however, not having the sense to take refuge in God, the maker of the universe, who endowed the race of mankind with wisdom, and gave them the faculty of invention, but wishing after the ways of their own heart to construct and to demolish theories, on finding themselves beset with difficulties and the most formidable perplexities of reasoning, presume next to declare that the world is eternal and had no beginning, for such assertions show to what straits they are reduced. How hard, for instance, are they pressed both with respect to man and bird, since the one is produced from seed and the others from eggs: and if this opinion of theirs is true, the question arises did men and birds —the products respectively of seed and of eggs—exist at the same

---

[1] Cosmas refers here to the work of Archimedes, which is still extant, on the Quadrature of the Parabola.
[2] Eccl. i, 1.   [3] Gen. i, 1.

183 time with God, or did they not? And if they did exist, the seed and the eggs will of necessity be found existing before God, and before men and birds; but if they did not exist they must submit to divine scripture, when it informs us through Moses: *God said, Let us make man in our image,* and through the Apostle at Athens on the Areopagus [tells us what we read in Acts xvii, 24-28]. So then, as has already been said, the sons of Seth, those namely who are called the sons of God, went in against the will of God but in obedience to their own self-will, to the daughters of men —that is, to the women of the race of Cain—and joined themselves to them in marriage. Wherefore God, taking occasion from this, made a new dispensation and destroyed those who had sinned by means of the Deluge, but him that was righteous he preserved by the Ark, and transferred to this earth of ours, which was a better one and almost equal to Paradise.

Text.

But to continue,—the divine doctrines, the structure of the world, and the prophecies cannot possibly be explained unless one learn them from divine revelation, or receive them from men divinely inspired, the Prophets themselves, and the Apostles, and all divinely inspired scripture; for it is impossible to acquire such learning from conjectures or arrogant assumptions or human wisdom. But that the structure of the world coincides with the doctrine of the Christians, the whole of divine scripture, as has been said, proclaims, namely, Moses and the Prophets, the Lord Christ and the Apostles, as we have repeatedly explained. For God divided the one place which extends from the earth to the higher heaven by interposing in the middle the second heaven, and thus made two places; and to this mortal and mutable state he assigned the lower place, and to the immortal and immutable state the higher, which is called also the Kingdom of Heaven, and about which the Lord Christ speaks thus in the Gospel of Matthew: *For in the resurrection they neither marry nor are given in marriage,* but are as the *angels of God in heaven;*[1] and again: *He shall to those on the right hand say—Come, ye blessed of my father, inherit the kingdom prepared for you before the foundation of the world,*[2] as if he should say prepared from that time; [see also] John xii, 32; Matt. xiv, 40; viii, 11, 12; Heb. iv, 11; Philipp iii, 20; Rom. viii, 17; Ephes. ii, 6; Philipp. iii, 14; Galat. iv, 26; Heb. iii, 1; Ephes. ii, 19; Heb. xi, 9, 10; *Ibid.* v, 16; *Ibid.* xii, 22-24; *Ibid.* xiii, 14; Luke xxiv, 51; Acts i, 10, 11; Heb. ix, 24; *Ibid.* vii, 26; *Ibid.* vi, 18-20; *Ibid.* x, 19, 23.

Can any one then be so infatuated, so lost in misery as to disbelieve such promises and such true prophecies, which both from the two places created in the beginning and made ready so to speak by God from the foundation of the world, and from such preparations are shown to be true and in harmony with the doctrine of the Christians? And this with regard both to the principles and the ends, namely, that when God had set apart the present mortal and mutable state of existence for the exercise of the reasoning faculty, and had led it through its trial, he at last releases the world from its toil and discipline, and reveals the future state, graciously bestowing everlasting benefits, exemption from penury and the sway of the passions, immortality, incorruption, immutability, perfect knowledge, righteousness, sanctification, redemption and blessedness for evermore, Amen! For the present state will not remain for ever, as the pagans are foolish enough to assert, supposing that God delights in evil, or rather that he is deficient in power or gives grudgingly, so that he is unable to grant the world release from its struggles and from corruption; yea, that day after day he adds destruction and sufferings, and death and trials, and is not strong enough to give the prizes of contests, or to award crowns,

---

[1] Matt. xxxii, 30.   [2] Matt. xxv, 34.

or to bring the toils with which men are exercised to an end. For as they suppose him to be merely the artificer who shapes the material which he has at his command, so even now they suppose that he is not able to make it better, disbelieving the resurrection of the body as a thing impossible, and disbelieving also the whole of divine scripture. Wherefore those miserable men admit the spherical form of the heaven to be true, disbelieving, yea, rather execrating, the whole of divine scripture, and turning away from the truth as from old wives' fables. Far however be it from us to boast except in the whole of divine scripture, through which the outside world is crucified to us and we to the outside world. Be it ours, O most pious Father Pamphilus, along with a good life, to embrace the divine oracles, and to repudiate those of our adversaries, according to the will of Him that is mighty, and by the help of Christ the saviour of us all, with whom to the Father, together with his holy and adorable Spirit, be glory now and evermore, world without end.—Amen!

BOOK IV.

A summary recapitulation and description of the figures of the world : also the refutation of the sphere.

T is written: *In the beginning God made the heaven and the earth.*[1] We therefore first depict along with the earth, the heaven which is vaulted and which has its extremities bound together with the extremities of the earth. To the best of our ability we have endeavoured to delineate it on its western side and its eastern ; for these two sides are walls, extending from below to the vault above. There is also the firmament which, in the middle, is bound together with the first heaven, and which, on its upper side, has the waters according to divine scripture itself. The position and figure are such as here sketched.[2] To the extremities on the four sides of the earth the heaven is fastened at its own four extremities, making the figure of a cube, that is to say, a quadrangular figure, while up above it curves round in the form of an oblong vault and becomes as it were a vast canopy. And in the middle the firmament is made fast to it, and thus two places are formed.

From the earth to the firmament is the first place, this world, namely, in which are the angels and men and all the

---

[1] Gen. i, 1.
[2] Gr. ἡ θέσις καὶ τὸ σχῆμα. For the sketch, see Plates 2 and 7 in the Appendix.

present state of existence. From the firmament again to the vault above is the second place—the Kingdom of Heaven, into which Christ, first of all, entered, after his ascension, having prepared for us a new and living way.

On the western side and the eastern the outline presented is short,[1] as in the case of an oblong[2] vault, but on its north and south sides it shows its length. Its figure is therefore something such as this.[3]

Note.

This is the first heaven, shaped like a vaulted chamber, which was created on the first day along with the earth, and of it Isaiah speaks thus: *He that hath established the heaven as a vaulted chamber.* But the heaven, which is bound to the first at the middle, is that which was created on the second day, to which Isaiah refers when he says: *And having stretched it out as a tent to dwell in.*[4] David also says concerning it: *Stretching out the heaven as a curtain,*[5] and indicating it still more clearly he says: *Who layeth the beams of his chambers in the waters.*[4] Now, when Scripture speaks of the extremities of heaven and earth, this cannot be understood as applicable to a sphere. Isaiah again says: *Thus saith the Lord, he that made the heaven and pitched it;*[6] and the Apostle in like manner says: *Of the true Tabernacle which the Lord pitched and not man.*[7] They both speak of the heaven as standing on and fixed on the earth, and not as revolving round it. Nay more, the extremities of the heaven are bound together with the extremities of the earth, and on both sides, and concerning this it is written in Job: *And he inclined heaven to earth, and the earth is poured out as dust, and I have fastened it as a square block to a stone.*[8] And with regard to the earth it is again written in Job: *He that hangeth the earth upon nothing;*[9] meaning, that it had nothing underneath it. And David in harmony with this, when he could discover nothing on

---

[1] The MS. has μακρὸν, which Montfaucon gives in his text, but in a note corrects into μικρὸν. [2] Gr. ὡς ἐπὶ θόλου μεγάλης.

[3] See Pl. 7 in the Appendix.

[4] Isai. xl, 22. [5] Psalm civ, 2. 3. [6] Isai. xlii, 5.

[7] Heb. viii, 2. [8] Job xxxviii, 38. [9] Job xxv, 7.

which it was founded, says : *He that hath founded the earth upon its own stability*,[1] as if he said, it hath been founded by thee upon itself, and not upon anything else.

To the best of our ability we have endeavoured to depict heaven having the firmament within it and the mountain peaks in the middle of the earth which we now inhabit, and the ocean surrounding it, and the four navigable gulfs which run into it— the Roman, the Arabian, the Persian and the Caspian or Hyrcanian. The ocean again we have depicted as surrounded by the land on its farther side, where also Paradise lies in the east. Then again we depict the breadth of the earth and of the ocean, and of the gulfs, and of the earth beyond, and Paradise, leaving out for the present the peaks, in order that a comprehensive view may be more readily gained by those who examine the delineation. Now the figure of the whole earth, with respect to this surface and to the breadth, is such as has been indicated.

With that earth which is situated beyond the ocean, the first heaven, which is like a vaulted chamber, is bound together at its extremities on all sides, and at its west and at its east side a wall is found rising straight upward, but at the south and at the north side there is a wall equal at the base until it takes what has evidently the form of a vaulted chamber, while at the top it rolls itself into a very lofty arch, like the spacious roof over a bath, with an arena-like floor below,[2] so that the wall itself forms a vaulted roof. Then, as we have just stated over and over again, the firmament which is spread out in the middle is at a certain height bound together with the heaven itself in order that two places may be formed—an upper place and a lower.[3] Now one of these places, namely, the lower, comprising the earth and the water and the other elements and the heavenly bodies, is this world which extends from the earth to the firmament, having the earth for its floor, the walls reaching down from the first heaven for its sides, and the firmament for its roof. The

---

[1] Psalm civ, 5.

[2] Gr. πέχμα, which Montfaucon translates by *lacunar*, a "ceiling", but no lexicon gives this as a meaning of the word. Sophocles gives "the area of a circus or of a theatre", as the meaning in Byzantine writers.

[3] Gr. ἀνάγαιον καὶ κατάγαιον.

188 other place again which extends from the firmament to the vault of the first heaven is, to wit, the Kingdom of Heaven into which the Lord Christ, after he had risen from the dead, ascended, and into which the righteous shall also afterwards ascend, and has for its floor the firmament or second heaven, and the first heaven itself for its walls and its vaulted roof. We further again depict the altitude and figure of this earth which we men dwell in, and which is encircled by the ocean, and contains the four navigable gulfs. Its eastern and its southern parts are low and depressed, while its northern and western are of very great elevation, but slope so gradually that the inequality is not perceived. The earth has therefore in its northern and western parts an elevation equivalent to its breadth. We therefore thus depict its figure according to the best of our ability.[1]

Note.

The earth taken as a whole is quadrangular according to the delineation already given. We have also indicated the altitude of its most central part and the heights in its northern and western parts. Hence we have delineated it as placed in the centre surrounded by the ocean and also by the earth on the opposite side of the ocean, with the heavenly bodies circling round it, so that the conical mountain[2] can project a shadow according even to the pagans, while in accordance with this figure eclipses can occur, as well as the vicissitudes of night and day. Divine scripture confirms the truth of this, saying: *The sun riseth and the sun goeth down, and draweth to his own place. On his rising he goeth then to the south and wheeleth his circles, and turneth round the air upon his circles;*[3] meaning that in circling through the air he comes back again to his own place.

Text.

In this view the inhabited parts of the earth are thus represented. In accordance therewith the sun rising in the east, and running through the south in the course of

---

[1] See Pl. 4 in the Appendix.   [2] See Pl. 8 in the Appendix.
[3] Eccl. i, 6, 7.

his *revolutions*, always, when giving light to the summit of
the earth, or even to the earth itself, makes night to the
ocean and the earth beyond it. Then again, when he is in
the west and the north beyond the summit of the earth, he
leaves us here in darkness, until in making his circuit he
again appears in the east where the earth is depressed, and
mounting the sky in the south again illumines all this side.
The eclipses of the moon therefore, even according to this
delineation, if at any rate what the pagans say is true, can
occur when either the sun or the moon is hidden by the
summit of the earth; for they say that a solar eclipse is not
produced by the shadow of the earth, but because in a
perpendicular line the moon is directly below the sun, so
that she is illuminated on that side which the sun sees, but
not on that which he does not see—yea, rather, she prevents
him from being visible by running under him, at the
occurrence at all events of the lunar new month, when the
moon is not enlightened on that side which is visible to us.
The opinion therefore which we hold is in no wise adverse
to such views, except only with respect to the motion and
revolution of the heaven—a theory subversive alike of all
divine scripture both of the Old and the New Testament,
and of Christian doctrine. But to enquire further into
these matters we have no leisure; for such knowledge is
unprofitable to us who have access to a more profitable
knowledge, which imparts to our soul a good and beneficent
hope which God hath promised he will give to those who
believe in him, while those who act unjustly he has doomed
to perdition. But with God's help we shall delineate the
figure of the earth on the reverse side in its northern
portion, that we may be able again in turn to delineate the
circuit of the heavenly bodies—and it is thus.[1]

When therefore the setting sun runs from here by the

---

[1] See Pl. 5 in the Appendix.

ministration of the invisible powers, according to the views of divine scripture, he makes night in the other part—that namely which is inhabited; but when he runs hither he makes darkness there. But we shall now concisely, according to our ability, delineate the heaven and the earth, and we do so thus:—[1]

Note 1.

This part of the earth situated beyond the north, where the luminaries pursue their course from the west through the north towards the east is uninhabited, and this stands upright like a wall, and when the sun comes to it, he leaves in darkness the other part which is inhabited. The earth therefore is found to have in this part, from the ocean beneath up to its summit, an altitude according with the measure of the breadth of its inhabited parts. Hence as it intercepts midway the light of the heavenly bodies, the nights and all the rest follow.

Note 2.

It is necessary for those who wish to be considered Christians to enquire into which of these eight or nine heavens Christ has ascended, and into which they themselves hope to ascend, and what is the use of the other seven or eight heavens. For having already delineated the world in accordance with the scriptural view, we assert that two places were created, one adapted to the present state of existence, and the other to that which is to come, since we have such a hope, one that is better than the life here. And you, if as Christians you hold such a hope, will of necessity be asked what is the use of the seven or eight other heavens. For the pagans who hold the theory of the sphere, if consistent with themselves, neither entertain such a hope, nor allow that there are waters above the heaven, nor are found to acknowledge that the heavenly bodies and the world will come to an end; but expect that the world in the state of corruption will continue for ever. If the sphere which has motion forces the others to revolve along with it from east to west, whence is pro-

---

[1] See Pl. 6 in the Appendix.

duced the motion, in the contrary direction, of the seven planets? Is it the spheres that have the contrary motion, or the stars themselves? If the spheres, how can they at one and the same time move both westward and eastward? And if the stars, how do the planets cut their way through the heavenly bodies? Is it not evident that a heavenly body cannot be cut asunder? For unless it were corruptible, it could not be cut through. How then do ye make such suppositions?

Since beyond this sphere neither place, nor body, nor element nor any of their parts anywhere exists, how do ye say it is moved? Tell us, begrudge us not an answer. For, except in some place or in space at large, it cannot possibly be moved. Show us therefore by what instrument—naming any one you please—it can be moved without place or body, or element or space. And do not, because you are adepts in the science of nature, jauntily treat us to nothing but empty phrases. But since some insist that the sphere rotates like a lathe by the shaft,[1] or like a waggon or a machine by the axle, let these show on what support the shaft and the axle rest, and then again on what this support rests, and so on to infinity. How then do you reason with respect to the natural world? and how does an axis not also pass through the earth, which is in the middle, and turn it round? And again tell me, ye who follow these men and yet wish to be Christians, into what place of the eight spheres, or of the ninth which is called by some the starless, hath Christ entered, or shall we ourselves enter? Or how can waters be contained on a rotating sphere? or how when the stars fall at the final consummation can such spheres as yours be preserved? or what can be the use of them? Is it not evident that you argue against the hope held out by the Christian doctrine? For these views cannot be consistently held except by Pagans, who have no hope of another and better state, and who consequently suppose that the world is eternal, in order that the rich abundance of the spheres in which the planets will accomplish their courses may be preserved for them—while in another sphere are the fixed stars—and their error has some show of reason in its favour. But ye advance arguments altogether incredible, and will have it that there is a multitude of spheres, and that there is no final consummation of the world since ye are

---

[1] Gr. ὑπὸ κλώτακος.

unable to tell what is the necessity of these things. And in like manner ye will have it that the waters above the spheres rotate—a most ridiculous idea and altogether idiotic, and ye advance arguments which are self-contradictory and opposed to the nature of things. And though ye allow that the universe was created in six days, yet ye find no mention of the making of a third heaven, and far less of the eight or nine which ye venture to affirm. How great is your knowledge! how great your wisdom! how great your intelligence! how great your inconsistency! *No man can serve two masters,*[1] as has well been said by the Lord, but if one will serve God, let him serve him, or if Mammon, then Mammon. And again he says, through Paul: *Ye cannot be partakers of the table of the Lord, and of the table of devils.*[2] And again: *Be ye not unequally yoked together with unbelievers: for what fellowship hath righteousness with lawlessness, and what communion hath light with darkness? and what concord hath Christ with Belial? or what part hath he that believeth with an infidel? and what agreement hath the temple of God with idols?*[3]

And how again was it possible for the earth, which according to you is placed in the very middle of the universe, to have been submerged by the deluge in the time of Noah? or how can it be believed that on the first and the second day it was covered by the waters, and on the third, when the waters were gathered together, that it made its appearance, as is recorded in Genesis? But with even greater wisdom ye suppose that there are men walking all the earth over with their feet opposite the feet of other men. We therefore depict according to your view the earth and the Antipodes,[4] and let each one of you who has sound vision and the power of reasoning justly turn the earth round whatever way he pleases, and let him say whether the Antipodes can be all standing upright in the same sense of the expression. But this they will not show even should they speak unrestrained by shame. Such then is our reply to your fictitious and false theories and to the conclusions of your reasonings which are capricious, self-contradictory, inconsistent, doomed to be utterly confounded, and

---

[1] Matt. vi, 24.
[2] I Cor. x, 21.
[3] II Cor. vi, 14, 16.
[4] See Pl. 10 in Appendix.

to be whirled round and round even more than that unstable and revolving mythical sphere of yours. Wherefore, O Christ-loving Father, since I have thus brought to an end the fourth book with a delineation of the Antipodes, I shall begin the fifth book, as I promised at thy pious desire, and it will contain a description of the Tabernacle prepared by Moses in the wilderness, if God will, who is the Saviour of us all.

BOOK V.

In which is contained a description of the Tabernacle, and in which the harmony is exhibited of the Prophets and Apostles.

OF the Tabernacle which was prepared by Moses in the wilderness, it is now time to give a description, as we have received it from that most divine man and teacher. And having made divine scripture our[1] starting point and accepted its testimonies, we begin with the exodus from Egypt, when the first-born of the Egyptians died, suffering the last of the plagues brought upon them through Moses—when also the Israelites, after having sacrificed, ate the Passover standing, having their loins girt, and holding staffs in their hands, ready prepared for their departure, on the first day of the first month at evening on the fourteenth day of the moon, which things were a shadow and type of the things that would be under the Lord Christ, namely, the deliverance from tyrannical bondage, the renovation of the world, accomplished by the resurrection from the dead, and

---

[1] According to the reading of the Greek text (ποιησαμένου, ἀρξαμένου), which Montfaucon follows in his Latin version, *his* should be substituted for *our;* but as Cosmas can neither have meant that *Moses* made divine scripture, which did not yet exist, his starting-point (τὰς ἀφορμὰς), nor that the narrative of Moses began with the destruction of the first-born of the Egyptians, I have taken as the proper readings ποιησάμενος and ἀρξάμενος.

the everlasting rest into which men shall enter. For at that very season of the year the world appears to have been created by God, and to have had its beginning. Likewise also in the time of Noah after the Deluge, there was again at that season a beginning of the world. It was the season again when there took place the deliverance of the Israelites from Egypt; and it was then also that there occurred the conception by the Virgin of the Lord Christ according to the flesh—of him who is the second Adam, the Chief Captain of the second state. In it again also occurred the resurrection from the dead of our Lord Jesus Christ according to the flesh, and it is said further that the general resurrection also shall then take place. The pagans moreover bear witness to the season, thieves that they are, deeming it to be an opinion of their own, and regarding Aries as the beginning of the Zodiac circle. In this sign there is, according to divine scripture, the first month of the year, and herein is a clear proof of their being plagiarists, especially as they assign a beginning to a circle—an idea scouted even by themselves as ridiculous. In fact they have nothing that is good but what they have purloined from divine scripture; but being puffed up with pride, and wishing to set themselves up as quite superior persons, they use as their own what is the property of other people.

But that the Law serves the purpose of foreshadowing some things that are future the Apostle testifies, exclaiming: *For the Law having a shadow of good things to come, and not the very image of the things*[1]—speaking of a shadow as when one draws a rough sketch of a man without taking a full likeness of him, that is without representing his features and all his different members, so that it can be known what sort of a man he is, whether old or young,

---

[1] Heb. x, 1.

whether comely or uncomely, but merely sketches an outline of his bodily figure; so by what he calls an image he means the characteristic features, that is, the mysteries celebrated by us, namely the regeneration through baptism, and participation in the mysteries.[1] But what he calls the real things themselves are the resurrection from the dead, the transformation of our bodies, the change from corruption to incorruption, the immutability of the soul instead of its mutability, perfect knowledge for that which is in part, an habitation, a rest, and an entrance into heaven, instead of earthly things heavenly, and instead of temporal things eternal. And all these boons have been secured for the human race through our Lord Jesus Christ. He therefore calls the Law the shadow of these things while the image and its characteristics are the mysteries celebrated by the Christians, as for instance, the lamb offered in sacrifice—a type of the Passion of Christ, in accordance with what the Apostle Paul says: *For Christ our Passover was sacrificed;*[2] and John the Baptist thus speaks: *Behold the Lamb of God which taketh away the sin of the world.*[3] Then after this, for the Israelites of that time there was their deliverance from the destroying angel and from the bondage to Pharaoh; for us, our deliverance from the devil and from our bondage to the very burdensome law. Then for them, their passage through the sea

---

[1] Gr. μετάληψιν μυστηρίων. *Metalepsis* is still in the Greek Church the term in use for the Holy Communion. By the *Mysteries* are meant the symbolic rites of the Christian faith, chiefly baptism and the eucharist. The mysteries recognised by St. Theodorus, abbot of the monastery of Studium, in Constantinople, who flourished towards the end of the eighth century, were baptism, eucharist, unction, orders, monastic tonsure, and the mystery of death or funeral ceremonies. The Greek Church now recognises seven mysteries: baptism, chrism or unction immediately after baptism, eucharist, priesthood, penance (μετάνοια), marriage and unction (εὐχέλαιον), administered by seven priests.   [2] II Cor. v, 7.   [3] John i, 29.

and their sojourning in the wilderness, and the giving of the law and the setting up of the Tabernacle; for us, our passage through baptism and our sojourning in the Church, and the gift of the Holy Spirit. For them, a copious supply of water from the rock to sustain their life; for us, the life-giving mysteries; for them, the land of promise as a place of rest; for us, heaven not made with hands as our place of rest; for them, temporal life; for us, life eternal and righteousness, and sanctification, and redemption and blessedness. The former things therefore serve the purpose of a rough sketch, but those that are ours are the images and characteristic features of the things themselves. And we are not yet within the things themselves, but it shall come to pass that we shall rise from the dead; for no one, save only the Lord Christ in the flesh, has been within the things, having been the first of all to rise from the dead.

When the Egyptians were accordingly hastening the departure of the Israelites from Egypt, these carried away on their shoulders the flour itself, which with their hands they had kneaded into cakes without any leaven, and without the dough being baked. So when they had taken their departure and were drawing nigh to the Red Sea, the Egyptian Pharaoh who had repented and collected an army, pursued after them and overtook them near the sea opposite the encampment in the midst of Migdol and right opposite Beëlsephon. Then evening at length coming on, the pillar of cloud or of fire, which always went before them and guided them on their way, that night came behind them and prevented the Egyptians from attacking the Israelites. Then afterwards when the day was about to dawn, and when the Israelites cried to God, God commanded Moses to smite the sea with his rod and to divide it. Moses, having therefore done as he was commanded, smote the water and divided it, so that it stood up as a wall on this side and on that side, and the Israelites passed through. But when the Egyptians with their chariots were in the midst of the sea pursuing the Israelites, the waters, driven by the anger of God, were turned back upon them and they were all overwhelmed in the sea and perished. Now that very place is in Clysma,[1] as they call it, on the right hand as you go to the mountain, where also the tracks of the wheels of their chariots are visible, and can be traced for a considerable distance as far as the sea, and are preserved even to the present day, as a sign to unbelievers and not to believers.

Note.

Regarding the conception of the Lord.

When Zacharias on the tenth day of the seventh month had gone into the temple, according to the tradition of the law, and it had been announced to him that John would be born to him by Elisabeth, word also came to the Virgin in Elisabeth's sixth month that her own first month had begun. For as Zacharias had received word on the tenth day of the month, and Elisabeth had conceived in that very month, it is evident that six months of the year had elapsed, and that six months were still left with the exception of those ten days, with two or three or seven others added, until Zacharias returned to his house, so that there would remain 161 or 167 or 163 days. The beginning therefore of the conception of the Lord, that is, the beginning of the first month, was Elisabeth's sixth month according to what is handed down in the Gospels. For God has always observed this order and continues to observe it. This we can know for certain, since

---

[1] The Heroopolitan, or Western Gulf at the northern extremity of the Red Sea, is called by Eusebius *Clysma*. As it was said to have been so designated from a town at the northern extremity of the gulf, Clysma was probably situated at, or somewhere near, Suez. Orosius mentions the wheel-tracks here spoken of by Cosmas, as does also Philostorgius in the abstract of his *Ecclesiastical History* made by Photius (Book III, c. 6). Athanasius, however, and others, thought Clysma was in Arabia, near the mountain to which Philo, an Egyptian bishop, was banished by Constantius.

we all celebrate the Nativity of Christ when the ninth month has been completed, reckoned from the beginning of the first month, that is Choiac 28. But the Christians of Jerusalem, as if on the authority of the blessed Luke, who says that Christ was baptised *when he began to be thirty years of age*,[1] celebrate his nativity on Epiphany.[2] And both the evangelist and they of Jerusalem say what is true, but their reckoning is not accurate, for on the day of his nativity fell also his baptism, as both Luke and the Christians of Jerusalem say. But from ancient times the Church, lest by observing the two festivals together one of them should be forgotten, ordained that twelve days, after the number of the Apostles, should be interposed, and that the Feast of Epiphany should then be celebrated; just as it also ordained that the fast of forty days, which the Lord endured before he entered on his contest with the devil, should be concluded by the resurrection of the Lord, in order that we also, taking example, should by fighting to the utmost of our power and imitating him, become recipients of the Passion and the Resurrection of the Lord, although the fasting did not take place on the self-same days. In like manner the Church therefore ordained that the Epiphany of our Lord Jesus should be observed twelve days subsequent to his nativity. But the Christians of Jerusalem alone, guided by probable conjecture but inaccurate calculation, celebrate his birth at Epiphany. But on his birthday they celebrate the memory of David and the Apostle James—not because they both died on that very day, but all, as I think, celebrate their memory lest they should remain excluded from the feast dedicated to all who were kinsmen of Christ according to the flesh, while glorifying God in all things. Amen!

The passage of the Israelites into the Desert after their departure from Egypt.

When the Israelites passed over to the other side to the place called Phœnicôn[3] they began to traverse the desert of Sur (Shur), God expanding a cloud over them by day to protect them from

---

[1] Luke ii, 22.

[2] The Manifestation of Christ to the Gentiles, with special reference to the day on which he was worshipped by the Wise Men of the East.

[3] This word means *a palm grove*. See Strabo's *Geog.*, XVI, ii, 41.

the scorching heat of the sun, and guiding them in it, while by night he appeared in a pillar of fire and led them on their way through all the wilderness, as it is written: *He spread a cloud for a covering: and fire to give light in the night.*[1] And all this can be thus depicted.[2]

Then again setting out from Merrha (Marah) they came to Elim which we now call Raithu, where there were twelve springs of water which exist to the present day.[3] But at that time the number of palm-trees was far greater than it is now. Up to this point they had the sea on their right hand, and on their left the wilderness, but thenceforth they advanced into the interior towards the mountain, leaving the sea behind them as they marched forward into the wilderness. When they were half way between Elim and the Mount Sinai, then the manna descended upon them, and there for the first time they observed the Sabbath, according to the commands which God gave to Moses at Marah, but not in writing. This also you can see thus depicted.[4]

When they had advanced to Elim from Marah, and had again journeyed into the wilderness in that place half way between Elim and Mount Sinai, the quails descended upon them at evening, and the manna in the morning. There again they began to keep the Sabbath, the manna not corrupting from the sixth day till the Sabbath, while on the other days it could not be kept, but it stank and was corrupted, and they were thereby taught to observe the Sabbath; for some wished to gather it even on the Sabbath but did not find it, according to what is recorded.

Then again they pitched in Raphidin (Rephidim), in what is now called Pharan (Paran). And when they thirsted, Moses according to the commandment of the Lord went with the elders (and his rod was in his hand) to Mount Horeb, which is in Sin near Pharan, being only about six miles off. And when he had there struck the rock, abundance of water gushed out, and the

---

[1] Psalm cv, 38.

[2] Note by Montfaucon: "This, with the figures that follow, we have purposely omitted, because they were either omitted by the copyists, or clumsily drawn and otherwise useless."

[3] See note 2, p. 56.

[4] The picture is not given in Montfaucon.

people drank, as David in the Psalms exclaims: *He clave the rock in the wilderness and gave them drink as out of the great depths;*[1] and again: *He opened the rock and the waters gushed out; they ran in the dry places like rivers;*[1] and again: *He brought water out of the rock, and caused waters to run down like rivers.*[2] But the Apostle says: *For they drank of that spiritual rock which followed them, and that rock was Christ;*[3] by which he meant that, just as the flood of water from the rock which followed them gave them without stint water to drink, so Christ supplies to us life-giving waters, through the mysteries of which the rock was a type. And in that place again, they routed Amalek in battle, and there also Iothòr (Jethro) met his son-in-law Moses, to whom he brought his two sons and his wife; for Moses had sent back to him his wife and his children. . . .

This hiatus is followed by a citation of the Ten Commandments.

Text.

Then when he had come down from the Mountain he was ordered by God to make the Tabernacle, which was a representation of what he had seen in the Mountain, namely an impress[4] of the whole world. *For see*, said He, *that thou make all things according to the pattern shown thee in the Mount.*[5] Now the blessed Apostle Paul in the Epistle to the Hebrews has declared that the first Tabernacle was a pattern of this world, for he says: *For the first had also ordinances of divine service and a worldly sanctuary; for there was a tabernacle made; the first wherein was the candlestick, and the table and the shewbread, which is called the Sanctuary.*[6] In calling it *worldly* he indicated that it was, so to speak, a pattern of the world, *wherein was also the candlestick,* by this meaning the luminaries of heaven, *and the table,* that is, the earth, *and the shew-bread,* by this meaning the fruits which it

---

[1] Psalm, lxxviii, 16.
[2] Psalm, cv, 41.
[3] I Cor. x, 4.
[4] Gr. ἐκμαγεῖον.
[5] Exod. xv, 30.
[6] Heb. ix, 1, 2.

produces annually: *which*, he says, *is called the Sanctuary*, by this meaning the first Tabernacle. Afterwards he speaks of the second in these terms: *We have such an high priest who is set on the right hand of the throne of the Majesty in the heavens; a minister of the sanctuary and of the true tabernacle which the Lord pitched and not man;*[1] and again: *But Christ being come a high priest of good things to come, by a greater and more perfect tabernacle, not made with hands, that is to say, not of this building; neither by the blood of goats and calves, but by his own blood he entered in once into the holy place, having obtained eternal redemption for us;*[2] and again: *for Christ is not entered into the holy places made with hands, which are the figures of the true, but into heaven itself, now to appear in the presence of God for us.*[3] In this last passage he says that heaven is the true tabernacle, while the things which were prepared by Moses are antitypes. He therefore calls the things of Moses things *made by hands*, but the real things *not made with hands*. Having then been commanded to make the Tabernacle he made it according to the pattern which had been shown to him, and also its appurtenances according to their pattern, the Ark of testimony, and the Mercy-seat above, and the two Cherubim stretching out their wings, and overshadowing the Mercy-seat above, and in like manner the veil and the table and the candlestick, and the hangings of the Tabernacle (namely the first coverings) and curtains made of goats' hair (that is stypta[4]) and these again were the second coverings of the Tabernacle. In like manner also the third coverings made of skins dyed red and sky-blue, that is, of what is

---

[1] Heb. viii, 1, 2.   [2] Heb. ix, 11, 12.   [3] Heb. ix, 24.
[4] This word (from στύφω, I contract) is to be found neither in Liddell and Scott's *Dictionary* nor in that of Sophocles. It is rendered by *ex tela* in Montfaucon's Latin version.

called leather, and all things cunningly worked and wonderful. We have depicted the Tabernacle thus.¹

Note.

We must here again observe that he (Paul) speaks of the Tabernacle which was pitched by God, namely heaven, as the true. Moreover he calls heaven that perfect Tabernacle not made with hands, as it was created by God. For he calls the Tabernacle which Moses prepared *made with hands*. And further in contrast with the Tabernacle prepared by Moses, he calls the other the true, because it abides for ever, while the former is dissolved. Then again he calls the curtains αὐλαία, and it is thus the pagans who use the Attic dialect call them, meaning by αὐλαία a large and variegated piece of tapestry. Hyperides the orator² in his speech against Patrocles speaks thus : *But the nine Archons were feasting in the portico, having fenced off that part of it from being seen, by means of an αὐλαία* (or curtain). Menander also uses the word [in the line]: Στρώμασι. ἱμάτια, μύρα, οἶνοι, αὐλαίαι.

The twenty pillars are twenty boards standing upright, one cubit and a half being the breadth of each of the boards, so that in the twenty pillars there are thirty cubits, and this is the length of the Tabernacle. But their sockets were double within and without, being placed on both sides of the board, and the sockets were of silver. The capitals again were simple but of gold, and in like manner the boards and the bars and the tenons. The tenons were two planks joined together and overlaid with gold and nailed to each board, turned to and falling against each other, in order that they might bind together all the boards. And the tenons and the bars, which passed through the rings called *psalides*, bound the whole Tabernacle securely together ; but the fifth bar in the middle was not borne up by passing through the rings, but was made to pass through the boards for the greater safety of the Tabernacle. The height again of each board was eleven cubits, and the breadth of the Tabernacle was likewise

---

¹ See the Tabernacle as Cosmas has depicted it in Pl. 12 in the Appendix.
² One of the *Ten Attic Orators*. He was the friend and political ally of Demosthenes. His orations are lost.

eleven cubits, and the wall opposite to this wall was similar to it. When the veil of the temple was rent in twain at the Passion of the Lord three things were indicated by this circumstance. First it proved the audacity of the Jews against the Lord, the divine temple, as it were, mourning and rending its garments; next, it showed the approaching dissolution and abolition of the Judaic ritual, by the taking away of the first Tabernacle; and it showed thirdly that the inner Tabernacle, which was invisible and inaccessible to all, and even to the priests, had become visible and accessible to men. Glory for all to Christ the King for ever and ever, Amen!

Text.

Here is a delineation of the Tabernacle without its pertinents. Its first coverings were woven of diverse colours, blue and purple and fine-twined linen, and scarlet, as was also the veil[1] which scripture calls hangings. And they were of similar length with the curtains.[2] The length of a curtain was eight and twenty cubits, and its breadth four cubits. But he says that five curtains were coupled together one to another, and likewise other five curtains, and that the couplings of the five with the five from the middle at the edge of the one set were loops, and at the edge of the other, clasps. And they put the clasps into the loops, and fastened the ten curtains together just as what are called *sigistropylai*, the bags for holding slaves' bedding,[3] or saddle-bags, are fastened.[4] But when they marched carrying the Tabernacle with its furniture, the five curtains were detached from the other five and were carried separately. This they did also in the case of the coverings of the second Tabernacle, which were made of goat's hair woven, and were called leather screens.[5] They were eleven in number, each being thirty cubits long, and thirty also broad. Five of them

---

[1] Gr. Καταπέτασμα, the inner veil, the outer being Κάλυμμα.
[2] Gr. Κορτίναι, a Latin word.
[3] Gr. στρωματοδέσμων.   [4] δισσακίων.   [5] δέρρεις.

were coupled together, and likewise the other six. They were joined together by clasps and loops, and the whole of them again became one. The length of the Tabernacle was therefore thirty cubits. For there were twenty pillars, that is, boards; each of which was one cubit and a half in breadth, thus making altogether thirty cubits. Then also there were the six pillars, each of them one cubit and a half in breadth, making nine cubits. Then there were at the corners two pillars of one cubit and a half each, and thus there were eight pillars of ten [twelve] cubits collectively, and these were made secure with bars on all sides. The ten curtains accordingly, when conjoined, made a breadth of forty cubits, and covered all the length of the Tabernacle, and the wall at the back which was ten cubits in height, altogether forty cubits. But the curtains, which together were eight-and-twenty cubits long, covered the breadth of the Tabernacle which was ten cubits. The two side-walls were ten cubits in height, the others twenty cubits, making together thirty cubits. There were besides curtains of eight-and-twenty cubits, and with the exception of one cubit, these covered the one wall, and also the other wall with the exception again of one cubit; but the screens of leather covered the other two cubits; for they were each thirty cubits in length, while the one leather screen which remained over was let down for the door of the Tabernacle. We therefore delineate their appearance along with the three coverings of skins and they are as you see.[1]

Note.

Here Moses, after he had been privileged to witness the terrible scenes on the Mount, is commanded by God to make the Tabernacle according to the pattern which he had seen in the Mount, this being a pattern of the whole world. *For see*, saith He, *that*

---

[1] See Pls. 14 and 17 in the Appendix.

thou make all things according to the pattern which was shown thee in the Mount.[1] Since therefore it had been shown him how God made the heaven and the earth, and how on the second day he made the firmament in the middle between them, and thus made the one place into two places, so he, in like manner in accordance with the pattern which he had seen, made the Tabernacle and placed the veil in the middle, and by this division made the one Tabernacle into two, an inner and an outer. The Apostle therefore declared the outer to be a pattern of this world, saying thus : *For the first Tabernacle had ordinances of divine service and a worldly sanctuary. For there was a Tabernacle prepared, the first, wherein were the candlestick and the table and the shew-bread which is called the Holy place,*[2] as if he said, it exhibits a pattern of the world, in which are the earth, and the monthly fruits and the luminaries (of heaven). And then when explaining the second Tabernacle he speaks thus : *But Christ having come a high priest of the good things to come, through the greater and more perfect Tabernacle, not made with hands, that is to say, not of this creation, nor yet through the blood of goats and calves, but through his own blood, entered in once for all into the Holy place having obtained eternal redemption ;*[3] as if he said : Just as the high priest once a year enters into the inner Tabernacle through the blood of goats and calves, making propitiation for the people, so also Christ entered into the Tabernacle not made with hands, that is, into heaven, having once for all procured eternal redemption. And again : *For Christ is not entered into the Holy place made with hands which is an image of the true, but into heaven itself ;* and again he says : *For the law had a shadow of good things to come ;*[4] for, as in an outline, by the inner Tabernacle he has signified the ascension of Christ after the flesh, and the entrance into it of just men. Wherefore he again admonishes us in these words : *Having therefore, brethren, boldness to enter into the Holy place by the blood of Jesus, by the way which he dedicated for us, a new and living way through the veil, that is to say, his flesh ; and having a great high-priest over the house of God, let us draw near with a true heart ;*[5] and again in declaring that Christ is in heaven he says : *Whom God set forth to be a propitiation by his blood ;*[6] since the

---

[1] Exod. xv, 30.   [2] Heb. ix, 12.   [3] Heb. ix, 11, 12.
[4] Heb. x, 1.   [5] Heb. 19, 21.   [6] Rom. iii, 25.

Propitiatory (Mercy-seat) was placed within the second Tabernacle. And many other such references are contained in the Epistles of the Apostle, and throughout divine scripture.

But perhaps again some one will still ask: Why did Moses ordain that the entrance to the Tabernacle should be in the east, and that the inner Tabernacle, that is the Holy of Holies, should be in the west? Such an enquirer will be answered very concisely, that since he was commanded by God to make the whole Tabernacle as an image of the whole world, according to the pattern shown to him in the Mount, he so made it, and at the same time has recorded that God, when he had created man, introduced him into the world in the east, and so commanded him, when in course of time he had increased and multiplied, to extend himself and to fill the earth towards the west. For this reason the door of the Tabernacle was placed in the east. And further, since the Tabernacle was an image of the heavenly mansions, at the end of the times it was determined that, through the high priest and the universal King our Lord Jesus Christ, it should be declared that the last dispensation had come. And since the human race had its origin in the east, and in the course of its progress advanced westward as it multiplied, for this reason the [inner] Tabernacle, as being the second and placed last, looked towards the west. From this circumstance also the Church has a tradition that Christians everywhere when worshipping God should turn towards the east, as it was there that He was first manifested to men. For she remembered the days of old, and now renders thanks to Him who has multiplied and extended the human race from the east unto the west. But the Jews, whose notions of the Deity were too anthropomorphic, worshipped God towards Jerusalem, where the temple stood.[1] On this point we can gain light from the story of Daniel, who, when he had opened the window of his chamber which looked towards Jerusalem, worshipped with his face turned towards the temple. One who finds himself in a place lying to the east of Jerusalem turns as a matter of course to the west when he worships; but if he be in the west, he turns to the east, if in the north to the south, and

---

[1] Irenaeus (76) and Epiphanius (Haer., 30, 13) inform us that the Ebionites (Jewish Christians) maintained the Jewish custom of turning in prayer towards Jerusalem as to the Holy City.

if in the south to the north, so that in a manner the four are shown as facing each other when worshipping. But the practice of the Christians is different, for in one and the same manner they offer to God, as being uncircumscribed, one spiritual worship with faces turned eastward, since it was from the east that in the beginning He was manifested to them, and that He multiplied them towards the west. To Him be glory for ever, Amen!

The seven lamps, tongs,[1] and oil-vessels.

This candlestick which had seven lamps and stood in the south of the Tabernacle[2] was a type of the luminaries, for, according to the wise Solomon, the luminaries rising in the east and running to the south, shine upon the north of the earth, and again, they are seven after the number of days in a week, seeing that all time, beginning with weeks, completes both months and years. He ordered them, however, to be lighted on one side, since the table was placed towards the north, in order that their light might from the south shine on the north; for Solomon speaks thus with reference to the luminaries: *The sun ariseth and goeth towards the south and moveth round to the north; the wind whirleth about continually and returneth again according to its circuits.*[3] Thus both Solomon and Moses have expressed themselves alike concerning the luminaries, in their general relations.

Note.

The table itself[4] is a type of the earth, and the loaves signify its fruits, and being twelve they are symbolic of the twelve months of the annual cycle. The four corners of the table signify the four tropics of the year, one occurring every three months; the waved border with which it is wreathed all round signifies the entire sea, or the ocean, as it is called by the pagans; and the crown which is round it indicates the earth that lies beyond the ocean where Paradise is.

Text.

The veil again he ordered to be made of blue and purple and fine linen and scarlet, variegated like the four elements,

---

[1] The Greek text has λάβιδες, which Montfaucon has corrected into λαβίδες. [2] See Pl. 15 in the Appendix.
[3] Eccl. i, 6. [4] See Pl. 19 in the Appendix.

or perhaps in order to produce a beautiful effect. For they were made evidently to serve not only for symbols, but evidently also for decorative and liturgical purposes. And he placed the veil in the middle of the Tabernacle, which he thus divided into two places. In the inner place was set the Ark of the Propitiation, which was concealed behind the veil, and was not seen by any one. The Propitiatory was a type of the Lord Christ according to the flesh, as saith the Apostle: *Whom God set forth to be a propitiation by his blood;*[1] and again the high priest was himself a type of the Lord Christ, according to the Apostle: *For*, saith he, *just as the high priest once a year entereth into the inner Tabernacle, so Christ, having come a high priest of the good things to come through his own blood, entered in once for all into the Holy place, having obtained eternal redemption,*[2] as methinks I have frequently mentioned. Here is a delineation of the Ark of propitiation [or the Mercy-seat].[3]

Note.

Zacharias then and Abia were both of them priests who alternately year by year entered *into the temple* to effect the remission of sins. It fell accordingly to the lot of Zacharias at the time of the Lord's conception to be exercising the priest's office; and having entered, as Luke records: *He saw a vision of an angel which also said unto him: Fear not, Zacharias, because thy supplication is heard, and thy wife Elizabeth shall bear thee a son:*[4] as if he had said, "Thou hast entered here to ask for the people remission of their sins, lo! I bring to you the good tidings that your prayer will be fulfilled, for there shall be born to thee a son by Elizabeth to be the forerunner of Him who of his grace will bestow upon the world a complete remission of their sins." John himself verily, pointing out with his finger the Lord Christ, exclaimed: *Behold the Lamb of God which taketh away the sin of the world,*[5] as if he said: Him who takes away and abolishes

---

[1] Rom. iii, 25. [2] Heb. ix, 11, 12.
[3] See Pl. 16 in the Appendix. [4] Luke i, 13. [5] John i, 29.

mortality and corruption and mutation, and makes us immortal and incorruptible and immutable and no longer capable of sinning.

Text.

The court of the Tabernacle had a length of one hundred cubits with twenty pillars, and a breadth of fifty cubits with twelve pillars. But to form the breadth of the Tabernacle on the east He ordered that there should be three pillars on this side, and three on that side, and that the veils like vestures of fine linen, alone measuring fifteen cubits, should be stretched over the three pillars. He ordered further that the four other pillars should be made the gate of entrance into the court, and that the veils should be variegated with four colours. But all the veils of the court were to be made of fine linen and of that alone. They were five cubits in height and were furnished with loops and pegs and cords, on which were stretched the coverings of the Tabernacle and the veils of the court. And the whole structure of the Tabernacle was at once awe-inspiring and of highest excellence. I must therefore to the best of my ability delineate these also, representing them in the form of what are called pavilions.¹

Concerning the garments of the priest.

The garments of the priest were the following: an embroidered tunic, and an ephod and a long robe and a turban and a girdle and a mitre and a plate, two shoulder-pieces² for the shoulders of the priest joined together the

---

¹ Gr. παπυλεώνων, incorrect for παπιλεώνων or παπιλιώνων. This is a Latin word (*pavilio*, a butterfly, a tent), and hence Cosmas may be excused for tripping in its spelling. See Pl. 18 in the Appendix.

² Gr. Χιτὼν κοσύμβρωτος, καὶ ἐπωμίς, καὶ ποδῆρες (should be ποδήρης, χιτών being understood), καὶ κίδαρις, καὶ ζώνη, καὶ μίτρα, καὶ πέταλον.
The word ἐπωμίς, as used by Greek writers, denotes the point of

one to the other and with the ends folded back from the left to the right and from the right to the left, and covering the bareness of his neck. These shoulder-pieces were interwoven with threads of gold and wrought and variegated with genuine purple, and with a blue dye and fine linen and scarlet. In the shoulder-pieces upon the two shoulders were set two stones of emerald[1] on which were engraved the names of the twelve tribes, six names on one stone and six on the other. But the oracular plate of judgment,[2] which was woven, was a square piece of cloth of a palm's breadth, doubly wrought with gold thread, variegated in the weaving with the four colours already mentioned, and set with four rows of stones, three stones being in each row, so that they were twelve in all.[3] The stones were enchased in gold, and were inserted in the oracular plate of judgment, and each of them had engraved upon it the name of one of the twelve tribes. He ordered also two small shield-shaped clasps of gold[4] to be placed

---

the shoulder where it joins the collar-bone, and also the part of the women's tunic which was fastened on the shoulder by brooches. The *ephod*, or vestment worn by the Jewish high priest over the blue tunic, consisted of two shoulder-pieces, one covering the back, the other the breast, and was therefore not unlike the Greek *epōmis*.

[1] Gr. σμαράγδου. The stones, however, were onyx-stones. See Exod., xxviii, 9.

[2] Gr. τὸ λογεῖον τῆς κρίσεως. *Logeion* denoted the place on the Attic stage from which the players spoke; *pulpitum* in Latin. Here it is used in the sense of λόγιον, an oracle. Κρίσις denotes *the judicial sentence by which one is justified or condemned;* and the wearing of the plate was meant to signify God's acceptance of Israel, grounded on the sacrificial functions of the high priest.

[3] Some think that in the breastplate there were inserted two images which personified Lights and Perfections, the mysterious Urim and Thummim. Others again take Urim and Thummim to be the breastplate itself, with its rows of precious stones. After the taking of Jerusalem it was carried to Rome, and with other spoils deposited in the Temple of Peace.

[4] Gr. ἀσπιδίσκας, lit. small shields; the *ouches* of our bible.

upon the two shoulders in the front, and fringes intertwined with gold and coloured tissues, to depend from these, and the oracular plate to hang suspended thereby upon the breast; as well as by means of two wreathen chains of gold drawn back from the two sides of the oracular plate underneath, and fastened together behind alternately at the two tips of the two shoulder-pieces at the back of the priest, so that the wreathen chains might be on the back of the priest, and serve to join diagonally the oracular plate to the shoulder-pieces before and behind. The undergarment was all of a blue colour, from the breast down to the ankles,[1] where a border was woven with it. But the hem underneath, being widened by a fringe of various colours, had golden bells and golden pomegranates adorned with flowers suspended around it, and so disposed that a bell alternated with a pomegranate. He had also a turban of fine linen,[2] and a girdle of various colours which at the top girt the under garment around under the breast. The priest wore the mitre on his forehead, and above the mitre a blue lace, having on its border a gold plate, on which was the seal of *Holiness to the Lord*,[3] namely, what is called a tetragram, and thus arrayed he entered into the Holy place. He wore also to cover his legs linen drawers[4] from his loins to his thighs for the sake of decency. The figure of the priest moreover can be thus delineated.[5]

---

[1] Hence its name, ποδήρης.

[2] Gr. κίδαριν βυσσινήν. Cidarim Persae regium capitis vocabant insigne: hoc caerulea fascia albo distincta circumibat.- Q. *Curtius*, iii, 3.

[3] Gr. σφραγὶς ἁγιάσματος Κυρίου. See Exod. xxviii, 36 : "And thou shalt make a plate of pure gold, and grave upon it, like the engravings of a signet, Holy to the Lord." The plate was worn in the mitre, or upper turban.

[4] Gr. βαμβωνάρια. A very rare word. It is used by the Byzantine historian Malala.

[5] See Pls. 20 and 21 in the Appendix.

It is evident therefore that the different parts of the attire were types of certain things, and that they were intended both for ornament and to impress the mind with awe ; for instance, the two stones of emerald which the priest wore on his shoulders, on which were the names of the twelve tribes, signify the twelve tribes which were descended from one ancestor Abraham, for this is shown by the fact that the emerald stone had been made into two, that there might be one for each shoulder. But he ordained that on the shoulders of the priest should be laid the burden of the twelve tribes, as it was he who wore the stones and went into God's presence on behalf of the tribes. But the oracular plate which was worn on the breast and was twofold, signifies the soul and the body. It was therefore twofold, and was placed upon the heart. The twelve stones were different from each other, because each man has his own peculiar mode of thinking, and because there were so many different tribes. Then, as there was one [common] ancestor, he commanded one stone, an emerald, to be set upon the shoulders, as one ancestor. But because the tribes and the ways of thinking are different, he commanded different stones to be placed upon the breast. And on the plate of the seal of *Holiness to the Lord*, which was on the forehead, he says that there were letters engraved. These letters formed the name of God, and what is called in Hebrew the tetragram. In fine, the other things were designed to please the eye by reason of their beauty. But the golden bells and the pomegranates were made to produce sound, a symbol by which the priest was instructed that he should not presume to enter into the Holy place until he had made the sound to be heard. For just as one who intends going into the presence of men of exalted rank, when he finds no one to announce him, begins to knock, not daring to enter without warning, so here the priest is enjoined to advance with the bells and set them ringing.[1] And such is our description of the Tabernacle and of the priest.

A cloud by day rested over the Tabernacle and fire by night, in the sight of all Israel as often as they resumed their march—according to what is recorded in scripture—and when merchants, chiefly Ishmaelites and Midianites, came to them with their loads, all their wants were through divine providence abundantly supplied, as is written in Deuteronomy ii, 7, and viii, 4; and also xxix, 5, where it is said: *He hath led you forty years in the wilderness: your clothes were not waxen old upon you, and your shoes were not worn off upon your feet;* for it is not the fact, as some marvelmongers, and especially they of the circumcision, have supposed, that their garments and shoes did really and truly not wear away, though Moses seems to say so, while, what he means is, that they lacked for nothing in the desert, since the merchants continually brought them necessary supplies; for how was it possible for the children born to them in the wilderness to wear the garments and shoes of their fathers, who were full-grown men while they were very small? And how could they have been ordered to make every day the twelve new loaves of shew-bread, unless the merchants had brought them corn? For ye know that with regard to this matter they murmured, saying: *Is he able to give us bread also, or to prepare a table for his people?*[2] Or how could they have procured the fine flour for making the cakes, or the skins for making the scarlet and blue leather curtains of the Tabernacle, unless they had purchased them from the merchants? And because, while the merchants, through the providence of God, supplied their wants, they still murmured both

---

[1] According to Josephus, the bells signified *thunder*, and the pomegranates *lightning*, or were meant to give notice to the people outside when the priest entered or came forth from the Holy place.

[2] Psalm lxxviii, 20.

against God and against Moses, even though they possessed the wealth of the Egyptians, he wrought wonders for them, ungrateful and unbelieving as they were, supplying them now with abundance of water from the rock, now with manna from heaven, now with quails from the sea for thirty days—and further, in teaching them to curb their lusts, he chastised them with plagues, at one time consuming a portion of their encampment with fire, at another visiting with death four and twenty thousand of them, at another sending serpents among them, while at yet another, under the wrath of heaven, the earth swallowed up the company of Dathan, Abiram and Korah, with all their families and their cattle, thus teaching them not to be distrustful and ungrateful to God, but to live soberly. And when they had received the law from God in writing, and had learned letters for the first time, God made use of the desert as a quiet school, and permitted them for forty years to carve out letters on stone. Wherefore, in that wilderness of Mount Sinai, one can see, at all their halting-places, all the stones, that have there been broken off from the mountains, inscribed with Hebrew letters, as I myself can testify, having travelled in these places. Certain Jews, too, who had read these inscriptions informed me of their purport, which was as follows: *The departure of so and so of such and such a tribe, in such and such a year, in such and such a month,* just as with ourselves there are travellers who scribble their names in the inns where they have lodged. And the Israelites, who had but newly acquired the art of writing, continually practised it, and filled a great multitude of stones with writing, so that all those places are full of Hebrew inscriptions,[1] which, as I think,

---

[1] Numerous inscriptions, partly Egyptian and partly Nabataean, are still to be found on the rocks of Sinai. The Egyptian are of great antiquity, even long prior to Moses, as they contain the names of Egyptian kings from Senefu and Cheops down to Ramses II.

have been preserved to this day for the sake of unbelievers. Any one who so wishes can go to these places and see for himself, or at least can enquire of others about the matter, when he will learn that it is the truth we have spoken. When the Hebrews therefore had been at the first instructed by God and had received a knowledge of letters through those tables of stone, and had learned them for forty years in the wilderness, they communicated them to their neighbours the Phœnicians, at that time first when Cadmus was King of the Tyrians, from whom the Greeks received them, and then in turn the other nations of the world.

The Israelites encamped in the desert, arranged in an order prescribed by God, as thus: the priests and the Levites encircled the Tabernacle and the twelve tribes were disposed around them—three on the east side of the Tabernacle, the tribe of Judah with Moses and Aaron being in the middle, as that tribe had the precedence of the others. Then there were three tribes on the south, three on the west, and three on the north side. And in this order they halted—and still observing it resumed their march, and went forward in the manner here represented.

In this manner then they encamped each day in the desert until at last when Moses and Aaron were dead, and Jesus the son of Nanê (Joshua the son of Nun) had obtained the leadership, and in a miraculous manner had

---

The discovery, moreover, of the cuneiform tablets at Tel-el-Amarna shows us that in the century before the exodus people were writing and corresponding with each other in the east from the Euphrates to the Nile. The Nabataean inscriptions, again, belong to the early inscriptions of the Christian aera, and the characters used are the Western Aramaic or Syriac. Cosmas, with easy credulity, took them to be as old as the time of Moses. Along with Eusebius and Jerome, he identified Mount Serbal with Mount Sinai. The famous monastery of St. Catharine was founded by Justinian in the time of Cosmas.

conducted them over the Jordan, he gave them for inheritance the land of promise in accordance with divine predictions and arrangements. Then the tribe of Judah obtained the Metropolitan city of Jerusalem, until from that tribe He should come forth who was expected and foretold by the law and the prophets—He through whom God wrought the great and eternal salvation and renovation for the world—I speak of the Lord Christ according to the flesh—according, that is, to the promises made by God to Abraham, and according to his purpose from the very beginning, as the Apostle also says in the Epistle to the Galatians, where, as if in answer to the question *What then is the law?* meaning, *Why was the law given?* he at once replies and says: *It was added because of transgressions till the seed should come to whom the promise hath been made: and it was ordained through angels by the hand of a mediator;*[1] whereby he means, that the reason why the law was added was this, that by means of it and of the priesthood the people which had received the promise should be under safe guardianship—the people, namely, sprung from Abraham—and that there should be no intermixture of this people with any other; so that thereby he who had been foretold might be recognisable by all—he, by whom the world is being renovated, and by whom also the purpose and economy which God had from the first designed is being fulfilled. For it was the purpose of God from the very beginning to make others participants of existence, and to give them a share of his goodness—reason and knowledge and immortality and blessedness, and of every good thing as far as the capacity of the participant might admit. And since the Deity, being by intuition in possession of all true knowledge, cannot be taught, while it is the proper nature of the brute creatures

---

[1] Galat. iii, 19.

to be moved by instinctive impulses without reason and true knowledge; and while again in like manner inanimate objects are altogether destitute of self-motion, of instinctive impulse, and of knowledge, God, having in his goodness been pleased to make, what was possible, an intermediate class of beings, endowed with reason and capable of acquiring knowledge by teaching and experience, subjected them to probation, and in accordance with his purpose from the beginning, made the future state, that is, the place on high.

So when in the first place he had set apart this present state, employing it as a school suitable for our needs, he made it mortal and mutable, in order that we, possessing the power of judging and reasoning, might enjoy our share of its blessings, and avoid its evils. Wherefore also the present dispensation has its joys and its sorrows, that we, who are every day living in the midst of them, might shun the one, and adhere to the other. For the same reason laws have been ordained, accompanied by threats and chastisements, to curb our vicious appetites; and lastly, death itself, which seems a token of his anger, but which in reality brings to a close this troubled life and our term of discipline, just as God also in his providence brought it upon the first man, to make his sin hateful to him and to make righteousness the object of his desires, thus encouraging him and all through him, to enter into the life prepared for us beforehand, and into the eternal Kingdom, and into righteousness, sanctification, redemption and blessedness, which the purpose of God from the beginning contemplated. God accordingly, as if moved by anger, wisely, yea most wisely, inflicted death upon the first-made man on account of his sin, that he might render sin a thing hateful to him. Then again afterwards, in order that the man might not sink into despair under his misery, he took care of him as a father takes care of his child, and made raiment for him. Then he avenged the blood of

Abel, and translated Enoch, that the sentence of death might have no power over him ; he saved Noah from the shipwreck of the world ; he chose Abraham by whom and his seed he accomplished the renovation of the world, Isaac also and Jacob, the patriarchs, and the children of these, and the twelve tribes sprung from them, which with a high hand he redeemed from Egyptian bondage and guided miraculously through the wilderness, and presented with a written law ; and when he had distributed the nation into ranks of war, he gave them the land of Palestine distributed into lots ; and he raised up for them prophets, David their first king, and Samuel, the great Elijah, his disciple Elisha, the twelve prophets, and the four great prophets who foretold the coming of the Lord Christ, who was to arise from among them according to the flesh, in whom and through whom is, and is fulfilled, God's purpose from the beginning, and his great scheme of salvation. For just as he ordained to introduce death on account of the sin of the first man, so also, through the obedience of the Lord Christ according to the flesh, he ordained the resurrection and the renovation and the gathering together of the whole creation. For, as Paul says, *as by man came death, so by man the resurrection from the dead*[1] has been brought into the world. This is the great salvation, and dispensation and wisdom of God, who has produced all things and has again restored them. Wherefore also he made the two states from the beginning, and the whole scope of divine scripture has regard to the future life, which succeeds this present life, as have also the Christian preaching and the hope of the Christians. For this reason in baptism the rite is not administered to any one unless he first confess his belief in the Holy Trinity and the resurrection of our flesh. Without doing this, he is neither

---

[1] I Cor. xv, 21.

accounted a Christian, nor pronounced to be one of the faithful. This is the scope of the whole of the divinely inspired scriptures both of the Old and of the New Testament, pointing out that, according to the pattern of the Tabernacle prepared by Moses in the wilderness, God made the whole world into two places, this world, namely, in which he thought fit that we, mortal and mutable creatures, should first spend our days as at school, and have experience of pain and of pleasure, for without education it is not possible there can be learning. *For no chastening*, saith scripture, *seemeth for the present to be joyous but grievous*.[1] On those accordingly, who have been rationally tested, he has decreed to bestow afterwards in the future state his good things that are everlasting, and to fulfil what has been his primary purpose from the beginning—having taken, as God, a providential care of what concerns us, as became him, and as was for our advantage. We sketch the encampment[2] of the Israelites in the wilderness, and their passage of the Jordan with Joshua the son of Nun after the death of Moses, and their rest in the land of promise, and Jerusalem, and how they got the land by lot and how they held it in possession.

While they dwelt in this land God at times raised up prophets to announce the advent of the Lord Christ according to the flesh, through whom the future state was to be revealed, while they also called to the remembrance of the people the promises which God gave to Abraham. Let us therefore sketch each of the men of old and each of the prophets, to show how each of them was thought

---

[1] Heb. xii, 11.

[2] Gr. Διαγράφομεν . . . τὴν στρατοπεδαρχίαν. The proper meaning of *stratopedarchia* is *the office of a military commander*. Cosmas seems to use it here instead of *stratopedeuma*—a camp. Neither these sketches, nor those of the men of old and the Prophets mentioned below, are given.

worthy to predict something about the coming of the Lord Christ, whether recording it by means of his words or by means of his deeds—if only he be deemed worthy to speak or do anything with reference to him, for this is in consonance with the argument of our work, wherein we would show from first to last what is the purpose which all divine scripture ever keeps in view.

Adam.

This is Adam,[1] the first-made man, who was held worthy to make a prediction concerning himself and his wife, who with the divine benediction were both through copulation united into one flesh, to which the Lord bears witness in the Gospels, saying tnat God had spoken this by the mouth of Adam, unto whom he had himself brought his bride; and the Apostle Paul has used this as an illustration, explaining it in a mystical manner, concerning the Lord Christ and the Church, saying: *This mystery is great, but I speak of Christ and of the Church.*[2] For just as Adam is the head of all men in this world, as being the cause of their existence, and their father, so also the Lord Christ according to the flesh is the head of the Church, and the father of the future age. Adam also was the first who had the honour to be, and to be called, the image of God, but with respect to the Lord Christ, this is in a still higher degree the case, as the Apostle says: *Who is the image of the invisible God.*[3] Adam again was the first and only one of men who from his side, through God, produced the female without seed, and the Lord Christ according to the flesh was, as a male, produced from the female without seed, thus preserving the equality of privilege and satisfying the debt of nature.[4] Adam was the first of men who

---

[1] See note 2, p. 164.   [2] Ephes. v, 32.   [3] Coloss. i, 15.
[4] Gr. τὴν ἰσοτιμίαν καὶ τὸ χρέος τῆς φύσεως ἀναπληρώσας. The debt was that which was due by the woman to Adam, and which she

sinned, having been beguiled by the devil. The Lord Christ on his account paid the debt, having opportunely annulled the bond and trampled the enemy under his feet.

Note.

In the first epistle to the Romans the Apostle has declared Adam to be a type of Christ, saying: *Who is a figure of him that was to come;*[1] and in like manner he has called Adam the first man, and Christ the second. Since God threatened the first man with death that very day should he transgress the commandment, and yet when he did transgress did not immediately visit him with death in accordance with the threatening, but was long-suffering towards him, and having disciplined him by means of the law, and cast him out of Paradise, and permitted him to live to a good old age before he died, God showed great forbearance and kindness towards man, particularly in having provided him with clothing, and in that he did not in wrath inflict death upon human nature, but instructed man in prudence and wisdom, and made sin hateful to him, and righteousness the object of his desires. Then, through the guarding of the tree of life, he taught men to love and hope for immortality. Glory to him who from the beginning to the end has bestowed his provident care upon man.

Note.

Any one who so wishes can learn that, in dispensing his lot to the man, God was not actuated by anger, but rather by benevolence and wisdom, and that after his transgression he not only treated him with forbearance, and provided for his wants, but even endowed him with the power of prophecy. For he said concerning his wife: *And he called her name Zōē (Life), because she was the mother of all living.*[2] For he could not possibly have foreseen that he would make the world of men from his wife, had he not been inspired with divine power and grace. And again when Cain had murdered Abel who had not yet begotten

acquitted by bearing Christ without seed. There seems to be reference also to the debt which Adam incurred by his sin, and which Christ paid by His death.

[1] Rom. v, 14.   [2] Gen. iii, 20.

offspring, but was still in immature youth, Adam, foreseeing that Cain who survived and his seed would be destroyed by a deluge, named the third son that he begat, Sêth, as if calling him the foundation of the human race—for such is the interpretation of the name *Sêth*. In one and the same prophecy he uttered two, both that the seed of Cain is to perish, and that he who had been begotten is, so to speak, a beginning and a new foundation of the human race. And not only Adam but his wife also herself speaking of her son, gave him his name, for it is of her that it is said: *And when she had conceived, she bare a son and called his name Sêth, for, said she, God hath raised me up another seed instead of Abel whom Cain slew:*[1] implying by this that Abel has died childless, and the seed of Cain is to perish; this hath God given me as a new foundation for the human race. So far Eve.

After the sacred historian had related the birth of Sêth and of his son Enoch he took up again the account of Adam and says: *This is the book of the generation of mankind. In the day that God created Adam, in the likeness of God made he him; male and female created he them. And he blessed them and called his name Adam in the day when he created them. And Adam lived 230 years and begat a son in his likeness and after his image, and called his name Sêth.*[2] In this place likewise he called his name Sêth, as being the foundation of the human race, and as bearing his own characteristics and the proper dignities. And here it must be observed that the historian says that it was God who gave the first man his name, and the man who gave the woman hers, and that they both gave the name to their son. By the merciful dispensation under which man was placed even the unseen powers, endowed as they are with reason, are instructed in the things which pertain to God. For since man is the bond which unites the whole creation, and is also the image of God, the dispensation under which he lives is a school for his own instruction, and for that of all rational beings. For when he had sinned and had received the sentence of death, these other beings began to lament, deeming all hope to be lost both for themselves and for the universe; but when again they saw that God cared for him, they were led to conceive a good hope both for him and

---

[1] Gen. iv, 25.   [2] Gen. v, 1-3.

for themselves. This, moreover, the Lord declares in the Gospels when he says: *There is joy in heaven over one sinner that repenteth*,[1] as on the other hand it is clear there is sorrow when any one sins. Nay, the Apostle even says that the angels were subjected to be under bondage to vanity on account of man, from a hope that God would also give them deliverance when men should receive the hope laid up for them when installed as the sons of God in glory. And again the Apostle testifies that the angels are taught the things that pertain to God by the dispensation under which man has been placed, for he says: *To the intent that now unto the principalities and the powers in the heavenly places might be made known, through the Church, the manifold wisdom of God:*[2] thus clearly showing that they are taught through the Church the wisdom of God.

Abel.

This is Abel the righteous, who, having been unrighteously put to death, was the first of all men who showed that the foundations of death were unsound. Wherefore also he being now dead yet speaketh, announcing the resurrection of the dead, which the Lord Christ the first of all, showed in his own person, and overthrew the supposed power of death. This is that Abel who is figuratively a representative of the Passion of Christ, seeing that, through the ill-will excited by his good works, he was unrighteously put to death by his brother. Of him the Apostle Paul also thus speaks in his Epistle to the Hebrews: *But ye have come into the Mount Zion and unto the city of the living God, the heavenly Jerusalem, and to innumerable hosts of angels, to the general assembly and Church of the first-born who are enrolled in heaven, and to God the Judge of all, and to the spirits of just men made perfect, and to Jesus the mediator of a new covenant, and to the blood of sprinkling that speaketh better than Abel.*[3]

---

[1] Luke xv, 7.   [2] Ephes. iii, 10   [3] Heb. xii, 22-24.

Note.

Here it is shown more clearly, when the righteous Abel came to his end that death was not brought upon man in anger, since he, who did not sin, died before him who did sin. Wherefore also an inquiry was made by God about the life of Abel, and vengeance was inflicted for his death. And since after his death he speaks, it is from this evident that he will come back again to life. And again, since death was not permitted to come first upon him who had sinned, but upon him who had not sinned, it is shown that death will be destroyed, inasmuch as he made his first assault not righteously but unrighteously—for he laid his foundations upon a righteous man and not upon a sinner, whence we can learn that death laid foundations that were unsound. Wherefore he was very quickly to be destroyed, and this came to pass under the Lord Christ, by whom his seeming power was destroyed. Glory be to him who from the beginning to the end has made the good of man his special care! And again, that death is not sent in anger is shown by this fact, that those who are acknowledged to be righteous come untimely to their end, while those who are acknowledged to be sinners, after fulfilling the number of their days, come to their end in a good old age. For *it is appointed by God unto all men once to die*,[1] as saith the Apostle, speaking of them in general; for neither do all die, nor did Lazarus and others whom the Lord raised die only once, but he refers to all men that are in this state of existence, and are mortal as God created them. Hereafter another and a better state will be introduced in which the righteous shall be discriminated from the unrighteous, the godly from the ungodly—a state wherein death no longer prevails. Some have further said that when the first man had sinned and received the sentence of death without being as yet invested with immortality, his lot was changed to mortality. And by way forsooth of explaining this they say: When God said: *In what day thou eatest of the tree, thou shalt surely die*,[2] he pronounced him to have become mortal, for we see that he did not die immediately according to the threat, so that it is evident the words hinted this: Immortal though thou art, thou shalt become

---

[1] Heb. ix, 27.   [2] Gen. ii, 17.

mortal, and, say they,[1] in order that the sentence pronounced by God may be proved true. Wherefore also his offspring, having fallen under the condemnation of their father, are born mortal. Well then, if all this be true, why was Abel, who, according to them, had fallen under this condemnation and was born mortal, but was declared to be righteous and virgin, why was he not only involved in this condemnation, but, as if it had not been sufficient, subjected also to a further punishment, that, namely, of an untimely death? Why was this punishment superadded to him, a righteous man and virgin, and more especially since, though he was born, as it is said, under the condemnation of his father, that is, was born mortal, mortals that are righteous can be exempted from death, as we see exemplified in Enoch, who also, as ye say, had fallen under the condemnation of his father, and had a wife and children, and yet did not taste of death, while Abel did so who had neither wife nor children. And why, when Cain petitioned for death through horror at his fratricide, did God not give it, but rather delivered him over to a still heavier punishment, namely, to remain on the earth lamenting and trembling— an evil from which he said death would be a deliverance? God therefore said: *Whosoever slayeth Cain, vengeance shall be taken on him sevenfold*,[2] thereby signifying that whosoever should slay him would take away from him many penalties, and would himself suffer his punishment. From this also we can see that, since God permitted a man who was righteous and virgin to be slain, death was not brought upon man in anger, as those marvel-mongers represent, but rather in benevolence and wisdom on the part of the merciful God for our discipline, as we have just said. And further, how came it, we ask, that when the first man had sinned by eating the fruit of a single tree, God according to them condemned him with all his posterity to mortality, while, when he had condemned the first murderer to lamentation and trembling, he did not condemn succeeding murderers to the same, but to a different punishment, which the first of such criminals asked to be inflicted on him, but without obtaining what he asked?

---

[1] Gr. φησίν, *saith he*, that is, the Apostle, which I think should be φασίν —*say they*.
[2] Gen. iv, 15.

Enoch.

This is Enoch on whom the sentence of death did not take effect, for he was translated by God that he should not see death, as is recorded in divine scripture, in order that thereby it might be declared to us that death shall not have power over man, but that his power over him shall be dissolved, as was exhibited in the case of the Lord Christ, when his power was entirely broken. This is Enoch who was translated to life, as a proof of the power of God to after generations, a power capable of warding off death from mortals, yea even of permitting them while living to undergo the change to a better state. This is he who along with Elias will in the last days withstand the Antichrist, and refute his error, according to the ecclesiastical tradition. This is he who through faith escaped the way of death.

Note.

In this case also it is shown still more distinctly that death has not been brought on man in wrath, nor even the sentence of death; but in order that, as we have said, God might make sin hateful to him, and righteousness the object of his desire. Wherefore neither the sentence of death, nor death itself has had power over him, nor will have power, for *By faith*, saith the Apostle, *Enoch was translated that he should not see death*;[1] clearly showing that he did not see death, yea even that while living he underwent the change to a better state, as shall also all those that are left alive at the coming of the Lord, and do not die before the resurrection and the future state. Then further, let those marvel-mongers who say that death is sent to us by the anger of God, and not by his providence and wisdom, tell us how comes it that, while all men ought once to die under the sentence passed upon their father, this man did not incur this penalty?

[*Here there is a gap in the text.*]

Now the length of the ark was 300 cubits, and its

---

[1] Heb. xi, 5.

breadth below, as has been said, 50 cubits, and at the top one cubit, for in summing up he saith: *Thou shalt make it, and in a cubit shalt thou finish it.*[1] The height then was 50 cubits. Those 50 cubits he therefore divided into three stories, each of which was 10 cubits in height—for saith he: *Of two stories and of three stories shalt thou make it ;*[1] as if he said, make within two chambers, and above make the third chamber that there may be three stories. And in the lowermost story he placed the wild beasts, and the venomous reptiles, because they were always wont to lurk in dens and holes under the earth. Then next he placed in the second story four-footed animals and those that bounded over the hills, because they lived on the surface of the earth and on the mountains. But the winged creatures and man he placed in the third story, because the former were denizens of the air, and the latter would become celestial. This is Noah who was a perfect man and righteous in his generation, who unwittingly made himself drunk, and when in that state had mysteries revealed to him. For the scripture saith: *And Noah awoke from his wine and knew what his younger son had done unto him.*[2] And after this statement, by way of cursing him, he tells the things to come, and to his other sons, by way of blessing them, he predicts the future and says: *Blessed be the Lord, the God of Shem ;* and again: *Let God enlarge Japhet and let him dwell in the homes of Shem ;*[3] for in a manner he did not curse the first, and bless those others, but uttered a prediction of the mysteries to be fulfilled through the Lord Christ. For the sons of Canaan did not serve their brethren, but rather it was the latter who served the former in Egypt. Nor did even the Gideonites, as some have supposed, serve them, but it was God whom they served. For the Israelites

---

[1] Gen. vi, 16.   [2] Gen. ix, 24.   [3] Gen. ix, 26, 27.

appointed the Gibeonites to be bondsmen and carriers of water to the temple of God, and not to themselves. What else then is it but just a prediction that they themselves also shall serve Christ, who according to the flesh was descended from Shem? But the exclamation: *Blessed be the Lord, the God of Shem;* is it only his God that is blessed? No, for Noah further says: *Let God enlarge Japhet and let Him*—that is God—*dwell in the tents of Shem;*[1] here making a transposition of the clauses, so that what he says is this: *Blessed be the Lord, the God of Shem, and let Him dwell in the tents of Shem*, and then: *Let God enlarge Japhet*, for he did enlarge both Japhet and Canaan, and again both of them serve Christ who sprang from Shem. For God made his dwellings among men partly in the prophets, but has now made them wholly and uninterruptedly and universally in the Lord Christ, who according to the flesh was descended from Shem, in the same way as it is written concerning the Lord Christ according to the flesh: *In whom dwelleth all the fulness of the Godhead bodily.*[2] By these visions therefore Noah was privileged to predict what was fulfilled in the dispensation of the Lord Christ.

Note.

And in the case of this man it is shown still more clearly that it was not in anger that death was brought upon man. For, though on a cursory view all men seemed to have perished in the deluge by the anger of God, yet in truth they so perished that, by their premature death, the burden of the sins which they had to commit might be lightened, and while this man like a jewel of great price was so carefully guarded and in this way provided for, the truth is, as we have said, that death has not been brought upon man in wrath, but for the benefit and discipline and cessation of this miserable life. For Noah himself, whom God so carefully protected and provided for, did not escape the way of

---

[1] Gen. ix, 27.   [2] Coloss. ii, 9.

death. And those who perished by the death which, as mortals, they would have had to suffer not long afterwards, suffered it as if, through its being premature, it had been sent in anger, whereas it rather benefited them, and relieved them of the burden of the many sins which, if living, they would have added to the account. But to Noah God renewed, and that in even greater measure, the same honour and blessing and promise which he had bestowed on the first man, saying: *And the Lord blessed Noah and his sons and said to them: Be fruitful and multiply and replenish the earth; and the fear of you and the dread of you shall be upon every beast of the earth, and upon every fowl of the air, upon all that moveth upon the earth, and upon all the fishes of the sea: into your hands are they delivered. Every moving thing that liveth shall be food for you: as the green herb have I given you all: but flesh with the blood thereof shall ye not eat.*[1] And a little afterwards: *Whoso sheddeth man's blood, by man shall his blood be shed, for in the image of God have I made man.*[2] Hence it is manifest that God, both before the transgression and long after its occurrence, gave to man the same honour and power and dominion. Nay, he now gave even more, because before the transgression in the garden he commanded the man to eat of every tree except one, and after his expulsion from the garden, he no longer commanded him to eat of the tree but of the seeds (fruits) of the earth. God accordingly, having disciplined those ten generations in the earth beyond (the ocean) which was overrun with thorns, and where he subjected them to an altogether austere and miserable existence, conveyed such of them as survived into this earth by means of Noah, and commanded them to dwell there as in a better country, and one that was nearly equal to Paradise, permitting them to eat of everything—of the fruits of trees and plants and still farther to eat even flesh.

Who is there that, on considering this wonderful providence and care on the part of the wise and compassionate God, would not find great difficulty in asserting that death has been inflicted on man by the anger of God, but would not rather wisely and with thankfulness reflect, that, since God wished to discipline the human race, he wisely brought death upon the first man for his

---

[1] Gen. ix, 1-4.   [2] Gen. ix, 6.

sin, in order that he might make sin hateful to him, and having expelled him from the garden where the tree of life was guarded, again brought him by discipline to entertain a longing after immortality? For when God said: *Lest he should put forth his hand and take of the tree of life and eat, and live for ever*,[1] he inspired man with a longing desire, and a love, and a good hope of immortality, and through him similarly inspired the invisible powers. For he did not exclude man from any of the promises given before the transgression, nor deprive him of them: nay, after having chastised him, he even gave him more, and through Noah augmented the dignity of his title as the image of God, for he said: *Because in the image of God made I man*.[2] For this, therefore, has God made man, that in the present life he should pass his days mortal and mutable, and after his course of discipline here should be rendered immortal. And this again you can more clearly see, because, from the beginning to the end, God gradually has led and is leading man to a better condition by discipline and instruction, while he also imparted to the first men the gift of prophecy. And Noah has some similitude to the Lord Christ according to the flesh. For just as, from out the mass of the first men, he was preserved and transferred to a better earth, in order that men might not suspect that the Lord God, as if repenting and reprobating his own handiwork, had destroyed men with the deluge, so also the Lord Christ according to the flesh was taken out of the mass of men for the salvation of the whole world, and was translated to a better and a heavenly kingdom.—Glory to God, Amen!

Melchisedek.

This is Melchisedek—that so great priest of God most high, who received tithes from the priests under the Mosaic law. This is the King of peace and righteousness, and at the same time a priest of God most high, who was made like to the Son of God—who neither received the priesthood in succession to other priests, nor transmitted it to other priests. This is he who did not perform the rites

---

[1] Gen. iii, 22.   [2] Gen. i, 27.

of divine worship according to the law of Moses, but exercised his priestly office with other and more excellent symbols. This is he who blessed the patriarch Abraham, he who was without father and without mother and did not trace his descent from them; the only person who was priest and king, who was made like to the Son of God, and was held worthy to be the revealer of so many good things.

Note.

After the deluge, when men had again multiplied, he, alone of them all, was by special choice appointed the priest of God most high and king of Jerusalem, after the likeness of the Son of God; and to God he presented sacred offerings, the choicest of all created things by which the human race is always sustained and gladdened, as scripture says. This is the king who habitually instructed the people under his rule to lead a religious life in the enjoyment of these things, whilst officiating himself in the order of his priesthood and making propitiation for his people. Though he was no doubt a Canaanite and king of the Canaanites and not of the race of the patriarchs, yet was he known to the patriarchs of the Abrahamic stock, and being such was declared to be a righteous man, a king, and a priest. He was the first who, when as a priest he had blessed Abraham and had given thanks to God, received tithes of all that Abraham possessed. Now I think, and perhaps shall be saying what is true, that Rebecca when she had gone, as is written, to inquire of the Lord concerning the twins then in her womb, heard through him the response: *The elder shall serve the younger*[1]—for to him as the priest of God was she wont to go, according to the custom of that time, to inquire of the Lord. The Apostle has declared him to be without father, without mother, and without pedigree, and to have neither beginning of days nor end of life, since he was not one of those men who were lineally descended from Abraham. In this respect, however, he had a likeness to the Lord Christ, who was without a father with respect to the flesh, and without a mother with respect to his divine nature, in virtue of which

---

[1] Gen. xxv, 23.

again he had no end of life, while in like manner in his human nature, he became immortal and immutable. God is therefore always reminding men, whether by words or by symbols, that after the life here there is a second state laid up in store for men.

Abraham.

This is the patriarch Abraham, the first of men who left his country, his kindred and his people and put his trust in God, and who for this, and for the promises which God made unto him, was declared righteous. This is he who from a body as good as dead and a womb also dead, produced myriads of men—who, as its root, produced for the world the blessed fruit by which the world is blessed and renovated ; who by his works and the promises made to him revealed to the world the resurrection of the dead— by promises and works [such as are mentioned in the following passages]: Gen. xxviii, 14 ; Gal. iii, 16 ; John viii, 56; Heb. xi, 17-19; Rom. iv, 17-25. Now the journey which Abraham made for three days until he reached the place which God showed him as that where he should offer up his son as a sacrifice on one of the mountains, as is written, and his showing the father a ram which he might offer instead of his son who was born to him in wedlock and in the course of nature—these were all symbols and types of the mystery of the Passion and Resurrection of Christ, for all scripture keeps this object in view.

Note.

Henceforth God begins with Abraham first to reveal both by words and by signs the future state of existence, for the great Abraham at the bidding of God meditated offering up his beloved son, in the belief that God was able to raise him up from the dead, and to bestow such boons upon him as are intimated in scripture. Wherefore also in the Gospels the Lord mentions the typical bearing of the sacrifice of Abraham, when he called it a type of his own day. And through the promises he showed it to Abraham himself, saying : *In thee and in thy seed shall all the nations be blessed*:[1] a promise which showed to him the dispensation according to Christ. Moreover, since God foresaw and from Abraham knew that He would come forth through whom the resurrection and the renovation of the universe are effected, He chose the faithful Abraham whom He had proved by every test, so that he was not chosen prematurely; and having found him the most faithful among the Chaldaeans, a people versed in astronomy and astrology, he transferred him to the enchanters called *Karēnoi*,[2] and having there shown himself faithful, he was commanded to inhabit the land of the idolatrous [Canaanites]. And since, while he dwelt there he was found to be superior to its inhabitants, and did not incline to any of the three ways that have been mentioned,[3] but rather submitted himself to the worship and to the commandments of God, he was thought worthy to receive the great promises and gifts of God, and to hear it said that from his seed should He come forth, who should first show to the world the blessing and the promise through him; He through whom also the creator and renewer of the world graciously bestows upon the world the resurrection and the promise. And they say that Abraham made the sacrifice of Isaac on that very mountain, where also the Lord Christ was offered up as a sacrifice for the whole world, and where he endured the saving cross.

Isaac.

This is Isaac the co-heir of the promises and the blessings of God given to Abraham his father—who was a type of the sacrifice of the Lord Christ, since for three days he travelled on to death, and afterwards returned alive—who on his own shoulders carried the wood for his own sacrifice, as also the Lord Christ carried his own cross on his shoulder—who died in intention and was given his life by God; he in exchange for whom a ram was slain, and whose father heard these words from God:

---

[1] Gen. xxii, 19.
[2] Montfaucon has here this note: "He (Cosmas) calls them *Carēni*, from Charan or Carrhae, whither Abraham withdrew on leaving Chaldaea." [3] Astronomy, Astrology, and Incantation.

Because thou hast not spared the son whom thou lovest,[1] so in like manner it has been said with reference to Christ the son of God: *Who spared not his own son but has given him up for us all;*[2] although the flesh alone is that which has been given for the life of the world, since it is impossible for deity to die; but since the flesh has thus been given, scripture saith that his own son hath been given, because the flesh is a substitute for and a counterpart[3] of the son, after the example of the blessed Isaac. For thus saith the Lord: *Abraham rejoiced to see my day, and he saw it, and was glad.*[4] This is Isaac who involuntarily transmitted to Jacob the blessing promised by God to himself and his father, saying: *Let peoples serve thee, and let their princes bow down to thee, and be thou Lord over thy brethren, and let thy father's sons bow down to thee; cursed be every one that curseth thee, and blessed be every one that blesseth thee.*[5] But we see not all these things accomplished upon Jacob, but see rather that Jacob, having prostrated himself seven times upon the ground, made obeisance to Esau. And thirty kings, sprung from Esau, reigned before ever a king reigned in Israel; so that these blessings await Him who was expected to descend from them, namely, the Lord Christ, whom the whole scope of divine scripture has in view.

And this man who was co-heir of the gifts and promises of Christ, and a type of the Lord Christ himself, was he who transmitted the blessing, which he himself had received from his father, not to the son whom he wished to inherit it, but to him to whom God ordained it should be given. Glory to our God who in supreme wisdom administers the affairs of men, Amen!

---

[1] Gen. xxii, 10.   [2] Rom. viii, 32.
[3] Gr. ἀντάλλαγμα καὶ ἀντίδειξιν. The latter is not a classical word. The *Dictionary* of Sophocles gives *demonstration* as its meaning.
[4] John viii, 56.   [5] Gen. xxvii, 29.

Jacob.

This is Jacob, himself also a co-heir of the promises of God, and one who looked for the city which hath the foundations, whose builder and maker is God—that is, the heavenly Jerusalem, into which, as our forerunner, Christ has entered—and to which state of existence the whole scheme of Christian worship looks, which new and living way the Lord Christ first of all instituted for us, which also the great Jacob predicts in transmitting it to Judah his own son, when he was blessing him; by whom also Jesus Christ is announced as the Lord of the promises in these words which he spake: *Judah, thee shall thy brethren praise: Thy hand shall be on the neck of thine enemies; thy father's sons shall bow down before thee; Judah is a lion's whelp; from the branch,[1] my son, hast thou ascended, he stooped down, he couched as a lion, and as a lion's whelp; who shall rouse him up? A ruler shall not fail from Judah nor a leader from his thighs until what is laid up in store for him shall come, and he the expectation of the nations. Binding his foal unto the vines, and to the tendril of the vine his ass's colt. He shall wash his garment in wine, and his vesture in the blood of the grape. Wine shall make his eyes sparkle with joy, and his teeth shall be whiter than milk.*[2] But the sons of his father did not bow down before him, nay, on the contrary he made obeisance to Joseph, even after the death of his father. It is evident therefore that the whole of this prophecy had its fulfilment in the Lord Christ who descended from him according to the flesh, and that it sets before the mind his kingly power, and his Passion, and his blessed Resurrection after his Passion.

---

[1] Gr. ἐκ βλαστοῦ—the reading of the Septuagint.
[2] Gen. xlix, 8-12.

Note.

And this Jacob, who is the third patriarch, being reckoned with the other two, married a wife whom he did not from the first himself wish to marry, namely Leah; and on the fourth son whom he begat by her, that is, on Judah, he conferred the blessings and the promises: so that from this it is manifest, that the blessing did not accrue to any chance person but to those from whom the Lord Christ according to the flesh, the Prince of the second life, was to spring. And from Judah himself we can learn, that it was not from his own wife, but from his daughter-in-law Thamar that the line of descent of his posterity, from which sprang the Lord of the promises, was reckoned. Most clearly still, when the patriarchs had received such great promises from God, namely, that in them and in their seed all the nations should be blessed, and this promise in like manner: *Unto you I will give this land, and unto your seed*,[1] and when they had received not so much of it as they could set their foot on, but dwelt in tents, they, being full of faith, showed themselves to be expecting and hoping for another dispensation in which they would receive the promises. Wherefore also each one of them in his dying moments transmitted the blessing to him whom God had ordained to receive it. Wherefore also again scripture, laying up, as it were, the fathers in a treasure-house, says with reference to each of them: *And he was gathered unto his fathers*, meaning that all of them together being treasured up for the future state, will receive possession thereof.

Moses.

This is that great Moses by whom marvellous signs and wonders were wrought, and by whom the history of the Creation was written; he, who was honoured to receive the shadows[2] of our true shepherd Christ; who by words and deeds announced beforehand the nature of the dispensation of the Lord Christ; by deeds, as, for instance, by redeeming Israel from the bondage of the Egyptians—

---

[1] Gen. xxviii. 15.
[2] *I.e.*, to receive the things which foreshadowed Christ.

by instituting the Passover and the shedding of blood—by making the passage through the sea, as in baptism—by foretelling through the cloud the setting of the law[1]—by pre-figuring under his sojourning[2] in the wilderness, our abiding in the Holy Spirit and in the Church; by his predicting the Passion of the Lord Christ on the cross, by lifting up on high the brazen serpent; by his describing beforehand the habitation in the heavens, when he procured an entrance into the land of promise by Joshua. O wondrous office of Mediator! by manifold miracles announced! And what need is there to speak of the Tabernacle which was an image of the whole world, in which was placed the mercy-seat, holding the office of the Lord Christ? But that we may not lengthen out the discourse, having before repeatedly said these things, let us come to the prophecy itself which was expressed by words—so then, he speaks thus: *A prophet shall the Lord your God raise up unto you—him ye shall hear. And that man[3] who shall not hear whatever that prophet shall speak in my name, that soul shall be cut off from his people.*[4] And again he records what was spoken by Balaam: *A star shall arise out of Jacob, there shall be raised up a man out of Israel—and he shall smite the princes of Moab—and destroy all the sons of Seth.*[5] By the sons of Seth he means the whole world. And this is not applicable to anyone except

---

[1] Gr. διὰ τῆς νεφέλης προμηνύων τὴν δύσιν τοῦ νόμου. The cloud here referred to is the *thick cloud* which rested upon Sinai at the giving of the law. Such expressions as: *We are not under law but under grace, We have been discharged from the law,* and others similar, used by St. Paul in his Epistle to the Romans, warrant Cosmas in speaking of the setting of the law under the Christian dispensation.

[2] Gr. διαγωγήν. The Latin version has *commemorationem* by a printer's error for *commorationem*.

[3] "We thus," says Montfaucon in a foot-note "restore the mutilated text, for in the Codex it is unlike the Greek Septuagint."

[4] Deut. xviii, 15, 18. [5] Num. xxiv. 17.

the Lord Christ, for *Sêth* is by interpretation *a foundation*
Since therefore Cain and his seed perished utterly in the
deluge, while Abel the younger died childless, Sêth was
posterior to these, from whom both Noah and all the world
are descended, and who is thus a foundation as it were of
mankind. Moreover for this reason Adam, inspired by
the deity, addressed him by the name of *Sêth*, that is,
foundation; and therefore he said: *And he will subdue all
the sons of Sêth*, that is, the whole world. Now this is
applicable to Christ, and to Him alone, whom all scripture
ever keeps in view.[1]

Note.

This Moses, who was a comely man born for God,[2] was brought
up in the royal court of Egypt and instructed in all the wisdom
of the Egyptians: and in after days, having been taken up to
Mount Sinai, he was taught also the wisdom of God, and was
sent back to Egypt in the character of a type of him who
redeems the world from bondage, and graciously bestows freedom
and adoption into sonship. For he redeemed the Israelites from
their bondage to the Egyptians, having prescribed beforehand
the shedding of blood and the Passover. Having led the people
through the Red Sea, he thus prefigured baptism. By the giving
of the law he foreshowed the descent of the Holy Spirit. By
the sojourn in the wilderness, he signified beforehand the discipline of the Church. By the entrance into the land of promise,
effected by his successor, he foretold the dwelling-place of
heaven. By the glory wherewith God made his face to shine,
he foreshadowed in part the future glories.[3] It was, however,
not only by types that he prophesied concerning the mystery as
to Christ, but he did so also by words; and again he was the
first who communicated to mankind and to the world the know-

---

[1] The Latin version has *collimat*, a printer's error for *collinet*.

[2] Gr. ἀστεῖος, τῷ Θεῷ γεννηθείς. The Latin version has *vir urbanus,
Deo natus*. In Exod. ii, 2, where Moses is described as a *goodly*
child, the Septuagint has, as the corresponding epithet, ἀστεῖον.

[3] τὰς μετὰ ταῦτα δόξας μερικῶς προδιεγράφετο. The Latin version has:
gloriam postea distributam per partes praenuntius adumbrabat.

ledge of letters and the practice of writing. Having seen the creation of the whole world, and the delineation of it revealed to him in mysteries, he committed what he had seen to writing, and showed the types of the first and of the second state of existence. Glory be to him who, through those whom he has reared up, has wisely provided for the interests of mankind.

Text.

223 After Moses and his successor Joshua the son of Nun, and after those who became Judges in Israel, and after Saul had been invested with the sovereignty and been rejected as unworthy, God raised up to them a King virtuous, righteous, and a prophet, who composed the book of 150 psalms, when moved by the Holy Spirit. These psalms were written metrically in accordance with the metre proper to the Hebrew language, and he chanted them with melody and rhythm, accompanied with the music of different instruments, and with dances and melodies. For he himself handled the harp, and he had under him a number of choirs of the minor prophets, for so they called those who attached themselves to the prophets, and who were also frequently designated the sons of the prophets. The instruments upon which they played were various: one part of the choir had cymbals, another flutes, another drums, another trumpets, another a psaltery and harp, while another played on what are called shepherd's pipes.[1] Each of the choirs had its leader;[2] one was called Asaph, another Idithum, others the sons of Core, another Aetham an Israelite, another Moses, a man of God.[3] When David therefore was moved by the Spirit, he would then predict something as to the captivity

---

[1] Gr. τοῦ δὲ ᾠδοὺς τοὺς λεγομένους, βουκολίους. lit., "another, the songs called *pastoral*." βουκολίους is not a classical form.

[2] Gr. ἔξαρχον. Cf. Ἀοιδοὶ θρήνων ἔξαρχοι. Homer, *Il.* xxiv, 271.

[3] Cosmas takes this to be a different man from the real author, the great Moses.

of the people, or as to their return therefrom—or he would inculcate lessons of morality, or take Providence for his theme, or the Lord Christ. Each psalm he composed in metre—and it turned upon a single subject—on which account some psalms are short and others long. On composing a psalm he would hand it over to one of the choirs which he had proved, or to the one which it fitted best, and that choir sang it first. And if again in the middle of a psalm he considered that he should make over the rest of the psalm to another choir, then that succession of the measure was called a *diapsalma*;[1] because those singers received in succession the rest of the psalm to be sung by them. But any one who so wishes can learn about this from what is written in the Chronicles of the Kings, namely: *And he sung this song by the hand of Asaph the prophet*.[2] But when the psalm had first been handed over in the manner stated, then each choir afterwards, both by itself and in conjunction with all the other choirs in responsive, joyous, and measured strains, some with these instruments and others with those, sang the psalm, along with dancing to the glory of God. But again we can learn with regard to this matter that David himself, when he had received the Ark from aliens, danced before it, and when reproached for so doing by his wife Melchol (Michal), said: *I will play and laugh for gladness before the Lord*.[3] For not only did he not cease doing so, but promised that he would long persist in the practice. But some, neither understanding this ordinance and the real truth of the matter, nor wishing to be instructed by those who know, have betaken themselves to allegorical interpretations, and have maintained that all the psalms are not David's, but allege that they are manifestly the com-

---

[1] The word used in the Septuagint for the Hebrew *Selah*.
[2] 1 Chron. xxv, 6. [3] II Sam. vi, 21.

positions of those who received them from David to be sung. But never did either the Apostle or the Lord himself mention them as being the psalms of any other than David.

David.

This is that great David, the King and prophet—the man after the Lord's own heart, to whom, as to Abraham, God again correspondently gave the promises that his seed should remain for ever, and that the throne of his kingdom should likewise be perpetual. For when Abraham, having left his country and his kindred, trusted God, God correspondently promised that he would make him the father of nations, and that he would bless all the nations through him and through his seed, that is, through Christ. And to David also, since he was a king, and one with whom He was well pleased, He promised that both his seed and the throne of his kingdom should remain in perpetuity— and here again Christ is meant. This David was privileged to prophesy under inspiration of the Spirit concerning the Lord Christ, having composed four psalms which refer entirely to him, namely, psalms ii, viii, xlv and cx.[1] I say so because both the Lord Christ and the Apostles appear to have taken testimonies concerning him from these four psalms; as for instance, it is related in the Acts of the Apostles that, when the whole company of the Apostles were praying to God, they said: *For of a truth against Jesus whom thou hast anointed both Herod and Pontius Pilate have been gathered together in this city;*[2] accepting the second psalm as having reference to Christ. In like manner in the Acts themselves, Paul when he was discoursing in the synagogue of Antioch in Pisidia spoke thus: *And we bring you good tidings of the promise made unto the fathers,*

---

[1] The last two Psalms are numbered in the Greek text 44 and 109, as in the Septuagint.   [2] Acts iv, 27.

how that God hath fulfilled the same unto us their children in that he raised up Jesus, as it is also written in the second psalm, Thou art my son, this day have I begotten thee.[1] Paul here, by Christ's having been begotten, understands his resurrection, and he too has decided that the second psalm has been spoken concerning him, as all the Apostles also have affirmed. And these things have been said about his humanity, for it is about his deity that in this very psalm it has been said: *Thou shalt rule them with a rod of iron; as a potter's vessel shalt thou dash them in pieces;*[2] as if at the same time making known the force and might of his divinity, and indicating the renovation or regeneration of the human race—for the potter's vessel, though dashed to pieces, provided it has not as yet been subjected to the furnace, admits of being refashioned.

In like manner also David composed the eighth psalm with reference to Christ, speaking of his divine nature in the first verses of it, as the Lord Christ himself also testifies of it in the Gospel, when they strewed his way with branches and praised him with shouts of welcome, saying: *Hosanna to the son of David! Blessed is he that cometh in the name of the Lord!*[3] And when the Jews, finding themselves powerless to rebuke the multitudes and the children, (for it was a marvellous spectacle—to see boys, babes and sucklings, and the disciples and the multitudes joining in shouts of applause, and with loud voices praising him in song), took in hand to throw questions at him, and said to him: *Hearest thou not what these are saying?*[4] But another evangelist says: *Some from among the crowd said to him: Rebuke thy disciples;*[5] as if they would say—Why dost thou blaspheme, accepting a hymn which can be suitably applied to God alone? each of the parties who

---

[1] Acts xiii. 32, 33.
[2] Psalm ii, 9.
[3] Matt. xxi, 9.
[4] Matt. xxi, 16.
[5] Luke xix, 39.

addressed him having the same purpose in view. Unto them the Lord said—to the one party: *Yea, have ye never read; Out of the mouth of babes and sucklings thou hast ordained praise?*[1] clearly indicating that the eighth psalm had reference to him; and at the same time obscurely hinting that he did not take by robbery the things which belonged to God, since he was God; as the Apostle also declares: *He counted it no robbery to be on an equality with God, but emptied himself, taking the form of a servant;*[2] to the other party he said: *Why do ye wonder at the children and the disciples? If these should hold their peace the stones will cry out.*[3] But these men, knowing it had so been written, and seeing in very deed babes and sucklings in an astonishing manner with loud voices chanting the hymn, they reflected that if he could make babes beyond their natural capacity sing the hymn with loud voices, he could also make inanimate things cry out —and thus reflecting, they for very shame put a bridle on their tongues. O how amazing the power of the Lord Christ! O how amazing his loving-kindness! O how amazing his merciful condescension! How by his teaching regarding the form of a servant which he took upon him, did he deign to show mildly glimpses of his divinity, to receive accusations preferred against him by his own creatures, and to answer them, not with anger but with mildness and forbearance? O the excess of his long-suffering! as David was privileged still further to make such prophecies, for he speaks also concerning his human nature in the same psalm from the passage: *What is man that thou art mindful of him?*[4] on to the end, unto which the divine Apostle Paul bears witness in the following passages: Heb. ii, 9; ii, 5; ii, 6-8; Acts xvii, 30, 31; as does also Peter in Acts x, 42.

---

[1] Matt. xxi, 16.   [2] Philip. ii, 6.
[3] Luke xix, 40.   [4] Psalm viii, 5.

In like manner David again spake of him in the forty-second psalm (our 43rd) in which we again find him speaking both of his divine and his human nature. To whom again the blessed Paul in his Epistle to the Hebrews bears witness in these words: *And of the Son he saith, thy throne, O God! is for ever and ever; the sceptre of uprightness is the sceptre of thy kingdom.*[1] Having said this concerning his divinity, he forthwith speaks of his humanity and says: *Thou hast loved righteousness and hated iniquity, wherefore God, even thy God, hath anointed thee with the oil of gladness above thy fellows.*[2] For it is not his divinity which is anointed on account of his loving righteousness and hating iniquity, nor is it in any case anointed, nor has it another God [for fellow], for God exists by himself. But it is his humanity which is anointed with the oil of gladness (by which is meant, with the Holy Spirit) above its fellows— that is, above all the anointed. For his divinity has no other fellow, for God is one, the Father and the Son and the Holy Ghost, but the humanity of Christ has for its fellows all men, especially those who have been anointed. For by reason that the humanity of Christ was anointed above all others, since it was anointed with the Holy Spirit and with power, a distinction accorded to none of the others who were anointed, he used the words: *Above all thy fellows.* The whole psalm, moreover, he wrote with reference to Christ and the Church, speaking of the one as a royal bridegroom and of the other as a royal bride.

And in like manner also he uttered the 109th psalm (our 110th) with reference to him, as the Lord himself testified when he addressed the Jews in these words: *How then does David in the spirit call him Lord, saying: The Lord*

---

[1] Heb. i, 8.   [2] Heb. i, 9.

said unto my Lord, sit thou on my right hand till I put thy enemies underneath thy feet; if David then calleth him Lord, how is he his son?[1] The expression, *his Lord*, clearly indicates that he was God, and that other, *sit thou at my right hand*, is clearly suited to his humanity. For, the word *sit* he said to him who was not sitting. But Deity is established in its own blessedness, and honour and glory, and is neither conceded by one who is greater to one who is less, nor is one who is less invited to assume it. But the humanity of Christ is, by the Deity which is inseparably united, invited[2] in the words: *Sit thou at my right hand*, that is, in my dignity—for God being uncircumscribed has neither right hand nor left. But he says this to his humanity, sit in my dignity—that is, in my person, as the image of God, shown to all the world. For thus also Daniel speaks: *And there was given to him a kingdom and dominion*,[3] et cetera; and the Lord himself says: *There hath been given to me power in heaven and on earth*.[4] Farther down again in the same psalm he saith with reference to his deity: *Out of the womb before morning have I begotten thee*, as if the Father were saying to the Son, with reference to his deity, Thee before all creation have I brought forth from the womb (thus showing him to be consubstantial) and not afterwards, but having thee in myself without beginning and without limit, as if from the womb, from my own substance have I begotten thee, being with me and co-existing with me. Then immediately again with reference to his humanity he says: *The Lord hath sworn and will not repent, Thou art a priest for ever after the order of Melchisedec*;[5] for deity does not exercise the priestly office or render worship, but is rather itself

---

[1] Matt. xxii, 43, 44.
[2] The text has ἐπιτρέπεται, but this must be a mistake for προτρέπεται, and I have translated accordingly.
[3] Dan. vii, 14.   [4] Matt. xxvii, 18.   [5] Psalm cx, 4.

worshipped and the recipient of sacred services. The Apostle also mentions this passage, saying in the Epistle to the Hebrews: *Even as Aaron, so Christ also glorified not himself to be made a high priest, but he that spake unto him, Thou art my son, this day have I begotten thee ; as he saith also in another place, Thou art a priest for ever after the order of Melchisedec ;*[1] thus extracting all that referred to the humanity of Christ.

Thus then the blessed David spoke these four psalms with reference to the Lord Christ and to him alone, for he did not confound the things of the Lord Christ with those of servants, but he spake of the things which properly belong to the Lord as the Lord's, and of the things of servants as those of servants. But whatever other passages the Apostles quoted from the psalms, they did not extract them because they were specially spoken of him, but because they suited their argument. For example: *They parted my garments among them,*[2] and again : *They gave me gall for my meat,*[3] and : *I have set the Lord always before me,*[4] and : *Thou hast ascended on high leading captivity captive ;*[5] and other such like passages they extracted, when they suited the argument they had in hand. The blessed Paul in *like manner* did this, transferring the passage of Moses in Deuteronomy to his own argument which it suited : *Say not in thy heart, Who shall ascend into heaven ? (that is, to bring Christ down) or, Who shall descend into the abyss ? (that is, to bring Christ up from the dead),*[6] thus accommodating the passage to suit the requirements of his argument. For the remaining parts of the psalms from which they quoted are not applicable to the Lord Christ. For instance, the passage : *They parted my garments among them,* occurs

---

[1] Heb. v, 4, 5.
[2] Psalm xxii, 18.
[3] Psalm lxix, 21.
[4] Psalm xvi, 8.
[5] Psalm lxviii, 18.
[6] Deut. xxx, 12.

in the 21st (our 22nd) psalm. Is that psalm then speaking of him where it says: *Far from my safety, the words of my transgressions?*[1] No—that is out of harmony and at variance with divine scripture, and to cite such a passage as referring to Christ would be clear madness. As regards however those four psalms which speak concerning the Lord Christ, each of them is entirely throughout applicable to Him. For, as we have just observed, the blessed David discriminated what was said with reference to the Lord Christ from what was said with reference to any one else. For even the Saviour himself manifestly did this when the Jews accused him, saying: *Why workest thou on the Sabbath day?* and he replied to them saying: *My Father worketh even until now.*[2] And when they accused his disciples, he said: *Know ye not what David did when he was an-hungered and they that were with him, how he entered into the house of God and did eat the shew-bread, which it was not lawful for him to eat nor for those who were with him, but for the priests alone?*[3] thus expressly contradistinguishing[4] himself from the Father, as a son relatively to his father, and his disciples from the prophets, or, at any rate, the priests, as servants relatively to servants. When the Lord was transfigured on the mountain before Peter and James and John in great glory, and Moses and Elias talked with Him, the disciples, witnessing the exceeding glory, were thrown into amazement and rapturous delight, and desire and ardent longing

---

[1] Psalm xxii, 1.   [2] John v, 16, 17.   [3] Matt. xii, 3, 4.
[4] Gr. ἀντιδιαστέλλων. Montfaucon translates this by *comparat*, which not only reverses the meaning of the word, but makes the argument unintelligible. Cosmas means that the disciples having done, like David and his men, what was unlawful must, like them, be contradistinguished from the priests, though they were servants like themselves. In the last of the examples, Peter is rebuked for not having made a proper discrimination between Christ and the two prophets.

for that wondrous beauty. *But Peter*, after a manner identifying himself with the others in their common astonishment at the spectacle, *answered* and said to Jesus: *Lord, it is good for us to be here*,[1] as if he said, Lo! beautiful is the sight, and the place, the splendour and the transcendent glory. Wherefore should we go down hence, putting ourselves again into the hands of those who wish to plot against us and to oppress us, while we have to remove from place to place, and are persecuted? *If thou wishest therefore, let us make here three tabernacles, one for thee, and one for Moses, and one for Elias.*[1] And because Peter considered Moses and Elias to be equal in honour to the Lord, seeing that with reference to their equality he reckoned the number of the tabernacles, assigning one to each, the evangelist Luke notes this and in these terms: *Not knowing what he said*,[2] that is, Peter not knowing what he said with reference to the Lord. Straightway moreover a cloud overshadowed them, and separated Moses and Elias from them and hid them from the disciples, and as for Jesus, who was left alone in the midst, the Father pointed out and showed him to the disciples saying: *This is my son in whom I am well pleased, hear ye Him.*[3] Ye are mistaken, he says, in putting Him on an equality with the others, for He is my Son. They, like yourselves, are servants. Him therefore as Lord and as my Son, hear ye in all things.

Thus then the prophet David also, being moved by the Holy Ghost, did not indiscriminately confound what had an underlying reference to the Lord with what had an underlying reference to servants, but those four psalms which had a special reference to the Lord he was privileged to compose with prophetic foresight; while all the other psalms he gave out to the whole world for useful

---

[1] Matt. xvii, 4. [2] Luke ix, 33. [3] Matt. xvii, 5.

instruction with regard to other persons or things or histories, in order that they might be held fast and well remembered by all as calculated to delight. And this is abundantly clear that, in all the churches of the world, we shall find that the Psalms of David are sung, and that they are on the lips of nearly all men, whether small or great, and are more studied and remembered than the other prophets and scriptures. But bringing this subject also to an end, let us pass on to the great Elias and supply a worthy delineation of him also. Here then you see him thus delineated.

Elijah.

This is Elijah the first of men who showed to men the path to heaven—the first of men who showed to angels and to men the one way—who though his lot was to be an inhabitant of earth, all at once penetrated into heaven—who though a mortal yet vies even with the immortals—who walked upon the earth, and yet, as a spirit, treads with the angels the paths of heaven; who with his mantle of sheep-skin imparted to his disciple Elisha a double share of his own gifts—a man who has lived for ages and is from old age exempt—who is reserved to be leader against Antichrist, standing up against him and convicting him of deception and overweening pride—who from the error into which he has seduced them, leads back all men to God at the consummation of the age. This is he who is deemed worthy to be the fore-runner of the second and glorious advent of the Lord Christ. O the wondrous measure of his services, in which he competes with the angels! Glory to God who graciously bestows these gifts upon men. Amen!

Note.

This is the great Elijah, who having been taken up as into heaven shows to men and angels how highly human nature has been honoured, and by means of him God has again laid the foundations of a good hope, that it is possible for men. if God will, to ascend into heaven. For it is a great and wondrous thing to see this man, bridle in hand, riding his fiery chariot as he sweeps the fields of air. Oh! what wondrous kindness on his part who has bestowed the honour. Let those be ashamed of themselves who do not extol the mighty dispensation of God— who do not praise and admire how wisely and how dispassionately God, on the one hand, awards to men their punishments, and on the other, preserves the honour of man who was made in his image. Glory and praise to him for ever and ever, Amen!

The Prophet Hosea.

This is Hosea, the first of the twelve prophets who was privileged to speak concerning the Lord Christ in these terms : *When they are afflicted, let them rise early to seek me saying, Come and let us return unto the Lord our God, for he hath smitten us and he will heal us ; he that hath struck us will bind us up. After two days will he heal us. On the third day we shall be raised up again and we shall live!*[1] With reference to this passage the Apostle Paul says to the Corinthians : *For I delivered unto you first of all that which also I received, how that Christ died for our sins according to the scriptures.*[2] For that he was buried, and that he was raised up on the third day according to the scriptures, is not to be found anywhere else. The prophet still further says what is applicable to Christ : *My flesh is of them* ; and again he says : *Ephraim compasseth me about with falsehood, and the house of Israel and Judah with ungodliness. Now God knoweth them, and there shall be called a holy people of God, from the tribe,*[3]

---

[1] Hos. vi, 1-3.   [2] I Cor. xv, 3.   [3] Hos. xi, 12.

through him who appeared out of it, namely, the Lord Christ according to the flesh—the prophet calling Judah the holy people of God. Yet again the same prophet says: *From the power of the grave will I ransom them. Where is thy victory, O death! Where is thy sting, O grave!*[1]—a passage which the Apostle has used concerning the resurrection.

Note.

This prophet also clearly predicted the resurrection on the third day, saying: *On the third day we shall rise up.* In like manner also he foretold the destruction of death and the vengeance upon the sting of the grave. How should we not be lost in astonishment at the ineffable benevolence of God, which is at all times making provision for the human race. Glory to him for his unspeakable gift!

The Prophet Joel.

This is Joel the second in order who was privileged to prophesy concerning the mystery of the Lord Christ, for he speaks thus (chap. ii, 28-32): *And it shall come to pass afterward that I will pour out my spirit upon all flesh; and your sons and your daughters shall prophesy, your old men shall dream dreams, your young men shall see visions; and also upon the servants and upon the handmaids in those days will I pour out my spirit. And I will show wonders in the heavens and in the earth, blood and fire, and pillars of smoke. The sun shall be turned into darkness, and the moon into blood, before the great and terrible day of the Lord come. And it shall come to pass that whosoever shall call on the name of the Lord shall be delivered*—a passage which the blessed Peter mentions in the Acts of the Apostles as having been fulfilled when the descent of the Holy Spirit upon the Apostles occurred on the day of Pentecost.

---

[1] Hos. xiii, 14.

Note.

This prophet also foretold the wonderful things that took place in the time of the Lord Christ through the Holy Ghost, such as prophesyings, dreams and visions under his influence; likewise the day of the great, terrible, and glorious advent of the Lord Christ. For examples we may point to the revelations made, in different ways, to Joseph and to the Wise Men in sleep, as the Gospels relate; and to the revelation made by the Holy Ghost through visions to Symeon (Simeon) who took up the Lord Christ in his arms. Anna again the daughter of Phanuel gave thanks to the Lord because of him. There were also those who prophesied, such as Agabus and the daughters of Philip. And the women who were at the Passion of the Lord saw visions of angels, as did also the disciples. And why need I speak of the descent of the Holy Ghost upon the Apostles; yea, even upon Cornelius and upon all the faithful of whom the Apostle writes (1 Cor. xii, 8-14): *For to one is given the word of wisdom; to another faith in the same spirit; to another gifts of healings in the same spirit; to another workings of miracles; to another prophecy, and to another discernings of spirits, and to another divers kinds of tongues, and to another interpretation of tongues; but all these worketh the one and the same spirit, dividing to each one severally even as he will!* Glory to God who through all the prophets foretold these things, glory for ever and ever, Amen.

The Prophet Amos.

This is Amos the third in order, who also was privileged to tell of the coming of the Lord Christ and in these words: *Lo! I am he that confirms the thunder and that creates the wind and that announces to men his Anointed.*[1] And again he says (ix, 11, 12): *In that day will I raise up the tabernacle of David that is fallen and close up the breaches thereof; and I will raise up his ruins, and I will build it as in the days of old, that the rest of men and all the nations may enquire who have been called by my name, saith the Lord*

---

[1] Amos iv, 13.

who doeth these things. A passage of which James the Apostle makes mention in the Acts of the Apostles.

Note.

This Prophet, in agreement with the first, announces Christ, through whom the salvation of the whole world is effected. And through him God promises that he will raise up again the Tabernacle of David which had fallen, and will extend help to all the nations. And these are the same tidings which all the prophets proclaim.

The Prophet Obadiah.

This is Obadiah (Abdiou) the fourth in order, who also was privileged to prophesy concerning the mystery regarding Christ, and who speaks thus: *Because the day of the Lord is near upon all the nations.*[1] This taken in its obvious meaning is spoken of the Scythians, that is, of Gog and Magog, but it is most properly applicable to the Lord Christ, for the prophet shortly afterwards says: *But on Mount Zion there shall be salvation.*[2]

Note.

This prophet also again clearly proclaims that the day of Salvation in Zion is near at hand and upon all the nations. Glory to God evermore. Amen!

The Prophet Jonah.

This is Jonah the fifth in order, who not by words, but by what he did and by what he typified, predicted the resurrection of Christ. For the Lord says: *as Jonah was three days and three nights in the belly of the whale, so shall the Son of Man be three days and three nights in the heart of the earth.*[3] For as the whale vomited out Jonah uncorrupted, so also did the sepulchre vomit out the Lord to a better life.

---

[1] Obad. i, 15. [2] Obad. i, 17. [3] Matt. xii, 40.

Note.

This prophet prefigured through his actions the sepulchre and the miraculous resurrection and incorruption of Christ, through whom is dispensed the renovation of man and his summing up in him. Glory to God who doeth these things. Amen!

The Prophet Isaiah.

This is the great Isaiah the son of Amos, who in a figure foresaw the things concerning the mystery of Christ, when he saw the Lord sitting on a throne high and lifted up, while the Seraphim stood in a circle around him, the one having six wings, and the other six wings, with which they did cover themselves, and the one cried out to the other and said: *Holy, holy, holy Lord of Sabaoth! the whole earth is full of his glory.*[1] Thereupon one of the Seraphim was sent to him who with the tongs took [a live coal] from the altar, and touched his lips saying: *This will take away thy sins.*[2] Isaiah by the vision which was shown to him, and by the hymn of praise, and by the figure was instructed to prophesy the mystery concerning Christ, and further again in words he thus speaks: *He was led as a sheep to the slaughter, and as a lamb before the shearer, so was he dumb.*[3] The Ethiopian eunuch on reading this passage asked Philip to interpret it to him, and he at once explained that it was spoken by the Prophet with reference to the Lord Christ. And again he says: *A man who is under chastisement and knows what it is to bear sickness;*[4] and so in other passages—Isaiah liii. 9-11; xxviii. 16; lxi. 10; and in lxi., 1; *The spirit of the Lord is upon me*—a passage which the Lord having read in the synagogue on the Sabbath said: *Verily I say unto you, to-day is this scripture fulfilled in your ears.*[5]

---

[1] Isai. vi, 1-3. [2] Isai. vi, 7. [3] Isai. liii, 7.
[4] Isai. liii, 3. [5] Luke iv, 18.

Note 1.

Isaiah, that prophet of sublimest strain,[1] by his words and visions proclaimed beforehand to men the confession even of the Holy Trinity, that is, of the one God, and the resurrection of human nature which the Church of God also now proclaims. Glory to God who wisely dispenses all things for the good of the human race!

Note 2.

But he too did not prophesy things strange and unusual, but like the other prophets predicted the things that would be through Christ, and among them again that great day of the Lord on which he would send the Prophet Elijah still surviving. Glory to God who created all things and again created them anew!

The Prophet Micah.

This is Micah the seventh in order, who also was privileged to prophesy concerning the coming of the Lord Christ, and he says: *And thou Bethlehem, the house of Ephratha, art the least to be among the thousands of Judah. From thee, there shall come forth to me one who shall be for a ruler over Israel, whose goings forth have been of old from everlasting.*[2] The chief priests and scribes of the Jews, taking this passage, when Herod asked them where the Christ should be born, replied, *In Bethlehem of Judaea*, upon which he sent the Wise Men away to Bethlehem. This prophet further says: *He will turn again and have compassion upon us; he will tread our iniquities under foot, and all our sins shall be cast into the depths of the sea. He will perform the truth to Jacob and the mercy to Abraham, as he hath sworn unto our fathers from the days of old.*[3]

Note.

This prophet also in harmony with the others, predicts that he who was raised up from of old to be a ruler over Israel should

---

[1] Gr. μεγαλοφωνότατος. In the Greek Anthology this epithet is applied to Pindar.   [2] Mic. v, 2.   [3] Mic. vii, 19.

come out of Bethlehem and Judah, he through whom absolution is given to the world, the taking away of our sins and conducting us into the better state. Glory to God who all things dispenses wisely and foretells the things which concern man!

The Prophet Nahum.

This is Nahum the eighth in order who was also privileged to prophesy concerning the resurrection of the Lord Christ, and he says : *Feast, O Judah, keep thy feasts, perform thy vows, for they shall add to pass through thee no more.*[1] *It has been consummated, it has been taken away. He went up breathing upon thy face, delivering thee from affliction.*[2]

Note.

See how this prophet also exhorts us to rejoice over the resurrection of Christ and over our own, showing beforehand that we shall never grow old, proclaiming, that is, our incorruption and our immortality. Glory to God, Amen!

The Prophet Habakkuk.

This is Habakkuk the ninth in order, who was also privileged to speak concerning the resurrection of Christ in these terms : *Behold, ye despisers, and regard, and wonder marvellously, and vanish for ever, because I work a work in your days which ye will not believe though it be told you.*[3] This passage Paul cited at Antioch of Pisidia as having reference to the resurrection of the Lord Christ.

Note.

In like manner also this prophet is commanded to predict marvellous and incredible things to men, and especially to despisers, things namely concerning the resurrection. Glory to God, Amen!

---

[1] Gr. διότι οὐ μὴ προσθήσωσιν ἔτι τοῦ διελθεῖν διὰ σοῦ εἰς παλαίωσιν.
[2] Nah. i, 15.   [3] Habak. i, 5.

The Prophet Jeremiah.

235   This is Jeremiah the tenth in order, who was also privileged to prophesy concerning the mystery respecting Christ, saying thus: *And they took the thirty pieces of silver, the price of him that was priced, whom certain of the sons of Israel did price, and they gave them for the potter's field as the Lord appointed me.*[1] The evangelist Matthew mentions this passage as having been fulfilled at the time of the passion. The same prophet again says: *Lo! the days are coming, saith the Lord, and I shall make a new covenant with the house of Israel and with the house of Judah,*[2] etc. This passage is cited by the Apostle in the Epistle to the Romans.

Note.

This prophet in like manner predicts things which have reference to the Lord Christ who is the Prince of the second dispensation—for he describes in the clearest manner the first and second dispensation, the second whereof had its beginning in the Lord Christ. Glory to God for ever, Amen!

The Prophet Sophonias (Zephaniah).

This is Zephaniah the eleventh in order who was also privileged to prophesy concerning the Lord Christ, and he speaks thus: *The Lord will come suddenly upon them, and will utterly destroy all the gods of the nations of the earth, and men shall worship him, every one from his place, even all the isles of the nations.*[3] *From beyond the rivers of Ethiopia shall they bring offering to me;*[4] and again: *Rejoice greatly, O daughter of Sion; shout, O daughter of Jerusalem; be glad and rejoice with all the heart, O daughter of Jerusalem; the Lord hath taken away thine*

---

[1] This is a quotation from Zachar. xi, 12; see Matt. xxvii, 9-10.
[2] Jerem. xxxi, 31-34.   [3] Zeph. ii, 11.   [4] Zeph. iii, 10.

iniquities. The King of Israel, even the Lord, is in the midst of thee; thou shalt not see evil any more.[1] All things are more especially applicable to the Lord Christ.

Note.

This prophet most plainly points to the manifestation of the Lord, to the destruction of idols, and the conversion of the nations to God through the Lord Christ. Glory be to God for ever, Amen!

The Prophet Ezekiel.

This is Ezekiel who prophesied in Babylon, and who was also privileged to predict concerning the dispensation of Christ, and he says: *I will redeem them from all their transgression, wherewith they have sinned, and I will purify them, and they shall be to me a people, and I the Lord will be their God. And my servant David shall be ruler in the midst of them, he alone shall be the shepherd of them all, because they shall walk in my precepts;*[2] and again: *And he said unto me, This water, issuing forth into Galilee which lies towards the East, was going down into Arabia and came even to the sea, to the water at the outlet,*[3] *and it shall heal the waters. And it shall come to pass that every living creature which swarmeth in every place whither the river comes shall live.*[4]

Note.

This prophet, like the others, under a figure foreshows the great founder and ruler of our second state, and foreshows also its constitution. Glory to God for the wisdom of all his dispensations, Amen!

---

[1] Zeph. iii, 14, 15.   [2] Ezek. xxxiv, 23-25.
[3] Gr. ἐπὶ τὸ ὕδωρ τῆς διεκβολῆς. The Revised Version translates this passage thus: These waters issue forth towards the eastern region, and shall go down into the Arabah: and they shall go toward the sea; into the sea *shall the waters go* which were made to issue forth.
[4] Ezek. xlvii, 8, 9.

The Prophet Daniel.

This is Daniel who prophesied in Babylon and who was also privileged to utter predictions concerning the Lord Christ, and he speaks thus: *And thou shalt know and discern that from the going forth of the commandment to the response and the building of Jerusalem, until the anointed one a prince, shall be seven weeks and three score and two weeks*,[1] and so forth. And again: *A stone was cut without hands, and it brake in pieces the clay, the iron, the brass, the silver and the gold, and it filled the whole earth;*[2] and again: *Behold one like unto the Son of Man coming with the clouds of heaven, and he came even unto to the Ancient of days, and he was brought near before him. And there was given unto him dominion and glory and a kingdom, and all the peoples and nations and languages shall serve him. His dominion,*[3] and so forth.

Note.

And this prophet spoke out more clearly concerning the coming of Christ, intimating both his time and the power belonging to him, and his birth from a virgin and the propagation of his gospel throughout all the earth, which things have all come to pass with God's help and will still come to pass. Glory to God who through all the prophets has revealed these things beforehand, Amen!

The Prophet Haggai.

This Haggai was also privileged to utter predictions concerning the Lord Christ, as, under the person of Zerubabel, he says things which are applicable to the Lord Christ: *And I will make thee as a signet, because I have chosen thee, saith the Lord God.*[4]

---

[1] Dan. ix, 26. [2] Dan. ii, 45.
[3] Dan. vii, 13 *seqq*. [4] Hag. ii, 24.

The Prophet Zechariah.

This Zechariah was also privileged to prophesy concerning the coming of the Christ, saying thus: *Rejoice greatly O daughter of Sion, shout O daughter of Jerusalem; behold thy King cometh unto thee; he is just and having salvation; lowly and riding upon an ass—even a young colt.*[1] This passage he uttered with reference to Zerubabel, in a strain of hyperbole as regards him, for it had properly its accomplishment in the Lord Christ, whom Zerubabel as it were, personified. He further says: *And I will say unto him, What are these wounds between thine hands? And he shall say, wounds which I received in the house beloved by me.*[2] And shortly afterwards again he says: *I will smite the shepherd and the sheep of the flock shall be scattered.*[3] Of this passage also the Lord made mention at the time of his Passion, applying it to himself when he was on the point of being betrayed.

Note.

This prophet, while he said nothing alien to the utterances of the other prophets, indicated the sovereignty of the Lord Christ in the future state.

The Prophet Malachi.

This is Malachi, who also was privileged to prophesy concerning the things relating to the dispensation of the Lord Christ. And it is thus he speaks: *For, from the rising of the sun even unto the going down of the same, my name is great among the nations; and in every place incense is offered unto my name and a pure offering, for my name is great among the nations, saith the Lord Almighty;*[4] and again he says: *Behold I will send my messenger, and he*

---

[1] Zach. ix, 9.
[2] Zach. xiii, 6.
[3] Zach. xiii, 7.
[4] Mal. i, 11.

shall prepare the way before thy presence.[1] This passage the Lord applied to himself and to John the Baptist. The same prophet further says: *But unto you that fear my name shall the sun of righteousness arise with healing in his wings, and ye shall go forth and gambol as calves released from the stall. And ye shall tread down winds; for they shall be ashes under the soles of your feet, in the day that I do make, saith the Lord Almighty. And behold, I will send you Elijah the Tishbite before the great and notable day of the Lord.*[2] As the Lord said to the Jews, and if ye are willing, receive it of John the Baptist: *This is Elijah who was to come.*[3] And now at last having finished with God's help the twelve prophets we shall proceed to the four great prophets.[4]

Note.

Now this prophet did not utter predictions respecting what would be done by Christ different from the other prophets, but predictions of a similar nature: and he again prophesied the great and notable day of the Lord, in which he says that he will send before him the Tishbite Elijah, who is still surviving. Glory to God who created all things and who again creates them anew. Amen!

Text.

All the prophets predicted, and reminded the Jews of the promises of God which he had made to their fathers; how he promised to bless all the nations in the seed of Abraham through the dispensation of the Lord Christ. They reminded them how God in former times had

---

[1] Mal. iii. 5.   [2] Mal. iv, 2-5.   [3] Matt. xi, 14.
[4] Montfaucon has here the following note: Cosmas at first had placed the four great Prophets after the twelve minor; but afterwards either Cosmas himself or someone else mixed up the great with the minor as in the present text.

redeemed them with a high hand from bondage to the Egyptians and given them the land of promise, and predicted how they would be led away captives to Babylon by Nabuchodonosor and would return again with glory; and again, how they would suffer great miseries at the hands of Antiochus and the nations around them, and how by the divine power they would overcome them; and then He, who was expected from the seed of Abraham, would come for the salvation of the whole world according to the promises earlier given. This was the work of the prophets. Some of them accordingly wrote their own books. David, for instance, composed the Book of Psalms, and Daniel at the time of the Captivity was commanded to write what was revealed to him through visions, and there were others besides. But the rest did not write their prophecies with their own hands, but in the temple there were scribes who wrote the words of each prophet as in a diary.[1] And when a prophet was sent by God to proclaim anything, either concerning Jerusalem, that it would be led away into captivity, or concerning Samaria, or other places, or concerning the return from captivity, or concerning Antiochus, or the surrounding nations, or concerning the Lord Christ himself, on the day in which they prophesied, the scribes wrote, in the book of that prophet, what he announced, that is, concerning a single subject; and again after some time had elapsed, if he wished to announce anything about another matter, the scribe again committed it to writing, recording it in its order among the sayings of the same prophet, and inserting what he announced as the beginning of a new chapter; and so in this manner they compiled the whole of his book. Hence we may find in their books a chapter relating to the Captivity at Babylon, or to the Return, and imme-

---

[1] Gr. ὡς ἐπὶ ἡμερολογίου.

diately thereafter another chapter which has reference to
Christ, and then once more a chapter speaking again of
the Captivity and the Return. And to speak briefly,
unless one reads with close observation, he will find very
much apparent confusion. And not only the books of
the prophets, but the books of the kings were in this
manner written in the temple, part by part. Thus the
events under Saul were recorded for Saul in his time, part
by part, until the end of his reign. The events in the
time of David were thus also recorded to the end of his
reign, and similarly the events under each king were
committed to writing during his period. In like manner
they wrote also in the records[1] of the Kings what we call
Paralipomena.[2] It was Moses who wrote the Pentateuch—
which is a history of things past, present and future.
Joshua again wrote the book which bears his name. The
book of Judges was written in the temple, or it may be, in
the Tabernacle, and the same may be said of the book of
Ruth. Solomon again wrote his own works, Proverbs, the
Song of Songs, and Ecclesiastes. For though he had
received the gift of wisdom from God, and counselled
every man to conduct himself wisely in this life, he did
not receive the gift of prophecy. As many, therefore, as
we have found to have been privileged to prophesy concerning the dispensation of the Lord Christ, we have
arranged in their order. And we further write concerning
the four other prophets whatever things they were commissioned to predict—whereunto the whole scope of divine
scripture has respect. We bring forward therefore first
the sublimely eloquent Isaiah,[3] who both by figure and

---

[1] Gr. ἐν τοῖς σκρινίοις. This is an erroneous transcription of the Latin word scrinium, *a chest for keeping documents*.

[2] Gr. Παραλειπομένας sc. βίβλους. The two Books of Chronicles.

[3] See note 1, p. 200.

by word was privileged to see and prophesy concerning the mystery of Christ.

John the Forerunner.

This is the greatest of all men—John the Baptist, who was filled with the Holy Ghost while he was yet in the womb, and leaped in joy and eagerness to be the forerunner of his Lord—a man great in the sight of God, the forerunner of Christ, preparing for him a people put in readiness to receive him—a man superior to the prophets, born into the world before the Apostles, intermediate between the Old and the New Testament, the last under the law, the receiver of the new dispensation—the man who showed to all the Lord Christ as present among them, who surpassed all men in the austerity of his manner of life, and outdid all men in service rendered—who went before in the spirit and power of Elias, and surpassed Elias, in that he baptized the Lord—a lamp that was lighted before the sun of righteousness. He proclaimed the presence of the Lord, saying: *Behold the lamb of God which taketh away the sin of the world ;*[1] calling him a lamb as being a sacrificial victim, and taking away the sin of the world—as delivering the world from sin, rendering men incorrupt, and immortal and immutable through the resurrection. This great John was privileged to be the herald of such a ministry and of such great things.

Note.

This is John the greatest of all men, who had both his father and his mother as fellow-prophets, who not only shows the Lord Christ to be present as the Prince of the second state, but proclaims him to be the Judge of all, saying: *Whose fan is in his hand, and he will thoroughly cleanse his threshing-floor, and will gather the wheat into his garner ; but the chaff he will burn with*

---

[1] John i. 29.

unquenchable fire.[1] He again proclaims beforehand the kingdom of heaven, and prepares the way for Him who comes after him, and who shows in himself in very deed the kingdom of heaven, which is the second state. Glory to God who has produced all things out of nothing, and again creates them anew in Christ. Amen!

The Prophet Zachariah.

This Zachariah the priest, who was himself thought worthy of the power of prophecy, spoke both concerning his own son and the Lord Christ together, in these words: *And thou, child, shalt be called the Prophet of the Highest; for thou shalt go before the face of the Lord to prepare his ways.*[2]

The Prophetess Elisabeth.

This is the prophetess Elisabeth, who by the Holy Spirit was privileged to prophesy both concerning the Lord Christ and the Holy Virgin, speaking thus: *And whence is this to me that the mother of my Lord should come to me?*[3] Thus both the father and the mother of the forerunner were privileged to announce beforehand the Lord Christ. To him be glory with the Father and the Holy Spirit for ever. Amen!

The Virgin Mary.

This is the holy virgin, Mary, who brought forth her blessed offspring to the world without seed by the Holy Spirit, who even before his birth announced with great joy the dignity of her son, and said: *For behold, from henceforth all generations shall call me blessed;*[4] and again: *He hath holpen Israel his servant, that he might remember mercy, as he spake to our fathers, to Abraham and his seed for ever.*[5] To him be glory for ever and ever. Amen!

---

[1] Luke iii. 17. [2] Luke i, 76. [3] Luke i, 43.
[4] Luke i, 48. [5] Luke i, 51.

The Prophetess Anna, the daughter of Phanuel.

This is Anna the daughter of Phanuel, who gave thanks to God concerning Him in the temple, when His parents brought Him up into the temple in the days of their purification, *to present Him to the Lord, as it is written.*[1]

Simeon.

This is the righteous Simeon who, when he had taken up the Lord Christ in his arms, prayed to God to let him depart this life, as it had been revealed to him by the spirit, saying thus: *Lord, now lettest thou thy servant depart, in peace, according to thy word, for mine eyes have seen thy salvation, which thou hast prepared before the face of all people—a light for revelation to the gentiles, and the glory of thy people Israel.*[2]

The Lord Christ.

This is the Lord of all, Christ, concerning whom all prophecy made its predictions to men, unto whom all creation turns its eye, and to whom every tongue shall confess, bending the knee to the glory of God—Christ, in whom all prophecy terminates, the judge of the quick and the dead, the light from the light, the Son of the living God—unto whom the whole creation is subjected both of things in heaven, and things on earth and things under the earth, who also spoke through His own lips: *The law and the prophets until John predicted Christ.*[3] To Him be glory with the Father and with the Holy Ghost for ever. Amen.

Introduction concerning the Apostles.

We have now fulfilled our promise in accordance with the obligations it imposed upon us, namely to show that

---

[1] Luke ii, 22. [2] Luke ii, 28-32. [3] Luke xvi, 16.

the men of primitive times and all the prophets uttered predictions concerning the mystery of Christ, and that they all, from the first-created man, Adam, until John the Baptist, had the future state full in their view ; which also the Lord Christ and his disciples and Apostles afterwards explicitly proclaimed, setting forth that there is a future state far better than the present state, which the Lord Christ first showed in himself to us when he rose from the dead and ascended into heaven, which also the men of old with some purpose in view[1] [obscurely?] announced, and which those who came afterwards clearly set forth. We have also shown that not one of them whether of the later or the earlier ever proclaimed or imagined that besides those two states there was any other state at all either before or after them ; but that when God began to make the whole creation, he made these two states and these only, ordaining that this present state, in which we live as citizens, should be first, and then the future state, whereunto the whole purpose of God and of his prophets has respect. Let the Pagans then take shame to themselves, who suppose the world to be co-eternal with God, while they both advocate the doctrine of a previous life, and deny the resurrection of the body. And let those too take shame to themselves who are their followers, and who, while they regard themselves as Christians, nevertheless think as do the Pagans who assert that the heaven is spherical. For their views differ not at all from those which the Pagans proclaim ; as for instance, that the bodies of which the world is made are always in corruption, and that there is no resurrection of the body, nor any other state than the present. Let the Manichæans

---

[1] Gr. σκοπῷ τινι. Montfaucon translates : *aliqua ratione et scopo;* but Cosmas no doubt wrote σκότῳ, *with some obscurity*.

and the Marcionists[1] take shame to themselves, who reject the flesh, and maintain that it is the production of the evil principle. Let all be ashamed who contemn our souls with their intelligence, Eutychès to wit, Arius, and Appolinarius[2] and all their followers. Let all the heretics take shame to themselves who acknowledge not one God the Maker of heaven and earth, known and worshipped in three persons, and who acknowledge neither the resurrection of our flesh, nor the existence of angel or spirit. Let the unbelieving Jews take shame to themselves who have not received Him who was expected, and confess not the Christian resurrection, but only such a condition of life as our present, in which there is marrying and being given in marriage. But well-done! well-done! ye who are truly Christians, to you be joy and exultation, to you who believe all divine scripture, both the Old and the New Testament, who have been led by the law and have believed in Christ and all that he has proclaimed, especially when saying: *The law and the prophets prophesied until John;*[3] and: *From the days of John the Baptist the kingdom of heaven suffereth violence, and the violent take it by force;*[4] meaning that as many as do violence to themselves, and live righteously, and are not guided by their own notions, but have faith in God, all obtain that kingdom.

---

[1] Marcion flourished about the middle of the second century; Manichaeus, after the middle of the third.

[2] Eutychès, who belonged to the fifth century, was a Presbyter and Abbot at Constantinople, where he headed the party opposed to the Nestorian doctrines. He asserted that in Christ there is but one nature—that of the Incarnate Word. Arius denied that the Son was co-equal or co-eternal with the Father. He flourished in the earlier part of the fourth century. Apollinarius, called Apollinaris by Latin writers, was Bishop of Laodicea in 362. He was condemned as a heretic by the Council of Constantinople in 381, on the ground that his doctrine denied the true human nature of Christ.

[3] Luke xvi, 16. [4] Matt. ii, 12.

And to be sure, when the mother of John and James asked the Lord that one of them should sit on His right hand and the other on His left hand in His Kingdom, He answered her saying: *It is not mine to give, but it is for those for whom it has been prepared by my Father;*[1] that is, the gift of God is extended to all, the rising again from the dead, and becoming incorruptible, and immortal and immutable—but to be preferred in honour to another, this is not a gift, but what is prepared by God for those who believe and act aright. For the Lord again saith: *Come, ye blessed of my Father, inherit the Kingdom prepared for you;*[2] and when it was prepared he tells us by adding: *from the foundation of the world.*

243 Since Moses then, who describes the world, and all the other prophets, and the men of old have spoken of these two states and of these only, without making mention of any others, but proclaiming only these and committing them to writing—and since not these only but also the Lord when he came among us, and his disciples, Evangelists and Apostles have proclaimed nothing else than only these two states and these alone, what is there further wanting to confute the belief that these things are not true? Who will not pay regard to the multitude of predictions—to the fulfilment of prophecies—to the multitude of signs and astonishing miracles—to the very walk and conversation of all the saints and of the Lord Christ and his Apostles—to the harmony of the Old and the New Testament? Which of these dissented from the others, and maintained that the heaven was spherical, or proclaimed the pre-existence of this world, or represented that the world was eternal, or denied the resurrection of the body, or the dispensation of Christ, under which righteous men go up to heaven? But all of them,

---

[1] Matt. xx, 24. [2] Matt. xxv, 34.

as being guided by one divine Spirit, predicted the same things by words and by acts and by figures, and all of them direct their view to the future state. And the Lord Christ himself shows in the Gospels in what place perfect righteous men, intermediate men, and impious men shall have their abode. And concerning the perfect righteous, he shows their place when he calls them to himself saying: *Come, ye blessed of my Father, inherit the Kingdom prepared for you from the foundation of the world;*[1] and concerning the impious he shows theirs, when he says to those on his left hand: *Depart from me, ye cursed, into everlasting fire prepared for the devil and his angels,*[2] as if he said, to the righteous, come above to the inner heaven beyond this visible firmament, and to the impious, go down to the place about the earth,[3] into which the devil also was hurled down. We are left under the necessity of seeking the place of the intermediate men. Christ says then in the parable of the ten virgins, that the five who were wise went in with the bridegroom into the bride-chamber, that is, into heaven, because, since they were wise, they chose virginity and alms-giving—but the foolish virgins who had, chosen the one of these but despised the other, remained outside of the bride-chamber, having found the door shut, and heard these words: *Depart from me, I know you not;*[4] being neither permitted to enter, nor condemned along with the impious, but remaining outside of the bride-chamber.

Thus then each one who has right and unfeigned faith and a worthy life enters with confidence into the Kingdom, but such, on the other hand, as have not even one of them, neither right faith nor an honest life, are condemned to spend their time along with the devil about the earth. But

---

[1] Matt. xxv, 34.
[2] Matt. xxv, 41.
[3] Gr. κάτω περὶ τὴν γῆν.
[4] Matt. xxv, 12.

those who have one and not the other, are the intermediate men, condemned to remain outside the bride-chamber, that is, the firmament. The particular nature, however, either of the good things or of the punishments, it is impossible for us to know, except by our actual experience of them; but by what was merely an example taken from the punishments and the good things of life here, He indicated what would be hereafter. For, since it was not possible for us before we had as yet acquired experience, to hear new things otherwise than in so far as they were figuratively stated, He said: *The Kingdom of heaven is likened unto a certain King who made a marriage feast for his son*,[1] having selected the highest of the good things of this life, and likened them to the good things of the future life. In like manner also to the worst things—fire, the undying worm, Tartarus, the gnashing of teeth, darkness and things similar to these, because they are the most frightful forms of earthly punishments, to these he likened the punishments of the hereafter. But it is possible to estimate neither the good things of the future life, nor its terrible things, nor the things that are intermediate. But that other state is far better than the present, and is altogether very far superior, just as this present life is far better than that when we were within our mother's womb. For we must consider what was our condition within the womb, where we existed in a confusion of darkness, blood, bad humours, bile and all kinds of impurity, while we were in ignorance of everything. But having emerged into this life we see things quite different, of which we had gained no previous experience—an extension of freedom, inspiration of the air, the enjoyment of the beautiful light, the framework of nature, the workmanship of an all-wise artificer, and this too while we are filled with the knowledge of God;

---

[1] Matt. xxii, 2.

not one of which things it was possible for us either to know, or to conceive, or to hear, or to enjoy, while we were still in the womb. In like manner also it is impossible for us, while we are still in this life, to understand or to conceive or to picture to our minds the future state which is altogether better than this, unless we are in the midst of the things themselves, for, saith He: *Things which eye saw not, and ear heard not, and which entered not into the heart of man, whatsoever things God prepared for them that love him*.[1] Just as God then has in this life freely bestowed a common gift upon all, making the sun rise upon just and unjust, and sending his rain upon good and bad, so also in the future state he bestows a common gift upon all, immortality and incorruption and life and immutability, but each one, according to his former deeds, procures for himself either the Kingdom, or the punishment due to him, or ascent into heaven, or remaining about the earth, or in the intermediate condition. All these things, moreover, are eternal and infinite, both the good things and the very worst. And altogether that state differs much, yea as much as can be, from the state here. In contrast to the good things which have been prepared for the righteous are set the things of the impious, punishment of the utmost severity, and judgment without mercy; for the judgment and punishment of this present state have their analogy in the future state. Let us then now come to the Evangelists and Apostles and show that they also speak in harmony with the ancients, declaring that these two states and these alone have been made by God: the first, being this in which we now exist, and the future, that unto which all we Christians direct our gaze. Let us therefore delineate Matthew the first of the evangelists who speaks concerning such things.

---

[1] I Cor. ii, 9.

Matthew the Evangelist.

This is the first of the evangelists who wrote a Gospel. A Gospel (Ἐυαγγέλιον) is so called because it is an announcement (ἀγγελία) of good things. When upon the outbreak in Jerusalem of the persecution in which Stephen was stoned to death, he was on the point of quitting the city, and certain of the faithful requested him to leave them his teaching in writing; he, who knew by personal experience the manner of life of the Lord incarnate upon earth, wrote for them an account thereof, for the purpose of setting before them an image of virtuous social intercourse, of a heavenly life, and of a divine walk and conversation. In carrying out this design he begins the narrative which he composed in these words: *The book of the generation of Jesus Christ the son of David, the son of Abraham*,[1] as if he said, addressing to you, O most faithful, my discourse of the miraculous generation, of our highest duty to others, of the heavenly life, and of the new state, I lay my book before you. And, seeing that God made promises to David and to Abraham that all the nations of the world should be blessed through their seed, and that their seed should reign for ever, I set forth the genealogy of Him who sprang from their seed, of Him, through whom God blesses the world and creates it anew, and on whom He bestows an everlasting Kingdom, and I show that He is the Prince of the future state, conceived and born in a new and becoming way, and that He directed His life in all righteousness and holiness and without sin. For just as the first-made man Adam was produced by divine power from earth which had not been sown nor tilled by man, so also the Prince of the second state was

---

[1] Matt. i, 8.

produced from human kind, that is to say, He was produced from the virgin earth without seed, without man, by the power of the Holy Ghost. And just again as formerly the female was produced from the male, so too in this case the male was produced from the female ; and just as the former, having been worsted by the devil, brought death upon the human race, so too the latter, having proved victorious, destroyed the power of death over the race, and procured for it, besides, immortality and life without end. The blessed Matthew, having in view to tell these and such like things, gave forth the work which he had written, wherein he showed how Christ had been conceived without seed by the Holy Ghost, and how, as He advanced in years, He lived without sin among His fellow men, and fulfilled the requirements of the law and gospel, and all other righteousness ; and how, when He was delivered over to the tempter, He came off victorious, having remained invincible, and having hurled out of the arena[1] the adversary of human nature; and how when the Jews plotted against Him and delivered Him over unjustly to death, He submitted willingly even to this, for the sake of our race—in order that having, as reason required, torn up the old bond, He might nail it to the cross, and might, as a reasonable sacrifice, pay the penalty of death that was due for all, by offering Himself to God spotless. Then afterwards, having after three days risen from the dead, He showed to all the destruction of death, and exhorted all to rejoice because He had taken away henceforth the power of death. Matthew also mentions the ascent into heaven, if not at the end of his book, yet in the course of his narrative, when he speaks concerning John the Baptist thus : *And in those days came John the Baptist preach-*

---

[1] Gr. ἔξω τοῦ σκάμματος ὑπερακοντίσας. *Scamma* is a place dug out and sanded for wrestling, leaping, &c.

ing in the wilderness of Judaea and saying, Repent, for the kingdom of heaven is at hand;[1] as if he said, the mansion in the heavens is now ready to be revealed, as the Christ is now near. But even in the Beatitudes and everywhere in his book, he mentions the kingdom of heaven, but more especially when the Lord in arguing with the Pharisees and Sadducees concerning the resurrection he speaks thus: *For in the resurrection they neither marry nor are given in marriage, but are as the angels of God in heaven.*[2] This is the design which the blessed Matthew the Evangelist had in view when composing his narrative.

Mark the Evangelist.

This is Mark, the second who composed a Gospel, a work which Peter in Rome enjoined him to undertake. He described, as the beginning of the Gospel or the Gospel dispensation, the baptism which was a type of the resurrection from the dead, through which we are born again into an immortal and unchangeable life. Then, after he had given an account of the temptations and the victory, and likewise of the plotting against Him, and the death, and the resurrection, he brought his composition to a close. He too mentions John the Baptist as proclaiming that the kingdom of heaven was at hand—and all that he announced was in harmony with the blessed Matthew.

Note.

And he also, being a preacher of the New Testament, wrote for us the same things as his predecessor, beginning with the account of the baptism, which is a type of the resurrection from the dead—that is, of the new and heavenly dispensation. He showed how Christ was baptized, and what was His manner of life, and how He was put to death, and rose again and ascended

---

[1] Matt. iii, 1, 2.   [2] Matt. xxii, 30.

into heaven, where there is the seat and the polity of the second state. Glory to God who from the beginning has prepared it, and announced it beforehand and has fulfilled it, and is fulfilling it. Amen!

Luke the Evangelist.

This is Luke the third of the Evangelists, who, having seen that many had taken in hand to write Gospels, and invented many things out of their own head, at once wrote to his own disciple Theophilus, warning him not to be carried away with their fictions, and not to be turned away from what he had learned at first: *That thou*, he says, *mightest know accurately the certainty of those things wherein thou wast instructed.*[1] He relates therefore to him what he had already delivered to him, beginning from the birth of John, announcing this, that the birth of the Forerunner also was miraculous. He then related the birth of the Lord Christ according to the flesh which was also miraculous, and, following the design of Matthew, who had preceded him, he enumerated his ancestors retrogressively, showing that he was descended from David and Abraham, and going still farther back he derived him from Adam. As he found no remoter ancestor he then at length fell back upon God, saying: *who was the son of God*, that is, of Him who, according to the sacred historian Moses, originated the creation, and made the first man Adam. Then again after having narrated things similar to the other evangelists, concerning the baptism and the temptations, and still further concerning His death and resurrection, he relates after these, both in the Gospel itself and in the Acts, His ascension into heaven, and states that He will in like manner come back again. And so he also closes his work directing his eyes to the object of

---

[1] Luke i, 4.

desire which all expect, and instructing in this also his disciple the God-beloved Theophilus.

Note 1.

This preacher of the New Testament also said the same things with the others, beginning from the generation of the Forerunner, and coming to the birth of Jesus, and showing what was the manner of His life. In like manner he also discoursed of the evangelical life—I mean baptism, death, resurrection, and finally of the ascent into heaven, which is the place of our habitation in the second state. Glory to God who from the beginning prepared these things and announced them beforehand, and who has now fulfilled and is fulfilling them. Amen!

Note 2.

It was he again who noted down the doxology of the multitude of the host of the angels, who were rejoicing and exulting at the birth of the Lord Christ according to the flesh, and saying: *Glory to God in the highest, and on earth peace, good pleasure among men,*[1] now putting away from themselves the old dejection brought upon them through the first-made man, and rejoicing at the birth of the second Adam.

John the Theologian.

This is the Theologian John, the Chief of the Evangelists, who was the most loved of all by Christ, who leaned upon the breast of the Lord, and who from thence as from an ever-flowing fountain drew forth the mysteries, to whom, when resident in Ephesus, there were delivered by the faithful the books composed by the other three evangelists, having received which he expressed his approbation of them. Some things, however, he said, had been omitted by them which it was necessary should be narrated. And having been requested by the faithful, he also gave to the world his book, which in a manner supplied what had been

---

[1] Luke ii, 14.

omitted; as for instance, the account of the marriage in Cana, the account of Nicodemus, of the Samaritan woman, of the nobleman, of the man who was blind from his birth, of Lazarus, of the indignation of Judas at the anointing of the Lord with myrrh, of the Greeks that came to him, of the washing of feet, and of further doctrines concerning the Comforter stated in the course of the narrative; but in particular he made clear proclamation also concerning the divinity of Christ, which he set forth in the outset of his work as its foundation—all which subjects had been omitted by the other Evangelists. Having begun therefore with the divinity of Christ he forthwith passed to his humanity also, stating such things as had been recorded before by the others, the baptism, temptations, death and resurrection. Then again he added such things as Christ had done after the resurrection, how He entered when the doors were shut, how He showed His hands and His feet and His side to His disciples, how He ate and drank with them, how He journeyed with them, how He held their eyes that they should not see Him, how, as often as He wished, He at once vanished from them, how by way of instructing her He said to Mary: *Touch me not*,[1] teaching her by these words that intercourse between immortals and mortals is not fitting, but rather intercourse with immortals must be in heaven. Wherefore also He directed her to go away and tell the disciples: I ascend into heaven into which ye also are to ascend. So when he also had written all these things, he brought to an end the book which he had written, having the same object in view as the other Evangelists, namely, to teach us that we ought to look away from this state to that which is to come, unto which all inspired scripture both of the Old and of the New Testament has reference.

---

[1] Luke xx, 47.

Note.

This illustrious preacher of the New Testament, having committed to writing the omissions of the other Evangelists, and filled up what they left defective, discoursed in like manner with the others[1] of baptism, manner of life, death, resurrection and ascent into heaven, which is the abode of immortal and righteous men and of angels, that is, it is the seat of the second state. Glory to Him who has prepared these things, and announced them beforehand and is still fulfilling them. Amen!

Peter the Apostle.

This is Peter the Chief of the Apostles, who was entrusted with the keys of heaven, who has the Church founded on his own confession, who thrice denied, and thrice confessed, who nobly prayed that he might sustain crucifixion with his head downward — and he, keeping in view the same object as the other evangelists, thus spoke in the Acts (see Acts ii, 22-24 and 32-36). Here I would have it to be observed, that within the compass of merely a few lines, he has described the whole of the argument of the Evangelists, making mention, when speaking concerning Him (Christ), of Nazareth where He was brought up, and saying that He was a man from God, as being the second Adam, and that through Him God wrought wonderful works; also that with His own consent He was put to death by lawless men, and that God raised Him up immortal and immutable (for so he said) having loosed the pangs of death, and that, having been exalted by divine power, He ascended into heaven, and sent down from thence the Holy Spirit. For no one else, not even David himself, ascended into heaven, but the Lord himself, concerning whom David said: *The*

---

[1] The Greek text reads: καὶ ἀναπληρώσας τὰ λοιπὰ τοῖς ἄλλοις. I have, however, translated in accordance with what must be the proper punctuation: καὶ ἀναπληρώσας· τὰ λοιπὰ τοῖς ἄλλοις ὁμοίως ἐξεῖπε.

Lord said unto my Lord, Sit thou at my right hand until I make thine enemies the footstool of thy feet.[1]

He says again when he addresses Cornelius—[For the 250 words see Acts x, 38-43]. In like manner when he healed the lame man, he said (what is recorded in Acts iii, 19-21). He mentions also the passage in Moses: *A prophet shall the Lord God raise up unto you.*[2] In several passages the blessed Peter bears his testimony in like manner as the Evangelists, and declares that all the Prophets had announced all these things beforehand—that God had made, and is making, a second new state, which also he announced beforehand by the mouth of all the Prophets, but neither said that before this state there existed another, nor did he declare that after the future state there would be another, but along with all the Prophets and Apostles he asserted that there were only two states—the present and the future.

Note.

At the time of the building of the Tower, when the men who fought against God wished to ascend into heaven, God, by dividing their tongues, frustrated their designs. But when, at the end of the times He had come for the salvation of men, and led up our nature into heaven, then on the day of Pentecost, by way of announcing beforehand the ascent of the rest of mankind, He brought the tongues together again, through the Holy Spirit from heaven, and gave them to the Apostles. And Peter, who was appointed to be the great preacher of the New Testament, when he was discoursing to the multitude, and carrying the keys of the heavens, which had been entrusted to him by Christ, proclaimed confidently the things which the Evangelists also had taught in their writings—baptism, holiness of life, death, resurrection, immortality, grace and incorruption. For this is the import of the saying: *Having loosed the pangs of death;*[3] and in like manner he calls the future state the ascent into heaven and

---

[1] Psalm cx, 1.   [2] Deut. xviii, 15.   [3] Acts ii, 24.

251 the times of refreshing, and this he calls the blessing which had been promised beforehand to Abraham, and says that it had been preached to all the nations by all the Prophets, and that the Prince of it was the Lord Christ, through whom all the nations will be blessed and honoured by God. Glory to Him who has prepared these things!

Stephen.

This is Stephen the first martyr of the New Testament and the first Deacon, who had for his slayer the great Paul while he was as yet zealous for the law—who alone by himself contended against the whole synagogue and made the Judge of the contest[1] rise from his seat to witness the spectacle. This is he who saw the heavens opened and the Son of Man standing on the right hand of God. For while the whole of divine scripture speaks of Him as sitting, this man saw Him standing; for the vehemence of the contest made the Judge rise up for the view.[2] Wherefore also on being invited to ascend to that glory, he prayed for those who were stoning him, saying: *Lord, lay not this sin to their charge, but do thou thyself receive my spirit*.[3] Lo! he also saw and preached the same things with the others, namely that Christ, the Prince of the second state, is in heaven, and of Him he entreated that He would receive him into that place.

Note.

And this man, who was a preacher and a zealous champion of the New Testament, with his very eyes saw within the firmament Jesus spiritually, whom also he entreated to receive his spirit. While addressing at great length an assembly of the Jews, he accused them of having been the murderers of Jesus. Wherefore he also has exhibited to us as trustworthy what those who

---

[1] Gr. ἀγωνοθέτην.
[2] This idea Cosmas borrowed from St. Chrysostom.
[3] Acts vii, 59.

had preceded him had taught—death, resurrection and ascension into heaven. Glory to Him who prepared these things and announced them beforehand, and has now fulfilled and is fulfilling these things. Amen!

Paul the Apostle.

This is the great Paul the Apostle, the leader of the heavenly phalanx, who has Christ speaking within him, who carries about the marks of Christ in his body—the great teacher of the Church, who endured daily ten thousands of deaths for the Church, who gloried in the Lord and in his own infirmities, who had the grace of Christ flowing in him, who spoke to all nations in their tongues, who was once a persecutor, but is now persecuted, who was once a sinner, but has now obtained mercy, who was caught up into the third heaven, and again into Paradise, who was the hearer of unspeakable words, the occult judge of spiritual gifts—Paul who prescribed the regulations of divine service, and surpassed the other teachers of the Church; whose salutation in all his epistles, to serve as a token, is *the grace of the Lord*. In all his epistles generally, as if he were already in the second state, he continues always rejoicing and full of assurance, saying: *He hath raised us up with Him and made us sit with Him in the heavenly places;*[1] and: *By hope have we been saved,*[2] and countless other expressions he uses which we cannot now conveniently cite. Some however we will mention that we may not too far prolong our discourse, I Cor. xv, 19; Heb. vi, 17-20; Heb. x, 34; xii. 28; xiii, 14; I Cor. vii, 31; I Tim. iv, 8; Philip. iii, 13-15; and 20, 21; Tit. ii, 13; Coloss. iii, 1, 2; I Thess. iv, 14-17; Heb. xi, 14, 15, 10; viii, 2; Acts xxvi, 7, 8, and 21-23. And if we cared to collect all the utterances of the Apostle on this subject,

---

[1] Ephes. ii, 6. [2] Rom. viii, 24.

we shall find references thereto in nearly all his fourteen epistles, namely, that we are hastening to run from this present state towards that which is to come, whence also he exhorts us in these words: *Let us be eager to enter into that rest;*[1] speaking of that rest as if there is no other after it, but a kingdom that cannot be shaken, meaning one that has no successor.

Note 1.

What need is there to speak of this chosen vessel—a new and mighty trumpet, sounding among the Gentiles, gathering together Jew and Gentile into one Church; since the choice of him at first was made by Jesus calling to him from heaven, and when he was instructed, he was not disobedient to the heavenly vision? He again when still sojourning in this present state was caught up into the third heaven, and saw the ranks of the angels, and beheld the worship observed by the invisible Virtues, the Principalities, the Powers and the Dominions—and having entered in and viewed, as in a glass, the ministrations of all the Virtues that have been named, he exclaimed: *Are they not all ministering spirits, sent forth to do service for the sake of them that shall inherit salvation?*[2] So also he spoke of the rank which the adversary once held, how he had the power of the air, and he announced his fall from heaven in consequence of his pride. He again exclaimed: *Know ye not that we shall judge angels?*[3] And again; *The saints shall judge the world.*[3] This is he who in all his Epistles exhorts us to think of heavenly things and to seek heavenly things and to make haste to run to heaven, and to press forward in order to obtain the things above. This is he, who, when he had declared that heaven was the city and habitation of the righteous, angels and men, and in a word of the whole Church, declared besides that the Lord Christ after the flesh was the supreme Head of the whole body. For he said that He was above all Principalities and Powers and Virtues and Dominions —and above every name that is named, not only in this world but in that which is to come.

---

[1] Heb. iv, 11.   [2] Heb. i, 14.   [3] 1 Cor. vi, 2, 3.

And, to speak briefly, this Apostle is the great teacher and interpreter of the heavenly hosts, and of the Church, and he makes mention of the present and the future state only, and of immortality and immutability and of all the good things in the world above—the power of which we are not able to reckon. To God who has prepared these things beforehand, and announced them beforehand and who has now fulfilled and is still fulfilling them, be glory for ever, Amen!

Note 2.

Paul at the very outset (of the Epistle) commends the faith of the Romans which was proclaimed throughout the whole world, and calls them his fellow-believers. But the Corinthians he reproves, because, as being recently philosophers of this world, after already believing in the resurrection of the Lord Christ, they make this as of no use to them, seeing that they do not believe our own resurrection. The Athenians therefore were right in calling him *a picker-up of sown seeds*,[1] since he tore up by the root the tares of their superstition. The Galatians he calls senseless both because they readily changed their opinions like insensate things, and because after baptism they had been deceived, and submitted to circumcision. To the Ephesians he reveals the whole counsel of God, and declares that in their city he had fought as it were with wild beasts, prophesying and saying to them that afterwards there would come some to them as wolves, and would tear them asunder; and therewith he said that from themselves would arise some who would, like wolves, ravage the Church. The Philippians he regards with the utmost admiration, praising them as those who alone displayed their great care and love for him in his bonds, and in his defence, and who often sent him supplies for his wants. The Colossians again he praises for their faith: if they continue in the same, having love to all the saints. The Thessalonians he calls lovers of the brethren, and speaks of them as being persecuted, and as suffering on account of their godliness. He calls them, in like manner as the

---

[1] Gr. σπερμολόγον. This word means figuratively *one who picks up and retails scraps of knowledge*, and is translated by *babbler* in Acts xvii, 18. See note on this word in Book VII.

Hebrews, faithful, and confirms them, in like manner as the Corinthians, in the belief of the resurrection of the dead, along with the belief of the second coming of the Lord. As a Hebrew and as a member of the Hebrew community, regarding its interests as his own, he designates them holy brethren, and called, and partakers of heavenly things, and speaks of them as persecuted and suffering for that godliness, *only however*, he adds, *if we hold fast the beginning firm unto the end;*[1] and he cautions them not to become faint-hearted from the fear of persecution, and not to run back again to the unbelievers. To Timothy again, who was then in Ephesus, he sends a message in writing, warning him against the teachers of a different doctrine, and against his giving heed to their fables, while he confirms him in the doctrines and delivers to him ecclesiastical canons, *That thou mayest know*, he says, *how men ought to behave themselves in the house of God.*[2] He says also that some heresies would show themselves at the last, and would subvert the truth. And he predicts that they would not make progress to what is better, but that they would become manifest, and that their foolishness would be evident to all. To Titus again, who was in Crete, he delivers ecclesiastical canons and confirms him in the doctrines, and administers rebukes to the Cretans, as being liars, and frivolous, and crafty, and led astray by those of the circumcision. Writing to Philemon, he bears witness to his abundant faith, to his piety, and to the love which he has for the saints, whose slave, Onesimus, when unprofitable, he had changed for the better, and made a pious man; and the great Apostle exhorts the master of this slave to receive him no longer as a slave but as a brother. In all his Epistles moreover he urges it upon all men to enter into the habitation in the heavens, through right faith and a good life, and not to miss the good things kept in store for the righteous—along with whom, unworthy as we are, deign, O Lord God, Maker of the Universe, in thy compassionate goodness, to number us. Amen! I must observe further that Paul being a Hebrew wrote to the Hebrews in the Hebrew language, but his Epistle was translated into the Greek tongue, as they say, by Luke, or by Clement, in like manner as the Gospel according to Matthew.

---

[1] Heb. iii, 6. [2] 1 Tim. iii, 15

Text.

It behoves us, O most beloved of God, to observe the harmony that exists between Moses, the historian of the world, and all the Prophets and the Evangelists and Apostles, how they all harmoniously assert that God made the whole world divided into two states. For to this end, when God began the work of creation, he made on the second day the firmament, and bound it together with the first heaven, having placed it midway between the earth below and the heaven above, thus dividing the one place into two places, and the lower of the two places he ordained to be this world, but the higher he prepared from the beginning to be the future world, according to his previous design. For it is not in this transitory life that our hope lies, but in that future life which hath no end, wherein is our adoption as sons, and redemption and immutability, and righteousness, and sanctification, and blessedness, and perfect knowledge and glory, and whatever other blessings are laid up for us to be received from God, after we have had here experience of things both good and bad, in order that as far as possible we may know the full strength of the good things reserved for us, who in a certain sense become the sons of God, and are exalted to glory and joy unspeakable. On this account, even here, we the faithful, after baptism, become partakers of the mysteries of the body of the Lord Christ,[1] in order that after the resurrection, by devoting ourselves to the Lord Christ, we may become partakers of His glory, attracting to ourselves glory from the glory that is His. Wherefore also the term *partaking*[2] is used according to what is written by the Apostle when he says:

---

[1] *I.e.*, of the sacrament of the Lord's Supper.
[2] Gr. μετάληψις. See note 1, p. 140.

But we all with unveiled face beholding reflected as in a mirror[1] *the glory of the Lord, are transformed into the same image from glory to glory even as from the spirit of the Lord;*[2] as if he said, when the Lord is nigh, all we the faithful, in the most manifest manner, without any veil, behold the glory of the Lord as in a mirror—and are transformed into the same image as the Lord has, partaking of his glory for our own glory. For the partaking of the mysteries indicates also our partaking of his glorified body, just as we behold him reflected as in a mirror and partake his glory. *For out of his fulness do we all receive,*[3] nor does he, in giving liberally, suffer any diminution of his fulness. But the expression *as from the spirit of the Lord* is intended to show us, that just as Moses received [glory] from the Lord, so do we receive [glory] through the Holy Spirit.

Note.

Just as we who are born in this world are nourished by the milk of our parents—that is, are organised for living from their flesh and their blood, so we are commanded to take our nourishment mystically from the body and blood of the Lord Christ; since in the future state, according to the view of scripture, He is our Father, from whom and through whom we receive glory, and are, so to speak, reborn into life eternal. In this state takes place the initial birth and the nourishment of milk in the mysteries, organising, suitably for living, him that has been generated—a type of the regeneration through water and the spirit, and the mystical nourishment of the body and blood of Christ inviting and strongly drawing to life eternal him that believes and partakes. In the future state again is the resurrection from the dead, whereby we rise up from our graves as from the womb, and are born anew and refashioned; and especially

---

[1] Gr. κατοπτριζόμενοι. I follow Beet's translation of this word—*beholding reflected as in a mirror*. The Revised Version has : *reflecting as a mirror*.

[2] II Cor. iii. 18.   [3] John i, 16.

there is the participation of the glorified, immortal and incorruptible and immutable body and soul of Christ. Glory to God the Creator and Renovator of the universe for ever. Amen!

Text.

Divine scripture is wont to speak of the creation as being from the Father, and the incarnation as being from the Son, and the regeneration from the dead as being from the Holy Spirit. Not that the Father does *this* alone, or the Son *that*, or the Holy Spirit *something else*, but the Holy Trinity conjointly effects the creation, and the incarnation and the resurrection. For, as has been said, divine scripture with a view to show that there is one God in three persons[1] is wont thus to distinguish them, namely—by ascribing to the Father as Cause, the causing the world to exist, by ascribing to the Son as begotten, the cause of the incarnation, as possessing a worthy adoption and being the fountain of knowledge, and by ascribing to the Holy Spirit as proceeding from the Father, in virtue of His life-giving and sanctifying power, the regeneration and redemption and sanctification of the future state. For just as the sun has in himself the power of giving light and heat, and without these cannot be perceived, so likewise the Father has two powers proceeding from himself, apart from which He cannot be seen, the Son, namely, and the Holy Ghost. And just as the sun is a fiery body and has as one of his powers to give light, and as another to

---

[1] Gr. ὑποστάσεων. Hypostasis denotes the real nature of a thing, as underlying its outward form and properties. It is thus equivalent to οὐσία, and to its own Latin etymological representative *substantia*. The Latin Christians, however, since they used *substantia* to translate *ousia*, found it necessary to use a different term to translate *hypostasis*, and adopted *persona* (πρόσωπον). *Hypostasis* thus came to differ from *ousia* as species differs from genus, so that it denoted the specific nature (ἰδιώματα) of a person or thing, in contra-distinction to the generic nature.

give heat; and neither the heat-giving is the light-giving power, nor the light-giving the heat-giving power, while the sun and his powers are inseparable the one from the other; so in the Father and Son and Holy Ghost there is one God—the Father with his two powers existing inseparably the one in the other, and these are seen by the mind in their proper Persons. For in this case, God is properly incorporeal, but the similitude, so far forth as it is such, is obscure. But we may take a further similitude from our own soul. For just as the soul has inherent in itself *word* (or discourse) and *understanding* (λόγον καὶ νοῦν), and the discursive faculty (τὸ λογικὸν) is one thing and the understanding faculty (τὸ νοερὸν) a different thing, and the *word* goes forth from the soul inseparably—not dissevered from it, [while the same is true of the understanding], nay, they are in the soul and from it and with it, so we must think of God.

Wherefore also John the Evangelist employing this illustration called the Son the Word as proceeding from the Father and being with Him, and being of the same substance; and the Apostle Paul taking an illustration from the material world called him the effulgence. But the Old Testament says: *Let us make man in our image and after our likeness.*[1] Here in both the words ποιήσωμεν and ἡμετέραν it expresses plurality, but the phrases *in our image* and *after our likeness* do not mean the same thing, but the former of them means one thing, and the other a different thing. The expression *in our image* has this sense, that man and man alone, as having all things in himself—things visible and things invisible, things perceived by the intellect and things perceived by the senses, things corruptible and things incorruptible, indicates that there is one Creator of all things that are, even God,

---

[1] Gen. i, 26.

and man is in this respect the image of God, through his knowing that there is one Creator of the universe, as the Apostle exclaims : *For a man ought not to cover his head, being the image and glory of God ;*[1] thus expressly declaring that man was made for the glory of God, and, in accordance with this, calling him His image, as man alone is capable of knowing that there is one Creator of the universe, even God, who formed man as the only living creature in whose composition are found all the natural qualities. But the other expression *after our likeness* has this sense, that Adam was a father and not a son, and, from his own substance by procession produced Eve, who is called neither a son nor a sister, and by generation produced his own son Seth, who again was of his own substance, producing him by generation, and her by procession, thus producing the one, one way, and the other, another way, out of his own substance. But inasmuch as Adam had a beginning, those also who spring from him have a beginning, but as God and the Father has no beginning, those who are of Him proceed from Him without beginning, and are eternally with Him, just as the effulgence and heat are with the sun, and just as the word and the intelligence are with our soul, according to the similitudes of divine scripture. And some of the Fathers have employed similitudes regarding the Holy Trinity drawn from the material world, some of them speaking of two rivers as flowing forth out of an ever-flowing fountain, and others of branch and fruit produced from a tree as the root. But all, whether Apostles or Fathers, as being but men, have spoken under the inspiration of the Spirit, in similitudes drawn from the natural world, which however fall altogether short of exhibiting the divine substance. But in the

---

[1] I Cor. xi, 7.

future state again, when we shall rise up spiritual beings, we shall know more exactly concerning God.

In this manner therefore divine scripture in these passages, having in view to set before us the Persons in the Trinity, frequently employs this phraseology, declaring the Creation to be, so to speak, from the Father, and the Incarnation to be of the Son, and the Resurrection to be of the Holy Ghost. But yet it is the Holy Trinity which does all things. The blessed Moses however, as if God were speaking, said: *Let us make man;*[1] here the word (ποιήσωμεν) though in the plural number can be understood to refer to two only. Since therefore it seemed good to God not to deliver to us at the first an acknowledgment of the Holy Trinity, lest we should think the Persons of whom it consists to have material bodies, and we should thus suspect that there are three Gods, when He came to the creation of man, He then expressed Himself ambiguously in the plural number, yet in such a way that it could be understood that He was speaking only of two. But after some time had elapsed, He is again found using an expression more distinctly plural when He says: *Come, let us go down and confound their language*[2]—an expression which can no longer be thought applicable to two only, but to three or more. Then again after an interval of a great many years, not to introduce a host of instances, God again used an expression ambiguously respecting the Trinity, repeating thrice through Isaiah the word *Holy* which he made applicable to one God, saying: *The Lord of hosts, the whole earth is full of His glory,*[3] showing both the number of the three Persons and the unity of the Godhead. But in the days of the Lord Christ according to the flesh, He taught this clearly, saying: *Go ye, and make disciples of all*

---

[1] Gen. i, 26.   [2] Gen. xi, 7.   [3] Isai. vi, 3.

the nations, baptizing them into the name of the Father and of the Son and of the Holy Ghost,[1] speaking indeed of one name, but distinguishing them into three Persons. And since he was going to proclaim these things clearly, giving intimation of them beforehand, through the form of the bond-servant, on his first making the announcement at the creation of man, He used the plural number: *Let us make man.* When therefore the Lord shall come from heaven, He takes with Himself into the kingdom of heaven the faithful, the righteous, the worthy, both angels and men; but as for the rest, some of them He permits to be outside of the firmament, and others He consigns to the nether parts around the earth, according to what He says in the Gospel in the account of the consummation of things: *Then there shall be two men in the field, one is taken, and one is left; two women shall be grinding at the mill, one is taken, and one, is left;*[2] as if He said *those in the field,* namely, all those that are in the world whether rich or poor or middle-class, that is to say whatever be their rank in life, whosoever is found worthy is taken into heaven; but if he be not worthy, he is left upon the earth. Then when He speaks of those grinding at the millstone, He means those that are bond-servants, and such of those bond-servants as are found worthy are taken into heaven, while those that are unworthy are left upon the earth. By His using the masculine form in the first instance, and then the feminine form[3] afterwards, He has indicated the difference of sex, whether they be males or females, whether they be righteous or sinners.

The Apostle Paul also, in his second Epistle to the Thessalonians, expresses himself to the same effect, saying:

---

[1] Matt. xxviii, 19.   [2] Matt. xxiv, 40.
[3] Referring to the text quoted above: ὁ εἷς παραλαμβάνεται and μία παραλαμβάνεται.

At the revelation of the Lord Jesus, from heaven, with the angels of his power, in flaming fire, rendering vengeance to them that know not God, and to them that obey not the Gospel of our Lord Jesus Christ, who shall suffer punishment, even eternal destruction from the face of the Lord and from the glory of his might, when he shall come to be glorified in his saints, and to be marvelled at in all them that believed;[1] he also showing that for the faithful saints, great and unspeakable glory is treasured up, but to the unbelieving, a doom of destruction,[2] that is, a punishment in congruity with that state. For in destruction, and sorest punishment and deep repentance, is every one found who does not enjoy the holy delights and glories, and the blessedness treasured up for the righteous. It is the duty then of every Christian in this life to bring himself into bondage, and thereby to make himself obedient unto God, and to believe the whole body of divine scripture both the Old and the New Testament, and to be a strict guardian of the doctrines, and to lead a life consistent with the faith; and, in accordance with what we professed and vowed when going forward to baptism, to thrust away from us and renounce all Satanic and Pagan error, and unbelief and folly and groundless hope. For by remaining in them they will incur the most grievous harm, while calculating and predicting eclipses as a divine science, without possessing any hope beyond this, and while leading others into the errors into which they have themselves been led. Now if any one resorts to these men, as to prophets, when he has lost a mantle or anything else, he hears from them of it, or recovers it through them, who deceive him as to the truth, but if not, then not even this. Such are the hopes of those weak-minded men who ascribe to the

---

[1] II Thess. i, 7-9.
[2] Gr. δίκη ὀλέθριος. The Latin version gives here *pœna æterna*.

heaven a spherical form ; nor are they able to hope for anything further, neither a resurrection, nor a kingdom of heaven, nor a better state, since they both lose the sphere, and ruin the hope itself which they have. May it be ours, O honoured head, at the revelation of our Lord Jesus Christ, through the prayers of our Lady the Mother of God,[1] and through those of all the holy patriarchs, prophets, apostles, martyrs, confessors and teachers, to be numbered along with those on the right hand, and to hear with them that surpassing and blessed utterance: *Come, ye blessed of my Father, inherit the kingdom prepared for you from the foundation of the world.*[2] To Him be glory for ever. Amen!

Note.

The whole scope of this work and of the delineations is to set forth that from the beginning, God, through all the men of old, and also through Moses the Cosmographer, and all the Prophets and Apostles, has shown that there are two states—the present state and the future ; and we have exhibited also the figure of the whole world, and have shown, that Christians prefer to follow their own principles, and that their ends are in conformity with their principles ; and herein we have proclaimed the goodness of

---

[1] Gr. τῆς δεσποίνης ἡμῶν Θεοτόκου. Latin : Dominae nostrae deiparae. Nestorius, the Primate of the Eastern Church, vehemently condemned the application of the term Θεοτόκος to the Virgin Mary. "The Blessed Virgin", says Gibbon, "he revered as the Mother of Christ, but his ears were offended with the rash and recent title of Mother of God, which had been insensibly adopted since the origin of the Arian controversy. From the pulpit of Constantinople .... he repeatedly preached against the use, or the abuse, of a word unknown to the Apostles and unauthorised by the Church." He thus kindled a controversy which raged so furiously that it threatened the disruption of the Church, led to the convocation of the Council of Ephesus (431 A.D.), and resulted in his deposition from his episcopal office. It seems singular that Cosmas, who was most probably a Nestorian, should use a term so much reprobated by his master.

[2] Matt. xxv, 34.

God, in the exercise of which He has set an end to this state of discipline, and to wrestlings, and to corruption and death. And we have set forth that in the Lord Christ immortality, incorruption, immutability, blessedness, sanctification and righteousness everlasting were prepared for all men, as he had prepared from the foundation of the world the second place, which is in heaven, and the second state, as again he showed it to us beforehand typically, by means of the Tabernacle. We have shown besides that the opinion of the Pagans is one which holds out no hope, for they neither expect a second state, nor believe that there will be a resurrection of our bodies, but they lead others into error and are themselves in error, their minds whirling round and round along with that sphere of theirs; and they think it to be impossible for God to raise the bodies of all men, although, as being wise, they ought to know that, if God is judge of the thoughts and hearts of all men, and can discern the thoughts of each man since the beginning of time, He should be able all the more to discriminate the bodies of men. For if he is able to discriminate the things of the spirit, much more is He able to discriminate bodies. For He shakes from its foundations the whole frame of nature, heaven and earth, together with the other elements at the final consummation, and each of these renders back whatever human body it possesses, God, by His power, making the discrimination. And just as one who sifts with a sieve will find the object which he seeks, so, when the whole creation is shaken, those who are sought for will be found amidst it; for saith He through the prophet: *For yet once more I shall shake not the earth alone but also heaven.*[1] But the word, *yet once more*, signifies, as the Apostle shows, the removing of those things that are shaken, as of things that have been made, that those things which are not shaken may remain. *Wherefore, receiving a kingdom that cannot be shaken, let us show*[2] *thankfulness whereby, we may offer service well-pleasing to God, with reverence and piety and supplication.*[3]

And the Lord referring to the final consummation says: [The texts here quoted are Matt. xxiv, 29 *seqq.*; I Thess., 15-17;

---

[1] Hagg. i, 7.
[2] Gr. ἔχομεν. A printer's error for ἔχωμεν.
[3] Heb. xii, 28.

I Cor., xv, 52, 53.] These are the good tidings of the Christians —these the great and wondrous hopes of the faithful—the resurrection of the dead, and the kingdom of heaven prepared from the foundation of the world for men, who, as soon as they have obtained immortality and incorruption and immutability, together with Christ shall inherit the kingdom of heaven, treading on high the paths of air, and shall reign as kings with Christ—shall with Christ possess heaven as their dwelling-place—being permitted to tread with Christ the entrance into the Tabernacle not made with hands, being called, along with Christ and the holy angels, citizens of the heavenly Jerusalem: rejoicing with Christ, exulting with Christ, exalted with Christ, wearing crowns along with Christ, glorified with Christ, enjoying with Christ the throne of grace, enjoying with Christ righteousness and sanctification and redemption and blessedness, and every eternal and unspeakable good. What nation, or what sect, can by believing possess such hopes except Christians alone?

The Pagans do not believe and are without hope, being in love with the wisdom of this world, which has not the power of itself to take hold of even one of the things, unless a divine illumination should follow. In like manner also the Jews, not believing in Christ, when He appeared and openly proclaimed these things, and confirmed them both by Himself and by His Apostles, have incurred the loss of all these things. The Samaritans[1] again, and the Montanists,[2] being more stiff-necked than the Jews, when they could not be taught by Moses and the figures of the world, and did not believe even the prophets, confessing neither angel, nor spirit, nor the immortality of the rational soul, but denying the same doctrines as the Pagans, even the resurrection of the body, suffer the loss of all these things.

---

[1] Members of this sect still exist at Nablus, as they have existed in that district from the time of Christ. In their creed and form of worship they closely agree with the Rabbinical Jews, but they reject the "Traditions". They retain, however, the sacrifice of a lamb at the Passover.

[2] This was a Phrygian sect founded about 171 A.D. The Montanists practised fasting, held the doctrine of the Millennium, and were noted for their austere manners and the severity of their discipline. Jerome wrote against them.

In like manner again the Manichaeans, who hate the body and do not confess its resurrection, but suppose it to be the workmanship of an evil deity,[1] and expect that it will be destroyed, these also are deprived of all good things, being condemned as impious, along with that deity whom they elected for themselves upon earth. In like manner also all the heretics, whosoever deny the assumption of our flesh and of our soul at the time of the Incarnation, and whosoever, by denial, take away the divinity of the Son, and seek to lessen the divinity of the Holy Ghost, are also deprived of all these good things. For those alone who acknowledge one God in three Persons, without beginning, eternal, uncircumscribed, invisible, intangible, incorruptible, immortal, imperturbable, incorporeal, unlimited, incomprehensible, uncompounded, indivisible, the Maker of heaven and earth and of all things visible and invisible, known and adored in Father, Son and Holy Ghost; who, in the last of the days, at the time of the Incarnation, desiring to renovate the world which He had created, and having taken again from the holy Virgin Mary our substance, God the Word, with the Father and Holy Ghost, without seed, with a view to renovate the microcosm which is the bond of the whole creation, namely, Man, by His own mere inclination, became united to him, in a union wondrous and indissoluble, in such a way that the assumption was not understood to precede the union, but the formation and assumption and union were simultaneous, and He consented to suffer and to be put to death; and when He had made man perfect through the resurrection, He led him up into heaven, and honoured him with a seat at His right hand, and appointed Him to be judge of all. Those also who, in like manner with Him, live uprightly, enter into the bride-chamber along with the bridegroom, those, to wit, who take away neither His divinity nor His humanity; these with Christ sing together for joy, and reign with Him in heaven, hearing from Him at the final consummation these words: *Come, ye blessed of my Father, inherit the kingdom prepared for you from the foundation of the world.*[2]

But of the day of the consummation no one knows except

---

[1] Manichæus, called also Manes, being a Persian, maintained the doctrine of two co-eternal principles, the one good and the other evil.
[2] Matt. xxv, 34.

God alone. They say however that, until men become equal in number to the angels, the consummation of the world will not take place. For Moses says: *He set the boundaries of the nations according to the number of the angels of God;*[1] as if he said: He set the bounds in this, in their becoming equal in number to the angels. The Apostle in point of fact also says: *But when the fulness of the Gentiles has come in, then all Israel shall thus be saved,*[2] here clearly speaking of the final consummation. Nay, even the Lord manifestly hints obscurely at this when He says: *At the resurrection they are equal to the angels.*[3] Ye then, as many as are Christians, and take hold of this hope, and have the Lord Christ as your example and model, when reading this book of mine, pray for me a sinner, that the Lord of all will not disdain me, but will in His mercy make me to be numbered along with you, in company with those on His right hand, while He overlooks our transgressions; and that I may not fail to obtain that blessedness unspeakable, through your prayers and supplications, and by the compassion and kindness and grace of Christ the Saviour of us all, to whom with the Father and with the Holy Ghost be glory both now and evermore world without end, Amen!

A Christian's *Christian Topography* embracing the whole world.

---

[1] Deut. xxxii, 8. This is the reading of the Septuagint. In our version the reading is: according to the number of the Children of Israel.

[2] Rom. xi, 25, 26.   [3] Luke xx, 36.

BOOK VI. SUPERADDED.

Regarding the Size of the Sun.

264 FTER my work had been finished, some questioned us about the figure of the world, saying: "How can the sun possibly be hidden, as you hold, by the northern parts of the earth, which according to you are very high, while he is many times larger than the earth? For in the case of the sphere which we advocate, however much greater the sun may be than the earth, he will always, when giving light to one part of her surface, leave the other in shadow." To those so questioning us we have made a very brief reply, that such a thing is false and a pure fiction, having shown first from the climates[1] which they themselves, recognise, that the sun projects shadows between which there is no difference, and next from what we ourselves saw with our own eyes in the parts of Axômis in

---

[1] Before it was known that the earth was a globe, it was supposed that its surface sloped from south to north, and this slope was called κλίμα. But as science advanced, this term was employed to designate different belts or zones of the earth's surface, as determined by the different lengths of the longest days on their southern and northern limits. Hipparchus (about 160 B.C.), first used this division. The term κλίμα came afterwards to denote the average temperature of each of the zones, and hence the present use of the word.

Ethiopia. For, at the beginning of the summer solstice on the twenty-fifth day of the month Paÿni at the sixth hour of the day when the sun is now at the meridian, we plainly saw that a man's shadow inclined to the south.[1] And when I was resident here in Alexandria, at the same time of the year on the twenty-fifth, that is of Paÿni, and until the thirtieth of Thôth at the sixth hour of the day when we were standing under the sun, I pointed out that the shadow inclined to northward only a single foot. And, according to them, Alexandria is the third climate. Now in this city there happened to be living that extremely pious and admirable man, Abbot Stephanus, the Presbyter of Antioch, a most Christian man and verily to be

---

[1] Mr. Ernest A. Floyer, in a letter sent from Egypt, which appeared in *The Academy* of 5th Oct., 1895, makes some interesting remarks about primitive sun-dials in Upper Egypt. He found that there the hours of work for a waterwheel were fixed by such sun-dials. " Two kinds were used. At Edfu a horizontal dhurra stalk lay north and south on two forked uprights. East and west were pegs in the ground, dividing evenly the space of earth between the sunrise and sunset shadows of the horizontal gnomon. Further south the gnomon was a vertical stick." Afterwards he says : " It is generally admitted that the Egyptians ascertained the length of the year to within a few hours. This approximation must have been obtained by measuring the shadow of a gnomon at the summer solstice, which coincided with their principal natural phenomenon, the rising of the Nile. It could hardly be otherwise. Given a constant and never-clouded sun, and a need to divide up the day, the upright stick is brought into use at once. But little time could have elapsed before it was noticed that the noon shadow was longer or shorter one day than the preceding day . . . . Thus the period from one summer solstice to another could not have remained long unknown". After tracing further the progress of discovery, the writer concludes with two remarks : " First, the effect of the use of a gnomon's shadow leaves its trace to this day on Arabic astronomy. Angles are called *shadows*. Secondly, measuring the exact length of a shadow on a somewhat rough plane was not easy. Perhaps better results were obtained by examining the faces of an obelisk. If the north face of an obelisk at Luxor sloped at an angle equal to the difference of latitude between Luxor and Syene, then at the summer solstice only all four faces would be equally illuminated.'

numbered among the perfect, and as he was accurately versed in lunar calculations, and moreover able, in accordance with the scheme of the world which we have laid down from divine scripture, to predict readily both solar and lunar eclipses, he willingly turned his attention to this subject. Accordingly when in the month Thôth of the current tenth indiction[1] he was asked by the erudite Anastasius, a man of science and learning, and superior to many in point of experience, to predict when an eclipse of the sun would take place, he stated that there would be one in that very indiction on the twelfth day of the month Mechir; and it did so occur. He predicted also a lunar eclipse for the twenty-fourth of Mesori in the same indiction. Anastasius was much surprised, and asked him next to tell what past eclipses there had been, and when he had declared them correctly great again was his surprise. There were present too some other scientific men, friends of ours, at this conversation. Now this God-beloved man, who has a curiosity to investigate such matters, and who lived in Antioch and, for many years also, at Constantinople, told us himself that he had measured the shadows in both these cities, and assured us that at Antioch the shadow projected a foot and a half at the time already mentioned,[2] while at Byzantium it projected two feet. Now Antioch is in the same climate as Rhodes, namely, in the fourth, but Byzantium is a little

---

[1] Regarding *indictions*, see last note to Book X.

[2] The height of a man who would cast a shadow of $1\frac{1}{2}$ foot in the latitude of Antioch, when the sun was on the meridian "at the beginning of the summer solstice", would be about $6\frac{3}{4}$ feet. This, however, can only be considered approximate, as there is some uncertainty about the length of the foot used, and of the exact declination of the sun at a time now so long past. In computing the height of the man, a plus correction of 12' has been applied to the sun's declination at the present day, and this may be taken as approximately correct.

beyond the fifth. For it is in the following way they distinguish the climates. The first is, they say, the climate of Meroë; the second of Syênê; the third of Alexandria, the fourth of Rhodes, the fifth of Hellespont, the sixth of the middle of Pontus, the seventh of the river Borysthenes and the Macotic lake, and the last of the Ocean. If therefore, as we have seen with our own eyes here, in the climate which, according to their own laying down, is the third, the shadow falls only one foot towards the north, and in the fourth one foot and a half, and in the fifth two feet, is it not manifest that the shadow is either lengthened or shortened by half a foot for each climate? And if this be true, as assuredly it is, the sun will be found to have the size of two climates and no more. For if, in the third climate, he throws a shadow of one foot, in the second he will beyond all question throw one of half a foot, while in the first he will throw none at all.[1]

[1] The sun is so far distant from the earth that its *mean* parallax is only about 8″, and therefore the rays of light falling on to the earth may be considered as parallel lines; and from the diagram below it will be at once seen that if the earth were flat, as Cosmas supposes,

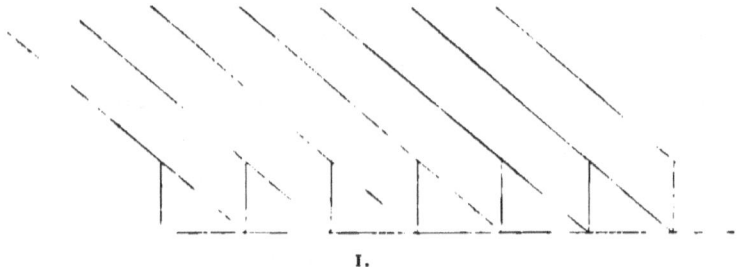

I.

the shadow of the gnomon would be the same length all the world over, at the same instant of time. Thus what is advanced by Cosmas in support of his theory of a flat earth proves the very opposite; for the fact of the shadows being of different lengths, as he had observed them to be, at the same season in different latitudes, is owing entirely to the curvature of the earth's surface. This, I think, is very clearly

But as we said by anticipation in the second book, there lie between Meroë and the Ocean in the south many of the

shown on diagram 2. If the sun were a small object and near to the

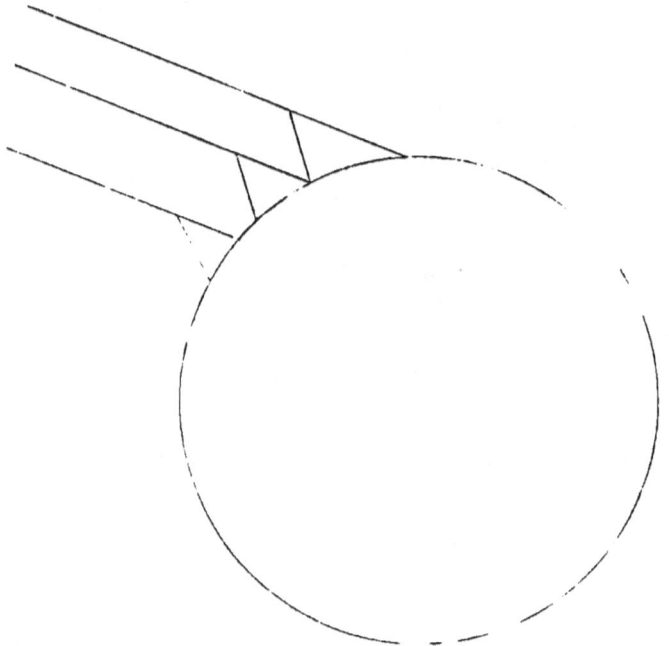

earth, of course the length of the shadows would be different for different latitudes, supposing the earth to be flat. This is shown in diagram 3. It is on the assumption of a near sun that the fallacy of

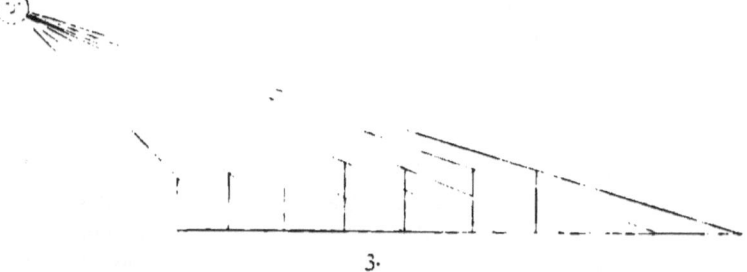

3.

the whole argument lies. Cosmas builds his whole theory on this false basis.

stages into which the earth is partitioned. For, from the Cataracts to the ocean we remember having stated that the number of halting-places in that distance was seventy more or less. But the number of climates which they suppose to exist they reckon at somewhere about twenty only.[1] So then quite clearly the shadow in the climate of Axômê, a city of the Ethiopians, is found projecting more than a foot to the south, so that everything goes to show that, if the sun in his passage through the summer tropic be between Syênê and Axômis, he has the size of two climates.[2] Is it not then false and fabulous what they say about the sun, that he is greater than the earth? And how too comes it, if, as they say, the earth is spherical, the shadow does not vary on the convex surface of the earth? For since they place the torrid zone in the centre, it follows of necessity that the parts on each side of that zone must be depressed. And they assert that none can inhabit the torrid zone—yea, even that the northern part of the world which is inhabited by us is many stages distant from the torrid zone. And I wonder again if, in those convex parts of the earth which they suppose to exist, the shadows are able to observe such a proportion that they increase or diminish by half a foot for each climate, as with God's help we have demonstrated and with our very eyes have witnessed to be the case, and have shown to the men with whom we have conversed —men by no means novices but adepts in science,

---

[1] Ptolemy reckoned nineteen climates. See Ukert, *Geog.*, vol. i, Pt. II, pp. 182 ff.; or Smith's *Dictionary of Greek and Roman Antiquities*, p. 297.

[2] The fallacy of this so-called proof lies also (as shown in note on pp. 247, 248) in the fact that Cosmas founds it on the supposition that the sun is near the earth. It falls through at once when we consider that the sun's rays are practically parallel lines, and the fact that the shadows vary in length, and in one place fall to the north and in another to the south, is owing to the spherical form of the earth.

and earnestly maintaining this opinion. But further again they affirmed most positively that when the illuminating body is large and the body which is illuminated small, and each of them spherical, the shadow produced is beyond question conical—for the rays of the larger sphere, passing beyond the smaller on this and on that side, necessarily make a very acute cone; and they endeavoured by means of geometrical demonstrations to circumvent us; but on this point we very concisely by optical experiments again showed the falsehood of what they alleged; for, fetching a small wooden globe, we drove a nail into it by which we held it in our hands, and on stretching it out to the sun, we saw that the shadow was round and not conical. And we said to them, look you now how small the sphere is which we hold out, and how great, according to you at any rate, the sun is, and yet he does not make a conical but a round shadow.[1] And we made the experiment both at a short and at a long distance—and they found nothing to show the truth of what they say, but with their specious sophistries they delude the multitude. We, again, fetching a cone-shaped vessel, then showed them that a conical body produces a shadow conical like itself. And, it is the truth I speak, O most God-beloved Father, through the power of Christ they went away dumbfounded and sadly crestfallen, having been put to shame by our exposure of their fictions. And now behold, we also, in accordance with an art of theirs, having drawn lines and imprinted one for each climate as they are wont to do, are able, if first

---

[1] Cosmas evidently misunderstood the phrase used: a cone casts a conical shadow when the rays are perpendicular (or nearly so) to its axis, and fall on a parallel surface, and the great distance of the sun prevents the cone of shadow from a sphere being observed, unless it be so small that it can be held more than 110 times its diameter from the surface on which the shadow falls. As the distance is increased, the circular shadow diminishes to a point, and then vanishes.

strengthened by the divine power, to show that the sun is not greater than two climates, in order that they may learn in this manner not to arch their neck proudly, but to bow submissively to divine scripture.

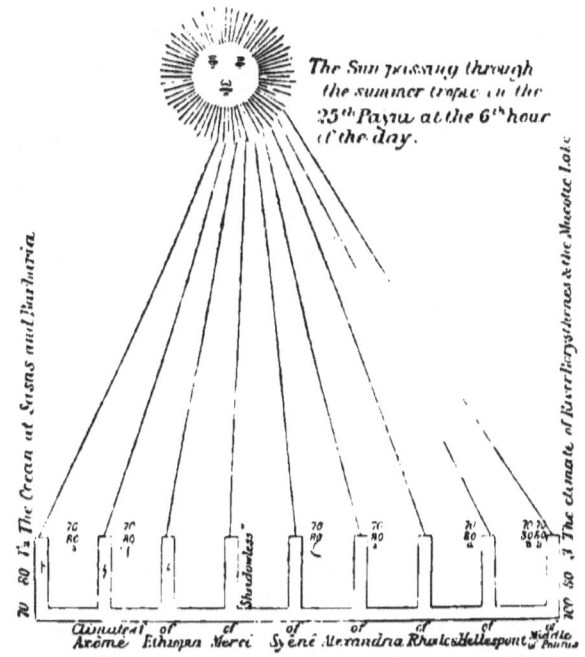

The straight (horizontal) line is the earth—the nine lines drawn perpendicular to it are so many bodies standing each of them for one of the climates. The lines drawn from the sun to these bodies are the rays of the sun which, falling simultaneously upon the bodies on this and that side, produce the shadows as we have depicted them in ink. That particular line which descends straight down, since it falls upon the top of the body perpendicularly, produces no shadow for it is greater than the body and shines all round it.

The Lord also bears me witness in the Gospels, when He calls the country of the Homerites, which is not more than a two days' sail by sea distant from Barbaria, the ends of the earth. It is evident again that I am right from the climates which they acknowledge, and from the places of which Ptolemy speaks, he who made war against Ethiopia, and of whom we made mention in the second book. And from the shadows themselves which are produced in each climate, it is proved that the sun does not exceed in size two climates, nay, even that the earth is flat, as the delineation shows, and not spherical.[1]

268 *A dissertation by which it is proved more clearly and comprehensively that, throughout the whole of divine scripture, we are taught that God has made two states—the present state and the future.*

First of all, it is proved from the account of the creation that God divided the one place which extends from the

---

[1] Cosmas is more plausible than lucid in his reasoning; his figure shows three climates from Syênê to Axômis, but possibly he meant to say between Syênê and Ethiopia. Taking the breadth of the two between Alexandria and Byzantium as about 635 geographical miles, this is his "size" of the sun. In order to appear with a diameter of about 33' of arc, its distance from the earth would be about 66,260 miles. But this is inconsistent with his argument from the length of the shadows. A gnomon 7 feet in height would cast a shadow of 11 inches at the summer solstice at Alexandria; of 1 foot $6\frac{1}{2}$ inches at Antioch; and of 2 feet 1 inch at the Hellespont, or 2 feet 2 inches at Byzantium; his measurements are, therefore, only approximate. But assuming them—that his gnomon was one of 7 feet, and that the earth were a plane, the sun's distance is easily deduced as about 4,400 miles, and his diameter as about 42 miles; a flat earth and a sun at a much greater distance than this would bring the shadows more near to the same length.

Cosmas was not the last to hold the theory of the earth being a plane. From 1848 to about 1865, Mr. S. Goulden, in various papers, propounded the doctrine that the earth is not a globe; he called his system Zetetic Astronomy. About 1865 was issued the prospectus of a book on the subject, in the contents of which was given "Distance of the Sun from London 4028 miles—How measured."—See De Morgan's *Budget of Paradoxes,* pp. 807-8.

earth to the first heaven, by placing in the middle the firmament, that is, the second heaven, thus making the one place into two places.

Secondly, it is proved from the very structure of man, inasmuch as he consists of two, namely, of mortal and immortal, evidently subjecting him through their contrariety to a life of conflict, in order that he may afterwards be honoured with gifts.

Thirdly, through the two trees which grew in the midst of Paradise, scripture shows that there are two states, one mortal and mutable, and one immortal and immutable. For the tree of the knowledge of good and evil is a type of this world as a school of discipline—and the tree of life is a type of the future state, in which neither death nor change has any power.

Fourthly, because the expulsion of the man from the Garden, by God, and his warning him and saying: *Lest he should stretch forth his hand and touch the tree of life and eat and live for ever*;[1] these are the words of one who imparts knowledge, and obscurely hints that some gift of life eternal is reserved for men after the life of conflict here.

Fifthly, again, we are taught through Lamech the father of Noah, who prophesied and said that his son would deliver us from toils and the curse, and would conduct us to the enjoyment of a better condition.

Sixthly, again, through this Noah we learn that from that first earth, all miserable and thorny, we were transferred to this earth, which we men now inhabit: an earth that is better, and almost equal to Paradise, whereby we are taught the difference between the first and the second state.

Seventhly, we learn that God chose Abraham out of the

---

[1] Gen. III. 22.

land of the Chaldaeans and transferred him to Palestine, and promised to give him great gifts and possession of the land, without giving him, however, so much of it as to set his foot on, according to divine scripture, and trained him to have faith, so that he knew to expect with confidence gifts to be bestowed afterwards. And in like manner He showed through Ishmael and Isaac the worth of the two covenants—namely, that one was servile, and the other free.

Eighthly, a second time through Isaac and Rebecca, when twins were born, it was said: *The elder shall serve the younger*,[1] thereby again showing there are two states, one of bondage and the other of freedom.

Ninthly, in the case again of Jacob and of Joseph, who could not bear to be buried in Egypt, but only in the Land of Promise, it was shown how each of them longed to obtain from God the hope which had been promised them—namely, of the second state.

Tenthly, the exodus itself in the time of Moses and the deliverance from the bondage of the Egyptians, and the freedom [thus obtained] and the entrance into the Land of Promise, accomplished through Joshua the son of Nun, clearly signified beforehand the two states.

Eleventhly, in like manner the construction of the Tabernacle and of the Temple, which, by means of the veil placed in the middle, was made from one into two—an inner and an outer—prefigured this state and the future state.

But what need is there that I should speak of the dispensations that existed through good men, for instance, the confidence Abel displayed after death, who yet speaketh, crying from the earth in bringing to birth the return of life.

If any reflects about the translation of Enoch, who

---

[1] Gen. xxv, 23.

because he pleased God, was translated that he should not see death, knows with the utmost certainty that there will be a better state, from an occurrence of this nature. Any one who is filled with astonishment, as he thinks of the ascension of Elijah and his passage in a chariot of fire, must see how much the nature of humankind has been honoured, as, it is thereby taught and has the hope, that it can pursue its way to heaven.

Any one who heard the multitudinous host of the heavenly ranks singing in chorus and rejoicing and exulting at the birth of our Lord Christ according to the flesh, and saying: *Glory to God in the highest, and on earth peace and good-will to men*,[1] would be astonished beyond measure as he reflected that the inhabitants of heaven and of earth had joined in making one confession, and that God was well pleased with men.

Any one who had seen the power of the resurrection from the death of our Lord and Saviour Jesus Christ would, with all his soul stirred up, celebrate without ceasing God the Saviour of all, who made the conflict of body and soul to cease, and brought into concord these two antagonistic parts of our nature, making them in things spiritual mutually conformable.

Any one who takes into view the ascension into Heaven of our Lord Christ, and the angels clothed in white raiment announcing to the Apostles his second coming, would never cease magnifying Jesus who showed and opened up to men the ascent into the future heavenly state, which He had prepared from the foundation of the world.

Any one who looks at the descent of the Holy Spirit upon the Apostles, and the speech of the great Peter in the midst of all the people, would in praying extol God

---

[1] Luke ii, 14.

the giver of all with loud praises, who gave such an earnest and pledge of the future state to men.

Any one who contemplates the calling of the great Paul made from heaven, and his being caught up into the third heaven, and again into Paradise, will lift up his voice to God and say: Glory be unto Thee who through all and unto all graciously givest gifts to men!

Any one who reads the writings of the company of the prophets and priests and righteous men, and also of the Apostles and Evangelists, and thinks of the miracles recorded by them, and of the prophecies and their exact fulfilment, will find that they make mention only of a first and a second state, and have not enumerated any others, as coming either before the first or after the second. Glory to God who spake and prophesied through them all, for ever and ever. Amen!

Any one who preserves deep in his heart remembrance of the second illustrious and glorious coming of our Lord and Saviour Christ, and who takes into mental account His blessed resurrection from the dead, and the change for the better which the world has undergone, and the unspeakable joy and hope laid up for men, will many a time beyond measure admire and extol in songs of praise the Cause of all, the Creator and Restorer of the universe. Yea, rather he will not be able in adequate terms to address Him, who is above all praise and glory and tribute of song, and who, in his supreme goodness from the beginning suitably for us, founded the two states, educating us in the first, and by instruction and reason teaching us to act prudently, and leading the human race and through it the whole creation into the second state. Glory to Thee, glory to Thee, glory to Thee, O thrice Holy, Creator, Maker of all and Restorer of the universe, for ever and ever. Amen!

By all these considerations the opinion of the Christians

is shown to be the best of all, and in accordance and harmony with the constitution of the world, and to be most true. It is in accordance with what those who are real and not pretended Christians acknowledge, that from the beginning God not unsuitably, but for apposite and useful ends, divided the one place into two places, preparing and making ready beforehand this place for this present state, and that other place for the future state. The Pagans accordingly, who suppose the world to be eternal, and deny the resurrection of our bodies and their ascension into heaven, looking upon this as foolishness, are properly, in view of their theory, deprived of future honours and of the ascension into heaven. The Jews, who read Moses and the prophets and understood not the great and wise dispensation of God, which through the prophets shows that from the beginning God made two states for the benefit of men, and who did not receive the Prince of the second state—nay, He proved even a stumbling-block to them; nor, even until now do they believe that there will be an ascension of men into heaven, but they expect, forsooth, one to come whom they call the Anointed, and who, they hope, will reign over their country, and subject to Himself all the nations, and make no account at all of things heavenly. They thus reject the counsel of God and think that the habitation in the heavens has been prepared without occasion, which Moses, however, shows to have been made not without occasion, saying that it was made on the second day, and that the firmament was placed in the middle, and that two places came to exist; and they themselves also are excluded from this habitation. The Samaritans in like manner, being ignorant of the same things as the Jews, and not believing, and entertaining doubts besides, about the resurrection of the body and the immortality of the soul, are also like the Jews banished

S

from the habitation in the heavens. The Manichaeans,[1] holding the same opinions as the Pagans, and supposing also the heaven to be spherical, and expecting the utter destruction of the body, these, along with their evil deity whom they elected for themselves about the earth, are condemned and driven away from the City above, which they denied. In like manner, every heresy which denies the perfect humanity of Christ, namely, a rational soul endowed with intellect, and a body, and which does not acknowledge all the distinctive qualities of the soul and of the body, but wavers in doubt; and the heresy which denies the divinity of Christ and impairs it, and which says that either He or the Holy Spirit is inferior to the Father,[2] all these fail to attain the heavenly mansions.

Blessed then are all those who, through the divine scriptures of the Old and New Testament, recognize the Maker of all things as one God in three Persons, namely Father and Son and Holy Spirit, a holy Trinity, consubstantial, equal in power, in strength, in glory and in honour, and without beginning, and who also recognize the great and wise and omnipotent dispensation of Him who is the Cause of all things; how wisely and harmoniously He established the two states from the beginning—the present state and the future—and through the perfect humanity of Christ who is like to us in all things both in body and soul, sin only excepted, and who sojourned among men in the last times when He declared and showed the future state, and gave assurance unto all by raising up that humanity from the dead. All the perfect therefore

---

[1] Manes, or Manichaeus, their founder, appeared about the year 270 A.D. The sect spread chiefly in Persia, Arabia, Egypt, and other parts of the East. St. Augustine at the age of twenty became a Manichaean, and continued to be one for nine years. See note 1, v. 242.   [2] The Arians.

who walk by this rule, peace be upon them and mercy, and at the judgment of God these shall of right hear Christ the Lord in the future state saying unto them from heaven: *Come, ye blessed of my Father, inherit the Kingdom prepared for you from the foundation of the world.*[1] To Him be glory for ever and ever. Amen!

The whole scope accordingly of the divine economy is this—for we must briefly recapitulate what that scope is—God of His goodness willed to let others participate in existence, and power, and reason, and knowledge, but, because those who participate in these cannot possibly know and possess all things in combination (for this belongs to God alone, to know all these things without learning and experience, being of Himself both power and reason and knowledge, while created beings participate in all these things from their Maker), He made those two states together, the first mortal and mutable, for the trial and discipline of rational beings, in order that, being exercised by the variety of the universe and the juxtaposition of contraries, we might have experience of pleasures and pains; then the second state, an immortal and immutable enjoyment of His gracious goodness, to the end that, from our acquired power of discernment, we may receive possession of the pleasures. To Him be glory for ever and ever. Amen!

No religion therefore, neither the Judaic, nor the Samaritan, nor the Pagan, nor the Manichæan, believes or hopes that there is a resurrection or an ascension into heaven for men; but such of these religions as think that heaven is a sphere, namely the Pagan and the Manichæan, are consistent with themselves in holding their unbelief. For, where are they able to find a place in the sphere for the kingdom of heaven? They are both of them there-

---

[1] Matt. xxv, 34.

fore justified in denying the resurrection of the body, and in saying that souls only are glorified or punished after the life here—or in saying, as some of them do, that souls are whirled round along with the sphere and see all things, or are condemned to be cast into Tartarus. Some of them even hold that souls are transmigrated into other bodies, while others deny the soul's immortality, and not one of them possesses any hope of the body after the present life. But those religions which do not believe in a sphere, namely the Jews and Samaritans, but think that the firmament, which is in the middle of the one place and thus makes two places, was made without occasion, these also, it necessarily follows, have fallen under the sway of unbelief; for the Samaritans acknowledge neither a resurrection nor an ascension into heaven, nor admit that the soul is immortal, but think that our race will continue for ever, while the Jews acknowledge a resurrection for men, but say that we shall live upon the earth and eat and drink and marry and be given in marriage, as, in the Gospels, the Sadducees proposed a question to the Lord, saying: *In the resurrection of which of the seven shall she be the wife?*[1] These the Lord very summarily convicted of error and of not knowing divine scripture, in which there is the power of God, saying to them: *For, in the resurrection, they neither marry, nor are given in marriage, but are as the angels of God in heaven.*[2] It is therefore proved against these, both from what is written and from the figure of the world prepared from its foundation, that the upper place was not made without occasion—but that there is a second heavenly state prepared from the foundation of the world. And, in like manner, every heresy among the Christians can be refuted; those also among the Pagans, the Manichaeans for instance, which suppose the

---

[1] Matt. xxii, 28.   [2] *Ibid.*, 30.

heaven to be a sphere, or those which embrace the theory of an antecedent life, or those which deny that in Christ there was aught of our nature, either body or soul or intellect, do greatly err, neither knowing the scriptures nor the power of God. For those only are perfect Christians who without error follow divine scripture, and who know, both from what is written and from the figure of the first and second state, the places and the figures which divine scripture mentions, for as this world consists of men and angels: *We*, saith the Apostle, *are made a spectacle to the world, to angels and to men*,[1] so also the higher place again has been prepared beforehand for angels and men. Glory for all to God the King of the Ages. Amen!

The heaven is bound together with the earth, and is divided into parts, for as it forms the two vaulted chambers and the two walls on each side, and after the manner of vaulted chambers has one of these walls curving round till it joins the other, and completes the entire figure (τὸ σχῆμα) of the world. And this figure, that is, the

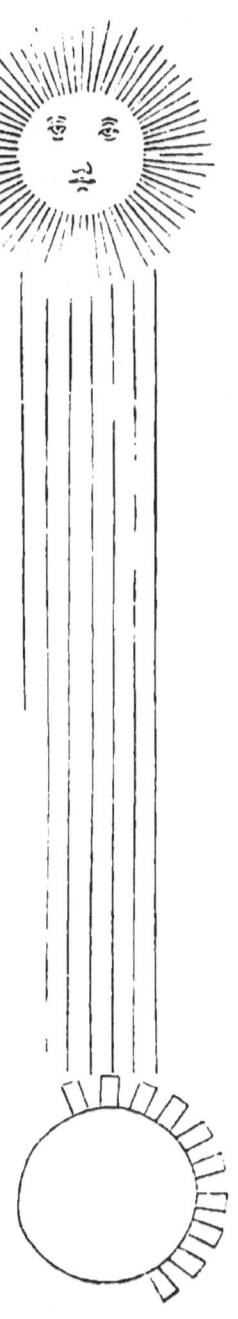

[1] I Cor. iv. 9.

magnitude of the sun and of the earth, we here delineate[1] in accordance with the views of those pagans, in order that any one who sees the two delineations may be able to compare the one with the other, how that in the delineation, which represents our view[2] in accordance with the reality, the rays of the sun falling upon bodies produce shadows for each climate agreeably to our previous description, these shadows showing a difference of half a foot for each climate—and how also that in the delineation here which represents their views, the rays do not fall upon the bodies, so that those climates which they speak of, bodies namely, cannot be illumined by the sun; and hence we see that they turn away from the truth and make a great boast in vain about their fables.

[1] See preceding page.   [2] See above, p. 251.

BOOK VII.

Concerning the Duration of the Heavens.[1]

 WILL not refuse, O most studious Athanasius, to comply with your request, that I should compose a discourse on heaven; but, for the sake of clearness, I shall first enquire whether divine scripture pronounces it to be indissoluble or dissoluble, for you have informed me that one of those who glory in being Christians, when wishing to speak against the Pagans, unconsciously agreed with them in their opinion, that heaven is a sphere which is always revolving; and yet that in the same work he proclaimed it to be dissoluble. I know not what induced him to make this assertion, and I could not but wonder that the wisdom of a man of so great learning should be blinded by his craving for distinction. For if, as a Christian, he had in view to refute the view of the Pagans, he ought first to have overthrown from the foundation their principles relating to the sphere and its revolution, just as we ourselves, by the will of God, have done in the other work, which as requested we composed. But if he admits their foundation and their principles, from which their demonstrations of eternal duration proceed, why does that wise man indulge to no

---

[1] "The Vatican Codex has Χριστίνου περὶ διαμονῆς, where we should, I think, read Χριστιανῷ"—Montfaucon. This reading would mean "To the Christian concerning duration".

purpose in idle talk, basing his nonsense not on a rock, but upon the sand? For no man of common sense would assert that what is in perpetual motion is corruptible and dissoluble, or that what is corruptible and dissoluble is in perpetual motion, but would admit that what is in perpetual motion is, in virtue of such motion, incorruptible, but that what is not in motion and dissoluble, is beyond question corruptible, because, by ceasing to move, it is not in perpetual motion. How then does that man who is so very learned, while admitting that the heaven is in perpetual motion, though divine scripture judges otherwise, determine it to be dissoluble? For among the philosophers whether of old or late times who are the most celebrated among the pagans, and have been of opinion that the heaven is a sphere, has he found one affirming that it is dissoluble? It is the fact rather that all of them, proceeding on the illative method, have declared it to be indissoluble. This man, observe, invents new absurdities, and neither following the teaching of those outside the Church, nor submissively accepting the spiritual tradition of those within her pale, but ignorant both of the diversity of the doctrines of the Pagans, and of the pure and simple learning of those within the Church, has taken in hand to teach new doctrines without previous examination, and without taking into account that his own statements are in mutual conflict, and without thinking of the questions to which they give rise; just as an inexperienced traveller, who has strayed from the highway, is cruelly pierced[1] and torn by thorns and briars and the points of jagged rocks, on whichsoever side he turns; so this admirable man, being wounded when taking his way into the enemy's country, is easily overthrown.

---

[1] Gr. ἀδύνη περιπείρεται, which Montfaucon renders inadequately by *anxius versatur*.

Wherefore, O Christ-loving! I deemed it sufficient that you, on reading our little treatise (for we must speak humbly of what we have done), namely, the *Christian Topography of the whole world*, should see how that in the first book we used arguments drawn from the natural world, against those, who, while seeming to be Christians, nevertheless supposed heaven to be a sphere—that in the second, we have exhibited the Christian theories concerning the figure and position of the whole world from divine scripture; that in the third we have shown how firm and sure, and how worthy of belief is divine scripture, and of what utility figures of the whole world are; that in the fourth we have given a summary recapitulation together with a drawing of the Tabernacle prepared by Moses, and shown also the harmony of the Prophets and Apostles; and that in the sixth we have treated of the size of the sun, and have thus brought our little work to its completion. Nevertheless I again, at the earnest desire and request of your Reverence, which, as has been said, I cannot disregard, will endeavour, agreeably to your command and to the best of my ability, to confute briefly from divine scripture those who hold that the heavens will perish, and, with the help of divine grace and your prayers, to prove their permanency. We shall state first, what forms of speech divine scripture employs when treating of heaven, and then shall show that it everywhere decides that the heavens are indissoluble.

Since the Old Testament was written for the Hebrews, it follows of necessity that it was written in the Hebrew tongue and in Hebrew characters. The Hebrew tongue then uses similarly the expressions, *the heaven* and *the heavens*, so that there is no difference between them, but the singular form is employed for the plural, and the plural for the singular, as when it says: *Praise him, ye heavens of the heavens*— instead of saying heaven of heaven—and adds: *And the water which is above the heavens*[1]—that is: this visible heaven—namely, the firmament—for the waters are above the firmament only, according to the sacred historian Moses. In like manner it says: *The heavens declare the glory of God, and the firmament showeth forth the work of his hands*[2]—here beginning with the plural number and ending with the singular—in order that by each form of expression it may indicate the same thing, that the very sight of the heaven, that is, of the firmament which we see, proclaims both the glory and the handiwork of God, through the order and magnificence which they display. In like manner again: *The heaven of heaven to the Lord, but the earth hath he given to the sons of men*,[3] here calling the first and higher heaven which is the heaven to this visible heaven, and which is placed above it—the heaven of heaven. In like manner again the great Moses says: *Behold the heaven of the Lord thy God, and the heaven of heaven;* as if he said: this heaven visible to us, and its heaven, that is, the heaven above it. Paul also uses this form of expression, exclaiming: *But our citizenship is in the heavens, from which also we look for a Saviour*,[4] here beginning with the plural number but ending with the singular, for instead of saying *from which* in the plural, he says *from which* in the singular.[5] For as two heavens were made by God, as the blessed Moses relates, and the two were bound together, sacred scripture speaks of them sometimes in the plural number and sometimes in the singular, in accordance, as has been said, with the idiom of the language, or even because the heavens at some of their parts are mutually conjoined and so become as one, as has been said.

Lest therefore you should be led into error when you

---

[1] Psalm cxlviii, 4. [2] Psalm xix, 1. [3] Psalm cxv, 16.
[4] Philipp. iii, 20. [5] Gr. ἐν οὐρανοῖς, ἐξ οὗ. Οὗ used for ὧν.

hear that the blessed Paul had been caught up into the third heaven, I must point out that there are not three or more heavens, and that he neither means to say this, nor contradicts Moses—but he means to say that he was caught up from the earth all the distance to the height of heaven except a third of it—as if he said: I was caught up from the earth so very far that there was left to me but a third of the distance to the height of heaven.[1] Such being the case it is now time for us to remark that divine scripture all throughout proclaims that heaven or the heavens are indissoluble. The Apostle Paul, then, speaks to this effect: *For we know that if the earthly house of our Tabernacle be dissolved, we have a building from God, a house not made with hands, in the heavens,*[2] in order that he may show that the earthly state here shall be dissolved, but that the future state, which is also a heavenly, is indissoluble and eternal. And again he says: *We have such a high priest, who sat down on the right hand of the throne of the Majesty in the heavens, a minister of the sanctuary, and of the true Tabernacle which the Lord pitched and not man*[3]—as if he said: the Lord Christ had been taken up into the heavens, into the true Tabernacle, that is, one which is permanent and indissoluble. For the expression *true* indicates that it is indissoluble, since that which was prepared by Moses was dissolved; this one as being indissoluble, by way of distinction and in contrast with the other, he calls the *true*—as being permanent and firm and indissoluble. And again he says: *But Christ having come a high priest of the good things to come, through the greater and more perfect Tabernacle, not made with hands, that is to say, not of this creation, nor yet through the blood of goats and calves, but through his own body, entered in once for all into the holy place, having obtained*

---

[1] See note 3, p. 116.   [2] II Cor. v, 1.   [3] Heb. viii, 1.

eternal redemption.[1] What he means is something like this: Since God commanded Moses to make the Tabernacle in imitation of the whole world, and he made it, dividing it by the veil in the middle, thus converting the one Tabernacle into two, an outer and an inner, thereby hinting, as it were, at this place, and at that which is above it—*And into the first Tabernacle the priests always enter, accomplishing the services, but into the second, the high priest alone, and but once a year enters, not without blood, which he offers for himself and for the people.*[2]

Wherefore the Apostle Paul says that *Christ having come as high priest* of the heavens, entered into the higher place with his own blood, just as the earthly high priest entered into the inner tabernacle with the blood of others; and just as the Tabernacle here is small and made with hands, and, as being but a type, is imperfect and dissoluble, so the heavenly is great, and not made with hands, and is steadfast and true and eternal and indissoluble, and in it is the eternal redemption. For the high priest being eternal, of necessity the salvation also and the Tabernacle are eternal, in accordance again with what is written: *And they indeed are many priests, because that by death they are hindered from continuing: but he, because he abideth for ever, hath his priesthood unchangeable. Wherefore also, he is able to save to the uttermost them that draw near unto God through him, seeing that he always liveth to make intercession for them. For such a high priest became us, holy, guileless, undefiled, separated from sinners, and made higher than the heavens.*[3] The expression *higher than the heavens* means, according to the idiom of the language, heaven; and, more clearly still, the expressions ἀπαράβατον (unchangeable), and τὸ μένειν εἰς τὸν αἰῶνα (the abiding for ever), and πάντοτε (always) indicate a state of things that

---

[1] Heb. ix, 11, 12.   [2] *Ibid.*, 6, 7.   [3] Heb. vii, 23-26.

is indissoluble. For if the priest is unchangeable, the Tabernacle also, wherein he exercises his office, must of necessity be unchangeable, that is, exempt from succession. And elsewhere again he says: *Wherefore we, receiving a kingdom which cannot be shaken*,[1] as if he said, one that is abiding and immovable and indissoluble and not liable to succession. And again he says: *Let us give diligence to enter into that rest;*[2] calling it a *rest* as not admitting of succession, and because when we are there, we shall not be transferred thence, but shall for ever rest in heaven itself. And again he says: *Having therefore a great high priest who hath passed through the heavens, Jesus the Son of God, let us hold fast our confession*[3]—the expression *who hath passed through the heavens*, that is *heaven*, according to the idiom of the language, means that He is within the two heavens, as in a Tabernacle not made with hands. And again he says: *Having therefore boldness to enter into the holy place by the blood of Jesus, by the way which he dedicated for us, a new and living way;*[4] the entrance into the Holies made by the blood of Jesus, he calls His entrance into the heavens, which He made after his Passion and Resurrection, when He was taken up into heaven; which also he calls a new and living way, dedicated for us, because He himself first of all in a new and fresh manner trod that living and holy way, leaving us an example for us to follow. And again he says: *And every priest indeed standeth day by day ministering and offering oftentimes the same sacrifices, the which can never take away sins; but this man, when he had offered one sacrifice for sins, for ever set down on the right hand of God, from henceforth expecting till his enemies be made the footstool of his feet. For by one offering he hath perfected them that are sanctified.*[5] If, as He says, he sits for ever at

---

[1] Heb. xii, 28. [2] Heb. iv, 11. [3] Heb. iv, 14.
[4] Heb. x, 19, 20. [5] *Ibid.*, 11-14.

the right hand of God after His Passion and Sacrifice, and for ever sanctifies those coming unto Him, how is it possible that heaven can be dissolved when He sits there for ever, and those coming unto Him are sanctified. And again he says: *For it is evident that our Lord sprang out of Judah, as to which tribe Moses spake nothing concerning priesthood;*[1] and again: *For it is testified of him, Thou art a priest for ever after the order of Melchisedec.*[2] Behold how in the clearest terms he speaks of Christ as a perpetual priest in virtue of His power and indissoluble life. How then is it possible for the Priest to be indissoluble whilst the Tabernacle, of which He is the minister, is subject to be dissolved? For he says: *A minister of the sanctuary and of the true Tabernacle which the Lord pitched and not man,*[3] thus here, as also in Heb. vi, 16, 17, and 20, and x, 34, expressly declaring it to be true and indissoluble.

See again, admirable Sir, how he speaks of that entrance into what is within the veil, that is, the firmament, into which Jesus entered, and into which we shall enter, that he declares it to be immovable and strong, and secure and steadfast, and abiding and eternal, and like an anchor holding us fast; and again he says: *For we have here no abiding city, but we seek that which is to come,*[4] meaning: We seek that ever-abiding and eternal heavenly Jerusalem, which is free and the mother of all the faithful, for, the one which is here is, he says, in dissolution, according to that which hath been said [in I Cor. vii, 31, and Coloss. iii, 1]. I have told you, Paul there says, the things that are above where Christ is now seated; seek therefore the things that are there, not the things here. But that he calls the city *prepared already*, you may learn again from Paul [Heb. xi, 16] and from Christ himself [Matt. xxv, 34]. And when

---

[1] Heb. vii, 14. [2] *Ibid.*, 17.
[3] Heb. viii, 2. [4] Heb. xiii, 14.

was the kingdom of which he there speaks prepared? From the foundation of the world, he tells us, as if he said, from the time at the beginning of the creation, along with the making of the heaven and the earth and the things produced along with them, the place of the kingdom of heaven was prepared, God having provided something better for us. For He says again further in the Gospel according to John: *In my Father's house are many mansions; if it were not so I would have told you. I go to prepare a place for you.*[1] He calls the habitation which is in the heavens, His Father's house. In this then, He says, is your habitation, which has been prepared for you by my Father. Then again He says: *And if I go and prepare a place for you, I will come again and take you unto myself that where I am there ye may be also. And whither I go ye know, and the way ye know.*[2] And again to the mother of James and John, who asked that the one of them should sit at His right hand and the other on the left in His kingdom, He answered, saying: *It is not mine to give, but for whom it has been prepared by my Father.*[3] Those that are worthy, therefore, shall obtain these things before I bestow them whether on your sons or on others that are worthy. But the expression *that where I am there ye may be also*, shows very remarkably that that place is indissoluble, and has been aforetime prepared, and not that another place is substituted (as those wise men imagine), in which we are to dwell after the resurrection, when this place of the heavens shall have been dissolved. And to speak briefly, the passages in divine scripture are almost innumerable which show that the heaven, into which Christ has entered and into which we also shall enter, is indissoluble.

And these things the Lord proclaimed to his disciples; but the Apostle Paul wrote to such of the Hebrews

---

[1] John xiv, 2. [2] *Ibid.*, 3. [3] Matt. xx, 23.

as believed in Christ, pointing out, as was suitable for them, the proper distinctions between all the things relating to the Tabernacle, both to the outer which has reference to this place, and to the inner which has reference to the upper and heavenly place. But to those from among the Pagans who believed, the Corinthians, I mean, men who cultivated learning and philosophy, and who already believed in the resurrection of Christ, but were in doubt concerning the resurrection of men in general, to them again he used the same arguments, and says: *Now, if Christ is preached that he hath been raised from the dead, how say some among you that there is no resurrection of the dead, neither hath Christ been raised? and if Christ hath not been raised, then is our preaching vain and your faith also is vain;*[1] as if he said: Your faith in Christ is of no use to you, unless our resurrection also is believed by you. For if ye have believed of one that he was raised from the dead, how is it not to be believed that it is possible for all others besides to be raised? For he that can raise one can also raise all. Then he observes: *Yea, and we are found false witnesses of God, because we have testified of God that he raised up Christ whom he raised not up, if so be the dead are not raised.*[2] But we, he says, who have testified unto you that God raised up Christ shall be found to be liars and impostors. And again he repeats this: *For if the dead rise not, neither hath Christ risen, but if Christ hath not risen, your faith is vain—ye are yet in your sins;*[3] from that which was confessed and believed in by them, he confutes them and says: for if He, concerning whom you have believed, when He was dead rose again, why do you doubt the resurrection of the other dead, so that you make it appear that you have believed in vain about the resurrection of but one. For he, who is able to

---

[1] I Cor. xv, 12, 13.   [2] *Ibid.*, 15.   [3] *Ibid.*, 16, 17.

raise one of the dead, is able also to raise all the others that are dead. So that by not believing in the resurrection of the dead, you revert to your former superstition, and have fallen away, for this he means by saying: *Ye are yet in your sins.*[1]

Then a little after he states also the reason saying: *For since by man came death, by man also came the resurrection.*[2] And by way of showing who the first man was by whom death was introduced, he adds; *For as in Adam all die, so in Christ shall all be made alive.*[3] Then shortly afterwards he says: *Else what shall they do which are baptized for the dead?*[4] *If the dead are not raised at all, why then are they baptized for the dead? Why do we also stand in jeopardy every hour?*[5] As if he said: Since we are baptized mystically for our dead bodies, being submerged in the holy water and emerging therefrom, thus imitating death and resurrection, from the hope and promise of the resurrection from the dead, why, he says, do we perform these acts in vain by not walking in accordance with them? And why, besides, do we stand in jeopardy every hour, proclaiming these things to so great a multitude, and fighting against the prejudices which prevail in the world? And further he endeavours again shortly afterwards by an antithesis[6] and an example taken from the natural world to persuade them on the point and says: *But some one will say, How are the dead*

---

[1] I Cor. xv, 17.   [2] *Ibid.*, 21.   [3] *Ibid.*, 22.

[4] Gr. οἱ βαπτιζόμενοι ὑπὲρ τῶν νεκρῶν. This expression is still generally taken in the sense in which Cosmas, as he shows below, understood it. It has, however, been supposed that Paul is referring to a practice in the early Church, according to which Christians underwent baptism on behalf of friends who had died in the faith, but before the rite had been administered to them. St. Chrysostom, in commenting on the passage, notices that this practice existed among the Marcionites.

[5] I Cor. xv, 29, 30.

[6] The antithesis between the grain and the plant.

raised? and with what body do they come? To that he has, be sure, an answer: *Thou fool!* he says, *that which thou sowest is not quickened, unless it die, and that which thou sowest, thou sowest not the body that shall be, but a bare grain, it may chance of wheat or of some other kind; but God giveth it a body even as it hath pleased him, and to each seed a body of its own.*[1] What he says is this: Consider, O men, that the bare grain when sown in the earth, in the first place undergoes dissolution, for if this, he says, first dies, it then grows up by the power and providence of God, and reappears richly endowed, artfully contrived and exceeding beautiful; instead of one grain, a great number, instead of being bare, enfolded in a sheath, instead of being easily plucked up and trodden underfoot, firmly rooted and aided by having ears to keep it safe from all that could do it harm. This very body then which has been corrupted and changed into earth, and again sprouts up from the earth multiplied and of an admirable beauty, is a work full of wisdom and art, and most fair to see—a product of the providence of God by whom all things were made.

Consider then that God gives it a body as it pleases Him, and gives to each of the seeds its own body, suitable for it; as if he said: When multiplying seeds God gives to each neither an alien nor a strange body, but a body similar and suitable to it. Then again, after having compared different kinds of flesh, and bodies earthly and heavenly, and shown that a great difference exists between them, he goes on to say: *So also is the resurrection of the dead. It is sown in corruption, it is raised in incorruption; it is sown in dishonour, it is raised in glory; it is sown in weakness, it is raised in power,*[2] and so forth. Then again he says: *But this I say, brethren, that flesh and blood cannot inherit the Kingdom of God, neither doth corruption inherit incorruption.*[3] Having

---

[1] 1 Cor. xv, 35-38.   [2] *Ibid.*, 42.   [3] *Ibid.*, 50.

here recourse to arguments from analogies in the natural world, he endeavours to convince of this those conversant with the wisdom of the world, and from the example about grain turns to the resurrection of the dead, saying: Just as corn is sown and is dissolved, so also the bodies of men, when planted as corpses in the earth, are dissolved; and just as the grain sprouts up with large increase, stability and beauty, so also the bodies of men are raised up with great honour and glory and power and beauty unspeakable, being discriminated by the omnipotent wisdom and ineffable might of God, who made and who renovates all things. For whatever be the element by which the human body may be found to have been absorbed and digested, He will at the last day restore to their proper souls their own particles, shaken after a thorough search out of countless other bodies. And just as in a sieve that which is sought for is found in the sieve's centre, so also with respect to the bodies of men, after the elements have been tossed and shaken, their particles that are sought for are brought together to the centre. Nor is this a wonderful thing for God to do; for as He is judge of the hearts and thoughts and intents of men, and discerns, from the beginning of time till the final consummation, the thoughts and intents of every man at each particular time, so He is able to do what is easier, namely, to discriminate one body from another: *For*, saith He, *yet once more I shake not the earth only, but also the heaven.*[1] *And this word " once more" signifieth the removing of those things that are shaken as of things that have been made, that those things that are not shaken may remain;*[2] as if He said: In the consummation I will shake yet once more all things, and throw them into commotion, in order that all things may be changed back into their proper state. For as these things have been made from

---

[1] Hagg. ii, 7.   [2] Heb. xii, 27.

the beginning, and have undergone corruption or change, I shall easily remodel everything into its proper nature, that they may thereafter remain in a better state and be no longer subjected to commotion and shaking.

But again some one will ask, how are our bodies raised the same, after having been already absorbed and changed into myriads of other bodies? To this we shall reply that just as when we are children we eat many kinds of flesh, of oxen and swine, for instance, and various others, also of fowl and fish, and these, when digested add to the size of our body without its being changed or transmuted from one thing into another, but still maintaining its identity, so also in the resurrection, when we are in the opposite state, and our bodies have been dissolved in the elements, you will see their forms by some kind of motion easily restored when separated by the divine power. For just as while we are living, our bodies, as God hath appointed, are not changed by their association with other bodies, so also when we die they are preserved from a transmutation into anything else, being readily kept distinct by His power. And again, admirable Sir, see how the Apostle speaks of heavenly and of earthly men: *And as we have borne*, he says, *the image of the earthly*, that is, the mortality and infirmity and corruption of Adam, *we shall bear also the image of the heavenly*,[1] that is, of Him who hath already gone before and ascended into heaven after the resurrection from the dead. I speak of Christ according to the flesh, who has become powerful and incorruptible and immortal and glorified, and we in like manner have, with Him, become heavenly. And after having said *we have borne*, well does he say, as if speaking next of the future, *we shall bear*; wherefore he again with joy and exultation adds: *But when this corruptible shall*

---

[1] I Cor. xv, 49.

have put on incorruption, and this mortal shall have put on immortality, then shall be brought to pass the saying that is written, Death is swallowed up in Victory. Where, O Death, is thy sting?[1] As if he said: Death being swallowed up shall disappear, life in us having become more than victorious. Wherefore let us exclaim: Where, O Death, is thy overweening pride? And where, O Hades, thy strength? Finally, he ascribes to God all things that have been procured and dispensed through Christ and says: *Thanks be unto God who has given us the victory through our Lord Jesus Christ;* as if he said: This victory over death accomplished by Jesus Christ hath He given unto us, He who is the God of all, to whom it becomes us to give glory and thanks for ever, Amen! And he wrote nothing to the Corinthians different from what he had written to the believers among the Jews: that we pass from this perishable state into that which is to come, that is, into the heavenly place, which he calls the kingdom of heaven, as if we had sovereign power over our passions[2] and corruption and death, and lived in a place most choice, eternal, and adapted to our nature, and where after being transformed from corruption to incorruption we have our heritage.

For the Apostle, as already quoted, has signified this in the example of the grain of wheat, wherein he uses the example of what is corruptible towards the illustration of incorruption, saying: Do not think that, in examples, the things compared are in all points similar, for, this I say unto you, that it is impossible for us being mortal and mutable (for it is this he means by blood and flesh) to inherit the kingdom of heaven, unless we first rise from the dead incorruptible and immortal and immutable. Yea, the

---

[1] I Cor. xv, 54, 55.
[2] Gr. τῶν παθῶν. "sufferings"? Montfaucon renders *mortos animi*.

Lord also used the same example when some of the Greeks requested Philip to show them Jesus, and Philip told the Lord their request, who answered saying: *Except a grain of wheat fall into the earth and die, it abideth by itself alone, but if it die, it beareth much fruit;*[1] as if he said: Why do they wish to see me now, when I am despicable in appearance and alone, like a grain of wheat; for except I die like a grain, and rise up like the wheat in ear and in the fulness of its bloom, having become incorruptible and immortal and immutable, and except mighty deeds and wonders shall be wrought in My name, they will not know My power and glory. In like manner also when John the Baptist was discoursing concerning the Lord, and was eager to show that in the future state He would be Judge of all, he also used the example about wheat and spake thus: *Whose fan is in his hand and he will thoroughly cleanse his threshing-floor; and he will gather the wheat into his garner, but the chaff he will burn up with unquenchable fire.*[2] And when Paul was addressing the Greeks themselves in Athens on the Areopagus [Acts xvii, 22-31], he said nothing to his hearers other than what he had said before to such of the Jews and the Pagans as believed, namely, that God, since He is uncircumscribed and omnipotent, will judge the world in righteousness by that man whom He raised from the dead, in order to give assurance unto all men, having appointed Him Judge of all.

The Apostle in like manner said concerning Him: *And he made him sit at his right hand;*[3] and John the Baptist in like manner said: *His fan is in his hand and he will sift the wheat from the chaff,*[2] giving over sinners to punishment when separated like chaff from the wheat. Accordingly some of them believed, as has been recorded, but some hearing of the resurrection of the dead mocked, and some

---

[1] John xii, 24.   [2] Matt. iii, 12.   [3] Heb. viii, 1.

again said: What does this picker-up of seeds[1] mean to say? as if they said: he is digging up the seeds we sowed; while others said: *We will hear thee again about this matter,* and others again: *He seemeth to be a setter forth of strange gods, because,* says Luke, *he preached Jesus and the resurrection;* and others again: *May we know what is this new doctrine which thou teachest?* In short, most of them derided Paul when discoursing about the resurrection of the dead. But when Paul was further accused by the Jews before Festus the Governor, and Agrippa the King, and stood on the tribunal, Festus, by way of explaining the nature of what had already been done in the case, said to Agrippa: *They have certain questions against each other of their own religion, and of one Jesus who was dead whom Paul affirmed[2] to be alive.*[3] Then Paul having received their permission to speak, in accents clear and loud, boldly entered on his defence [for which see Acts xxvi, 6-8 and 21-23]. And in like terms again he addressed the unbelieving Jews in Antioch of Pisidia, when he had been granted permission to speak [see Acts xiii, 16-41]. And having expounded things similar to these from the prophets, he said to them nothing else than what he had spoken of before, death, resurrection and the kingdom of heaven, being eager to persuade all men, God assisting him with signs and wonders and mighty works, which both Paul and all the Apostles wrought in presence both of the Pagans and the Jews, whether they were believers or unbelievers. God further,

---

[1] Cosmas uses the word σπερμολόγος here in its primitive sense. Montfaucon, however, translates it, according to its secondary meaning, by *verbi sator*, "a babbler", but the context shows this interpretation to be here inadmissible.

[2] Gr. ἔφασκε. By the use of this particular term the speaker implied that he had doubts as to whether Paul really believed that Jesus was alive. He might be *pretending.*

[3] Acts xxv, 19.

by prophecies and their fulfilment, confirmed them in all things which transcend this world. At the same time also *He made them*, as Paul writes, *sufficient as ministers of a new covenant, not of the letter, but of the spirit: for the letter killeth but the spirit giveth life;*[1] as if he said: We have been made sufficient by God by means of signs and of the Holy Spirit, while teaching such things, to persuade those who hear us ; for God hath appointed us ministers of the new and life-giving covenant, not of the old letter, that is, of the written law which threatens death, but of the life-giving power, that is, of the Holy Spirit. Wherefore, again he says: *Now some are puffed up, as though I were not coming to you. But I will come to you shortly, if the Lord will; and I will know not the word of them which are puffed up, but the power. For the kingdom of God is not in word but in power;*[2] as if he said that the word of the kingdom of heaven surpasses all words, and that some are in vain puffed up while endeavouring to establish themselves by word. For that word only, which comes from the power of the Holy Spirit and from the signs which accompany it, merits belief.

And again he says : *Seeing that ye seek a proof of Christ that speaketh in me; who to youward is not weak, but is powerful in you;*[3] as if he said : It is powerful from the signs that are wrought in you in His name—and so much on these points. Some, however, assert that the angels are not in the world, but that they are in the higher place above, against whom in turn we shall quote a few words from divine scripture, showing that the angels spend their time along with us in our place here, and that as yet not one of them has been privileged to obtain the things above. The Lord, then, first thus addresses Nicodemus: *And no one hath ascended into heaven, but he that descended*

---

[1] II Cor. iii, 6.   [2] I Cor. iv, 18, 19.   [3] II Cor. xiii, 3.

out of heaven, even the Son of Man which is in heaven[1]—thus very clearly showing that no one at all had ascended into the upper place except the Lord Christ Himself. Then the Apostle Paul says: *We have been made a spectacle to the world,* and to show whom he means by the world, he adds: *to angels and men,* as if he said: We are seen by all as in a theatre in this place, and by *all* I mean angels and men, as both these and those are in one place. Then again he says: *For the earnest expectation of the creation waiteth for the revealing of the sons of God;*[2] and, as if some one was uncertain as to his meaning and asked him: For the sake of what or by doing what, does the creation await this? he proceeds and says: *because the creation was subjected to vanity not willingly;* as if he said: in this corruptible and mutable world. For this he calls vanity—when creatures by the command of God were ordered to serve even against their will. Whence we learn by the expression *not willingly* that he is speaking of rational beings, and this is the law laid down for them. Should some one, he then says, put the question, And how again shall they serve, they who now move all things? They do serve, he replies, but as far as concerns the sin of Adam through which he was condemned to death, they could not endure to serve longer and toil in vain on our behalf. But I say this, he adds, on account of him who hath subjected them in hope, this namely, that God has given them a hope that some good will result to men in the course of time, and for this reason they were subjected, and do render service in expectation of their freedom, when men also are freed from death and corruption and these vanities, and shall receive the hope of God, and the glory which is reserved for them. Accordingly he adds: *Because the creation itself shall be delivered from bondage into the liberty of the glory*

---

[1] John iii, 13.   [2] Rom. viii, 19.

of the sons of God[1] and again he says elsewhere: *Are they not all ministering spirits sent forth to do service for the sake of them that shall inherit salvation?*[2] saying here, that all of them together have been ordained for service to men, as living with them in this place. And again he says: *To the intent that now unto the principalities and the powers in the heavenly places might be made known through the Church the manifold wisdom of God.*[3] Clearly has he again signified that they are not only here, but he also says that they had been taught by those things which had been dispensed to man. For by using the expression *through the Church*, he evidently signified through men.

Then again in the Old Testament, the Patriarch Jacob saw a ladder which reached from the earth up to heaven. And at the top of it he saw God standing, and the angels ascending and descending on it. He shows them at first ascending and then descending. Then again this same Patriarch saw a multitude of angels and called them an embattled host.[4] In like manner Moses had recorded that only two heavens were made, namely, the first which in the beginning was made along with the earth, and the second which was made on the second day, and which he calls the firmament. He likewise frequently speaks of angels as in this place of ours, ministering among others to Hagar and to Abraham and to Lot and to Jacob himself. And in the great song[5] he says: *Rejoice, O ye heavens, with him, and let all the angels of God adore him;*[6] here, after the heavens, speaking of the angels as being in this place of ours; whence he added: *Rejoice, ye nations with his people*; here again referring to those who are in this place. In like manner also David, having the same object in view as

---

[1] Rom. viii, 21.   [2] Heb. i, 14.   [3] Ephes. iii, 10.
[4] Gr. παρεμβολήν. See Gen. xxxii, 2.
[5] The Song of Moses, given in Deuteronomy xxxii, 1-43.

Moses, and having himself become a prophet after Moses, thus speaks, discriminating between the things that are in heaven and the things that are on the earth: *Praise ye the Lord from the heavens, praise him in the heights. Praise ye him, all his angels; praise ye him, all his host;*[1] here properly beginning with the firmament and the place on high, and then proceeding to the place below, he speaks next of the angels, calling them at the same time God's host. Lastly again he mentions the things that are with them: *Praise ye him, sun and moon, praise him, all ye stars of light.*[2] From this he recurs to the upper place, and says: *Praise him, ye heavens of heavens,* instead of saying, heaven of heaven, calling the first heaven the heaven of heaven, since it is the heaven of the visible firmament. Then he says: *and the water which is above the heavens;* that is above the heaven. Having now spoken clearly of the things above, he evidently recognizes the first mentioned things as below.

Then when he had called upon all things that are in the heavens to praise God, he states the reason why they ought to praise him with hymns, and says: *For he spake and they were made; he commanded and they were created. He hath also established them for ever and ever; he hath made a decree which shall not pass away.*[3] Then finally he passes on to all things on the earth, and mentions all things that live in the air and in the waters and upon the land, whereon also he places man, and again enjoins them thus: *Let them praise the name of the Lord,* and tells them for why: *Because his name alone is exalted.* At last he takes them all conjointly saying: *The confession of him as above earth and heaven;*[4] thus at the same time showing that all things are within earth and heaven. In like manner also God Himself,

---

[1] Psalm cxlviii, 1, 2.
[2] *Ibid.*, 3.
[3] *Ibid.*, 5, 6.
[4] *Ibid.*, 12, 13.

speaking through Moses, says: *For in six days God made the heaven and the earth and all things that are therein ;* [1] thus still more clearly showing that all the angels are within heaven and earth and are circumscribed by them. Then again David elsewhere says: *Who stretcheth out the heaven like a curtain, who layeth the beams of his chambers in the waters ;* [2] here manifestly speaking of the firmament which has the waters on its surface, as serving us for a covering. For the coverings overhead of a tent are properly called screens (δέρρεις) whether they be made of canvas or of hair. Then in continuation he says: *Who maketh the clouds his chariot, who walketh upon the wings of the winds, who maketh his angels spirits, and his ministers a flame of fire.* Having here again mentioned things from the firmament above to the clouds and winds below, he adds as being among these, angels, whom he also calls ministers. So far David. And now let us pass on to Daniel that Prophet most nobly endowed. What saith he in the hymn which he puts into the mouth of the three children. *Bless ye the Lord, all ye works of the Lord, praise him and exalt him on high for ever. Praise the Lord, O ye heavens.*[4] He also mentions the angels after the heavens, not leaving unnoticed the waters which are above the heaven ; and—employing again the consecutive order, he resumes his theme, and proceeding from the lowest, he mentions next after them the angels, whom he calls powers, and with whom he conjoins the sun, moon and stars, showers, dews and winds, fire and frost and heat, clouds and snows and lightnings, and all things that are in the air and the waters and the earth— and, following David and Moses, he at last mentions man, on whose account all the things before enumerated were created. For since man is a kind of bond and pledge of the union in

---

[1] Exod. xx, 11. [2] Psalm civ, 2, 3. [3] *Ibid.*, 4.
[4] Dan. iii, 57, 58 (*Song of the Three Children*).

love of the whole world, man of necessity includes to a certain degree all the things already said. For it has well been said by the pagans : Man is a microcosm.

Accordingly all the inspired men—Prophets and Apostles, men who have been adorned by most holy lives, and have exposed themselves for their religion to countless sufferings and deaths, *of whom*, as it is written, *the world was not worthy*,[1] and who wrought miracles without number and beyond the power of description, and performed a variety of mighty deeds, and were by God made fit to teach and persuade and visit all the earth under heaven,[2] and to draw all the nations to religion and piety—these men have spoken concerning two such states without mention of any others. And all of them with one consent have spoken of this place as that of angels and men, and have declared that the place on high will, after the resurrection, be likewise the place of angels and men. What kind of a defence then have those pretended Christians for their disbelieving all these things, and saying that the heavens shall be dissolved, on which hangs our firm, immovable and indissoluble hope, which is laid up in store for us by God, and concerning which Paul exclaims : *Which eye hath not seen, nor ear heard, nor has it entered into the heart of man what things God hath prepared for them that love him ;*[3] and again : *The sufferings of this present time are not worthy to be compared with the glory which shall be revealed to usward.*[4] Again in like manner : *For our light affliction which is for the moment worketh for us more and more exceedingly an eternal weight of glory, while we look, not at the things which are seen, but at the things which are not seen ; for the things which are seen are temporal,*

---

[1] Heb. xi. 38.
[2] In the Greek text γῆν is, by a printer's mistake, omitted.
[3] I Cor. ii, 9.　　　　　　　　　[4] Rom. viii, 18.

but the things which are not seen are eternal.[1] By this he means that if you weigh in the balance against the afflictions of this world the good things of the future state, these will be found to surpass in glory and to outweigh beyond measure the lightness and insignificance of the afflictions of this world, which in comparison are of exceeding brief duration, and which at last utterly disappear. For, he says, the things which are seen, that is, the things of this world, are temporary, but the things which are not seen, that is, of the heavenly place or world on high, are eternal. Now we must turn to the Epistles General and adduce their testimony on this subject. And there it is said: *Into which things the angels desire to look;*[2] as if he said: They also have not yet obtained the good things laid up for us in heaven—yea, they have not so much as the privilege of seeing them. For this is similar to what the Apostle says: *For the whole creation groaneth and travaileth in pain together until now;*[3] as if he said, even the angels are heavily burdened by the change, and groan along with all creation, eagerly longing for liberty. How then is it possible to expect that the heavens will be dissolved, and other new heavens be produced? For, were it so, all that has been said before is shown to be false, namely, that they have been prepared and are indissoluble, and that we shall enter the place whereinto Christ hath entered. According, however, to the fables of the pretended Christians, all is imposture and deception that is written in divine scripture. But above all, if the heavens be dissolved, as they say, and others be put in their place, then Christ who is in them must of necessity be dissolved, and another new Christ must be introduced along with the other new heavens, provided of course that we are to be with the Christ. But away with this trifling! and let the

---

[1] II Cor. iv, 18, 19.   [2] I Pet. i, 12.   [3] Rom. viii, 22.

blasphemy recoil on their head. For saith the Apostle: *Our citizenship is in heaven, from whence also we expect the Saviour the Lord Jesus;*[1] as if he said: I speak of those heavens from which we expect the Lord will come, who will transform us from corruption to incorruption, and take us up where He himself has entered before us. For this also he says elsewhere: *The forerunner himself hath for us entered.*[2]

Since, therefore, some corrupting the meaning of the divine scriptures have misinterpreted the saying of our Lord, namely: *The heaven and the earth shall pass away, but my words shall not pass away*,[3] failing to recognize that the mode of expression is hyperbolical, we shall interpret what their meaning properly is; for he says: It is possible for them to be dissolved, but for my words, never. And again it was said by David: *Thou, Lord, in the beginning didst lay the foundation of the earth, and the heavens are the work of thy hands; they shall perish, but thou shalt remain.*[4] This they distort, not understanding that here also in contrast to the uncreated deity he speaks of created things as perishable, because these things, having been previously non-existent, afterwards came into being; and if he wished the annihilation of existence, then, just as he produced these things when non-existent, so now that they exist, he is able to destroy them. For that which has not been made by any one cannot be destroyed by any one; but that which has been made can also be destroyed, especially if its Maker should so wish. Something similar is asserted in the Epistles General: *In which the heavens being on fire shall be dissolved, and the elements shall melt with fervent heat.*[5] But in their ignorance they misinterpret the new heaven and the new earth as well

---

[1] Philipp. iii, 20.   [2] Heb. vi, 20.   [3] Matt. xxiv. 35.
[4] Psalm cii, 26, 27.   [5] II Pet. iii, 12.

as His promises, through their not understanding what is said, but they actually assert that these heavens shall be dissolved, and other new heavens be created—a view which is opposed to all divine scripture. For if these heavens, into which Christ after He had risen from the dead, and having become incorruptible in body and immutable in soul has now ascended, and into which we also shall enter when we have risen from the dead; and if divine scripture pronounces this hope and this life to be indissoluble, how is it possible that these heavens can be dissolved and other new heavens be produced? For if the place in the heavens is the habitation of those who are now incorruptible and immortal and immutable, how shall it not receive us when we have risen and become incorruptible and immortal and immutable? Away with such madness! For God does not repent of what He hath done, so that He should destroy these and produce others. He will, however, renew the whole creation to better its condition, as we have frequently said. For if man, who is the bond of the whole creation, shall be renewed, becoming incorruptible and immortal in body, and immutable in soul, is it not evident that all the elements of which the body of man is composed, and all rational beings, as being akin to the soul of man, shall be renewed and brought into a better state? For all things, saith the Apostle, are summed up in Christ, both the things that are in the heavens and the things that are on the earth. And again, he says: *If any one be in Christ he is a new creature—old things are passed away, behold! all things are become new;*[1] here speaking of all things as new, or of the renovation of all existing things; for, when he speaks of the summing up and the new creation, he signifies by each the same thing, that each is effected in Christ. For just as Christ according to the flesh, when

---

[1] II Cor. v, 17.

risen from the dead was not a different Christ from the Christ who had died, but was the same who had suffered death, yet in like manner as He was victorious in His resurrection over sufferings and death, so also the whole creation, while not perishing but retaining its identity, is changed into a better condition. *For*, as the divine oracle says, *He hath established them for ever and ever; He hath made a decree which shall not pass away*.[1] Wherefore God takes not hold of angels, but of the seed of Abraham, according to what is written. For had He taken hold of the angels, rational beings only, as being of a kindred nature, could have hoped to be renovated. But now having taken hold of the seed of Abraham, that is, of a body and a rational soul, and conducted it into the heavenly place, He laid the foundation beforehand of a hope for all creation. Whence the declaration in the Epistles General: *In which the heavens, being on fire, shall be dissolved, and the elements shall melt in fervent heat but* [we look for] *new heavens and the new earth*,[2] has this as its purport, that with a great noise, as in the twinkling of an eye, all the elements, being on fire as in a furnace and being thus purified, undergo the change for the better. And as regards the heavens and the earth—these shall be made new and the conditions of life in them shall be changed in accordance with the saying of Paul: *The fashion of this world passeth away*;[3] as if he said: the present order of things shall be changed, the succession of day and night shall cease, the stars shall no longer accomplish their courses and the air shall no longer be in motion, and neither the water nor the earth shall any more produce their harvests, but a new state of things shall be introduced suitable for immortal and incorruptible men and angels.

---

[1] Psalm cxlix, 6.   [2] I Peter iii, 12.   [3] I Cor. vii, 31.

But we say nothing of the fact that the Church from the first has held the Catholic Epistles to be doubtful. No one certainly of those who have commented on the divine scriptures has taken any account of these Epistles. Nay, even those, who have drawn up the list of the canonical books of divine scripture, have all of them placed them in the doubtful category. I refer to Irenaeus the Bishop of Lyons, a man of eminence and of illustrious life, and who flourished not long after the Apostolic age,[1] and to Eusebius Pamphili,[2] and to Athanasius the Bishop of Alexandria,[3] and to Amphilochius who became Bishop of Iconium and was the friend of, and in communion with,[4] the blessed Basil, and who in the iambic verses which he addressed to Seleucus declared the Epistles

---

[1] Irenaeus, who was a native of Smyrna and a disciple of Polycarp, became Bishop of Lyons in Gaul, A.D. 177. Like his contemporaries, Clemens Alexandrinus and Tertullian, he accepted as canonical the four Gospels, Acts, the thirteen Pauline Epistles, the first Epistle of Peter and the first of John, and the Apocalypse.

[2] Eusebius, who took the surname of Pamphili, in token of his devoted friendship for Pamphilus, Bishop of Cæsarea, was born in Palestine about 264 A.D., became Bishop of Cæsarea in 315, and died about 340. He recognised three classes of New Testament Scriptures: 1. *Homologoumena*, those universally recognised which embraced those enumerated in note 1, above, with the exception of the Apocalypse; 2. *Antilegomena*, those not universally recognised, which included, among others, the Epistles of James and Jude, the second of Peter, and the second and third of John: 3. *Notha*, that is spurious, such as the Acts of Paul, the Shepherd, the Apocalypse of Peter, the Epistle of Barnabas, and others (see his *Hist. Eccles.*, Book III, c. 25).

[3] Athanasius was born in A.D. 296 in Alexandria, of which he became the Archbishop in 326. In his Festal Letter written in 373, announcing to the churches (as he did annually) the date of Easter for that year, he gives a list of the sacred books which were known and recognised as authoritative, and in this list he places the seven Catholic Epistles and the Acts.

[4] Gr. φίλος καὶ κοινωνικός.

to be doubtful.[1] In like manner Severianus also, the Bishop of Gabala, proscribed them in his work *Against the Jews*.[2] In fact most of the authorities deny that these Epistles were written by the Apostles, but assign them to some other authors—simple Presbyters. Hence Eusebius Pamphili in his *Ecclesiastical History*[3] informs us that there were two tombs in Ephesus—one of John the Evangelist, the other of John the Presbyter who wrote two of the Epistles General [of John]—the second and the third, of which the former is inscribed thus: *The Elder to the Elect Lady*, and the latter thus: *The Elder to Gaius the beloved*. For he, as well as Irenaeus, says, that with the exception of the first Epistle of Peter and the first of John, the Epistles General were not written by the Apostles, while others say that they were all written by Presbyters, and not by the Apostles. For the first and second and third of John are so written that it is evident that the three are the productions of a single person. But others receive also the Epistle of James along with these two (I John and I Peter) while others receive them all.

---

[1] St. Amphilochius became Bishop of Iconium in A.D. 273-4. On his elevation to this office he received from St. Basil a congratulatory letter which is still extant. At Constantinople, to which he had gone to attend the Œcumenical Council in 381, he signed as a witness the will of St. Gregory of Nazianzus. The iambic poem here attributed to him consisted of 333 lines. The Seleucus to whom it was addressed was the nephew of St. Olympias, who had herself been brought up by the Bishop's sister. Other testimonies, besides that of Cosmas, have been adduced in support of the authority of the poem. Its object was to instruct Seleucus in a godly life, and to warn him against prevailing vices, but its principal value consists in the list of canonical scriptures with which it closes.

[2] Severianus, in the year 400 A.D., if not earlier, became Bishop of Gabala, a town in the northern part of the sea-coast of Syria. He united with Serapion, and Theophilus the Archbishop of Alexandria, in the conspiracy against St. Chrysostom, who had formerly been his friend.

[3] Book III, 39.

Among the Syrians, however, none are found except only the three already mentioned, namely, the Epistle of James and that of Peter and that of John—while the others do not even find a place among them. The perfect Christian ought not therefore to depend upon books that are doubtful, seeing that those which have been admitted into the Canon, and which are commonly acknowledged[1] suffice to declare everything concerning both the heavens and the earth and the elements and the whole scheme of Christian doctrine.

Those accordingly seem to me to be wanting in sense and to have no inner knowledge at all of the divine scriptures—those inventors of the new doctrines, who think that the heavens will be dissolved. For since God from the very beginning has knowledge and fore-knowledge, and is always cognisant, and never receives any accession to His knowledge, and whereas He wished to give to others a share in existence, and to fill them with his own goodness and knowledge and wisdom, He made the whole world, comprising it within the compass of heaven and earth, but placing the firmament in the midst, and binding it to the first heaven; and when He had made the one place into two places, He allotted to the mortal and mutable state, this place, while He prepared beforehand the upper place for the future state, according as the delineation of its figure at the end of my work shows, as well as the structure of the Tabernacle, which was itself an image of the whole world. And it was His pleasure that we should for the present live in this state as in a useful school, where there are pains and pleasures, in order that we may be disciplined by the pains, and may be kept from fainting by the pleasures, being instructed in the knowledge of the

---

[1] Gr. τῶν ἐνδιαθέτων καὶ κοινῶς ὡμολογημένων γραφῶν. Ἐνδιάθηκος like ἐνδιάθετος is used to signify *canonical*.

Maker and attracted to it by the diversity of the things created, and the all-wise harmony, and the difference between beings; while the Maker himself, who has at times been seen, has given us laws in aid of our weakness, inducing rational beings, as has been said, to seek the knowledge of His supreme loving-kindness and goodness, which is the chief end of all such beings. For since we are created beings, and have our being from another, we always need that other for the continuance of our existence and the acquisition of knowledge. For it could not be that, as soon as we were made, we could possess all knowledge, for this is an attribute which belongs only to God who is unoriginated.

Since then God in His goodness has, for mysterious reasons, made the lower animals devoid of knowledge, for the instruction and assistance of ourselves who are rational, He has made, as was possible, the rational to be intermediate between himself and the irrational, in order that by the variety in the universe, and by the laws imposed upon us and by the pursuit of knowledge, we may, through a longing produced by our experience of pains and pleasures, be induced to seek part by part a knowledge of the world. *For the invisible things of him*, saith the divine Apostle, *are clearly seen, being perceived through the things that are made, even his everlasting power and godhead; so that they may be without excuse;*[1] as if he said: The invisible things of God, namely, His power and wisdom and providence and goodness and His eternal godhead, we apprehend and see from things existent and visible, and through all His works we, in our measure, perceive the Creator, so that we cannot offer any excuse of ignorance (for this is what *without excuse* signifies) since we have it in our own hands to know from all these things in

---

[1] Rom. i, 20.

our measure the Creator of ourselves and of the universe. In like manner again he says: *God, having of old time spoken unto the fathers in the prophets by divers portions and in divers manners, hath at the end of these days spoken unto us in His Son,*[1] thus distributing the word into portions and manners, into the prophets and His Son. By portions, he means the difference of the places in which God appeared and spake to the men of old through the prophets, and by manners, the diversity of the visions themselves, which He, when seen at one time and another in cases of immediate necessity, exhibited either in person or through the Prophets, having a desire to signify this, that God in every way, both by real things and by visions, did not neglect to instruct rational beings in the knowledge of Himself, placing it before them at one time through the prophets, and now through His own Son; then for them, when they had at last been proved, He prepared the future state, in which, after having made us incorruptible and immortal, He would place us, filling us, as having acquired experience, with the perfect knowledge of Himself as far as we ought to know. For this reason He has made two states from the very beginning, since we could not, as has been said before, receive the whole knowledge of Him in one collective mass without a process of instruction. For the Deity only is self-taught, and is the foundation of knowledge, receiving no accession to it from any other, but able to impart it to others, while we are again taught when we are immortal and immutable, by the hardships we have undergone. Since the Apostle says: *All discipline seemeth for the present to be not joyous but grievous;*[2] for without discipline and suffering it is impossible there can be learning. For the purpose of discipline therefore, He made this

---

[1] Heb. i, 1, 2.   [2] Heb. xii, 11.

world mortal and mutable and diversified, in order that by the affliction of learning and the variety of the universe, we may, by this experience, ascend to the knowledge of God. For if He had made us from the beginning immortal and immutable, we would have differed nothing from the non-rational animals which have by nature something good and useful, though without their knowing what they possess—just as the bee which with wisdom constructs its honeycomb, and the spider which with great skill weaves its network, and the ant which in summer prepares its store of food, do not do these things with any rational knowledge, but are as unconscious of their art as gold and pearl are of the beauty which adorns them.

God therefore with wisdom—yea, with supreme wisdom—made from the first two states, in order that having had experience here of pleasure and pain we may in the second state have perfect knowledge of the power of His goodness, through the unspeakable and everlasting good things bestowed upon us, and may recognize from what things into what things we have passed. These and similar things the whole of divine Scripture proclaims, and this is its whole scope. For those admirable men, who destroy the heavens and produce others for us that are new, are ignorant of the scope of the divine scriptures. For it is not to be imagined that God was at one time ignorant, but has now come to know better, how to make other heavens and a better state, according to the fable of these demented and pretended Christians; but He is always the same, existing after the same manner and principle, knowing how and when and how great, and where and what like He would make the whole world. But nevertheless they propose to us, quite reasonably of course, the difficulty which emerges from this, asking us: Why then do embryons which have died in the womb advance to the knowledge of God without having had experience of pleasures and pains, but have been taught at a distance from hence concerning God?—to whom we shall reply that the embryon which is rational, having been in close touch, so to speak, with the maternal womb, and the maternal womb being in a dim sort of way a symbol of this world in which are heat and cold and dryness and moisture, the embryon when gathering knowledge in the future state, has a remembrance, and an awakened consciousness of the maternal womb, in which it had some partial experience of this present world. It sees moreover even the elements themselves and the whole world standing as its teacher; and reflecting with itself in virtue of the perfect knowledge, it arrives straightway at a knowledge of its past life, and thereafter at the knowledge of God as the Maker of all things. But as concerns the judgment to be pronounced on them, we leave that to God himself, for it is not possible for us to know all things in this life. We say only, and this is all it behoves us to say, that they form an intermediate class, neither destined to receive crowns, nor to undergo punishments, for they are exempted from punishments, because they have not enjoyed the good things of this life, but they fail to obtain crowns, as they have not undergone toils in this life.

But if any one should say that God will judge them according to what he knows would have been their manner of life and conduct had they survived, we do not reject this notion, but leave it to those who know better than ourselves. For we have no perfect knowledge how God judges, deeming that whatever seems good to Him will be altogether fair and wise, acknowledging with the utmost pleasure that the matter is beyond us, and even pluming ourselves on[1] our ignorance regarding it, in accordance with the great Apostle

---

[1] Gr. στεφανοφοροῦντες ἐπὶ.

Paul when he says: *For we know in part and prophesy in part; but when that which is perfect is come, then that which is in part shall be done away;*[1] for we shall then know perfectly, as we ought to know, when we have all risen from the dead perfect, as the Apostle again says: *Till we all attain unto the unity of the faith and of the knowledge of the Son of God, unto a full-grown man, unto the measure of the stature of the fulness of Christ.*[2] But they will yet again question us on this point: How does one who is diminutive in body rise perfect? And how can the maimed and the lame or he that is mutilated in one of his limbs rise up sound and quite perfect? Let them listen to us replying from scripture and from what is seen in Nature thus: Just as God took Adam's rib, a very small member of his body, and constructed out of it a perfect woman, mysteriously supplying what was deficient; and just as a man and woman copulate, of whom one or the other is, as is often the case, blind or maimed, and their offspring is born sound and entire, so it is to be believed and understood with respect to the resurrection of the dead, in which we are born anew from the tomb into a better birth than from the womb. But I will delineate for thee, O most beloved, the figure of the heaven and the earth, and of the firmament in the middle—also the Tabernacle prepared by Moses which is a pattern of the universe, and also that famous sphere of the pagans,[3] in order that you may know by the sight itself agreeably to the figure, what divine scripture and the Christian teaching alike declare, and how altogether different therefrom is the sphere of the pagans.

---

[1] I Cor. xiii, 9.   [2] Ephes. iv, 13.

[3] See Pls. 2, 7, 9, and 10 in the Appendix.

Notes from divine scripture in mutual harmony concerning the figure of heaven and earth.

In the beginning God made the heaven and the earth.[1] He speaks of these as comprehending other things, and at the same time time signifies the things that are within them and which were produced along with them. And again: *The heaven and the earth were finished and all the host of them,*[2] as if again they comprehended other things, and the whole host of things were within them. And again: *In six days God made the heaven and the earth and all that in them is,*[3] as if again all things exist within them, and they were comprehensive of them. And again: *And God rested on the seventh day from all the work which he began to make :*[4] meaning that He began to create and ceased from creating; and again: *This is the book of the generation of heaven and earth ;*[5] meaning, this book records the coming into being of the whole world which is circumscribed by heaven and earth. And again about its figure Isaiah says : *He that hath established the heaven as a vaulted chamber and stretched it out as a tent to dwell in ;*[6] the expression *as a vaulted chamber* has reference to the first heaven, but the other expression *stretched it out as a tent,* to the second heaven, which he speaks of as a house where people live and make their abode. And again David says : *Stretching out the heaven as a curtain,*[7] speaking here of the firmament—and speaking of it as a curtain, that is, as the coverings which made the roof over the Tabernacle, whatever these coverings were, whether made of hair or of canvas—for the coverings above which roofed the Tabernacle are properly called δέῤῥεις (leather curtains). He no doubt says : *Who layeth the beams of his upper chambers in the waters :*[8] here more clearly speaking concerning the firmament itself as if it were a covering. But that there is nothing under the earth, is thus declared in Job : *He hangeth the earth upon nothing,*[9] meaning that there is nothing underneath it. In like manner again in Job: *Whereupon were the foundations thereof fastened ?*[10] meaning that

---

[1] Gen. i, 1.
[2] Gen. ii, 1.
[3] Exod. xx, 11.
[4] Gen. ii, 2.
[5] Gen. v, 1.
[6] Isai. xl, 22.
[7] Psalm civ, 2.
[8] Psalm civ, 3.
[9] Job xxvi, 7.
[10] Job xxxviii, 6.

there is nothing underneath on which it is fixed. And David says: *He hath founded the earth upon its own stability ;*[1] as if he said that it has been founded upon itself and not upon anything. But with regard to the heaven being fastened to the earth he declares in Job: *He hath inclined heaven to earth; dust is poured out as earth,*[2] *but I have cemented it as if with stone a square block ;*[3] intimating that the heaven is inclined to the earth and at its lower part fastened to it like a cube, that is, at the four corners.

The Tabernacle, as a whole, is therefore a pattern of the whole world, as the divine Apostle explains to us—speaking in these terms of the outer Tabernacle: *For the first Tabernacle had ordinances of divine service, and its sanctuary, a sanctuary of this world :*[4] calling it *of this world* as being a pattern of this world ; but with regard to the inner tabernacle he speaks thus : *For Christ entered not into a holy place made with hands like in pattern to the true, but into heaven itself :*[5] calling heaven the true holy place, and the inner tabernacle its antitype. Let the reader then consider the figure of the heaven and of the earth and their model— *i.e.*, the Tabernacle—how, to wit, that all are in harmony with the Christian doctrine—that there are two paths[6] of the whole world—this here and the upper, prepared from the foundation of the world. This here has been given in the present state to men and angels, and the upper is given, in the future state after the resurrection from the dead, to men and angels. For the famous sphere of the pagans does not harmonize at all with what Christian doctrine proclaims ; but is adapted rather for those who hope neither for a resurrection of the dead nor for another state after it, but assert that the whole world is in an endless process of generation and corruption.

Another Note.

If those teachers of error say that the Lord Christ entered into the first sphere where the moon is, it is, in the first place, in beautiful agreement with their error, that they should admit that

---

[1] Psalm civ, 5.
[2] The Greek text has γῂ in mistake for γῇ.
[3] Job xxxviii, 38.   [4] Heb. ix, 1.   [5] Heb. ix, 24.
[6] Gr. πόροι. Cf. πόροι ἁλός, *paths of the sea*, *i.e.*, the sea itself (Odys. xii, 259).

He abides with their goddess. In the second place, since their sphere is solid, let them tell us whether, along with the moon, He cleaves His way, like a fish in the water, through the body of heaven, going in the opposite direction to that which it pursues, or whether, along with the universe, He is violently whirled round in its direction—which is all the most ridiculous nonsense. In the third place, it is in agreement with your error, that above Him are the other planets which are gods of yours, namely, Mercury, Venus, the Sun, Mars, Jupiter, Saturn, the father of your gods—gods to whom ye have been seen offering sacrifice—then also those fixed houses of the twelve signs of the Zodiac, and the six-and-thirty *decani*.[1] And how shall the Apostle not lie, according to you, when he says that Christ is above these: *Far above all rule, and authority, and power, and dominion, and every name that is named.*[2] But if they shall say that He is in the second sphere, they will be confronted again with the same difficulties, and so will they be if they say that He who is above all is in the third, fourth, fifth, sixth, seventh, eighth, and ninth[3] and what is said by the Apostle will be found false, that from the first tabernacle, that is, from this world, Christ entered into the second, that is, into the heavenly place, having obtained eternal redemption—the second, observe, and not the ninth. He therefore, who sincerely desires to be a Christian, follows divine scripture and puts no reliance on the fallacious theory of the pagans which teaches the plurality and the equality of gods, and brings destruction on the souls of men.

Text.

Since therefore all the spheres lie in a continuous series and are solid, how is it possible to conceive that in such a configuration there can be a resurrection of the dead, and that men can ascend into heaven, and reign in heaven, that is, in the second Tabernacle, whereinto Christ also,

---

[1] *Decani* is a Latin astrological term, having *gradus* in the plural understood. It is thus equivalent to the Greek δεκαμοιρία, "ten degrees of the zodiac", or a thirty-sixth part of its whole circuit.

[2] Ephes. i, 21.

[3] These are the spheres of the seven planets.

saith scripture, hath already entered the first of all? to which add all that has been said before. For the pagans who think that there is a sphere, in consequence neither acknowledge a resurrection of the dead, nor say that the dead ascend into heaven, nor admit that there are waters above the heaven, nor admit that the fashion of this world, that is, the revolution of the heavenly bodies, will be changed and all things one after another, nor that any one at all has ever ascended into heaven with his body, or will go up thither. Some of them, however, say that their souls and these only move round with the sphere, and see or know all things,[1] while others maintain that souls migrate into other bodies, and others again believe in the pre-existence of the soul, and these consequently say that the sphere will be dissolved—that is, that every corporeal nature will be utterly destroyed, while the souls will revert to their original condition—an opinion held also by the admirable Origenes[2] and his disciples. Others again maintain that the heavens had no beginning and will never have an end—and that the world is continually undergoing renovation and destruction; from which it is inferred that they speak of God as delighting in evil, or as powerless or jealous, nay, think that there is no god at all. For it is repugnant to the divine nature to permit the world to be constantly subject to renovation and destruction—and hosts of other difficulties besides, that their views involve, start up for all these. The Christians then alone are

---

[1] This high conception inspired Byron to compose the noble and impressive lyric beginning:

"When darkness wraps this suffering clay,
Ah! whither strays the immortal mind?

[2] Origen, the father of biblical criticism and exegesis, was born at Alexandria in 185 A.D., and died at Tyre in 254, from sufferings which he had undergone not long previously, during the Decian persecution.

perfect, being like wheat-plants of piety in the midst of tares and thorns—believing as they do in the whole of divine scripture, both in the Old and New Testament—and neither saying that there had been any state before this present state, nor asserting that after the future state there will be any other ; but that there are only two states, which our delineation in conformity therewith shows, that we shall be transferred from this state to that which is future and heavenly ; and again, that we shall live with the Lord, as the whole of divine scripture argues—namely, that when God began to create and had made the two places, He rested from his work according to His purpose from the very first. Things very different from these, most excellent Sir, did that person write, whom you mentioned, a pretended Christian, who says that the heavens, which he also thinks to be spherical, shall be dissolved according to the theory of the pagans, and to be always revolving, thus committing to writing old wives' fables rather than Christian doctrines, and following in general no authority, unless in part the worthy Origenes, for his writings are completely at variance with Christian opinion.[1]

For it will be your part next to judge and compare each dogma and question, and to consider to which dogma and figure one, who is truly a Christian and wishes to live piously, ought to adhere. For I see much fallacy and guile on the part of the present writer of the fables, who bestows a spherical figure on the heavens and says that they shall again be destroyed. As for myself, dearest friend, I am of one mind with divine scripture, and I am confident that you also are such as I am—a Christian following the divine scriptures, and the tradition of the

---

[1] In 232 A.D., Origen was excommunicated, chiefly because of his denial of eternal punishment.

Holy Church when saying: I believe in one God, that is, Father and Son and Holy Spirit, the consubstantial Trinity, and in the Resurrection of the flesh, in one Holy, Catholic and Apostolic Church—as also the Creed says: I believe that there will be a Resurrection of the dead and that there will be a life to come ; and as the priests in like manner pray, using these words with reference to those presenting offerings: *The thank-offering of thy servants receive on thy heavenly and estimable altar, on the amplitude of thy heavens, giving back to them for corruptible things incorruptible, for temporal things eternal, for earthly things heavenly*—and for the dead these words : *Give repose, O Lord, to his soul—collecting also together again his flesh on the day that thou hast appointed, according to thy true promises*[1]—with whom I also joining in prayer, add what is left over : Grant us of Thy grace to have before Thy presence a Christian and happy end—for ever. Amen !

---

[1] " Prayer for the dead".—*Note by Montfaucon.*

BOOK VIII.

On the Song of Hezekiah and the going back of the Sun.

AS I know well, my dear Peter, how hard it is to please the race of man, I hesitated long to comply with your request, for there be some men who cast reproach on those who choose to commit their thoughts to writing, on the ground that they immerse themselves in business, though it be in their option to abstain from all exertion and to enjoy a life of leisure and repose. Others again, since they set no value on writing, put out of sight what is laborious, and seek quiet in seclusion. Some too there be who begin to read books with unbounded eagerness, but afterwards, consigning them to utter neglect, play the part of the poor brutes that walk on all fours; while others, who are conversant with literature, do what is still worse, for in the case of new writers, aware though they be that these have reached the very pinnacle of fame, they will not condescend to peruse their works, even when they are compositions of most sterling merit. Persons again of the common sort, led by their ignorance, disparage even what is said to the purpose,¹ and, to speak plainly, calumny is ever inventive, and has

---

¹ Gr. τὰ καλῶς λεγόμενα may perhaps mean *what is finely said or expressed.*

no lack of material for sneering and indulging in censorious remarks, the grounds for which envy supplies without stint. When I turned over all this in my mind, I put off, notwithstanding you besought me with great importunity, to give a written interpretation of the Song of the blessed Hezekiah. But you have now, my admirable friend, I know not how, prevailed over me and done away with my reluctance, representing to me that there is no lack in this world of those who are willing to labour hard from their eagerness to read the works of all, and to approve those that are excellent,[1] according to the injunction of the divine Apostle (Rom. ii, 18), and among such thou thyself rankest as one. For this is a worthy subject on which to bestow your pains, anxious as thou art to ascertain whether anything tending to profit is to be gained from the Song; for it would be quite in keeping with your good sense in such matters, were you to be convinced that what appears of least importance in divine scripture is capable of affording no little help; and certainly an eager desire to learn the use of everything is a point in your character, which stands not far remote from your devotion to work. So then, as I had with God's help all but completed my exposition of the Song of Songs, which our common and admirable friend, Theophilus, had invited me to take in hand, as you are yourself aware, I put off the matter until now; but as I have just quite completed that work, I shall at once proceed to fulfil your request,[2] if the Holy Spirit will, without whom there can be

---

[1] Gr. δοκιμάζειν τὰ διαφέροντα, translated in the Revised Version "to approve the things that are excellent", but in the margin thereof "to prove the things that differ." Cosmas seems to have understood the words in the former sense. The expression has occasioned much controversy.

[2] Gr. ἄρξομαι καὶ τὴν σὴν αἴτησιν. Βουλήσει .... πληροῦν. As αἴτησιν is governed by πληροῦν, the reading should be αἴτησιν βουλήσει, &c.

no good thing in us. I shall state first with what purpose in view he uttered the Song, and shall then proceed to its detailed exposition, and shall at the same time point out what is useful in each passage, for in this way the point of what is said will become clearer.

The blessed Hezekiah then, who was King of the Jews, and a very pious and virtuous man and an object of God's especial care, entertained the idea that the blessed David had spoken of him prophetically in many of the Psalms, such as the nineteenth, the twentieth,[1] and many others besides, and having moreover applied to himself the prophecy which had once been made in his father's time by Isaiah: *Behold a virgin shall conceive and bear a son*,[2] he was uplifted in mind by the workings of human passion, and imagined himself to be the Christ who had been predicted. He was in consequence at first unwilling to take a part in the common offices of life, through the existence of another opinion among the Jews, that Christ when He comes, never dies, but abides for ever, as they also said in the Gospel: *We have heard out of the Law that Christ abideth for ever*.[3] So Hezekiah being of this opinion abstained from taking a wife and providing for the succession of his line by having children, being under the belief that he would live always. But when it came to pass that Senachéreim (Sennacherib)[4] the King of the Assyrians warred against Judæa and went up to Jerusalem to plunder it, Hezekiah on hearing what had been said by the impious Rapsacus (the Rab-shakeh)[5] as well

---

[1] The Psalms here meant are the twentieth and the twenty-first of our Bible. In the Septuagint the ninth and tenth psalms appear as but one, and hence the difference in the numeration.

[2] Isai. vii, 14.   [3] John xii, 34.

[4] Sennacherib the son of Sargon was the King, according to *Herodotus* (ii, 141), of the Assyrians and Arabians. He invaded Judæa in the fourteenth year of the reign of Hezekiah, who ascended the throne in 726 B.C. and died in 697. Sennacherib died in 681.

[5] Rab-shakeh is a title, meaning *Commander-in-Chief.*

as what had been written by Senachereim himself, rent his royal robes, and went into the temple clad in sackcloth, and besprinkled with ashes, and there supplicated God to deliver him from the Assyrians. But when his prayer was heard, and 185,000 men of the Assyrian army had been destroyed in one night by the angel, and when a victory so great and so marvellous had been wrought for him by God, he held more firmly than ever the estimate of himself which he had formerly entertained, claiming that he was beyond all doubt the Christ who had been predicted. Wherefore, as he was again uplifted in mind by this conception of himself, he did not go after his victory into the temple, as was his duty, to render thanks and give glory to God, but he was uplifted with pride, as it is recorded in the second Book of Chronicles (xxxii, 26): *That he humbled himself for the pride of his heart*, and, *God left him, to try him, that he might know all that was in his heart* (*ibid.*, 31).

But God who, in mercy to man, always works for his salvation, desiring to dispossess Hezekiah of that notion which his erring human judgment had suggested to him, and remembering also his virtues, did not permit him to be deluded to the end, but sent him such a sickness as led him to despair of his life. Then Isaiah the prophet going in unto him said: *Set thy house in order, for thou shalt die and not live*;[1] and thus at once took away the two opinions he had entertained. For some of the Jews said that the Christ never dies, while others held that he does really die, but rises again from the dead. So by saying *thou shalt die* the prophet took away from him one opinion—that according to which he thought he would never die, but when he added thereto and said: *thou shalt not live*, he took away the other opinion, according to which others asserted that he rises from the dead. For, being under the

[1] Isai. xxxiii, 1.

test of sickness, he was taught by both expressions that he was not Christ. But the Prophet with great wisdom suggested to him by the power of the Holy Spirit, that he was not the Christ, when he said to him: *Set thy house in order, for thou shalt die and not live;* as if he said, arrange thine affairs, settling to whom thou wilt transmit thy kingdom, in order that the promise of God may be guarded against the possibility of failure, for thou art not the Christ proclaimed by the Prophets, who has a kingdom without successor, but thou shalt undoubtedly have a successor, and thou hast not done well in neglecting to beget children to succeed thee in thy kingdom. It must therefore be thy concern now to arrange thine affairs, and to declare whom thou wilt have to be thy successor in the kingdom. As he had fancied that he would have but himself for his successor, Hezekiah on coming to know otherwise wept bitterly, and having repented and turned himself on his bed to the wall—the quarter in which the Temple lay, in accordance with the practice obtaining among the Jews—he made his supplication with his thoughts, you may be sure, directed to the Temple.[1]

But when he had changed his estimate of himself, and corrected his false notion, inasmuch as his prayer had been heard and he had recovered from his sickness, and been deemed worthy of an addition to his life, of fifteen years, and had been assured of this by another very wonderful sign, namely, by the retrogression of the sun, of which I shall state the cause a little farther on, then he sang the song to the Lord, wherein he set forth each of the circumstances already mentioned, for he speaks thus [see Isaiah xxxviii, 10-20.] *I said in the noontide of my*

---

[1] Thus Daniel prayed at three distinct times of the day with his face turned towards Jerusalem. The Ebionites maintained this Jewish custom of turning in prayer towards the sacred city.

days I shall go,[1] as if he said, I always cherished this thought in my heart, saying to myself, that I shall live always and never die. For by his saying: *In the noontide of my days I shall go*, he indicated that his days would never be shortened; and as if some one, while he was silent, had asked: while you were absorbed in these meditations what happened to you? he continues and says: *At the gates of the grave I shall leave the residue of my years*;[1] meaning, while I was thus meditating, I was all at once seized with a dreadful sickness, and could no longer cling to my former notion, but thought I should spend the rest of my years in the grave. Then: *I shall no longer behold the salvation of God upon the earth*.[2] The salvation of God here signifies Christ; for thus also Symeon, when he took up Christ in his arms, prayed God to be allowed to depart from this life, since his eyes had seen the salvation of God, namely Christ himself, for it had been revealed to him by the Spirit that *he should not see death, until he had seen the Lord Christ*.[3] What Hezekiah then meant to show was this: I not only abandoned that idea and ceased to entertain those lofty imaginations concerning myself, but I do not even think I shall be privileged to see the Christ upon the earth, as I have only other fifteen years to live. *I shall no longer see a man of my own kindred*[4]—this means, after the fifteen years which God has granted to me as an addition to my years, I shall, when dying, not only not be counted worthy to see Him, but not even to see any man, nay, not so much as one of my kindred. *I am deprived of the residue of my life*;[5] this means, having thrown away therefore my former estimate of myself, and considering what was my duty for the future, I recognised that my life would come to an end.

---

[1] Isai. xxxviii. 10.   [2] *Ibid.* 11.   [3] Luke ii. 26.
[4] Isai. xxxviii. 11.   [5] *Ibid.* 12.

After this he says: *It has gone out and gone away from me, as one takes down the tent which he had pitched;*[1] meaning: And so completely has my former overweening arrogance departed from me, that I am like one, who, after having pitched a tent, forthwith takes it down again. *The breath within me is as when a weaver is preparing to cut away the web from the loom;*[2] meaning: My very soul had all but left me, just as when the web of a woman who is weaving is ready to be cut. *In that day I was delivered till morning as to a lion, he did so break all my bones—from day even to night was I delivered over;*[3] meaning: In the time then of my sickness, I was delivered over to the fever as to a terrible lion that was crushing all my bones, so that, as it raged, I was tortured incessantly from morning till evening and from evening till day-dawn. *As a swallow so shall I chatter, and as a dove so shall I mourn;*[4] that is, In the time of my sickness I would utter cries like the sharp and quivering notes of the swallow, and in my pangs I would wail after the wont of doves. The words, *I shall chatter*, and *I shall mourn* are used instead of *I chattered* and *I mourned*, one tense being put for another—this being an idiom of frequent occurrence in divine scripture; as when Isaiah says: *He was led as a lamb to the slaughter,*[5] instead of he will be led. *Mine eyes failed me in looking at the height of heaven towards the Lord, who rescued me, and took away the anguish of my soul, O Lord; concerning it, it was told unto thee;*[5] meaning: And so much did I strain the eyes of my mind in looking up to the height of heaven, laying upon Thee, even upon God the Preserver of all, the anguish of my soul, which Thou didst remove from me, having changed my arrogance into humility and obedience to religion, on account of which, O Lord, I shall for

---

[1] Isai. xxxviii. 12.   [2] Ibid.,   [3] Ibid., 13.
[4] Ibid., 14.   [5] Isai. liii. 7.

ever give thanks unto Thee. *And thou hast resuscitated my breath, and having been comforted by thee I lived. For thou didst rescue my soul that it might not perish, and thou hast cast behind me all my sins ;*[1] meaning: For by comforting me Thou didst resuscitate my breath and I lived ; having rallied my soul that was perishing, Thou hast cast my sins behind, and not suffered them to be spread out before me. *For they that are in the grave cannot praise thee, nor can the dead celebrate thee ; nor can they that are in the grave hope for thy mercy. The living shall praise thee, even as I also do ;*[2] meaning: For if Thou hadst not granted me still to live, how could I have been converted, or have repented and been saved, or have hope of Thy mercy, since the dead who are in the grave can do nothing of this kind, but in Thy compassion Thou hast graciously granted me this.

It is a light thing for the shadow to decline ten steps ;[3] *nay, but let the shadow return backward ten steps.*[4] Accordingly after the shadow of the sun, as he proceeded [from mid-heaven] had declined the ten steps, then by the divine power, through the prayer of the Prophet, the sun returned backward till he was again in mid-heaven, and the shadow was found to have gone back the ten steps, according to sacred scripture. For if, on the contrary, it had been the

---

[1] Isai. xxxviii, 17. [2] *Ibid.*, 18, 19.
[3] Gr. ἀναβαθμούς. "Cyril of Alexandria and Jerome thought that the *steps* were really stairs, and that the shadow (perhaps of some column or obelisk on the top) fell on a greater or smaller number of them according as the sun was low or high. The terrace of a palace might thus easily be ornamented." Smith's *Dictionary of the Bible*. Josephus quotes a passage from Apion to the effect that in Egypt "Moses set up pillars instead of gnomons, under which was represented a cavity like that of a boat, and the shadow that fell from their tops fell down upon that cavity, that it might go round about the like course as the sun itself goes round in the other." See Whiston's *Josephus—contra Apion. Book II*, near the beginning.
[4] II Kings xx, 10.

third hour of the day, the shadow having by this time gone forward, could neither have gone back, nor could the sun have moved backward, if even it had so happened that the door and the steps of the house of Hezekiah looked to the west. And so much with regard to the position of the house. But the reason for such a sign being accorded was this—that most of the nations and perhaps all of them, serving especially the host of heaven, honour the sun as a greater god than all the others, and, as the father of lights. God therefore by ordering him to go backward, showed to all the nations that He himself was Lord of all, and that the sun was His servant, and was not God. For if He ordered so great a luminary to go back contrary to his use and wont, much more can He order those that are smaller, and treat them as His servants. But with God's help I shall now declare what advantage thence accrued. When the sun then went backward, the circumstance became known to all the nations, even to the ends of the earth, so that even the King of Babylon, Merodach,[1] the son of Baladon, who lived far off and yet beheld the sign, was struck with consternation, and a desire of searching into the nature of this dread and strange miracle. For amazement and terror overcame the king himself and his courtiers, who eagerly sought to learn from all that were conversant with astronomy the cause of this dread and mighty sign. And after much inquiry had been made, he learned that Hezekiah the King of Judæa having fallen into a sickness, and been brought to despair of his life, made prayer unto God, and God restored him to health and gave him an extension of his life of fifteen years, and with a view to give him a sure belief in the promise, He wrought for him this dread and mighty sign because He is the God of gods,

---

[1] According to Bérôsus, this king, whom he calls Mardocampados, was himself, like Hezekiah, tributary to the Assyrians.

who made heaven and earth and all things that therein are.

The Babylonian having learned this, and having been taught by the occurrence that He by whom it was wrought was the God of the universe, lost no time in sending many gifts and an embassy to Hezekiah, as being a true and beloved servant of the God of all. On this occasion he was likewise taught that heaven is not a revolving sphere, according to the opinion of the Babylonians, who at first suspected it to be such, when they were engaged in building the Tower to a lofty height, but that it was stationary and fastened to the earth as a vault. For if it were a sphere, then while the universe was wheeling in a forward direction, the sun, since he could not but be carried along with it, could not be advancing in the opposite direction so as to move backwards for the space of three hours, that is, the fourth part of a day, and again another fourth part, until he came back to the place from which he had retrograded. But about all these figures we wrote in the *Christian Topography*, as you yourself, admirable Sir, know, at the exhortation of the God-beloved Pamphilus of Jerusalem. For the very Prophet through whom the retrogression of the sun was effected, when, by means of the dread sign, he had in reality confuted the theory of the Babylonians, by showing that the heaven is not a revolving sphere, and that they held an opinion that is erroneous, this very Prophet not long afterwards speaks thus of the figure of the heaven: *He that established the heaven as a vaulted chamber;*[1] and again: *The Lord God who made the heaven and fixed it,*[2] thus declaring at once that it is a vault, and that it is established and fixed and not in revolution. But by committing such things to writing it is manifest that he did a good service to the Babylonians. For whoso

---

[1] Isai. xl. 22. [2] Isai. xlv, 18.

wishes can learn this from what took place in the time of Cyrus the King of the Persians. For taking into his hands the book of Isaiah he found as he read the section which contained the prophecy concerning himself; since Isaiah says in that section: *Thus saith the Lord to his Anointed, to Cyrus, whose right hand I have holden to subdue nations before him, and I will loose the loins of kings. I will open the doors before him, and the gates shall not be shut. I will go before thee and will level mountains. I will break in pieces the doors of brass, and cut in sunder the bars of iron; and I will give thee the treasures of darkness, and hidden riches of secret places will I present to thee, that thou mayest know I am the Lord, which call thee by thy name, even the God of Israel. For Jacob my servant's sake and Israel my chosen, I have called thee by thy name and I will accept thee;*[1] and shortly afterwards: *I have raised him up a king in righteousness, and I will make straight all his ways. He shall build my city, and lead back the captivity of my people, not for price nor reward, saith the Lord of hosts.*[2] Cyrus, struck with wonder at the foreknowledge and the prediction, and finding his own name expressly announced by the Prophet beforehand,[3] ordered the people to go up to Jerusalem, after having released them from captivity, and given them funds wherewith to build their city and their temple. And not only did he do this, but those also who came after him did the same until the City and the Temple were finished.

The decree of Cyrus, which is committed to writing and

---

[1] Isai. xlv. 1-4.   [2] *Ibid.* 13.

[3] The foregoing quotations are taken from the forty-fifth chapter of Isaiah. Some biblical critics contend that the latter chapters of this Prophet (40 to 66) were written by a deutero-Isaiah who was about a century later than the first. One of their arguments in support of this view is, that Cyrus is mentioned by name, and that an intimate knowledge is exhibited of his career.

recorded in Chronicles and in Esdras (Ezra), and which enjoined all the people to go up, runs thus: *In the first year of Cyrus King of Persia, that the word of the Lord by the mouth of Jeremiah might be accomplished, the Lord stirred up the spirit of Cyrus King of the Persians that he made a proclamation throughout all his kingdom and put it also in writing, saying: Thus saith Cyrus King of the Persians, all the kingdoms of the earth hath the Lord, the God of heaven, given me, and he hath charged me to build him an house in Jerusalem which is in Judaea. Whosoever there is among you of all his people, be God with him and let him go up!*[1] See, my admirable friend, how he acknowledges that he had read the book of Isaiah, and believed in what was written, and fulfilled what was written in scripture with all diligence and without sparing the expense. How then is it not manifest that much benefit to religion accrued to all nations from all these circumstances? And how could those who had such faith in the scripture of Isaiah disbelieve what he said concerning the figure of heaven in his book. *He that hath established the heaven as a vault?*[2] especially when in that age the miracles of the overthrow of Senachereim and of the retrogression of the sun were still recent events; whence also all the men of rank among them being convinced as to the truth of these world-renowned miracles, and convinced also by the prophesying of Isaiah, agreed to the opinion of the king, and released the people with honour. Since then the Babylonians were the first who conjectured and suspected that the heaven was a sphere, they again were the first to be taught, through Isaiah the Prophet, that it is not a sphere but a vault. From these sources having derived all the figures we have also depicted them in the *Christian Topography*, in the preface thereto, giving the name of the master who taught

---

[1] Ezra i. 1-3.   [2] Isai. xl, 22.

us, namely, the great Patricius,[1] who came here among us from the country of the Chaldaeans—and so much again on these matters.

When the ambassadors of the Babylonian king came to Hezekiah, his heart in a fresh access of human weakness was lifted up with pride, and he received them with all gladness, for his own glory; and contrary to the will of God, he led them into the palace, displaying to them his treasures and all his riches. Then again Isaiah was sent to him to correct his frame of mind, and said to him ironically: *What do these men say, and whence came they unto thee?* And Hezekiah said: *From a far country have they come unto me—even from Babylon.* Then said Isaiah again: *What have they seen in thine house?*[2] But the King, seeing that the Prophet put the question knowing how matters stood, told the truth and said to him: *All that is in my house have they seen, and there is nothing in the house which they have not seen—yea they have even seen all my treasures.*[3] Then he told him, by way of a threat to chastise the pride which uplifted his heart, what would come to pass after him and says: *Hear the word of the Lord of Hosts. Behold the days come, that all that is in thine house, and that which thy fathers have laid up in store until this day, shall be carried to Babylon: nothing shall be left, saith the Lord. And of thy sons that shall issue from thee, which thou shalt beget, shall they take away, and they shall be eunuchs in the palace of the King of Babylon;*[4] as if He said, For you ought to have been instructed by your former experiences that, not so much for your glory as for Mine, were the mighty signs wrought, in order that the nations also may be made acquainted with My greatness, which thou again didst think lightly of, and wert uplifted with pride, not giving

---

[1] See note 2, p. 24. [2] Isai. xxxix, 3.
[3] *Ibid.*, 4. [4] *Ibid.*, 5-7.

Me thanks. But since without My sanction thou didst receive the ambassadors, and didst show them the wealth which thou hast obtained from Me, be therefore henceforth taught that hereafter, in the time of thy successors, I will deliver over to the Babylonians all thy wealth to be plundered and captured, because thou hadst again no regard for My glory, but didst honour thyself in preference to Me. But inasmuch as thou hast ever been virtuous and pious, none of these things shall happen in thy times. Hezekiah, on hearing and understanding this, humbled himself, as he was a righteous man and obedient to God, and giving thanks said to Isaiah: *Good is the word of the Lord which he hath spoken. Let there be peace in my days.*[1]

But that all things happened according to the word of the Prophet is a clear matter of fact, for Nabouchodonosor (Nebuchadnezzar) the King of Babylon having plundered Jerusalem took all the spoils to Babylon, and having selected young men of the royal line, Daniel, Ananias, Azarias, Misael and their companions, he made them eunuchs and appointed them to his own service; for it was a custom for the King to be served by eunuchs, as they were his personal attendants. In divine scripture certainly there is no record of the marriage of any one of them, or of child born to them, nor was any thing of this nature heard regarding them. But tradition and custom alike, according to the prophecy, represent them, as shown in their pictures, to be beardless snd smooth-skinned. But that, in their time, there were many miracles and prodigies and revelations and predictions which proved of great benefit to the Babylonians, Medes and Persians, thou art not unaware, O admirable Peter, and that in consequence the Kings greatly honoured them, and among their own subjects published decrees touching religion, which pro-

---

[1] Isai. xxxix, 8.

claimed, with reference to the God of all, that He is the God of gods and the Lord of lords ; and they moreover ordained that such as uttered blasphemy against Him should be punished. Thus God who continually directs all things, by means of His own people, teaches all the nations by raising to honour those who do righteously, while He punishes those who sin, and sends them into captivity—thus teaching the nations by each of these dispensations to recognize His beneficence and His majesty ; in order that they also may take their share in the duties of religion, being trained beforehand for the faith to be afterwards revealed through our Lord Jesus Christ. For not one jot or one tittle of scripture has been written needlessly, but all that is therein has been recorded for some useful end and for the common and manifold advantage of men. Wherefore, my Christ-loving friend, I beseech, through you, those who fall in with this composition of mine to read constantly divine scripture, and to reap therefrom all the gain wherewith it can help every man in affairs human and divine. God grant that we may obtain the divine blessing and promises through the prayers of our teachers and of thy brotherhood, O thou who lovest Christ with thine whole heart.[1]

Just as the twelve loaves of shew-bread which lay on the table are a type of the annual cycle and of the fruits of the earth, as was said when we treated of the Tabernacle, and as is described in the ninth book, so also now we have delineated the cycle of the twelve months of the year, and the fruits produced in each month, giving thanks to God the giver of all, as also David moved by the Holy Spirit thus in a psalm addresses God : *Bless thou the crown of*

---

[1] Montfaucon has here this note : Cosmas here again delineates the figure of the conical mountain which causes nights and eclipses, as he thought it would contribute much to the understanding of the

the year of thy goodness;[1] thus in a remarkable way styling the cycle of the twelve months of the year a crown of goodness, as crowning the surface of the earth with beauty, and fostering the growth and maturity of its monthly fruits through the tempering of the elements which the invisible powers accomplish. Wherefore he further adds: *And the plains shall be filled with thy fatness;*[1] and again: *Thou hast prepared their food, for thou hast so prepared it.*[2] And elsewhere again he speaks thus: *They all look to thee to give them their food in due season;*[3] as if he said, Thou nourishest us, preparing our food from the products of each season. And elsewhere he thus speaks concerning our most necessary food, which the summer tropic perfects, and continues to give us for three months successively: *They have been increased with their corn and wine and oil*[4]— here again in a remarkable way, in the giving of thanks, observing the order in nature and mentioning first corn, then

things said before, and of the ninth book, regarding the course of the stars. For the cycle of the twelve months, see Pl. 23 in the Appendix.

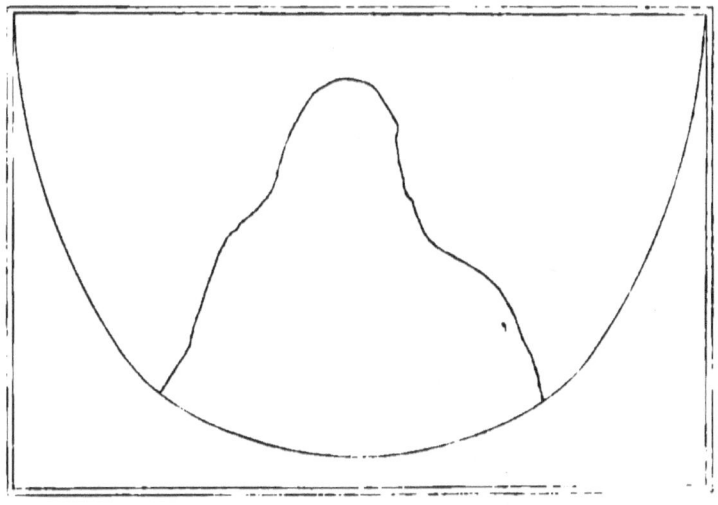

[1] Psalm lxv, 12.
[2] *Ibid.*, 10.
[3] Psalm civ, 27.
[4] Gen. iv, 7.

wine, and thirdly oil, in accordance with the order, in which by the blessing of God, they are produced during the three summer months, by the agency of the rational orders, namely, angels and men. It is therefore the duty of every Christian to read divine scripture neither in a cursory nor perfunctory way, but with studious care and in a suitable order, as in the outset we advised, in order that the divine grace, accepting our resolution, may coöperate in enabling us to know the mighty works of God. To Him be glory for ever, Amen! Be strong, ye Christians, in the Lord.

BOOK IX.

Concerning the course of the heavenly bodies.

HE circle of the twelve months is the uppermost, that of the sun is lower, and that of the moon is lower still.[1] Divine scripture signifies this by the structure of the candlestick, whereby the circular branches spring out from its shaft three on the one side and three on the other in such wise that one branch precedes another branch,[2] and each day the circle of the twelve months outruns the sun one degree, so that the sun is found in thirty days running through one month, and thus in twelve months completing the year, falling short, as has been said, one degree each day.[3] The circle again of the sun outruns the circle of the moon[4] twelve degrees each day,[5] so that it is found that the moon in thirty[6] days falls short of accomplishing the whole of the circle, that is, one month. But if any

---

[1] See Pl. 9 in the Appendix, depicting the *celestial sphere* of Ptolemy.

[2] See Pl. 15 in the Appendix.

[3] More exactly 59′ 8⅓″.

[4] Gr. Τὸν δὲ κύκλον τῆς σελήνης, ἡ τοῦ ἡλίου προτρέχει. As προτρέχει governs the genitive, the reading should be τοῦ δὲ κύκλου, and ἡ should be ὁ.

[5] More exactly 12° 11′ 26¾″.   [6] 29½+days.

should choose to consider the matter in the reverse way,[1] then the circle of the moon falls short of that of the sun every day twelve degrees and some minutes, and the circle of the sun falls short of the uppermost circle of all, that is, of the twelve months, every day one degree. But these bodies are moved by the invisible Powers in an orderly and rational manner according to the will of God, these Powers having received this as a law, according to what is written in David: *Bless the Lord, all ye his angels, ye mighty in strength, that fulfil his word, hearkening unto the voice of his word. Bless the Lord all ye his hosts, ye ministers of his that do his pleasure.*[2] To Him be glory for ever and ever, Amen!

And these courses of the twelve mansions of the twelve stars and of the two great luminaries, according to the length of their three circles, we have explained to the best of our power in terms consistent with Christian doctrine, being moved by divine assistance, and at the same time drawing our conclusions from optical appearances. But as to the course of the two great luminaries in respect of latitude, and as to their transitions, their ascensions and declinations, conjunctions and seasons of full moon, nodes and elongations of their courses,[3] parallaxes and phases, regular and irregular motions, and their northern and southern limits, and other terms which the pagans are pleased to employ, whereby they calculate the eclipses of the same luminaries, we resign the calculation to those who know and investigate such subjects with a view to calculate and foretell eclipses, since by this our withers are unwrung, and we are

---

[1] Gr. Ἐι δέ τις ἐξ ἀντιστρόφου βουλειθείη νοεῖν. Montfaucon translates this wrongly: Quod si quis *facta comparatione* rem considerare voluerit.

[2] Psalm ciii, 21, 22.

[3] Gr. ἐκδιαμέτρων δρόμων. Montfaucon renders: de diametralibus cursibus.

even more confirmed in our views. For if terms of this kind, namely, transitions, ascensions, declinations, etc., hold [as they do] a place in our scheme, contention is futile. Now we have not cared to show anything else by this treatise of ours than that these eclipses of the two luminaries do occur, and are in harmony with our scheme, although the heaven should not be moved at all from east to west, or from west to east, and whether it be spherical or consist of many spheres; while at the same time the stars and luminaries in the air, by the agency of the rational powers, complete their course in observance of their order, and the figure of the two heavens and of the earth is preserved in accordance with divine scripture—a figure in which from the beginning God prepared two states —the present and the future, namely those circles which we have described, and not heavens that are spherical, continuous, solid of body and transparent—according to the nonsensical babble of the pagans.

We remember to have stated in the second book that the angels move the luminaries and the stars and all else, as having been ordained for the service of men, and there also we have delineated the scheme as far as it is possible to exhibit it graphically. For we have testimonies from divine scripture showing that this is so. For that these bodies have a circular motion David shows when he says: *Thou shalt bless the crown of the year with thy goodness;*[1] here with wonderful propriety styling the circle of the twelve months a crown, as crowning the face of the earth with beauty, whence he added: *And the fields shall be filled with thy fatness.*[1] For by the circular motion and the succession of returns from the tropics, the fruits of the earth grow and reach maturity. Yea, even Moses placed upon that which was typical of the earth, namely, upon

---

[1] Psalm lxv, 11.

the table all round, the twelve loaves of shew-bread, three at each corner, signifying by the corners the four tropics, each distant from each three months, and by the circle the twelve months, and by the loaves the fruits of the earth, thus mystically representing the months by a circle crowning the earth above. In like manner also he arranged the twelve tribes in a circle around the Tabernacle, three on the east, three on the south, three on the west, and three on the north, beginning from the east, going up to south, descending again to the west and then lastly running through the north in accordance with the motion of the stars and the position of the earth.

This circle the pagans call the Zodiac which we have ourselves delineated in accordance with their theory.[1] But the other seven stars, which they call planets, Moses obscurely represented by placing seven lamps in the candlestick, which he placed in the south, so that it cast its light upon the table towards the north, while by the lamps he signified a week of seven days, signifying by all these the days, the weeks, the months, the tropics, and the year. By the daily loaves which were each day laid down new upon the table, he indicated the days, and by the seven lamps the week, and by the number of the loaves the twelve months, and by the four corners the tropics, and by the circle the year, concerning which things the divine Apostle speaks in the Epistle to the Hebrews :[2] *Now if he were on earth he would not be a priest at all, seeing there are those who offer the gifts according to the law ; who serve that which is a copy and shadow of the heavenly things, even as Moses is warned of God when he is about to make the Tabernacle : For, see, saith he, that thou make all things according to the pattern which was shown thee in the Mount.* And Solomon says : *The sun ariseth, and the sun goeth down, and hasteth to*

---

[1] See Plates 9 and 22 in the Appendix.   [2] Heb. viii, 4, 5.

his place. Arising he goeth there towards the south and wheeleth round in his circuit, and the wind goeth on its circuits.[1] He also, in what he says, agrees with Moses and David, namely, that the sun proceeding from the east ascends to the south, and by making a circuit through the north, causes the tropics, and completes the great circle of the year in his passage through the air; for this is what the expression *the wind goeth on* means, as if he said, *in the air*. And that the heavenly bodies are moved by the invisible Powers, divine scripture intimates this also, when it says: *For the creation was made subject to vanity not of its own will, but by reason of him who subjected it in hope that the creation itself shall be delivered from the bondage of corruption into the liberty of the glory of the children of God;*[2] meaning by this, that at the final consummation, the angels shall be delivered from this bondage, and from the ministrations which they render on account of men, for men, having then become immortal and immutable, will no longer be in need of such ministrations, as the Lord also in the Gospels speaks thus concerning the consummation: *For the powers of heaven shall be shaken*,[3] thus calling the angels the powers of heavens, and by the expression *they shall be shaken*, He means they shall be set free from their former office. As the angels, therefore, who move the stars themselves and other things, are certainly set free from this office and ministry, He declares that the stars fall to the earth.

The language of the Apostle also: *Are they not all ministering spirits sent forth to minister for the sake of them that shall inherit salvation?*[4] very clearly shows that they all for the sake of man are occupied night and day in their ministrations and services, and in doing everything else

---

[1] Eccl. i, 5, 6.   [2] Rom. viii, 20.
[3] Matt. xxiv, 19.   [4] Heb. i, 14.

towards giving men relaxation from their toils and towards supplying their wants. For, when we shall no longer need them, they shall be set free from this bondage and service, and shall cast down the stars upon the earth. As Paul endured many toils and afflictions and persecutions for the Church, and at last, from the multitude of his impending dangers, was driven to despondency, the divine grace consoled him by means of frequent visions, encouraging him not to despair, but to persevere, and to minister to the growth and propagation of the Church. He therefore sets forth from these things for us two causes [of the visions], one pointing to labour, and the other to reward. For what does he say? *I know a man in Christ fourteen years ago (whether in the body I know not, or whether out of the body I know not, God knoweth), how that he was caught up into the third heaven;*[1] and again he says: *And I know such a man that he was caught up into the third heaven and heard unspeakable words which it is not lawful for a man to utter;*[2] here manifestly setting forth things concerning himself in the person of another. I know, he says, O Corinthians, if I needs must myself come to visions and revelations of the Lord, that I was, in a wondrous manner beyond all conception, caught up to a vast height, that of the distance from the earth to the firmament, two-third parts, so that only one third of the whole height of heaven remained to me to be ascended.[3] And what was the cause of his being thus caught up I will with God's help explain. Since the invisible powers in this height up to which Paul was caught, in obedience to the divine ordinance, for the sake of man move the heavenly bodies unceasingly and unhesitatingly by night and by day, He

---

[1] II Cor. xii, 2.   [2] *Ibid.*, 3.

[3] From this it would appear that Cosmas took the distance from the earth to the firmament to be double the distance from the firmament to the summit of heaven. But see note 3, p. 116, and its text.

therefore caught up Paul, and conducted him thither, to show him the incessant service which they perform for the sake of men—to show him in what a rational, orderly, rhythmical and intelligent a manner, and with what toil and assiduity and solicitude, they render their service, and fulfil their work, that he might thus in a measure comfort Paul, so that in labouring for the Church, he might not give way to despondency, but persevere in his ministry, as he saw the angels were doing in theirs. Paul therefore had the boldness to reveal how they ranked in dignity, naming Principalities, and Powers, and Virtues, and Thrones, and Dominations. For some of them perform the work while others superintend the workers, and others exercise power as commanders of squadrons; and to say all in a word, all of them alike, groaning and travailing in pain together, perform their labour with great anxiety and solicitude, and in rational order, all of them being together desirous to gain their freedom from that bondage under which they serve for the sake of men.

I shall here speak again, God helping me, concerning the being caught up into Paradise. Since, after their departure from the body, the souls of the righteous, who are thought worthy to enter into the kingdom of heaven, are consigned to Paradise (as we learn from the case of the thief who was crucified along with the Lord), until the resurrection, being there kept as in a choice and honoured place by the invisible Powers, who entertain them with hymns and every mark of honour; God caught up Paul thither, and by way of comforting him, showed him, but in part only, the crowns which were the prizes of his toils and struggles; whence he was unable to give a perfect description of the things there; yea, he rather declared them to be unspeakable and incomprehensible, but he had the boldness to write, that for him, as one who had finished his course of service, and had kept the faith, there was laid up a crown of righteousness by the Lord, and not for him only, but also for all who are like him. And so much we have said with regard to the visions.

But here it is to be noted that all the heavenly bodies are under the firmament, and are moved and wheeled in their orbits below the two-thirds of the height of heaven,[1] by the ministry and the arrangement of the invisible Powers. And from this we learn that an angel does not ascend beyond the heavenly bodies. For if *they are all ministering spirits sent forth to minister for the sake of them that shall inherit salvation*,[2] let any one who is opposed to this opinion declare in what service the angel, who goes above the firmament, is engaged; and if he is at a loss to point this out, let him submit, I do not say to us, but to divine scripture. For it is impossible for any of us, while still mortal or corruptible or mutable, to go beyond the stars, unless we receive from God incorruption and immortality and immutability by the resurrection from the dead; unless the angels also are, in like manner, along with us, delivered from bondage, and casting down the stars to the earth, likewise obtain immutability and freedom, we do not go beyond the stars and cleave the firmament to enter into the kingdom of heaven. For this the Apostle shows when he says: *Flesh and blood cannot inherit the kingdom of God*;[1] here by the word *flesh* meaning mortality, and by *blood* mutability. He declared therefore that it is impossible for one who is mortal or mutable to inherit the kingdom of heaven. He subjoins immediately: *Neither doth corruption inherit incorruption*[3]—and he repeated this, by way of showing that nothing that is corrupt can go up and enter there, for harm rather than any advantage would

---

[1] That is two-thirds of the height of heaven above the earth. See note 3, p. 116, and note 3, p. 326.
[2] Heb. i, 14.   [3] 1 Cor. xv, 50.

result. For just as we, who are far away from the sun, have not the power, should we direct our eyes to his disc, to continue doing so, but would be injured and blinded rather than profited, so would it fare with any one if, while still mortal or mutable or corruptible, he should seek to overstep the boundaries, and approach the way which leads to the kingdom of heaven, while still far off therefrom. So then, just as the Lord Christ when He had risen from the dead, having become incorruptible in the body and immortal, and in soul immutable, then passed beyond the heavenly Powers, and when He had approached the firmament, having become, as it is written, better than the angels, He pierced it and entered into the kingdom of heaven; as Paul also declares when he says that he ascended far above all principality, etc., so we also and the angels, having obtained these attributes, enter therein. Again, the two trees in the middle of Paradise mystically presignify the present state and the future, and the tree of the knowledge of good and evil is a type of this world which is mortal and mutable, having pleasures and pains, and being a school of discipline,[1] just as Adam was taught by this tree both good and evil. Now the tree of life is a type of the future heavenly world, in which life and blessedness reign, for the saying: *Lest he stretch forth his hand and take of the tree of life*,[2] signified the vast height of the tree and thereby signified the mansions above. As therefore He commanded the Cherubim with the flaming sword which turned every way, to guard the way to the tree of life, so He commanded the angels and the luminaries which revolve round the height of the firmament, to guard the way which is there that leads into the kingdom of heaven; intend-

---

[1] According to the Greek text there should be a full stop after discipline; but it seems better to place it after the clause which follows. [2] Gen. iii, 22.

ing to signify that the mansions above are meanwhile inaccessible to men. At His Passion therefore the Lord Christ carried with Him the soul of the thief into Paradise, having suspended the guardianship of the Cherubim and of the flaming sword, which turned every way. But after His resurrection, when He came to his ascension, He opened a passage through the host of the invisible Powers, and the luminaries and the firmament itself, and entered into the kingdom where immortality, and immutability, and blessedness reign. At the final consummation therefore, when the angels cease to make the luminaries revolve and when the stars fall, then the Cherubim and the flaming sword waving both ways no longer prevent men from entering into the true life, but the righteous, raised on high and traversing the new way and piercing the firmament with the Lord Christ, shall inherit the kingdom of life. Do Thou, who hast compassion and great pity, deem us also, along with Thy righteous, worthy of this life and inheritance.

BOOK X.

Passages from the Fathers.

CERTAIN of those [Christians] who delight in wrangling, on reading this book and finding it no easy matter to face such a weight of testimony as we have adduced in this treatise from the divine scriptures, thus addressed us : " You and the Fathers on whom you rely interpret divine scripture in a peculiar way to make it correspond with your own opinions, for nothing is conveyed by it about figures and types such as you assert. But the Fathers on whom we rely, who could not but have known accurately the true scope of divine scripture, have in their expositions transmitted to us nothing such as you say, since scripture tells us : *God hath set in the Church, first Apostles, secondly Prophets, thirdly Teachers.*[1] To the Apostles indeed and to the Prophets you seem to have attached yourself in your interpretation, but as for the Teachers who are the exponents of the true scope of divine scripture, you hold aloof from them entirely, and travel a strange road, known to none but to yourself and your friends." On this account, therefore, we are constrained to make manifest once more to all their love of contention, and to this end we have placed together in this book the testimonies of

---

[1] I Cor. xii, 28.

the Fathers, even those whom they themselves adduce
either in pretence or in sincerity, in order that they may
be refuted by their own authorities, and be convinced how
admirably our treatise is confirmed by the testimonies of
all the Apostles and Prophets and Teachers. And first
let step forward the great Athanasius[1] who proclaims the
same views as ourselves.

From the Festal Epistles of Athanasius.[2]

316-319   Observe, pray, how this great Teacher is constantly in
agreement with ourselves and our doctrine, in the view he
takes of the whole figure of the world, calling the kingdom
of heaven a great and supramundane hall, sufficient for
the whole creation, and proclaiming that the Lord Christ
as our forerunner is therein, and that we shall enter into
it along with him at his second coming; And the saying:
Enter into the joy of thy Lord[3] he refers to that very hall,
that is, to the heaven of heavens which is the kingdom of
heaven—and he says that this has been prepared for men
by God from the foundation of the world, and that the
Tabernacle erected by Moses is a type of the heavens.
Can the lovers of contention show how this great Teacher
does not agree with us, or how we have been going a
strange road different from that of the Church? But away
with the vain labour of these men! We will add to
Athanasius, Gregory of Nazianzus[4] with whose praises

---

[1] For a notice of Athanasius and his Festal Epistles, see note 3, p. 290.

[2] Montfaucon here notes that he had published the passages adduced by Cosmas in vol. xxvi, column 1431, of the *Patrologia*. So they do not appear either in the Greek or Latin texts.   [3] Matt. xxv, 21.

[4] St. Gregory, the son of Gregory Bishop of Nazianzus, was born in the year A.D. 329, and was eminent for the zeal with which he defended the Nicene creed against the attacks of the Arians. When offered by his friend St. Basil the See of Sasima, he declined it, but he was afterwards installed as the Patriarch of Constantinople,—an

they make the world ring, and who yet proclaims the same views as the previous authority and ourselves.

Extract from the discourse on the Passover by Gregory of Nazianzus.

"But let us sacrifice to God a sacrifice of praise upon the altar on high along with the choir above; let us go through the first veil, let us draw near to the second, let us glance into the Holy of Holies." How then is it not manifest that we have not gone a strange road different from that of the Church? Let the men of strife therefore be ashamed of themselves when they see the harmony of the Church, and let them not be intolerant of us, for it is hard for them to kick against the pricks. But let us introduce a third after him, one who was his contemporary, even Theophilus Bishop of the Church at Alexandria,[1] who also bears testimony to our opinions, yea rather, to the truth.

From the first Festal Epistle of Theophilus of Alexandria.

"In order that, being engaged in higher than earthly 320 doings in the sublime mansion of virtue, we may, like the disciples, eat the Passover in the upper chamber, having with us Christ, who was sacrificed for us, while we eat Him all, as our life."

From the same Festal Epistle of the same.

"In order that, having again drawn back the veil of the word, we may with unveiled face behold the festival of the

---

office which he resigned after only a brief tenure. He died in 389 or 390.

[1] Theophilus became Bishop of Alexandria in 385 A.D. He was one of the most violent and unscrupulous ecclesiastics of his time. He opposed Chrysostom, persecuted the Origenists, and took violent measures to drive all the Pagans out of his diocese. His turbulent career came to an end in 412.

divine Passover,[1] appealing thus to Jesus : *Where wilt thou that we prepare to eat the Passover with thee?*[2] On receiving his reply that this feast was to be celebrated in an upper chamber, a chamber, that is, of second things,[3] the disciples with alacrity of heart betook themselves with all speed to enter the Holy of Holies, into which Christ Himself hath entered for us, and hath done away with any further need of the typical High Priest, having obtained eternal redemption for us, and on our behalf presenting Himself before the face of God. Formerly indeed the High Priest alone once a year entered into the Holy of Holies, the people remaining without by reason of the littleness of their power. But the Saviour having entered in, has given full liberty of access to all who wish."

Observe how this authority is also in harmony with us in calling the upper chamber a house, into which the Lord Christ as forerunner hath entered for us (of whom the High Priest in the Tabernacle of Moses was a type) to present Himself before the face of God, and hath given full liberty to all who wish, to enter into the Holy of Holies, that is, into the kingdom of heaven. Let those who are on the side of the schismatics reply to the following questions. How have we gone a strange road different from that of the Church? How is it that they do not regard the words of their own Fathers? but falsely traduce them as if they were heretics. But passing from this Father, let us turn to the fourth who was his contemporary and fellow mystic, Severianus, namely, the Bishop of Gabala,[4] who can be taken as a witness to confirm all that is written in my work.

---

[1] Gr. τὴν διαβατήριον τοῦ Θείου Πάσχα "transitoriam divini paschatis celebritatem" *Montfaucon*. Philo also uses διαβατήριον to designate the Passover.   [2] Matt. xxvi, 17.

[3] Gr. δευτέρων πραγμάτων.

[4] Regarding Severianus, see note 2, p. 291.

From the first book of the Hexaëmeron (Six days of the Creation) of Severianus, Bishop of Gabala.

"For on the first day He made the matter out of which things were created; but on the other days He gave their form and arrangement to the things created. For example, He made the heaven which was before non-existent—not this visible heaven, but the one above it, for the visible was made on the second day. God made the higher heaven— *the heaven of heavens to the Lord*,[1] and it is higher than this visible heaven, and, as in a house of two stories,[2] between it and the earth another heaven is interposed. God having thus created the world as one house, placed this visible heaven as a roof in the middle, and the waters above it. Wherefore, David says: *Who covereth his upper chambers with waters.*[3] God then made the heaven when it was not, the earth when it was not, the abysses when they were not, and wind, air, fire, water; of all the things that came into existence He made their matter on the first day. But some one will say that it is recorded that He made the heaven and the earth, while nothing is recorded of waters and fire and air. In the first place then, brethren, when He said that the heaven and the earth were made, He indicated by the things which contain, the things that are contained. Then after the interposition of a few passages, hear Him next relate when the air was made: *And the spirit of God moved upon the face of the waters.*[4] Here He does not speak of the Holy Spirit, for the uncreated is not numbered along with what is created, but it is the motion of the air which He calls *spirit*. *God said, Let there be light,*[5] and the nature of fire came into being. And again proceeding He says: But our souls He

---

[1] Psalm cxiii, 5.   [2] Gr. ἐν οἴκῳ διωρόφῳ.
[3] Psalm civ, 3.   [4] Gen. i, 2.   [5] *Ibid.*, 3.

fenced round with the body, while He made the angels bodiless. So then, what we see to be the case with respect to human souls and to angels, the same is the case with respect to fire, for the fire above subsists without matter, but the fire below with matter, for the fire above is akin to the fire below, just as our souls are also akin to the angels. How so? because the former are spirit and the latter too are spirit. And again: All of them were then brought into existence, fire, abyss, winds, the four elements, earth, fire, water, air; for whatever Moses omitted he comprehended in that marvellous summary where he says: *For in six days God made the heaven and the earth and all the things that therein are.*[1] And just as in the case of the body he did not speak of all its members, so in the case of the creation he did not enumerate all its parts, although all things were created simultaneously with the world. But if there was not fire in the world, it could not at the present day be struck from rock and from wood; for the friction of wood against wood generates fire, but if Nature did not hold it, from what source does she produce it?"[2]

From the same, from the second book.

"On the second day God said: *Let there be a firmament in the midst of the waters, and let it divide the waters from the waters.*[3] He made this heaven, not the one above, but the visible heaven which he crystallised from the waters like ice. But I shall endeavour to place the matter before your eyes, for many things are better explained by ocular than by oral demonstration. This water, let us suppose, overflowed the earth five cubits. Then God said: *Let there be a firmament in the midst of the water,*[3] and

---

[1] Exod. xx. 11.
[2] Gr. πόθεν γεννᾷ. Montfaucon renders this by *quomodo generabit.*
[3] Gen. i, 6.

thereupon a solid ice-like substance was produced in the midst of the waters, which made lighter the upper half of the water, and left the other half underneath, as it is written: *Let there be a firmament (στερέωμα) in the midst of the water, and let it make a division between the waters.*[1] But wherefore does he call it the *firmament?* It is, because God made it *firm and solid (ἐστερέωσε)* from waters which are of rarer and less compact substance. Wherefore David also says: *Praise him in the firmament of his power;*[2] and, to take another example, we may adduce smoke, which when emitted from burning wood is rarified and attenuated, but when it mounts up high into the air becomes transformed into the density of a cloud. In this wise, when God had made the waters, which are by nature rarified, ascend on high, He there made them solid. And that this example is to the point, and true, Isaiah testifies where he says: *The heaven was made firm and solid as smoke.*[3] The heaven having therefore become solid in the midst of the waters made the upper half of them light, but the other half He left underneath. Why then and for what purpose were the waters placed above? Was it that we might drink them or that we might sail on them? For that there are waters above, David testifies, saying: *And the water which is above the heavens.*[4] Observe then the wisdom of the Creator; the heaven was crystalline, having been consolidated from the waters; but since it was to receive the flame of the sun and of the moon and the countless hosts of the stars, and was entirely filled with fire, then in order that it might not be dissolved, nor burned with the heat, He spread over the upper surfaces of heaven those sea-like expanses of water, with a view to soften, and as it were to anoint the upper

---

[1] Gen. i, 6.   [2] Psalm cl, 1.
[3] Isai. li, 6.   [4] Psalm cxlviii, 4.

surface and thus render it capable of resisting the scorching heat of the flames. An example of this is ready at hand: if, for instance, you to-day put a pot on the fire, with water therein, the pot withstands the fire, but if you do not supply water the pot will crack or melt. Accordingly, against fire He opposed heat as its counteractive, in order that the upper surface of heaven being, as it were, anointed with the waters, might be well enough able to maintain its existence. And observe what is here marvellous; in the body of heaven which is assailed by so much fire, the moisture is so superabundant that it lends a constant supply to the earth. For whence cometh the dew of the cloud? from nowhere? The air holds no water; so it is clear that the heaven drops it from its superabundance. Wherefore also the Patriarch Isaac when blessing Jacob said: *God give thee of the dew of heaven and of the fatness of the earth*"[1]—And later on he[2] thus continues: "Observe, I pray you, that the waters above the heaven render another service, for not only do they preserve the heaven, but they also send down the flame of the sun and the moon, since, if the whole heaven were transparent, the rays would mount upwards; for, as it is the nature of fire to ascend, it would leave the earth destitute of light. On this account, therefore, He compressed the heaven above with a boundless expanse of waters, in order that the rays, being confined, might be sent downwards. Behold then the wisdom of the Architect. And thou hast even in thyself the image of the Architect. So attend particularly, I pray you, to what I shall now say: Suppose this head to be the heaven above, and what is above the tongue to be the other heaven, namely, the firmament, whence also [the palate] is called the little heaven,[3] or roof of the

---

[1] Gen. xxvii, 23.   [2] Severianus.
[3] Gr. οὐρανίσκος. Aristotle uses οὐρανός itself in this meaning: τοῦτο δ' εἰς μὲν τὸν ἐγκέφαλον οὐκ ἔχει πόρον, εἰς δὲ τὸν τοῦ στόματος οὐρανόν.—*Hist. Anim.*, i, 11.

mouth; now, above, in the invisible parts is the brain not manifest to sight, while in the lower heaven is the the tongue, a thing manifest to sight, just as the upper heaven is classed with things discerned by the intellect, but the world, with the things we ordinarily talk about."[1]

From the same discourse.

"For on the third day the fruits were produced, and in order again that it might not be supposed that they were produced by the influence of the sun, it was not until their creation was finished, that He made the sun and the moon and the stars. But whence did He make them? For it has been said that on the first day He made all things of nothing, but on the other days, out of things existing. Whence then the Sun? Why, out of the light created on the first day which the Architect modified at His pleasure and transformed into objects of varied aspects, creating, in the first place, the substance of the light, and then producing the luminaries, just as if one should bring forward a mass of gold, and should then coin it into pieces of money, and by so doing make it a thing of beauty. For just as He divided the abyss, which was then one mass of water, into the water on high, into seas, into rivers, into fountains, into lakes, into wells, so also did the Architect divide the light, which was a single uniform mass, and distribute it into the sun, into the moon and into the stars." And subsequently we read: "He made therefore the heaven, not a sphere, as those vain babblers conceive—for He did not make a rolling sphere, but, as the prophet says: *Who hath made the heaven as a vaulted chamber and stretched it out as a tent to dwell in;*[2] for none of us is so impious as to be persuaded by these triflers, and not by the words of the Prophet, which declare that the heaven has a beginning and an end. For this

---

[1] Gr. ἐν τοῖς λαλουμένοις.   [2] Isai. xl, 22.

reason therefore the sun is not said by them to *ascend* but *to go out*, for the scripture saith: *The sun goeth out upon the earth*,[1] not goeth up; and again he says: *From the end of heaven is his going forth, and at the end of heaven is his goal*.[2] Not a going up then—but if it is circular, it has not an end—for where are we to find an end of what is perfectly round? Does then David only say this, or does the Saviour also say so? Hear then this which is spoken by the Lord: *When the Son of Man cometh he shall send forth his angels with a great sound of a trumpet, and they shall gather together his elect from the four winds, from one end of heaven to the other*.[3] But, we ask again, where does the sun set, and where does he pursue his course by night? as we have said. Well, according to the pagans, under the earth, but according to us who speak of it as a tent, consider, I pray you, whether what we assert be false, or has the seal of the truth to attest it. Now, with my expression the place too [where we are met] coincides;[4] for such things are better explained by a reference to what is seen than by words addressed to the ear. Suppose a dome to be placed over the church with its east towards sunrise, its north in this direction, its south here, and its west there. Suppose next the sun rising and then going down—going down not under the earth, but pursuing his course through the northern parts, and hidden from view as by a wall, the waters not permitting his path to be seen—pursuing his course, I say, through the northern parts, and reaching again the quarter in which he rises. But whence is it made clear that this is so? By the blessed Solomon then, when in the book of Ecclesiastes, a book attested [to be inspired], and not rejected [from the canon] he says: *The sun ariseth, and the*

---

[1] Psalm xix, 5.   [2] *Ibid.* 6.   [3] Matt. xxiv, 30, 1.
[4] Gr. Συντρέχει δέ μου τῇ φράσει καὶ ὁ τόπος. The expression to which he refers is σκηνή, a *tent*, and the place must be the *church* in which the address was delivered.

sun goeth down, and hasteth to his place ; arising there he goeth to the south, and wheeling in his circuits, wheels towards the north ; the wind goeth and turneth about in its circuits.[1] Behold then the sun running his course in the south, and wheeling round to the north, and be instructed." And further on he says : " All things, therefore, obey the law of God. The heaven stands, not as upheld by its own power but firmly compacted by the divine word. For should I be at a loss to understand how the heaven was consolidated out of the waters, the blessed David resolves the difficulty when he says : *By the word of the Lord were the heavens made solid ;*[2] because made from the waters—for in no passage elsewhere is the [heaven] said to be *solid ;* it is one thing *to be made solid*, and another *to be solid*. The expression *being made solid* is used when that which is rarified and attenuated becomes consolidated."

From the same—from the sixth discourse.

"So then that tree had not a power in itself to produce a knowledge which would result in death, but it got its name from the dire calamity that befell Adam in connection with it. I shall briefly explain the matter ; for divine scripture presents no difficulty. To-day we have the saving food of which the faithful partake. That tree then has a natural salutariness. If, through the glory invoked,[3] you have a pledge from things that are present, why do you doubt about those that are past ? There the food was death-giving, here it is life-giving. If this saves by its natural properties, and not by grace—then that also killed by its natural properties, and not by the purpose he put before him ; if this food saves by its natural properties and

---

[1] Eccl. i, 5.   [2] Psalm xxxiii, 6.
[3] Gr. διὰ τὴν ἐπικαλουμένην δόξαν. Montfaucon renders : *gloriam te advocantem.*

not by grace, that also kills by its natural properties and not by the breaking of the commandment."

325 *From the same—from the fourth discourse.*

"For the angels having been created beings were not co-workers with God, but His ministers who praised Him in song, and expressed their gratitude for being brought into existence, being aware that, as they had no previous existence, they had been created by the Spirit of goodness. So they stood as spectators merely, beholding the things made along with them, and after them; for they beheld the heaven made of nothing, and were struck with astonishment; they beheld the sea parted off, and were lost in wonder; they saw the earth in her beautiful apparel, and were thrilled with delight. But that the angels were not co-workers, but admiring spectators, God says in Job: *When I made the stars, all the angels praised me and celebrated me in song;*[1] subsequently he says: "He beheld Adam sinning, but He foresaw his posterity acting righteously; He saw him being cast out from Paradise, but He foresaw that a kingdom had been prepared for him. And what is wonderful is this, that even before Paradise the kingdom had been made. Why then do you wonder at his having been cast out of Paradise, when the real wonder is that before Paradise existed, the kingdom of the heavens had been prepared for him?—as saith the Saviour: *Come, ye blessed of my Father, inherit the kingdom prepared for you from the foundation of the world.*"[2]

From the same—from the third discourse.

"It now remains to be examined why God made the moon at her full. Pray attend closely, for the subject to be considered is deep, as she required to be made on

---

[1] Job xxxviii, 7. [2] Matt. xxv, 34.

the fourth day in order to present a fourth day's appearance. And again, if she appeared four days old, she could not have occupied the extremity of the west. She was found therefore having an advantage of eleven days—for on the fourth day she appeared full, as she would have appeared on the fifteenth day. By eleven days then the moon is in advance of the sun, not by the act of her creation, but by her shining.[1] Wherefore what advantage she then gained, she paid back to the sun, for as the number of days in the lunar month is twenty-nine and a-half she makes in twelve months a year of three hundred and fifty-four days. For if you reckon twenty-nine and a-half days for each month there are in the year three hundred and fifty-four days, in order that the moon may pay back annually to the sun the days which she then gained. Let any one who can count make the calculation."

(*Cosmas now speaks*).

What will those lovers of strife say to this, when they hear that there is such harmony between this author and myself, both as regards the figure of the first heaven and of the second, and as regards the two places made by the interposition of the firmament—that the first heaven, according to divine scripture, is not a sphere, but a vaulted chamber,—that this second heaven, which is visible, was consolidated from the waters, and carries the waters, that it may not be dissolved by the heat of the heavenly bodies, but be preserved therefrom by the chillness of the waters—that the dew falls from the firmament—that the heavenly bodies pursue their course through the northern parts during the night—and that the angels were created along with the heaven, and were

---

[1] That is, by her being fully illuminated in advance by eleven days.

spectators of God's six days' handiwork, and were taught thereby, and filled with astonishment; and what will they say as to his reasoning concerning souls, that they are enclosed within the body and operate in the body. How then shall not every mouth be stopped that speaketh unrighteousness against God, and against ourselves who carefully study divine scripture, and argue therefrom agreeably to the tradition of the Church? For, observe, I pray, it was shown that the Prophets and the Apostles, and the Evangelists, and the Lord himself and all divine scripture—yea, moreover even those who in common report are called Fathers and Teachers, whether in truth or pretence, differ not from my opinions, but all bear testimony to my words, so that by them all the truth may be established, and every mouth be stopped that speaketh unrighteous things. But, taking our leave of this author, let us pass on to his fellow-servant, Epiphanius the Bishop[1]—the fifth in order, to show that he also testifies to our words and is in agreement with them.

From the work of Epiphanius, Bishop of Cyprus, On Measures and Weights.

"Two and twenty works, O lover of the good and the beautiful, did God make from the beginning until the seventh day, namely these. On the first day He made the higher heaven, the earth, the waters from which come snow, ice, hail, frost and dew; then the spirits which minister before His face, such as these—the angels standing in His presence, the angels of glory, the angels of the clouds and darkness and snows and hail and frost—the angels of sounds, of thunder and lightning; the angels

---

[1] The Bishop of Constantia (the ancient Salamis) in Cyprus, and the Metropolitan of that island. He was the first of three of the same name who held the same office.

of cold and heat, of winter and autumn, and the angels of all the spirits of His creatures which are in heaven and upon earth and in Chaos; then the darkness and the brooding over the abyss, the waters which once covered the earth, out of which darkness comes evening and night, the light of day and of the dawn. These seven mighty works did God make on the first day. On the second day was made the firmament which is in the midst of the waters. On the same day the waters were divided, one half of which ascended above the firmament, while the other half was underneath the firmament, upon the face of all the earth. This was the only work which God made on the second day."

This author also agrees with us testifying as to the figure, declaring the heaven to be above, and the firmament, which also carries the waters, to be underneath. And with regard to the angels he says what is in explicit agreement with our own views, namely, that they are all in this world, and are all engaged in moving all things, and ministering for the sake of man, and that they also were brought into being on the first day along with the upper heaven and the earth. And hearing this, do not, O men, fret and fume, overmastered by the spirit of strife and envy, but rather from a love of truth, recognize the ecclesiastical, yea rather, the veritable harmony. For when ye are unable to face the truth, it is of no avail to take to reviling. Regard then with all due deference the great host of witnesses. But, if we have not yet adduced a sufficiency of them for you, let us leave this authority for the Bishop of the Capital—the admirable John, who was treated contemptuously by the three foregoing writers, and let us show that this illustrious champion [of the Church], who was devoted to deeds of mercy, bears testimony to our argument and is in agreement therewith.

From the work on Alms by John Chrysostom.[1]

"A human being is a great thing, and a man, if merciful, is to be honoured. Behold, how great a thing is mercy—the merciful man God likens to Himself; for He saith: *Be ye merciful, even as your Father which is in heaven is merciful.*[2] Should death come, there your riches abide."

From the Commentary by the same on the Epistle to the Ephesians.

"*In all wisdom and prudence*, he says, *having made known unto us the mystery of his will*,[3] as if one should say: he made known to us the things in his heart. For this is the mystery which is full of all wisdom and prudence. For what seekest thou that is greater than this wisdom? Those who were nothing worth—even those He found out, that He might lead them to great riches. What is there that can compare with this inventive skill?[4] He that was an enemy, He that was hated: this very man has on a sudden been raised on high, and not only so, but at this particular time, and this was done in wisdom also. And that this was done by the Cross, it would require a long discussion to show. What a matter of wisdom this was, and how it has made us wise!"

Again.

"*According to his good pleasure*, he says, *which he purposed in him;*[3] that is, He longed for this, He was in throes, as one may say, to bring forth this mystery. And of what nature is this? It is that it is His will to set man on high,

---

[1] John, surnamed Chrysostomos (the golden-mouthed), from the force of his eloquence, was born in Antioch 347 A.D.; succeeded Nectarius as Archbishop of Constantinople in 397; died in exile at Comana in Pontus in 407.

[2] Luke vi, 36. [3] Ephes. i, 9. [4] Gr. εὐμηχανίας.

and this He desires with a view to a dispensation of the fulness of the times to sum up all things in Christ, the things in the heavens, and the things upon the earth." [328]

From the Commentary of the same on the Epistle to the Hebrews in the chapter where it is said: "Now in the things which we are saying the chief point is this."[1]

"Where are those who say that the heaven is in motion? Where are those who think it to be spherical? For both these opinions are here swept away."

From the same Commentary of the same on the chapter which says:

"Wherefore he is the Mediator of a new covenant."[2]

"And how come these to be patterns of the things in the heavens? And what does he call the things which are now in the heavens? Is it heaven? is it the angels?[3] No, none of these, but our things, for heavenly things are ours, yea, even though they be accomplished on the earth, since the angels also are on the earth, and are nevertheless called heavenly. And the Cherubim too appeared on the earth, and yet they are heavenly. But what am I saying?— that they appeared? Is it upon the earth then they spend their time as if in Paradise? Nay, not so, for they are heavenly and our citizenship is in the heavens, although we spend our life with those that are here." And subsequently he says: "I show by actual facts those that attain to this height. And who be these? I mean Paul and his followers, who, though they were on earth, sojourned in heaven. But what am I saying?—in heaven? Nay, they

---

[1] Heb. viii, 1.   [2] *Ibid.*, 6.
[3] Gr. Ἄρα τὸν οὐρανὸν. ἀλλὰ τοὺς ἀγγέλους; ἀλλὰ is evidently a press error for ἆρα.

were higher exalted than heaven, yea even than the other heaven, for they ascended to God Himself."

And this great and wise teacher, again, expresses opinions which are marvellously in accordance with our own and with those of such as hold with us with regard to the figure of the world. For with regard to this figure he gradually advances upward from the regions of the earth to the sovereign throne, and describes finely the gradations of the ascent. He places the air first, then the moon, then the sun; in the next place, the firmament, then again, the heaven of heaven, without saying there are more than two heavens, and he ridicules those who say that it is a sphere, and maintain that it is in motion. And with regard to the angels and the cherubim, he declares that they are all in this world along with ourselves, and that up to this time not one of them has winged his way beyond this world. And with regard to doctrine again he expounds it clearly, making a safe use of the figure in doing so. *For why?* he says, *He that was an enemy, He that was hated, all of a sudden this Person has been raised on high.* And again he says, *that it is the will of God to set man on high,* etc. For when God had made the heaven and the earth, on the second day He made the firmament, and, having placed it midway on high, He divided the one world into two worlds, namely this and the one above. And when He had on the sixth day finished all this world, last of all, as a bond to unite the whole world of things visible and invisible, He made man—the one living being compounded of all the natures. At the end of the days therefore, when it behoved that the second world also should be displayed, God, having taken him who was the bond of the whole world of things visible and invisible, namely, Man; and having renovated him by raising him from the dead, and made him better, he conducted him in presence of all into heaven, namely, into the second place—that is, into the second world.

For a restoration and a renovation was effected by the dispensation of God in man as the bond between heavenly and earthly things, that is, of all things visible and invisible.

This Father then, knowing these things and the mystery of the will of God, took pleasure in declaring them, and proclaimed that he who had been expelled from Paradise as hated on account of his disobedience, had suddenly through God's good pleasure become heavenly, for the summing up in him of the universe.[1] Oh! how wonderful the concord of the Church! how wonderful the spiritual unanimity of the teachers! How is he not to be condemned who sets himself in opposition to them? O Lord God of the universe, confirm us evermore in Thy mysteries, Amen! Let the lovers of strife cease from wrangling, and let them rather submit their necks to the Church. For from a habit such as this we, along with the Church, turn away with aversion. But having ended our citations from this authority, let us adduce a seventh witness who completes the testimony of the divine Testament both the Old and the New. For if in divine scripture it is said that *in the mouth of two witnesses or three every word shall be established*, how much more then in the mouth of seven; for the company of seven witnesses shows the testimony of the perfect testament. It is Philon then the Bishop of Carpathus[2] who gives the same testimony as the other six.

---

[1] Gr. ἐπὶ ἀνακεφαλαιώσει τοῦ παντός. See Ephesians, i, 10. Montfaucon renders *ad universi restaurationem*.

[2] Philon was ordained Bishop of Carpathus, an island between Crete and Rhodes, by Epiphanius of Cyprus, about the beginning of the fifth century. His surname was probably *Carpasius* rather than *Carpathius*, as there is a town called *Carpasia* in the north of Cyprus. He is principally known from his Commentary on the Canticles, which he treats allegorically.

From the Commentary on Canticles, by Philon Bishop of Carpathus on the passage: The King brought me into his inner chamber.[1]

"The banqueting-house of the heavenly King, that is, His body which He built up for Himself as His house, and then also the kingdom of heaven."

From the same on the passage: Let him kiss me with the kisses of his mouth.[2]

"For the son of God assumed humanity, which He put on [received] from the Church, and in return gave back His sacred flesh to be partaken of in the sacrament."

From the same on the passage: The King fettered in his movements to and fro. Why wert thou made beautiful, and why wert thou established?[3]

"For when He passed from heaven to earth, and when He descended to hell, yea to the very lowest depth of hell, He thence will draw up the dead." *And farther on he says:* "It was not His divine nature that was in reality made beautiful, and that was established, for this does not admit of increase or diminution, but it was the flesh which He assumed, and the humanity which He wore. He was beautified by being conformed to the beauty of divinity—and was established in the kingdom of heaven at the right hand of God."

From the same on "The six days," where he discourses on the man that was born blind.

"For although thou wert looking at the man himself, yet thou oughtest from those very works to see God in man."

Consider pray, how this Father also maintains the same view with ourselves concerning the figure of the world and

---

[1] Song of Sol., ii, 4. [2] Song of Sol., i, 2. [3] Not in our Bible.

as to the figure remark how he calls the kingdom of heaven
God's *tamicion*—the *tamicion*[1] being the innermost and
securest apartment of the house, and this he speaks of as
the kingdom of heaven. And concerning the doctrine,
remark, how he represents man, whose nature God assumed,
and whom God recalled from death, and deemed worthy of
the place of honour at His right hand, as being seated and
established in the *tamicion* itself, that is, in the kingdom of
heaven. How then do those lovers of strife cry out against
us, as if we have gone a strange road—a road that is known
to nobody? Let them desist from that voluntary madness,
and no longer assail us with slanders: *for it is God who
justifieth, where is he that condemneth?*[2] For it is God who
first confirms our opinions, then the Prophets and Apostles
and the Evangelists and the renowned company of the
Fathers—Fathers from among whom ye yourselves profess
to accept some, while moreover there are even old pagan
writers who in some points are in agreement with our
opinions. But that we may not unduly prolong the
discussion, we have deemed it sufficient to advance solely
the testimonies already offered for the sake of the lovers of
strife, and for their sake only who have the assurance to
challenge our principles, or rather, I should say, the truth
itself; and this we have done, in order that they may have
an absolute refutation of their ill-timed madness, and from
a desire to make manifest to all that the motive, by which
they are actuated, is a sheer love of strife. And in order
that what we have written may be supported not solely
by the testimonies of these ancient authorities I will adduce
the testimony, and that even in abounding measure, of a
recent schismatical Father of theirs, one who is still living,
and resident in Constantinople, and who whether from

---

[1] Cosmas has not quoted the passage where this word occurs.
[2] Rom. viii, 34.

ignorance, or from being constrained by the truth itself, agrees with what we have written.

331 *From Theodosius, Bishop of Alexandria—On the fortieth day of the Ascension of the Lord.*

"To-day human nature is conveyed into heaven—to-day heaven is thrown open and man enters therein."

What will our opponents say to this? How has he not borne testimony to our opinions both with regard to the figure of the world and to the doctrine? Oh how wonderful the force of the truth, which attracts to it even its enemies against their will!

From the same—in another exposition.

"It is no great thing if God overcame the devil."

Oh how wonderful! Here also the truth reveals their ill-timed love of strife. For if he says it is no great thing for God when contending with the devil to overcome him, why then—to say the opposite is downright madness; for to God, not only the devil but the whole of creation is subordinate, and will be counted as nought. How then is it not manifest that he means, that it was man who contended with the devil and overcame him? Now this is even a great point, for he had before spoken of man, as having entered as a conqueror into heaven. And that he holds to this meaning is shown when again he exclaims: *For it behoved, it behoved, I say, that this nature, which had been foiled in wrestling, should be adorned with a crown*—as if he said: This nature which was overcome by the devil in Paradise, as he says, namely man, whom he declares frequently and at great length to have been bettered by the resurrection—him, I say, he pronounced with all frankness to have been carried up into heaven.

From an exposition by the same given in the great Church when the Gospel was read: "Father, if it be possible, let it pass from me,"[1] etc.

"The sufferings of this flesh—and the tokens of suffering, anguish, and sweat, grief and perturbation of soul—all these are indicative of human nature."

Oh what a marvel is here! They say such things and yet they quarrel with us, making divisions in the Churches in defiance of all authority.[2] For where is it written that He was in agony and sweated, if not in Luke where it is said: *And being in an agony he prayed more earnestly, and his sweat became as it were great drops of blood falling down upon the ground—and there appeared unto him an angel from heaven strengthening him.*[3] How dare they say these words, and on the other hand condemn those who dare to expound them? Is not the love of strife on the part of such men manifest? But dismissing this authority, let us pass over to one who was his predecessor in office, Timotheus the younger,[4] who recently died, and show that he also unwillingly assents to what we have written. He writes, then, in explanation of the passage which, at the sacred period of Easter in the Church of St. Victor, was read from the Prophet Isaiah, who says: *He was led as a sheep to the slaughter, and as a lamb before her shearer is dumb so he opened not his mouth;*[5] and when in his exposition he referred to the passage: *Father, if it be possible, let this cup pass from me,*[6] he spoke to this effect:

---

[1] Matt. xxvi, 39.   [2] Gr. τυραννοῦντες. See note 2, p. 92.
[3] Luke xxiii, 44.
[4] So called to distinguish him from Timotheus, nicknamed *Aelurus* or *the Cat*.
[5] Isai. liii, 7.   [6] Matt. xxvi, 39.

Timotheus on the passage: "*Father, if it be possible,*" *etc.*

"For it is natural for the soul to love to dwell always in the body, and to be vexed at taking leave of life." And again in the Church of Sarapammon he exclaimed: "And greater things than those will be given unto Me by the Father—resurrection from the dead, renovation of nature, and vivification, instead of corruption."

From a discourse of the same at the festival of the Holy Nativity—on the birth of Christ, on the 30th of Choiac in the 10th Indiction.[1]

"The Virgin brought forth a son who was perfect and sinless"—and a little subsequently he says: "Let us be circumcised with Christ, that we may also be purified along with Him."

And again in the Church of St. Theodorus on the 8th of Tybi in the 10th Indiction.

"For through that which was apparent he showed the power of that which was concealed."

---

[1] Gr. *Ἰνδ. ί.* The time from which reckoning by *Indictions* began was the 1st, but, according to others, the 15th of September, 312 A.D. The *Indiction* is a cycle of fifteen years, which was used in reckoning time chiefly by ecclesiastical historians onward from the time of Athanasius, and it is still used by the Popes, who reckon it as commencing 1st January, 313. See Gibbon's *Decline and Fall*, chap. xiv, n. 62; also chap. xviii, n. 170. The word originally meant *a summons to pay a tax*, and only gradually came to be a mode of reckoning time. The expression, *the Tenth Indiction*, does not mean the tenth period of fifteen years from 313 A.D., but the tenth year of any current Indiction. We express ourselves similarly when we say, for instance, *the tenth January* instead of the tenth of January.

From an exposition by the same in the Church of Quirinus on the Lord's Day on the 22nd[1] of Pachôn in the 5th Indiction, when the passage in the Gospel of John had been read. "Now Jesus being wearied with his journey was sitting."[2]

"Since therefore He is at once both God and man He is proved to be both by His works, and this cannot escape the notice of the spectators. For, that He is by nature God, is shown both by His works and His signs, cleansing the lepers, giving sight to the blind, strength to the paralytic, and life to the dead—and what is greatest of all (for the Prophets also equally succeeded in doing these things) He expressly and unreservedly said: *I and my Father are one*.[3] But, by the things mentioned, the might of His divinity is fully proved—and that He is also truly man, this He does not wish to go unobserved; thus in anticipation refuting those who erroneously think He assumed a body in appearance only, for He showed clearly that He submitted to sufferings—and to what kind of sufferings? to those, forsooth, which are assigned to flesh by reason of its infirmity and not by reason of sin—I mean, for instance, hunger and thirst and the need of sleep, and fatigue. For as these things happen to us by nature and not by our choice, they do not affect with sin those who have to endure them. By these sufferings then which were not incurred by sin the Lord declared that His flesh obeyed, showing clearly that He had become man in nature and in truth, and not in seeming."

From a discourse of the same in the sanctuary at the Pachôn Festival.

"It belongs to God to work miracles, to command the

---

[1] Gr. Πασχῶν κβ'. Montfaucon translates *Pachon decima quarta*. The circumflex on ω shows Paschôn to be a misprint for Pachôn.
[2] John iv. 6.
[3] John x. 30.

elements, and to make predictions of future events, but to man when civilized and leading a social life, it belongs to honour parents, to maintain kindly intercourse with brothers, and to converse with disciples and acquaintances. Accordingly our Lord Jesus Christ being both God of God, and having become man for our sake, exhibits both the power of His divinity, and observes also the laws of our humanity, proving what He was and is by His miracles, and showing by His actions what He deigned to become."

From a discourse by the same on the fortieth day from the Ascension of the Lord, on the 25th Pachôn in the 9th Indiction—the text, taken from the Gospel of John, being: " It is expedient for you that I go away."[1]

" But let us consider the words now spoken by Him to His illustrious disciples—namely: *It is expedient for you that I go away*. For your salvation have I come down to the earth, for your benefit it is well that I go up into heaven. For your sakes did I, hitherto bodiless, come down—it is expedient for Me to be there with the body; your race did I resolve to draw up to heaven; it behoves Me in the flesh to take My seat on the right hand of the Father. It behoves Me to open up a way that before was strange, as a new way, and to show that heaven is accessible to man. I take my way first through the air, in order that you also afterwards may be caught up into the air in clouds to meet Me." And I fancied I heard him, as he was reading, expressly proclaim[2] how that this man shrinks from departure from life, and " how that He through suffering and the resurrection received incorruption and renovation of His nature and vivification—how that through prevailing infirmity He was formerly subject to sufferings and fatigue—how that more-

[1] John xvi, 17.
[2] These words seem to be added by Cosmas himself.

over He was drawn to heaven and deemed worthy of the seat on the right hand, and was the first to traverse the strange way, and the first to make heaven accessible to men." 334

O harmony of those not in harmony with us! Oh! the involuntary agreement of the schismatics with us! Oh! the unwilling laudation, the assent, that is, of our revilers to our opinions! How have we not all round shown ourselves to be the children of the Church? They say, forsooth, we have not trodden the beaten way. How are they not to be utterly condemned who disbelieve all these things or argue against them? How is our work not in all things attested to be the true offspring of the tradition of the Church? God is our witness, then the Apostles, Prophets, the glorious company of the holy Fathers.

BOOK XI.

A description of Indian Animals, and of the Island of Taprobane.

HIS animal[1] is called the rhinoceros from having horns upon his snout. When he is walking his horns are mobile, but when he sees anything to move his rage, he erects them and they become so rigid that they are strong enough to tear up even trees by the root, those especially which come right before him. His eyes are placed low down near his jaws. He is altogether a fearful animal, and he is somehow hostile to the elephant. His feet and his skin, however, closely resemble those of the elephant. His skin, when dried, is four fingers thick, and this some people put, instead of iron, in the plough, and with it plough the land. The Ethiopians in their own dialect call the rhinoceros *Arou*, or *Harisi*, aspirating the *alpha* of the latter word, and adding *risi*. By the *arou* they designate the beast as such, and by *arisi*, ploughing, giving him this name from his shape about the nostrils, and also from the use to which his hide is turned.[2] In Ethiopia I once saw a live

---

[1] In the Codex the pictures of the animals and plants precede the description of them. See the Plates in the Appendix.

[2] Salt states that the name, by which the rhinoceros (two-horned) is designated to this day all over Abyssinia, is absolutely the same as that given by Cosmas. Hence he was convinced that the language spoken at the Court of Axum was Gheez.

rhinoceros while I was standing at a far distance, and I saw also the skin of a dead one stuffed with chaff, standing in the royal palace, and so I have been able to draw him accurately.[1]

The Taurelaphus, the Bull-stag or Ox-deer.

The taurelaphus is an animal found in India and in Ethiopia. Those in India are tame, and are used for the transport of pepper and other stuffs packed in saddle-bags. They are milked, and from the milk butter is made. We also eat their flesh, the Christians killing them by cutting their throats and the Pagans by felling them. The Ethiopian kind, unlike the Indian, are wild and have not been domesticated.

The Camelopardalis—the Giraffe.

Cameleopards are found only in Ethiopia. They also are wild creatures and undomesticated. In the palace[2] one or two that, by command of the King, have been caught when young, are tamed to make a show for the King's amusement. When milk or water to drink is set before these creatures in a pan, as is done in the King's presence, they cannot, by reason of the great length of their legs and the height of their breast and neck, stoop down to the earth and drink, unless by straddling with their forelegs. They must therefore, it is plain, in order to drink, stand with their forelegs wide apart. This animal also I have delineated from my personal knowledge of it.

---

[1] The animal, however, as depicted by Cosmas is more like a horse than a rhinoceros. A description of the rhinoceros and its mode of fighting with the elephant is given by Agatharchides in his work on the Erythraean.

[2] Cosmas here uses the Latin word: παλατίῳ.

The Agriobous or Wild Ox.

This wild ox is a large Indian animal,[1] and from it is got what is called the *toupha*,[2] with which commanders of armies decorate their horses and banners when taking the field. If his tail, it is said, catches in a tree, he does not seek to move off but stands stock-still, having a strong aversion to lose even a single hair of his tail. So the people of the place come and cut off his tail, and then the beast, having lost it all, makes his escape. Such is the nature of this animal.

The Moschus or Musk-deer.

The small animal,[3] again, is the Moschus, called in the native tongue *Kastouri*. Those who hunt it pierce it with arrows, and having tied up the blood collected at the navel[4] they cut it away. For this is the part which has the pleasant fragrance known to us by the name of musk. The men then cast away the rest of the carcase.

The Monoceros or Unicorn.

This animal is called the unicorn,[5] but I cannot say that I have seen him. But I have seen four brazen figures of

---

[1] This is evidently the *yák*, the *Bos grunniens* of naturalists.

[2] The *Chowries* or fly-flappers used in India, particularly on occasions of state and parade. Tupha is the Turkish name of the horse-tail standard.

[3] It is little more than three feet in length.

[4] The cyst of the male, which is about the size of a hen's egg, contains a clotted, oily, friable matter, dark-brown in colour, and this is the true musk.

[5] The first author who has given a description of the unicorn is Ctesias of Cnidos, a physician who spent seventeen years at the Court of Artaxerxes Mnémôn, where he heard all manner of marvellous stories about India. The one-horned animal which he describes under the name of *the wild ass of India*, and which Aristotle speaks of as the *Indian ass*, is best identified with the rhinoceros, notwithstanding all the errors of the description.

him set up in the four-towered palace of the King of Ethiopia. From these figures I have been able to draw him as you see.[1] They speak of him as a terrible beast and quite invincible, and say that all his strength lies in his horn. When he finds himself pursued by many hunters and on the point of being caught, he springs up to the top of some precipice whence he throws himself down[2] and in the descent turns a somersault so that the horn sustains all the shock of the fall,[3] and he escapes unhurt. And scripture in like manner speaks concerning him, saying, *Save me from the mouth of lions, and my humility from the horns of unicorns.*[4] And again: *And he that is beloved as the son of unicorns;*[5] and again in the blessings of Balaam wherewith he blessed Israel, he says for the second time: *God so led him out of Egypt even as the glory of the unicorn;*[6] thus bearing complete testimony to the strength, audacity, and glory of the animal.

The Chœrelaphus or Hog-deer and Hippopotamus. 336

The hog-deer I have both seen and eaten. The hippopotamus, however, I have not seen, but I had teeth of it so

---

[1] Lobo, in his history of Abyssinia, describes the unicorn as resembling a beautiful horse, and in the picture of it by Cosmas its body is not unlike that of a horse. For a remark on this picture, see Yule's *Marco Polo*, vol. ii, 273.

[2] Gr. εἰς κρημνὸν ἐφάλλεται, καὶ ῥίπτει ἑαυτὸν ἐκ τοῦ ὕψους. Montfaucon's rendering of these words: "deorsum in praecipitia sese conjicit," does not give their full import.

[3] This is said to hold true of the oryx.

[4] Psalm xxii, 21. The Revised Version has here: *from the horns of the wild ox.* To the influence of the Septuagint Version, which rendered the Hebrew word for the *wild ox* (reém) by *unicorn*, may be traced most of the fables about the unicorn.

[5] Psalm xxix, 6. [6] Numb. xxiii, 22.

large as to weigh thirteen pounds,[1] and these I sold here.[2] And I saw many such teeth both in Ethiopia and in Egypt.

Piperi—pepper.

This is a picture of the tree which produces pepper. Each separate stem being very weak and limp twines itself, like the slender tendrils of the vine, around some lofty tree which bears no fruit. And every cluster of the fruit is protected by a double leaf. It is of a deep green colour like that of rue.

Argellia—The Narikela of Sanskrit—Cocoa-nuts.

The other tree [represented] bears what are called argellia, that is, the large Indian nuts. It differs nothing from the date-palm, except that it is of greater height and thickness and has larger fronds. It bears not more than two or three flower-spathes, each bearing three nuts. Their taste is sweet and very pleasant, like that of green nuts. The nut is at first full of a very sweet water which the Indians drink, using it instead of wine.[3] This delicious drink is called *rhongcosura*. If the fruit is gathered ripe and kept, then the water gradually turns solid on the shell, while the water left in the middle remains fluid, until of it also there is nothing left over. If however it be kept too long the concretion on the shell becomes rancid and unfit to be eaten.

---

[1] Gr. λιτρῶν. This word is the Siceio-Greek form of the Latin *libra*. The coinage system of the Dorians of Sicily was borrowed from Italy.

[2] In Alexandria and probably in his earlier years, when he was a merchant.

[3] "Possibly," says Yule, "Cosmas has confounded the cocoa-nut milk with the coco-palm toddy. For *sura* is the name applied on the Malabar coast to the latter. *Roncho* may represent *lanha*, the name applied there to the nut when ripe, but still soft."

The Phoca or Seal, the Dolphin and the Turtle.

The seal, the dolphin, and the turtle we eat at sea[1] if we chance to catch them. When we want to eat the dolphin and turtle we cut their throat. But we do not kill the seal that way, but strike it over the head as is done with the large kinds of fish. The flesh of the turtle, like mutton, is dark-coloured; that of the dolphin is like pork, but dark-coloured and rank;[2] and that of the seal is, like pork, white and free from smell.

Concerning the Island of Taprobanê.[3]

This is a large oceanic island lying in the Indian sea. By, the Indians it is called Sielediba, but by the Greeks

---

[1] Gr. κατὰ θάλατταν. Montfaucon renders *ad oram maris* "on the sea shore."

[2] Gr. ὡς χοίρου, μελαμψὸν δὲ καὶ βρομῶδες. Montfaucon in his rendering overlooks the δέ, and thus makes Cosmas say that pork is black and foul-smelling. βρομῶδες is an incorrect form of βρωμῶδες, an epithet applied by Strabo to the district of Puteoli, which was noted for its foul smells.

[3] Ceylon has been known by many names. In Sanskrit works it is called Lankâ, an appellation unknown to the Greeks. Megasthenes, who wrote his work on India about 300 B.C., calls it Taprobanê, a compound which is generally regarded as a transliteration of Tâmraparnî, *copper-coloured leaf*, a name given to the island by its Indian conqueror, Vijaya. This name is found in its Pâli form, Tambaparni, in Asóka's inscription on the Girnâr rock. Some are, however, of opinion that Taprobanê is a slightly-altered form of *Dwîpa-Râvana* (Island of Râvana), as the country was called by Brahmanical writers. From the *Periplûs* and Ptolemy we learn that Taprobanê was anciently called *Simoundou*, but in his own time, *Salike*, i.e., the country of the *Salai*. Here we have in a slightly-altered form the *Siele-diva* of Cosmas, for *diva* is but a form of *Dwîpa*, the Sanskrit for *island*. Both *salai* and *siele* have their common source in *sihalam* (pronounced as *Silam*), the Pâli form of the Sanskrit *sinhala*, a lion. To the same source may be traced all its other names, such as Serendivus, Sirlediba, Serendib, Zeilan, Sailan, and Ceylon. As there are no lions in Ceylon, *sinhala* must be taken to mean a lion-like man—a hero—the hero Vijaya.

Taprobanê, and therein is found the hyacinth stone.[1] It lies on the other side of the pepper country. Around it are numerous small islands[2] all having fresh water and cocoa-nut trees. They nearly all have deep water close up to their shores.[3] The great island, as the natives report, has a length of three hundred *gaudia*, that is, of nine hundred miles,[4] and it is of the like extent in breadth. There are two kings in the island, and they are at feud the one with the other.[5] The one has the hyacinth country, and the other the rest of the country where the harbour is, and the centre of trade.[6]

---

[1] Some think this is not our jacinth, but rather the sapphire; others take it to be the amethyst.

[2] The Laccadives. The name means, *islands by the hundred thousand*.

[3] Gr. Ἀσσοβαθαὶ δὲ ὡς ἐπὶ τὸ πλεῖστον πᾶσαί εἰσιν. Montfaucon renders *alia aliam proxime sitae*, thus taking no account of Βαθαὶ, the predominant partner in the compound. Ἀσσοβαθὸς is a barbarous form of ἀγχιβαθής.

[4] "The Hindus" says Tennent in his *Ceylon*, Chap. I., "propounded the most extravagant ideas, both as to the position and extent of the island: expanding it to the proportions of a continent, and, at the same time, placing it a considerable distance south-east of India." The Classical and Arab writers were no less extravagant in their estimates than the Hindus. Even Ptolemy, who determined correctly the general form and outline of the island, as well as its actual position with reference to the adjoining continent, represented it as some fourteen times larger than it is. Its extreme length from north and south is 271½ miles, its greatest width 137½ miles, its circuit somewhat under 700 miles, and its area one-sixth smaller than that of Ireland. With regard to the word *gaudia*, Tennent says (*Ceylon*, vol. ii., p. 543, *note*): "It is very remarkable that this singular word, *gaon*, in which Cosmas gives the dimensions of the island, is in use to the present day in Ceylon, and means the distance which a man can walk in an hour. . . . . A *gaon* in Ceylon expresses a somewhat indeterminate length, according to the nature of the ground to be traversed."

[5] Gr. ἐναντίοι ἀλλήλων. Tennent (*ibid.*) prefers to render this expression by " ruling at opposite ends of the island."

[6] Tennent (*ibid.*) rejects Thevenot's notion that by *hyacinth* Cosmas meant here "the part of the island where jacinths are found;" on the ground that the region which produces gems, namely, the south

It is a great mart for the people in those parts. The island has also a church of Persian Christians who have settled there, and a Presbyter who is appointed from Persia, and a Deacon and a complete ecclesiastical ritual.[1] But the natives and their kings are heathens.[2] In this island they have many temples, and on one, which stands on an eminence, there is a hyacinth as large as a great pine-cone, fiery red, and when seen flashing from a distance, especially if the sun's rays are playing round it, a matchless sight.[3] The island being, as it is, in a central position, is much frequented by ships from all parts of India and from Persia and Ethiopia, and it likewise sends out many of its own. And from the

---

part of the island, is that which also has the port and the emporium. The King who possessed the wonderful gem (called by Gibbon *the luminous carbuncle*) ruled the northern part of the island. The emporium, according to Gibbon, was *Trinquemale*, but Tennent takes it to be *Point de Galle*.

[1] Gr. καὶ πᾶσαν τὴν ἐκκλησιαστικὴν λειτουργίαν.

[2] Gr. ἀλλόφυλοι. Tennent renders the sentence thus: "The natives and their kings are of different races." Cosmas, however, here uses the term in the sense in which the kindred compounds ἀλλοφυλέω and ἀλλοφυλισμός are used in the Septuagint. The latter word in II Maccab. iv, 13, means *the adoption of gentile manners and customs*. Montfaucon rightly renders: *alieni cultûs*.

[3] The Chinese pilgrim Hiouen Thsiang, who was a century later than Cosmas, relates that at Anarajapura, on a spire surmounting one of its temples, a ruby was elevated which with its transcendent lustre Illuminated the whole heaven. Marco Polo again relates that the King of Ceylon was reputed to have the grandest ruby that ever was seen—one that was flawless and brilliant beyond description. "It is most probable" says Tennent—quoting the authority of Dana's *Mineralogy*, vol. ii, p. 196, "that the stone described by Marco Polo was not a ruby but an amethyst, which is found in large crystals in Ceylon, and which modern mineralogists believe to be the 'hyacinth' of the ancients." There is no authentic record of the ultimate history of this renowned jewel, unless it be the "carbuncle" of unusual lustre which was purchased early in the 14th century for the Emperor of China. See Tennent's *Ceylon*, vol. i, pp. 543-4, note.

remotest countries,[1] I mean Tzinista and other trading places, it receives silk,[2] aloes, cloves, sandalwood[3] and other products, and these again are passed on to marts on this side, such as Male,[4] where pepper grows, and to Calliana[5] which exports copper and sesame-logs, and cloth for making dresses, for it also is a great place of business. And to Sindu[6] also where musk and castor is procured and androstachys,[7] and to Persia and the Homerite country, and to Adule. And the island receives imports from all these marts which we have mentioned and passes them on to the remoter ports, while, at the same time, exporting its own produce in both directions. Sindu is on the frontier of India, for the river Indus, that is, the Phison, which discharges into the Persian Gulf, forms the boundary between Persia and India.[8] The most notable places of trade in India are these: Sindu,

---

[1] Gr. τῶν ἐνδοτέρων. The countries inside of Cape Comorin, that is, to the east of it.

[2] Gr. μέταξιν—μέταξα and not μέταξις is the usual form of this word. Metaxa is a Latin as well as a Greek word, and means properly "yarn." It was used, however, by the mediaeval Greeks to signify silk in general. Procopius, who was contemporary with Cosmas, says that clothing was made from it, and that of old Greeks called this clothing *mēdikē*, but in his time, *sērikē*. See *Note* 2, p. 47.

[3] Gr. τζανδάναν.

[4] The Malabar littoral.

[5] Calliana, now Kalyâna, near Bombay, is named in the Kanhéri Bauddha Cave inscription. Mention is also made of it in the *Periplûs of the Erythraean Sea*, which states that it was raised to the rank of a regular mart in the times of the elder Saragones, who was probably one of the great Sâtakarni or Andrabhritya dynasty.

[6] Probably Diul-Sind at the mouth of the Indus. See Yule's *Hobson-Jobson*, p. 247.

[7] Gr. ἀνδροστάχην. This word, so far as I know, is not met with elsewhere. I take it to be an error in transcription for νάρδου στάχυν or ναρδόσταχυν, Latin *spica nardi*, whence our *spikenard*.

[8] The Persian empire when overthrown by Alexander the Great extended to the Indus, and even embraced some territory in Sindh lying along the eastern bank of that river.

Orrhotha,[1] Calliana, Sibor,[2] and then the five marts of Male which export pepper: Parti, Mangarouth,[3] Salopatana, Nalopatana, Poudopatana.[4] Then out in the ocean, at the distance of about five days and nights from the continent, lies Sielediba, that is Taprobanê. And then again on the continent is Marallo, a mart exporting chank shells,[5] then Caber[6] which exports alabandenum, and then farther away is the clove country, then Tzinista which produces the silk.[7] Beyond this there is no other country, for the ocean surrounds it on the east. This same Sielediba then, placed as one may say, in the centre of the Indies and possessing the

---

[1] Pliny, in his list of the Indian races, mentions a people called the *Horatae*, whose country adjoined the Gulf of Khambay. Their name is an incorrect transcription of *Sorath*, the popular form of *Saurishtra* or, as it is called by the author of the *Periplûs* and by Ptolemy, *Surastrênê*, i.e., Gujarât. Some have therefore identified *Orrhotha* with *Surat*, but as *Surat* was not a place of any importance till the arrival of the Portuguese in India, this view cannot be accepted. Yule took it to be some place on the western coast of the peninsula of Gujarât.

[2] Yule identifies Sibor with Chaul or Chênwal, a seaport situated 23 miles to the south of Bombay. It is the Simylla of Ptolemy, and the Saimûr or Jaimûr of the Arabian geographers.

[3] Mangarouth is now Mangalôr.

[4] These three ports appear to have been situated on the coast of *Cottonarikê*, the pepper country, somewhere between Mangalôr and Calicut. The termination *patana* means "town". *Poudopatana* means "New town", and the place so called may be identified with Ptolemy's *Podoperoura*.

[5] Gr. κοχλίους.

[6] *Caber* is the emporium called by Ptolemy Chavêris, which Dr. Burnell identified with Kâvêripattam—a place situated a little to the north of Tranquebar, at the mouth of the Podu-Kâvêri (New Kâvêri). Kâvêra is the Sanskrit word for *saffron*. What its export, *alabandenum* was, is unknown.

[7] Gr. ἡ τζινίστα τὴν μέταξιν βάλλουσα. Anciently *Seres* was the name of the Chinese nation as known by land, and *Sinae* as known by sea. In the *Periplûs* the country is called Thina. Cosmas was the first who laid down its correct boundary on the east by the Ocean.

hyacinth receives imports from all the seats of commerce and in turn exports to them, and is thus itself a great seat of commerce.

338   Now I must here relate what happened to one of our countrymen, a merchant called Sopatrus, who used to go thither on business, but who to our knowledge has now been dead these five and thirty years past. Once on a time he came to this island of Taprobane on business, and as it chanced a vessel from Persia put into port at the same time with himself. So the men from Adulè with whom Sopatrus was, went ashore, as did likewise the people of Persia, with whom came a person of venerable age and appearance.[1] Then, as the way there was, the chief men of the place and the custom-house officers received them and brought them to the king. The king having admitted them to an audience and received their salutations, requested them to be seated. Then he asked them: In what state are your countries, and how go things with them? To this they replied, they go well. Afterwards, as the conversation proceeded, the king inquired Which of your kings is the greater and the more powerful? The elderly Persian snatching the word answered: Our king is both the more powerful and the greater and richer, and indeed is King of Kings, and whatsoever he

---

[1] "Cosmas", says Tennent in his *Ceylon* (vol. i, p. 542, note 2), "wrote between A.D. 545 and A.D. 550; and the voyage of Sopatrus to Ceylon had been made thirty years before. Kumaara Daas reigned from A.D. 515 to A.D. 524." He further states (*ibid.*, p. 393) that of the eight kings who reigned between A.D. 515 and A D. 586, two died by suicide, three by murder, and one from grief occasioned by the treason of his son. The Malabars, taking advantage of the anarchy prevailing, made frequent descents on the island then and afterwards. This author, following the French version of Thevenot, has been misled into saying that *Sopatrus sailed from Adulè in the same ship with the Persian bound for Ceylon*. Cosmas describes the Persian as a πρεσβύτης, *i.e.*, *an old man*, and not an *orator* (*i.e.*, an ambassador), as Montfaucon renders the Greek word.

desires, that he is able to do. Sopatrus on the other hand sat mute. So the king asked: Have you, Roman,[1] nothing to say? What have I to say, he rejoined, when he there has said such things? but if you wish to learn the truth you have the two kings here present. Examine each and you will see which of them is the grander and the more powerful. The king on hearing this was amazed at his words and asked, How say you that I have both the kings here? You have, replied Sopatrus, the money[2] of both — the *nomisma*[3] of the one, and the drachma, that is, the miliarision[4] of the other. Examine the image of each, and you will see the truth. The king thought well of the suggestion, and, nodding his consent, ordered both the coins to be produced. Now the Roman coin had a right good ring, was of bright metal and finely shaped, for pieces of this kind are picked for export to the island. But the miliarision, to say it in one word, was of silver, and not to be compared with the gold coin. So the king after he had turned them this way and that, and had attentively examined both, highly commended the *nomisma*, saying that the Romans were certainly a splendid, powerful, and

---

[1] "Vincent has noted the fact that in his interview with the Greek, he (the King) addressed him by the epithet of Roomi, "σὺ 'Ρωμεῖ", the term which has been applied from time immemorial in India to the powers who have been successively in possession of Constantinople, whether Roman, Christian, or Mahommedan" (Tennent's *Ceylon*, vol. i, p. 542, note 2).

[2] Gr. τὰς μονίτας. This is a Latin word, and should be μονήτας. Moneta was a name of Juno, in whose temple money was coined. *Proprie, nota numinis impressi moneta est.*

[3] Gr. νόμισμα. This would be an *aureus*. Constantine the Great coined *aurei* of seventy-two to the pound of gold, and at this standard the coin remained to the end of the empire.

[4] This word is generally written μιλιαρήσιον, a silver drachma of which twenty made a *daric*, which was equivalent to an Attic *stater*. Among the imports of Barygaza (Bharoch) enumerated in the *Periplûs* we find *gold and silver denarii*—δηνάριον χρυσοῦν καὶ ἀργυροῦν.

sagacious people.¹ So he ordered great honour to be paid to Sopatrus, causing him to be mounted on an elephant, and conducted round the city with drums beating and high state. These circumstances were told us by Sopatrus himself and his companions, who had accompanied him to that island from Adule ; and as they told the story, the Persian was deeply chagrined at what had occurred.

But, in the direction of the notable seats of commerce already mentioned, there are numerous others [of less importance] both on the coast and inland, and a country of great extent. Higher up in India, that is, farther to the north, are the White Huns.² The one called Gollas when going to war takes with him, it is said, no fewer than two

---

¹ "This story," says Tennent (*Ceylon*, vol. i, p. 542), "would, however, appear to be traditional, as Pliny relates a somewhat similar anecdote of the ambassadors from Ceylon in the reign of Claudius, and of the profound respect excited in their minds by the sight of the Roman denarii."

² Gr. λευκοὶ Οὖννοι. The absence of the rough breathing from the name is notable, since another form of it is Χοῦνοι. About the year 100 of our aera the most warlike tribes of the Huns, impatient of bearing longer the Chinese yoke, turned their faces westward, and having left behind them the mountains of Imaus, directed their march, some to the Oxus, and others to the Volga. "The first of these colonies", says Gibbon in his 26th Chapter, "established their dominion in the fruitful and extensive plains of Sogdiana, on the eastern side of the Caspian, where they preserved the name of Huns, with the epithet of Euthalites or Nephthalites. Their manners were softened, and even their features were insensibly improved by the mildness of the climate, and their long residence in a flourishing province which might still retain a faint impression of the arts of Greece. The *white* Huns, a name which they derived from the change of their complexions, soon abandoned the pastoral life of Scythia." Sir William Hunter, at p. 170 of his work on *The Indian Empire*, says : "The latest writer on the subject (the fortunes of the Scythian or Tartar races in Northern India) believes that it was the White Huns who overthrew the Guptas between 465 and 470 A.D. He (Dr. J. Ferguson) places the great battles of Korur and Maushari, which 'freed India from the Sákas and Húnas', between 524 and 544 A.D. Cosmas Indicopleustes, who traded in the Red Sea about 535 A.D.,

thousand elephants, and a great force of cavalry. He is the lord of India, and oppressing the people forces them to pay tribute. A story goes that this king once upon a time would lay siege to an inland city of the Indians which was on every side protected by water. A long while he sat down before it, until what with his elephants, his horses and his soldiers all the water had been drunk up.[1] He then crossed over to the city dryshod, and took it. These people set great store by the emerald stone and wear it set in a crown. The Ethiopians who procure this stone from the Blemmyes[2] in Ethiopia take it into India and, with the price it fetches, they invest in wares of great value. All these matters I have described and explained partly from personal observation, and partly from accurate inquiries which I made when in the neighbourhood of the different places.

The kings of various places in India keep elephants,[3] such as the King of Orrhotha, and the King of Calliana, and the Kings of Sindu, Sibor and Male. They may have each six hundred, or five hundred, some more, some fewer. Now the King of Sielediba gives a good price both for the elephants and for the horses that he has. The elephants he pays for by cubit measurement. For the height is

---

speaks of the Huns as a powerful nation in Northern India in his days."

[1] Even as the army of Xerxes and his beasts of burden drank up the Scamander.—See *Herodot.* vii, 43.

[2] The Blemmyes were fierce predatory nomads of the Nubian wilds and the regions adjacent. Emeralds were found in the mines of Upper Egypt, and were no doubt shipped from Adulé for the Indian markets by the Ethiopian traders who bought them from the Blemmyes. If taken to Barygaza (Bharoch), they could be transported thence by a frequented trade-route to Ujjain, thence to Kabul, and thence over the Hindu Kush to the regions of the Oxus.

[3] Pliny has preserved from Megasthenes a section of his *Indika*, in which he states the number of elephants kept by each of the Indian kings in his time.

measured from the ground, and the price is reckoned at so many *nomismata* for each cubit, fifty it may be, or a hundred, or even more. Horses they bring to him from Persia, and he buys them, exempting the importers of them from paying custom. The kings of the continent tame their elephants, which are caught wild, and employ them in war. They often set elephants to fight with each other for a spectacle to the king.[1] They keep the two combatants apart by means of a great cross beam of wood fastened to two upright beams and reaching up to their chests. A number of men are stationed on this and that side to prevent the animals meeting at close quarters, but at the same time to instigate them to fight one another. Then the beasts thrash each other with their trunks till one of them gives in. The Indian elephants are not provided with large tusks, but should they have such, the Indians saw them off, that their weight may not encumber them in action. The Ethiopians do not understand the art of taming elephants; but should the king wish to have one or two for show, they capture them when young and subject them to training. Now the country abounds with them, and they have large tusks which are exported by sea from Ethiopia even into India and Persia and the Homerite country and the Roman dominion. These particulars I have derived from what I have heard.

The river Phison separates all the countries of India [lying along its course] from the country of the Huns. In scripture the Indian region is called Euilat (Havilah). For it is thus written in Genesis: *Now the river goeth out from Eden to water Paradise. And from there it was parted and became four heads. The name of the first is Phison (Pishon); that is it which compasseth the whole land of Euilat, where there is gold; and the gold of that land is good; there is the*

---

[1] A custom still in vogue.

carbuncle and the jasper stone;[1] where the writer clearly calls the country Euilat. This Euilat, moreover, is of the race of Ham. For thus again it is written: *The sons of Ham, Cush and Misraim, Phut and Canaan the sons of Cush, Sabà and Euilat*; that is the Homerites and Indians, for Sabà is situated in the Homerite country, and Euilat is in India. For the Persian Gulf divides those two countries. And that country has gold according to sacred scripture. It has also the pezerôs[2] which Scripture calls *anthrax* (carbuncle) and the jasper stone, by which it designates the leek-green stone.[3] Clearly therefore does divine scripture, as being really divine, relate these things, even as the whole of our treatise goes to show.

[1] Gen. ii, 10-12.
[2] This is an incorrect form of παιδέρως, a kind of opal.
[3] Gr. λίθον πράσινον.

NOTICE TO THE READER.

(From the Latin of Montfaucon.)

WE wish to apprise the reader that this twelfth book of Cosmas Indicopleustes which is contained in the Laurentian Codex, but in a mutilated state at the end, is not found in the Vatican Codex of the eighth or ninth century. For, as one may see in the course of perusing the work, the books which compose it were written at different times by the author, who, when he had published in the outset only five books on the figure of the world, added the sixth book, and at intervals the seventh, eighth, ninth, etc., against the champions of the opposite view, who clamoured against the work immediately after it appeared. As his opponents did not remain silent, and afterwards started new objections, Cosmas manfully, in his new books which he added to the original work, replied to those who stood out against him as best he could ; and since it is probable that copies of the published books had got into circulation before he could add new books to the original, it seems to have come about that that copy, from which the text of the Vatican Codex was derived, was in the hands of the public before the twelfth book had been added. Nor will it be out of place to point out that Cosmas Indicopleustes not only added new books to those already finished, if the case so required, but even altered, added, deleted much and made marginal notes ; whence it happens that the Vatican is not altogether in unison with the Laurentian Codex. For, as we have already stated, that copy, from which the Vatican text is derived, makes the beginning much shorter, whence it can be plainly seen that the copy of Cosmas, from which the Laurentian text was derived, had been revised and extended by subsequent labours of the author.

BOOK XII.

Yet another book showing that many of the old Pagan writers testify to the antiquity of the divine scriptures uttered through Moses and the prophets. And that the Greeks appear to have learned letters the last of all, and to have their unbelief with regard to the divine scriptures deeply rooted.

N the Chaldaean books of Bêrôsus[1] and certain others it is thus written: that ten kings reigned over the Chaldaeans 2242 myriads of years, but, under their tenth king Xisuthrus, as they called him, there was a great flood, and that Xisuthrus being warned by God embarked in a ship with his wife and kindred and cattle, and that having been brought over in safety, as their story goes, to the mountains of Armenia, he offered sacrifices of thanksgiving to the Gods after the flood. These writers have thus presented in a new form nearly all the account given by Moses; for men continued to live in the earth beyond [the Ocean]

---

[1] Cosmas seems to have derived his knowledge of the works of the historians whom he cites in this book mainly from Josephus.

Berôsus was a priest of Belus at Babylon. He was born in the reign of Alexander the Great, and in that of Antiochus Theos wrote in the Greek language the history of Babylonia. This work, which includes notices of the history of Chaldaea, Assyria and Media, is now lost, but some fragments of it have been preserved in Josephus, Eusebius, and some of the Christian Fathers. Berôsus was acquainted with the Jewish scriptures, and hence his statements are often in agreement with those of the Old Testament.

2242 years for a course of ten generations, and, under Noah who was the tenth the flood having occurred, they passed over to this earth by means of the Ark. For Noah is he whom they call Xisuthrus. But by having changed the days into years, they asserted that those ten kings had lived 2242 myriads of years, since the number of years reckoned by Moses to have elapsed from Adam to the deluge of Noah was 2242. In like manner the philosopher Timaeus[1] also describes this earth as surrounded by the Ocean, and the Ocean as surrounded by the more remote earth. For he supposes that there is to westward an island, Atlantis, lying out in the Ocean, in the direction of Gadeira (Cadiz), of an enormous magnitude, and relates that the ten kings having procured mercenaries from the nations in this island came from the earth far away, and conquered Europe and Asia, but were afterwards conquered by the Athenians, while that island itself was submerged by God under the sea. Both Plato and Aristotle praise this philosopher, and Proclus has written a commentary on him. He himself expresses views similar to our own with some modifications, transferring the scene of the events from the east to the west. Moreover he mentions those ten generations[2] as well as that earth which lies beyond the Ocean. And in a word it is evident that all of them borrow from Moses, and publish his statements as their own.

---

[1] Timaeus the Locrian was a Pythagorean philosopher, and is said to have been one of Plato's teachers. In the dialogue which bears his name, Plato puts into his mouth, on account of his deep knowledge of physics and astronomy, a long and learned discourse on the origin of the universe and the formation of man. It is not Timaeus, however, who in that dialogue delivers the myth about "the island Atlantis which was larger than Libya and Asia put together," but Critias. See chap. vi. of the *Dialogue*.

[2] The *Timaeus* merely states that in the Atlantic island there was formed a powerful league of kings, but their exact number is not specified as Cosmas would have us believe.

For the writers of Chaldaean history as being more ancient, and living farther east, have mentioned in their works both the deluge and the building of the Tower, since they saw that Tower with their own eyes under the process of construction, being no doubt well aware that the men of that time, in fear of another flood, erected it for themselves as a place of refuge and safety. But the men of later times, when they had read Moses also, and found that Noah, in whose time the deluge occurred, was the tenth from Adam, they feigned that they also had ten kings, who had reigned 2242 myriads of years, as has already been said. Of these the first was Alorus, that is, *Adam*; the second Alaaprus, *Sêth*; the third, Almêdôn, *Enoch*; the fourth, Ammeôn, *Cainân*; the fifth, Ammegalaros, *Mahalaleel*; the sixth, Daonus, a keeper of sheep, *Jared*; the seventh, Euedôrachos, *Enoch*; the eighth, Amempsinachus, *Methuselah*; the ninth, Otiortês, *Lamech*; the tenth, Xisuthrus, *Noah*. In his time they say the great flood recorded by Moses occurred.

The writers again of Egyptian history, namely, Manethô,[1] and Chaerêmôn,[2] Apollônius surnamed Molôn,[3] Lysima-

---

[1] Manethô, who flourished in Egypt during the reign of the first Ptolemy and survived till that of Philadelphus, was, like Berôsus, a priest, and like him, wrote a history of his own country based upon its priestly records. As many fabulous stories were circulated by other writers under his name, his work, which was written in Greek, and gave an account of the religion, history and chronology of the Egyptians, sank into discredit, and it was not until quite recent times that his authority as an historian has been restored, the inscriptions on the Egyptian monuments having been found to confirm such portions of his works as have come down to our times.

[2] Chaerêmôn, who flourished in the earlier part of the first century of our aera, and was by birth an Alexandrian, was chief librarian of the famous Alexandrian library, and was also one of Nero's preceptors. He wrote a work on the history of Egypt, in which, according to Josephus, he advanced wilful falsehoods. Only one or two fragments of this work have been preserved.

[3] This is the famous rhetorician of Rhodes, who went to Rome, where he pleaded causes and had the honour of giving instructions in

chus[1] and Apiôn the Grammarian[2] mention Moses and the departure of the children of Israel from Egypt. For, as being Egyptians and the historians of Egypt, they also agree in their relations of local transactions, and traduce Moses as a promoter of sedition, who stirred up a mob of rascally beggars and lepers,[3] and say that these had gone away to Mount Sinai and Jerusalem, and were called Jews. And in a word the Chaldaeans and Egyptians, as being older nations than the Greeks, testify in a manner to divine scripture, asserting that both the deluge in the days of Noah did occur, that a Tower was built, and that there was a departure of the children of Israel from Egypt. But the Greeks, who are later than these, and were later in learning the art of writing, and who are settled, far away from the east, in the regions of the west, and live far remote both from Judaea and from Egypt, knew nothing about these events, either by seeing them or hearing about them. Wherefore even unto this day they refuse to believe both

---

rhetoric to Cicero and to Julius Caesar. In one of his works, mentioned by Josephus, he wrote against the Jews. Not one of his writings is extant.

[1] Lysimachus was an Alexandrian grammarian who flourished during the latter half of the second century. Josephus cites a work called 'Αιγυπτιακά, which is supposed to have been written by him.

[2] Apiôn, who was a native of Oasis, but wished to be considered an Alexandrian, taught rhetoric at Rome in the reigns of Tiberius and Claudius. He was so loquacious and so boastful of himself that the former of these emperors was wont to call him the *cymbalum mundi*. Among the numerous works which he wrote was one, highly valued, upon Egypt, in which he frequently attacked the Jews. He attacked them also in a separate work, entitled *Against the Jews*, and of this the contents are known from the reply made by Josephus. The largest fragment of his writings is that which has been preserved by Aulus Gellius, containing the story of Androcles and the lion.

[3] Gr. πλῆθος τῶν ἀγυρτῶν καὶ λελωβημένων. This is Manethô's description of the Israelites. See Josephus, *Contra Apion*. i, 28.

the Old and the New Testament, thinking that what they relate is fabulous.

But the Chaldaeans and the Medes and Persians, having a somewhat wider knowledge, were instructed by the building of the Tower, and the deluge, and by what happened in the case of Hezekiah and Jonah, and by the Captivity, and by Daniel and the Three Children, and also partly by the writings themselves. In like manner also the Egyptians were instructed by the affairs of Joseph and of Moses, and by the people of Israel, and these nations were thus better prepared for a ready acceptance of Christianity. Even the Greeks, however, did believe later on through the Apostles, when they saw the wonders which they wrought. And when still later again signs ceased, and time rolled on, you will find Greeks who have believed, and have been baptized, lapsing, nevertheless, many of them into unbelief, and ignoring the Old and the New Testament, that is, divine scripture, as persons who have not long had the root of religion and the foundation of faith deeply implanted. Wherefore in their writings they have not mentioned, as the early Chaldaeans and Egyptians have done, anything about the deluge and the building of the Tower, and the departure of the children of Israel from Egypt, and about the first historian, Moses. But though they regard themselves as very superior persons and the wisest and foremost of men, they are nevertheless from their swelling vanity ignorant of many things. Wherefore one of the Egyptians, whose name was Solomon, said to Plato: *The Greeks are always children, and no Greek is ever old, nor is there any learning among you that is of hoar antiquity.*[1] Yet some, for instance Dius and Menander,

---

[1] Cosmas must here be quoting the *Timaeus* of Plato from memory, for he misrepresents what is there stated—namely, that the charge

who translated the antiquities of the Tyrians into the Greek language, in the works they composed bear testimony to Solomon and the Jews; and further, the whole, I may almost say, of Ethiopia, and the regions to the south of it, bear testimony to divine scripture. But the Greeks alone, who are wise in their own conceit, know not wherein their salvation lies. Timaeus alone, who has been already mentioned, drawing from what source I know not, but perhaps from the Chaldaeans, recast the story of those ten kings, feigning that they came from the earth beyond the Ocean into the island of Atlantis, which he says was submerged below the sea, and that taking its inhabitants as mercenaries, and arriving in this earth, they conquered Europe and Asia—all which is a most manifest invention, for as he could not point out the island, he gave out that God had consigned it to a watery grave.

But those Greeks already mentioned who are admired for their wisdom, when at a late period they had acquired letters and had become possessed of laws, imagined that they alone had rained wisdom upon the world. I refer to their Lycurguses and their Solons and their Teucers of the Locrians, and all the rest of them, who are but men of yesterday, if put in comparison with the renowned Moses, in whose time not so much even as the name of *Law*[1] was known among the Greeks. Homer is my witness, who nowhere in his poetry uses the word. For there was not

---

advanced against the Greeks of *being always children* was made to Solon by an Egyptian priest. It is well known that Solon, after his legislation had been adopted, withdrew from Athens for ten years, and that one of the countries which he visited during that time was Egypt, where he conversed with two learned priests—Psenophis of Heliopolis and Sonchis of Saïs. It seems singular that Cosmas should have converted a name so well known as that of Solon into Solomon. Had he only a hearsay knowledge of the dialogue?

[1] Gr. νόμος. The laws of Solon were called νόμοι, those of Draco θεσμοί.

in his days such a thing, but the people were governed by the best judgments and the commands of their kings; and from that time till long afterwards, they continued to use unwritten customs, and to alter many of them from time to time according to circumstances. For the Lacedemonians and Cretans conducted education by the training of the habits and not by oral instruction, but the Athenians and nearly all the other nations prescribed by law what ought to be done, while neglecting to accustom the people to conform in practice to the law. Yet one nation after another made a gradual advance to a fixed and authoritative code of laws, not imposed from the beginning like that of Moses of old, who educated his nation in the knowledge of letters and of fixed law, being the first who showed both by word and deed the firm and permanent nature of the law and of letters, until, after a long course of time, he conducted the nations, guided and guarded by the firm nature of the law, to the predicted Lord Christ and his teaching.

The Phœnicians accordingly, being next neighbours to the Jews and having learned letters from them, both wrote inscriptions earlier than the Greeks,[1] and prepared the Greeks to learn letters; for Cadmus, taking the letters of the alphabet from Tyre, carried them into Greece. Let not the Greeks then show any supercilious pride, as if they had been the first to invent any thing new of benefit to the world, seeing that they have borrowed from others letters and laws and the notion of the sphere, and astronomy

---

[1] One of the earliest known Greek inscriptions is that which is to be seen in Nubia near Abu Simnel. It was made in the reign of Psamatik II, King of Egypt, by his generals Apollonius and Amasis, and its date is about 595 B.C. Kadmos, according to Mr Sayce, is certainly Phœnician. The question has been settled by a cuneiform tablet, which informs us that Qadmu was the name of the "god". See *The Academy*, 22nd September, 1894, p. 217.

and astrology. For as it was late before they made a figure in the world, they imagined the world to be eternal; having been taught by others to regard the heaven as a sphere, they, as if they were the first who held this opinion, claimed as a discovery of their own the laws of astronomy; and although they were taught letters by others, they suppose themselves to be the oldest and earliest writers; although they have been taught by others to frame laws, they have depicted themselves as the legislators of old times, and founders of just government; although they have received a copious language and an elegant mode of speech from the bounty of God, yet, being unthankful to God the Giver, they are disobedient to His words; and while they have received everything from God and their predecessors, they set them aside, and with swaggering insolence ascribe everything to themselves. For, contending against the divine words, which say: *He that established the heaven as a vault*,[1] these most superior persons cry out in opposition and say: "It is not so, for it is spherical, and this is manifest from the eclipses which we have already adduced." But further, when they hear the resurrection preached to them, they pronounce this to be impossible, for how, say they, can one who has been used up to form countless bodies in succession, rise up? And, to be brief, they attack with sophistries the Giver of their speech in their endeavour to overthrow the doctrines of His Church. And yet He has not left them without a witness to Himself, that He was working for their good and taking thought for it beforehand, for He manifested to them some tokens of His goodness, some four hundred years or more[2] before the coming of Christ, in the days of Alexander the Macedonian, long after the Trojan war, when the Greeks were still

---

[1] Isai. xl, 22.
[2] Not more but less by about 70 years.

flourishing. Let me give an instance of this: When Alexander the Macedonian was passing by Jerusalem in prosecution of his war against Darius, the High Priest of the Jews, arrayed in the robes of his office, came forth to meet him, whereupon Alexander dismounted from his horse and in a very kindly manner embraced him. And when his attendants reproached him for so doing and said: Why hast thou done so? he excused himself and said: When I set out at first from Macedonia, a man dressed in this style was seen by me in a dream who said to me: Go forth and conquer. The result was that the King himself offered sacrifices to God and bestowed many gifts on the Temple, and accorded many privileges to the country of the Jews.[1]

In subsequent times Ptolemy surnamed Philadelphus, after having made careful inquiry from Tryphon the Phalerean[2] about the Jewish books, and learned the truth concerning them, earnestly solicited them from the High Priest Eleazar, to whom as well as to the Temple he sent many presents. These books he received along with seventy elderly men, who translated them from the Hebrew into the Greek tongue, and he deposited them on the shelves of his own library. This also was a work of divine providence, that the translation had been prepared before the coming of Christ, lest, if it were done afterwards in the days of the Apostles, it would be exposed to general suspicion, as if they had interpreted what had been said of old by the prophets both concerning Christ and the calling of the Gentiles in a way to suit their own predilections.

---

[1] This story is now discredited, as is also that which immediately ollows concerning the Septuagint, of the origin of which little or nothing is known for certain. Both stories are taken from Josephus's *Antiquities of the Jews*.

[2] *Tryphon* is evidently a slip of memory on Cosmas's part for *Demetrius*.

When Ptolemy Physcôn[1] again had conquered the Jews, and wished to destroy those here in Alexandria by means of his elephants, but God had unexpectedly turned the rage of the animals against his soldiery, he was taught to revere God, and he honoured thereafter with sacrifices and oblations of gifts Him who was the true God, and His people, namely, the Jews. And other kings of the Macedonian empire there were who invited them to be their allies in war; while others, again, who preferred to war against them and held them under subjection for a long time afterwards, witnessed Providence turning to work in their favour, and aroused for their help, and even saw themselves conquered by men who were insignificant and few in number.

And to speak briefly they were trained by wars and miracles and dreams and their sacred books, and were thus taught to know Him who was truly God, Him whom the Jews revere and worship, in order that they also might be the better prepared for the reception of Christianity, so that, at the time when our Lord sojourned upon earth, many nations of Greece, seeing the signs wrought by the Apostles, assented to the faith of Christ, confessing His resurrection and His ascension into heaven. But now, after a long lapse of time and the cessation of signs, they have fallen into a sort of oblivion of that faith, and have reverted to the former superstition, declaring it impossible that there can be a resurrection of the dead and an ascent into heaven. Wherefore you find them observing baptism, and yet thinking that the heaven has a spherical form, in order that the resurrection of their bodies and their ascension into heaven may be denied. These men one will mostly

---

[1] Physcôn (so called from his obesity) was the seventh sovereign of the Ptolemaic dynasty, and reigned from B.C. 170 to B.C. 117. Cosmas has copied the story here related of him from Josephus, *Contra Apion.* II, 5.

find discussing philosophy with the Pagans alone, and setting forth eclipses as arguments to prove the world of a spherical figure, as if that were a divine doctrine, in this themselves deceived while they deceive others. Wherefore we, by undertaking to exhibit the figures and the places of the whole world, and the revolution of the heavenly bodies, controvert their views from divine scripture, doing our best by means of all these[1] * * *

---

[1] The last leaf of the Florentine MS. is wanting. Hence the abrupt breaking off in the middle of a sentence.

APPENDIX.

Plate I   Figures 1 to 8

„ II   „ 9 „ 10

„ III   „ 11 „ 21

„ IV   „ 22 „ 37

Explanation of the Plates.

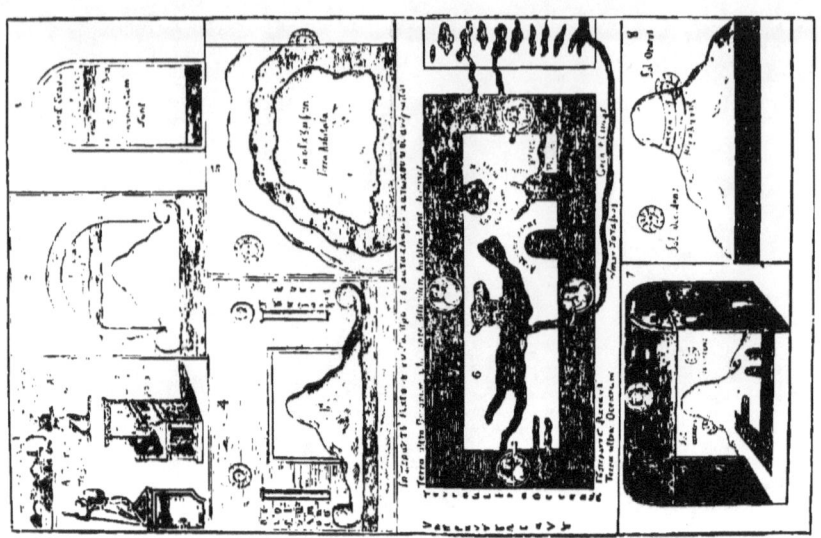

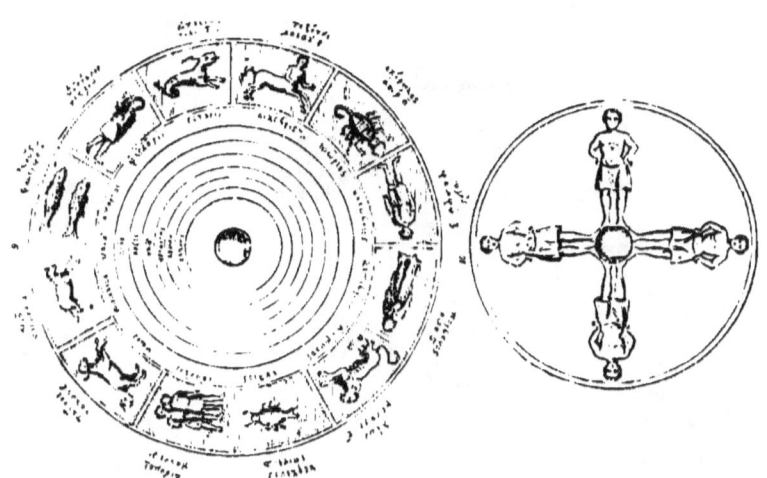

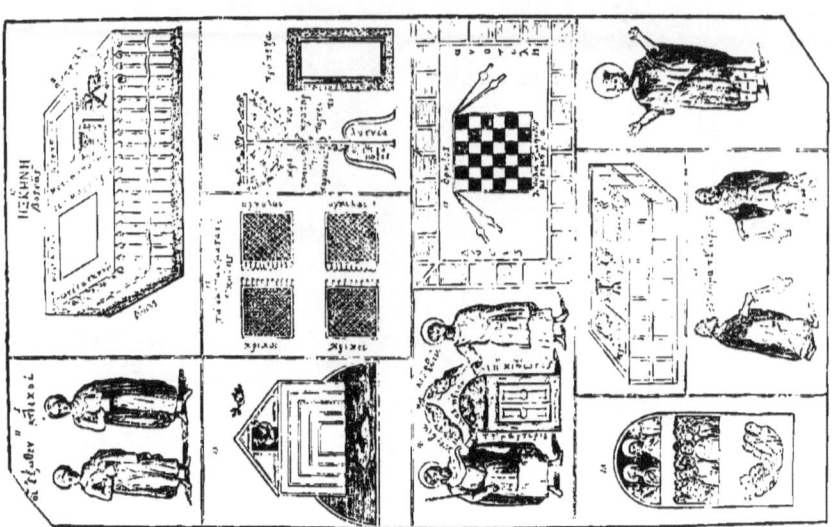

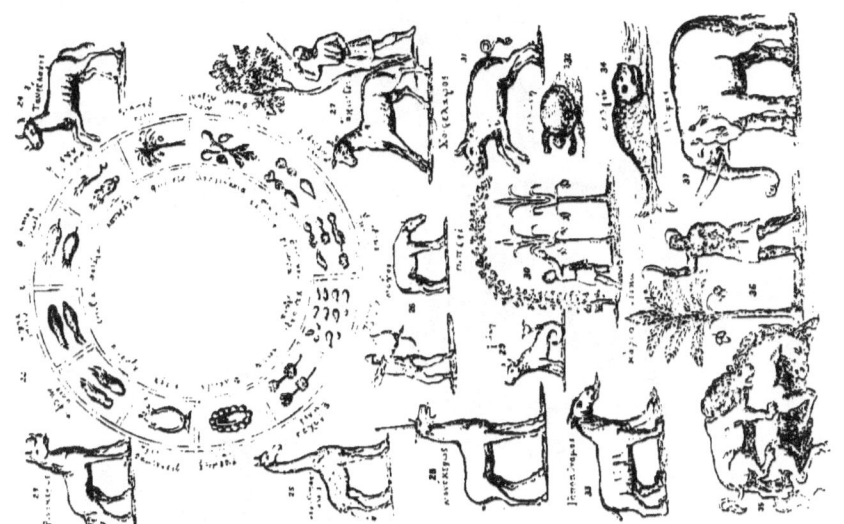

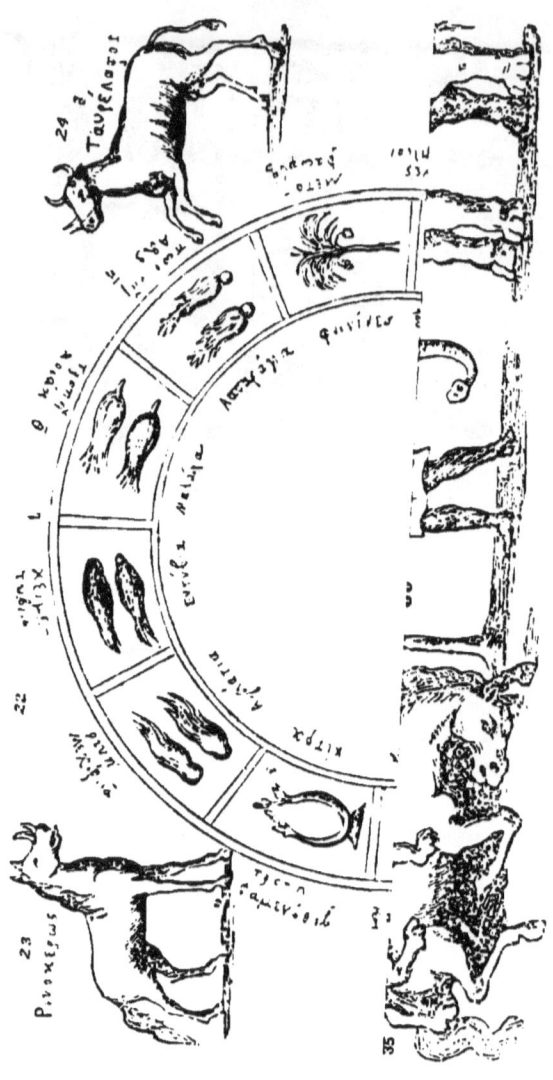

Plate 1. – The picture on the left represents the City of Adulé – that on the right an Ethiopian travelling from Adulé to Axômê. The lower picture on the left is the tablet with the Greek inscription copied by Cosmas. It is surmounted by the figure of Ptolemy Euergetês, standing in a warlike attitude. The throne represented on the right is ascribed to the same Ptolemy by Cosmas, but erroneously. It was placed at Adulé by an Axumite conqueror. The writing on the right of it is Δίφρος Πτολεμοϊκός, Ptolemy's chair.

Plate 2. – The figure of the earth and the heaven, as Cosmas and the ancient Fathers conceived it. The cross-bar represents the firmament.

Plate 3. – A picture of the waters above the firmament.

Plate 4. – A representation of the conical mountain, and also of the sun and the moon under the firmament. The inscription along the pillars is : οἱ στύλοι τοῦ οὐρανοῦ, the pillars of the heaven.

Plate 5. – A tracing of the inhabited world 'γῆ οἰκουμένη'.

Plate 6. – A representation of the oblong rectangular figure of the earth which we inhabit, with its surrounding ocean, which is itself surrounded by the other earth which was the seat of Paradise and the abode of man before the Flood. The four gulfs which penetrate into our earth from the ocean, and the rivers which flow into it from Paradise, are also depicted. Above the ocean in the outer earth is this inscription : Γῆ πέραν τοῦ ὠκεανοῦ ἔνθα πρὸ τοῦ κατακλυσμοῦ κατώκουν οἱ ἄνθρωποι, the earth beyond the ocean where men dwelt before the Flood. The lateral inscription is: Γῆ πέραν τοῦ ὠκεανοῦ, the earth beyond the ocean. The inscription in the figure of the great gulf coming from the west is Ῥωμαικὸς Κόλπος, the Roman gulf. *i.e.*, the Mediterranean. The gulf coming from the north Cosmas calls Κασπετὰ Θάλασσα, the Caspian Sea. The name of the northern river is Φεισῶν, and of the southern Γηῶν ποταμός, the Pison and Gihon of our bibles.

Plate 7.—A representation of the earth with the walls which come down to it from heaven. The four gulfs are shown, and the conical mountain in the north-west whence the earth slopes downward to the south.

Plate 8.—A picture of the conical mountain with three circling lines to show the paths of the sun as he moves round it at different altitudes, thus making the nights shorter or longer. The words written here are μικρὰ νύξ, μέση νύξ, μεγάλη νύξ, short night, night of medium length, long night.

Plate 9.—The figure of the world according to the Ptolemaic system. The twelve signs of the Zodiac are shown, and the names are given of the Roman and Egyptian months. The earth, in the form which Cosmas so much abhorred, is in the centre, encircled by the orbits in succession of the Moon, Σελήνης; of Mercury, Ἑρμοῦ; of Venus, Ἀφροδίτης; of the Sun, Ἡλίου; of Mars, Ἄρεος; of Jupiter, Δίος. The names of the Roman months are given in Greek characters, thus: Γεναρις, Φλεβάρις, Μάρτιος, Αυριλλιος (υ=ν), Μαιος, Ιουνιος, Ιουλιος, Αυγυστος, Σεπτεβριος, υκτωβριος, Νοευριος, Δικεβρις. Above the outer rim of the Zodiac are given the names of the twelve signs with the names of the corresponding Egyptian months: Αἰγό-κερως Tybi; τοξότης Choiac; σκορπίος Athyr; ζυγὸς Phaophy; παρθένος Thôth; λέων Mesori; καρκίνος Epiphi; Δίδυμοι Payni; ταῦρος Pachôn; κριὸς Pharmouth; ἰχθῦς Phamenôth; ὑδρόχοος Mechir.

Plate 10.—Antipodes drawn to deride the idea of their possibility.

Plate 11.—A delineation of the figure and dress of the pagan inhabitants of Attica, οἱ ἔξωθεν Ἀττικοί, as seen in the time of Cosmas. These figures are meant for those of Hyperides and Menander, mentioned in p. 147.

Plate 12.—A representation of the outward form of the Tabernacle, ἡ Σκηνή. The words written outside indicate the directions, ἀνατολή, east; βορρᾶς, north; Δύσις, west. The double line in the centre drawn from north to south represents the veil, καταπέτασμα, dividing the Tabernacle into the inner and outer sanctuary. The division to the right represents the outer, which contained the table of shew-bread, ἡ τράπεζα; the candlestick, λυχνία; Aaron's rod, ῥάβδος; the vessel of sprinkling, στάμνος; the two tables of the Law, αἱ πλακές; the serpent, ὄφις. In the inner Tabernacle, ἐσωτέρα σκηνή, is depicted the Ark of the Testimony, ἡ κιβωτός τοῦ μαρτυρίου. See pp. 148-154.

Plate 14.—A delineation of the coverings of the Tabernacle, τὰ σκεπάσματα τῆς σκηνῆς: the loops, ἀγκύλαι, and clasps, κρίκοι, by which they were joined.

Plate 15.—A picture of the table of the Tabernacle turned by the lathe, τράπεζα τορνευτός, and another of the candlestick with its seven lamp-wicks, λυχνία ἑπτάμυχος; its shaft, καυλός; its ball, καρύισκος, in the middle of the shaft; its spherical bowl, σφαιρωτὴρ κρατὴρ; its lily, κρίνον; and its branches καλαμίσκοι, three on each side of the shaft, making, along with the terminus of the shaft, seven in all, and representing, according to Cosmas, the seven days of the week. See p. 152.

Plate 16.—The Ark of the Testimony, ἡ κιβωτός τοῦ μαρτυρίου. Above it is the Propitiatory or Mercy-seat, ἱλαστήριον. Above it the Cherubim χερουβίμ, and the figure of Zacharias on one side, and that of Abia on the other.

Plate 17.—A delineation of the Court of the Tabernacle, ἡ αὐλὴ τῆς σκηνῆς; the other words denote the directions: ἀνατολὴ, δύσις, ἄρκτος, μεσημβρία, east, west, north, south.

Plate 18.—The upper figures represent the celestials; the middle, the terrestrials; and those below, the subterraneans or the buried. See pp. 300-303.

Plate 19.—A delineation of the order in which the contents of the outer Tabernacle were arranged. On the left is the table (τράπεζα) of shew-bread, with three loaves at each of its four corners, to represent the fruits of each of the four seasons (see p. 152); then follow the candlestick, λυχνία; the vessel of sprinkling, στάμνος; the tables of the Law πλακές; the serpent ὄφις.

Plate 20.—Melchisedek arrayed in his royal robes. See p. 175.

Plate 21.—A front and back view of Aaron wearing his priestly robes τὸ σχῆμα τοῦ ἱερέως. Montfaucon states that Cosmas, in explanation of this sketch, wrote for the figure on the right: 'Ααρὼν μέγας ἀρχιερεὺς ἐμπροσθοφανής front view of Aaron, the great high priest; and for the figure on the left: 'Ααρὼν μέγας ἀρχιερεὺς ὀπισθοφανής back view of Aaron, the great high priest.

Plate 22.—A delineation of the circle of the twelve months and the fruits produced in each month. Outside the circle are written the names of the Egyptian months Μηνές 'Αιγυπτίοι, and of the four seasons, which he designates respectively, ἐαρινή τροπή the spring tropic; θερινή τροπή the summer tropic; μετοπωρινή τροπή the autumn tropic; χειμερινή τροπή the winter tropic. The fruit produced in Egypt in Pharmouth (April) is σκόροδα, garlic; in Pachōn (May), κίννα a kind of pulse; in Paÿni (June), κάρυα 'Αρμένια Armenian nuts; in Epiphi (July), σῖτος κοπύμωμα. Montfaucon takes the latter word to be a mistake for συκόμορος the fig-mulberry, called also συκάμινος ἡ 'Αιγυπτία: in Mesori (August), σῦκα σταφύλια, figs, grapes: but to judge from the picture only one kind of fruit is indicated; in Thôth (September), ελαιόδακνα an unknown fruit; in Phaophy (October), φοίνικες, palms or palm-leaves; in Athyr (November), ἀσπαράγια asparagus; in Choiac (December), μαλάχια mallows; in Tybi (January), ἐντύβια, endives; in Mechir (February), ἀγλάται: this is unknown; in Phamenôth (March), κίτρα fruit of citron?

The remaining plates are pictures of the animals and plants which Cosmas has described in the earlier portion of the eleventh book.

INDEX.

Aaron, officia robes of, 123
Abel, 168-170
Abia, 153, Plate 16
Abraham, 177, 253-4
Abraham of Cascar, 24
Abyssinia, 55, 60
Acesinés, R., 75
Adam, 78, 79, 81, 165-7, 218, 235
Aden, 63
Adulé, vii, x, 54, 61, 66, 366, 368, 371
Aeolis, 35
Agamé, 60
Agau, vii, 52
Agriobous (Wild-ox), 360-1
Agrippa (King), 217
Albatrosses, v, 40
Alexander the Great, 18, 36, 69, 72, 74, 75, 119, 366, 375, 382-3
Alexandria in Egypt, viii, xviii, 23, 50, 54, 245, 247
Aloes, 366
Angels, creation of the, 102; their functions, xix, xxiv, 76, 78, 81, 105, 228; 320-7, 345; their place of abode, 280-7, 328, 347; their destiny, 82-3
Anastasius, 246
Angabe, 61
Anna the Prophetess, 210
Annine, 62
Antigonus, 69
Antioch, 18, 25, 120, 246
Antioch of Pisidia, 201, 270
Antiochus I, 18, 72
Antiochus II, 72
Antiochus IV (Epiphanes, Theos), 69, 207, 375
Antipodes, xx, 5, 14, 17, 86, 136-7
Apion, 378
Apocalypse of Paul, 290
Apollinarians, ix
Apollinarius, 213
Apollonius Molon, 377
Amethyst, 364, 365
Amos, 198-9
Amphilochius (of Iconium), 290
Apostles, teaching of the, 212
Arabah, the, 203
Arabia Felix (Sabaea, Yemen), 35, 37, 38, 64, 66, 120
Arabitae, 64, 66
Ararat, Mt., 33
Archangels, functions of, 88
Archimedes, 125
Argellia (cocoa-nuts), 362

Arians, ix, 258
Aries (Zodiac sign), 13, 139
Arius, 213
Aristotle, 4, 11, 18, 117, 121, 125, 360, 376
Ark (Noah's), 33, 44, 46, 91, 171-2, 376
Armenia, 375
Arsaces, 72
Arsinoé, Queen, 57
Arsinoé, city of, 120
Aromatics, country of, *see* Barbaria
Artaxerxes Mnémôn, 360
Arts, invention of the, 122-5
Asia (Minor), 120
Asóka, inscription of, 363
Assyrians, 37
Astronomy, the Ptolemaic, 6-8
Atalmó, 62
Athara R., 60, 61, 62
Athagaûs, 61
Athanasius (B. of Alexandria), festal letters of, 290, 332
Athanasius (friend of Cosmas), xxiii, Book VII addressed to him, 263
Athenians, the, 229, 381
Atlantis, island of, 376, 380
Aua, 61
Augusti, line of the, 71
Augustine, St., 17, 258
Axum, Axômis, vi, 39, 50, 54, 59, 61, 120, 245, 249, 350

Babel, Tower of, 91-93, 225, 377-9
Babylon, Babylonians, 36, 58, 68, 91, 313, 315, 316, 375
Bactrians, 37, 49, 120
Balaam, 182
Balkh, 37
Baptism, 183-4, 220; for the dead, 273
Barbaria (frankincense country), vii, 34, 38, 39, 48, 51, 65, 66, 67, 252
Barygaza (Bharoch), 369, 371
Basil, St., 290, 332
Beazley, Mr. Raymond, quoted, xiii, xxiv
Bega, 62
Bells, the golden, 156, 158
Berenicê, Queen, 57
Berenicê, hair of, 58-59
Berenicê, or Ptolemais Thérôn, 58
Berenicê, city of, 126
Bérosus, 312, 375
Bigot, Emeric, i
Blemmyes, 64, 371

Borysthenes, R., 247
Brachmans, 48
Bulgarians, 121
Byron, quoted, 301
Byzantium, *see* Constantinople

Caber, 367
Cadmus, 381
Cæsar, Julius, 378
Cain, 123, 120
Calliana, 119, 366
Cambyses, 58, 59
Canaan, 36, 173
Canopus, Synod of, 58
Cappadocia, 120
Captivity, the Babylonian, 208
Carbuncle, 373
Carrhae, 178
Caria, 57
Caspian Sea, 39, 50, 131, 370
Cassaniti, 37
Castor-oil, 366
Cataracts of the Nile, 24, 50
Catholic Epistles, 290-2
Ceylon, vi, viii, xx, xxiv, 48-9, 118-9; its different names, 363; its size, 364; its kings, 364-5; its trade, 365-7
Chaeremon, 377
Chair with Greek inscriptions, 54-68
Chaldaeans, 24, 91; their kings, 375
Charton, M., xiii
Cherubim, 111, 146, 329, 330
Chosroes, 18, 72
Christ, His conception, 139, 142; birth, 143, 221, 236, 242; earthly life, 219; temptation, 220; miracles, 98, 115, 116; transfiguration, 192-3; passion, 81, 140-1, 205, 253; resurrection, 196-201, 229; ascension, 219, 220-1, 356-7; second coming, 237-8, 256; two natures, 84, 258, 359
Christianity, nations converted to, ix, 384
Chrysostom, St., 17, 291, 333, 349; quoted, 345-8
Ciborium, 75
Cicero, quoted, 11, 17, 378
Cilicia, 58, 120
Cimmerii, 35
Cinnaedocolpitae, 64, 66
Circumcision, 27, 119
Cleopatra, 70
Climates, 247
Cloves, 366
Clysma, xx, 142
Cocoa-nuts, *see* Argellia
Colchos, 120
Colossians, the, 229
Comana, 346
Comorin, C., 39
Cone, shadow cast by a, 250
Constantinople, x, xi, xviii, 24, 50, 239, 246; Council of, 213, 291
Constantinus, 2
Corinth, 18
Corinthians, the, 229, 230

Cosmas, name of, iv; his biography, iv-viii; sect, ix; veracity, xii; cosmology, xv-xvii; maps and sketches, xxv; place in history, xxv; work on geography, 2
Cretans, 230, 381
Crimea, 35
Ctesias of Cnidus, 360
Cupping-glass, 19
Cush, 36, *passim*
Cyclades, 57
Cyprus, 35, 36, 37
Cyrênê, 120
Cyrus, 68, 314-5

Dalmatians, 121
Daniel, 204, 207, 308, 317, 370; interpretation of his vision and the image, 68, 73
Darius the Mede, 68
David, 184
Day and Night, vicissitudes of, 132
Death, why inflicted on man, 162-3; how introduced, 219
De La Croze, ix, xiv
Denarii, 370
Devil, *see* Satan
Diapsalma (Selah), 185
Dillmann, 61, 64, 65
Diodorus Siculus, quoted, 75
Diodorus (of Tarsus), ix
Diodorus, Island of, 60
Dionysus, King of Egypt, 70
Dioscorides, *see* Socotra
Dolphin, 363
Dumb barter, 51-54

Earth, one here and one beyond the ocean, 33; the one here divided between the sons of Noah, 34-37; its length and breadth, 49-51; its shape, 132; its position, 136; its flatness, 252
Earth beyond the Ocean, 376
Earthquakes, 17-18, 86
Easter, 122, 353
Ebionites, 308
Eclipses, 4, 9, 116-7, 121, 133, 238, 246, 322-31, 385
Eden, *see* Paradise
Edessa, 25, 72
Edfu, 245
Egypt, 2, 18; *passim*
Elamites, 37, 120
Elanitic Gulf, 54
Elbe R., 75
Elements, the four, 10-12, 15, 20, 85-6; fire and water, 338
Elephants, 57, 58, 370, 371; fight of, 372
Elesboas, King of Axum, vii, x, 52, 54, 55, 359
Elijah, 115, 194-5, 200, 206, 255
Elim, 56, 143
Elis, 35
Elisa (Elishah), 35
Elisabeth (John Baptist's Mother), 210

INDEX. 395

Embryons dying in the womb, destiny of, 296-7
Emeralds, 371
Enoch, 167, 171, 254-5
Entelecheia, meaning of, 11
Epicycles, 8, 13
Ephesians, the, 229; Epistle to the, 346
Ephesus, 222, 230; council of, 239
Ephorus quoted, 73-75
Epiphanius (B. of Cyprus), 349; quoted, 344-5
Epiphany, 143
Erythraean Sea, 38
Esau, 179
— Ethiopia, vi, 20, 34, *passim*
Eunuch, the Ethiopian, 199
Eunuchs, 317
Euphrates, R., 41, 58, 76
Eusebius Pamphili, 72, 111, 142, 290-1, 375
Eutychês, 213
Eutychians, ix
Euxine Sea, 35
Eve, 167, 235
Exodus, the, from Egypt, 141, 142, 254
Ezekiel, 203

Festus, 279
Firmament, the, 231, 336-9, *passim*
Flood, the Noachian, 114, 136, 375
Floyer, Mr., quoted, 245
Franks, the, 121

Gabala, 62, 66
Gadeira (Cadiz), 34, 35, 36, 38, 50, 75, 120, 121, 376
Galatians, the, 229
Galaxy, the, 14
Galilee, 203
Gallandi, xiii
Gambela, 61
Ganges R., 48
Garamantes, 120
Gaudia, 364
Gazé, 60
Gellius, Aulus, 378
Geon R., 41
Gibbon quoted, xiii, 25, 120, 121, 230, 354, 365, 370
Giraffe, 359
Glaser, Dr. E., 60, 61, 64, 65
Gog and Magog, 198
Gold mines, 52, 53
Gollas, 370-1
Gomer, 35
Goths, 121
Gravitation, law of, illustrated, 28-29
Greeks, invective against the, 382; relapse of the, into infidelity, 385-6
Gregory, St., 332
Gregory (B. of Nazianzus), 332-3
Guardafui, C., v, vii, 36, 60
Gulfs, the four, 101, 131
Guzerat, 48

Habakkuk, 201
Haggai, 204
Ham, 34, 36, 373
Harrar, 60
Havilah (Euilat), 372
Heavenly bodies, 76, 101; motions of the, 84-85; course of the, 321-330
Heavens, the, indissolubility of, xxiii, 268; fixity of, 16; number of, 114, 134, 267; sphericity of, denied, 230, 347-8; duration of, 263-266
Hebrews, the, 230
Hedjaz, 60, 64
Hellespont, 58, 247
Hercules, pillars of, 36
Herod, 200
Heruli, 121
Hezekiah, song of, 305-311; sun dial of, 311-313
Hieroglyphics, 94
Himyari, *see* Homerites
Hiouen Thsiang, 365
Hipparchus, 244
Hobia, cr Obbia, 64
Hog-deer, 361-2
Homer, 380-1
Homerites, vii, x, 37, 39, 52, 55, 251-2, 366, 372
Homologus, 3
Horatae, 367
Horeb, Mt., 144
Horses, Persian, 372
Hosea, 195-6
Huns, 37, 120, 370-1
Hunter, Sir W., 370-1
Hyacinth-stone, 364, 365, 368
Hydaspes, R., 75
Hyperidês, 147
Hypostasis, 233
Hyrcanian Sea, *see* Caspian Sea
Hyrcanians, 72

Iberia (Spain), 50
Illyrians, 121
Image, man the, of God, 235
India, 36, 37, 49, *passim*; Further India, 39; India tertia, 39
Indiction 246, 354
Indus, R., 48; identified with the Phison, 372
Inscriptions at Adulé, ii, vii, 54-68
Ionia, 58
Iouuia (Iounnia?), 49
Irenaeus, 290
Isaac, 177-9, 254
Isaiah, 199, 200, 307-8
Ishmaelites, 158
Israelites; how fed and clothed in the Wilderness, 158

Jacob, 179-181; ladder of, 282
Japhet, 35, 173
Jasper-stone, 372
Jeremiah 202
Joel, 196-7

John St., Gospel of, 222-4
John the Baptist, 142, 206, 209-10, 219-220
Jonah, 98, 198-9, 379
Joseph, 254
Joshua (son of Nun), 115, 117, 160-1
Josephus, 111, 311, 375
Judah, 181
Judas Iscariot, 223
Judgment, the last, 278; oracular plate of, 155-6
Jupiter, the planet, 11, 13
Justinian, 18, 48, 55
Justinus I, x. 55

Kalaa, 61
Karinoi, 178
Kasu, 64
Katoptrizomenoi, 232
Kâvêra, 367
Kâvêripattam, *see* Cabor
Kelts, 73
Kêtioi (Cyprians), 36
Khartum, vii
K'lima, meanings of, 244
Kidaris (turban), 156

Laccadive Islands, 364
Lacedemonians, 381
Lactantius, quoted 17
Laodicea, 213
Lazarus, 169, 223
Lazica, 120
Lazinê, 62, 66
Letters, knowledge of, given to Moses, 110, 112
Leuce Cômê, 64
Libya, 36, 37, 40, 57, 120
Lotus, the, 75
Ludolf, Job, 56
Luke, St., 221-2
Luxor, 245
Lycia, 57
Lysimachus, a grammarian, 377-8

Maccabees, 69
Macedonia, 68, 69, 70
Maeotic Lake, 247
Magi, the, 72
Magog, 35
Malachi, 205-6
Malala, John, 55
Male (Malabar), 48, 119, 366, 367
Man, God's image, 104; creation of, 104-5; how constituted, 104-6; upright figure of, 108-9
Manetho, 377
Mangarouth (Mangalôr), 367
Manichaeans, ix, xxi, 212, 242, 258, 259
Manna, 144
Marah, or Merrha, 144
Marallo, 367
Mareb, R., 60
Marcionites, ix, 213, 273
Marco Polo, 365
Mark, St., 220-1

Marmora, Sea of, 54
Mars, the planet, 11, 13
Martin, V. de Saint, 59-60, 63, 65
Mary, the Virgin, 69, 71, 210, 354; *Mother of God*, x, 25, 239
Masius, Mt., 50
Massâwa, 60
Mauretania, 120
Media, 35, 58, 68, 120
Megasthenês, 363, 371
Melchisedec, 175-7
Menander, 147
Mênas, vii, 56
Mercy-seat, the, 111, 146
Merodach, 312
Meroê, vii, 36, 37, 38, 64, 247
Meshech, 35
Mesopotamia, 58, 120
Mesraim (Egyptians and Ethiopians), 36, 373
Metalêpsis (H. Communion), 140, 231-3
Metaxa (silk), 366
Metine, 62
Micah, 200-1
Midianites, 158
Migdol, 141
Miliarision, 369
Millennium, the, 241
Mingrelians, 120
Mithras, xx, 115
Mithridates I, 72
Money, the Roman, 73, 369
Montanists, 241-2
Montfaucon, Father, ii, *passim*
Moon, circle of the, 321-2; created at full illumination, 342-3
Moses, 94-7, 181-4, *passim*.
Mountain, the conical, xviii, xxiii, 132, 134
Music, instruments of, 184
Musk, 366
Musk-deer, 360

Nablus, 241
Nahum, 201
Nalopatana, 367
Nebuchadnezzar (Nabuchodonosor), 68, 70, 115, 207, 317
Neo-Platonists, Pantheism of, xxi
Nestorius, 239
Nile, 41, 52, 245; sources of the, vii, viii
Nisibis, 24, 48, 49
Noah, 44-5, 172-6, 253
Nomisma, 369
Nubia, 36, 62, 120, 371

Oasis, the Greater, 25
Obadiah, 198
Origen, 301
Origenists, 333
Orrhotha, 367
Oryx, 361
Ouraniskos, 338
Ousia, 233
Oxus, R., 370, 371

INDEX. 397

Palestine, 35, 36, 58, 120
Palibothra (Patna), 58
Pamphilus (of Jerusalem), 3, 4, 23, 90, 128, 313
Pamphilus (B. of Caesarea), 290
Pamphylia, 58
Paradise, xx, 33, 47, 76, 81, 89, 123, 131, 152, 174, 253, 329, 342, 347, 349, 372
Paralipomena (Chronicles), 208
Paran, 144
Parthia, 72
Parti, 367
Passover, the, 138-9, 182, 241, 333-4
Patana, 367
Patricius, ix, 24, 316
Paul, St., 227-230 ; rapture of, into heaven, xxv, 116-7, 227-8, 256, 267, 326-8
Pentapolis, 120
Pepper, 119, 366, 367
Pepper-tree, 362
Perdiccas, 69
Persarmenia, 41, 76, 120
Persia, 48, 49, *passim*
Persian Christians, Church of, 365
Peter (friend of Cosmas), xxiii, 304, 317-8
Peter, St., 224-6
Petra, 64
Pharaoh, 94, 141
Phasis, R., 120
Phazania (Fezzan), 120
Philémon, 230
Philippians, the, 229
Philometor, 70
Philon (B. of Carpathus), 349-51
Phison, R., 366, 372
Phœnicia, 35, 57, 120, 381
Phœnicôn, 143
Photius, iii, xi
Phut (Libyans), 36, 373
Physcon, 384
Pisces (Zodiac sign), 13
Plagues of Egypt, 95-8
Planets, the, 35, 300, 324 ; motions of the, 8, 13, 14
Plato, 91, 117, 121, 125, 376
Pliny, 367, 370
Phoca (the seal), 363
Point de Galle, 365
Polycarp, 290
Pomegranates, the golden, 150, 158
Pontus, 120
Poudopatana, 367
Priests, garments of, 154-8
Proclus, 376
Proconnesus, Island of, 54
Procopius, 366
Prophecies, how written, 207-8
Propitiation, Ark of, 153
Psalms, contents of the, and how composed, 184-194
Ptolemais, 120
Ptolemy Sôtêr, 57, 66, 70
Ptolemy Philadelphus, 57, 383

Ptolemy Euergetês, 54, 57, 58, 70, 252
Ptolemy, the astronomer, 117, 125, 249, 364
Punishments, the future, 216-7, 238
Pythagoras, 91, 121
Pytheas, 74, 75

Quadrature of the circle, 125

Rae, Dr. Milne, xiv
Rain, how produced, 18-20, 86
Red Sea, or Arabian Gulf, *passim*
Resurrection, the, 220, 240, 260, 274-7, 382
Rewards, nature of the future, 216-7, 231, 241
Rhaithu, vii, 56, 143
Rhapsii, 63
Rhaptum, 39
Rhinoceros, 358-9, 360
Rhodes, xviii, 36, 246, 247
Rhongoosura, 362
Rome, 50, 220
Roman Empire, 70-3
Ruby (the Ceylonese), 365
Ruth, Book of, 298

Saba, *see* Arabia Felix
Sacrament (the Holy), 241-2
Salopatana, 367
Salt, Mr., 54, 66, 359
Samaritans, 241-2, 257-260
Sandal-wood, 366
Sassanidae, 72
Sasu, 51-2, 64, 66
Satan, 76, 78, 83, 102, 105, 215, 219, 228, 352
Scamander R., 371
Scete, desert of, 24
Scythia, 35, 40, 370
Scythians, 121, 198
Seleucia, 49, 50
Seleucus Nicator, 18, 58, 69
Seleucus, Iambic verses addressed to, 290-1
Self-identity, retention of our, 276
Semenoi, the, 61, 62, 67
Senaar, 40
Sennacherib, 309-7
Septuagint, the, 361, 383
Seraphim, 199
Sêres (Northern Chinese), 367
Sesame, 366
Sesen, 63, 65
Seth, 167, 182-3
Severianus (B. of Gabala), 17, 291 ; quoted, 334-343
Shadows, 244-252 ; various lengths of, 262 ; retrogression of, on Hezekiah's sun-dial, 311
Sheba (Sabaea, or Yemen), Queen of, 52
Shem, 34, 173
Shew-bread, 318, 324
Sibor (Chaul), 367
Sidonians, 37

Sieledība, *see* Ceylon
Sigyē, 60
Silk, 48, 49, 366
Simeon, 197, 211
Sinae (Southern Chinese), 367
Sinai, desert of, viii; inscriptions on rocks of, xx, 159-60
Sindh, 366
Sindu, 366
Socotra, island of, xx, 119
Socrates, 121
Sôlate, 63
Solomon, 208
Solon, 380
Somalis, 60
Song of songs, xxii, 305
Sopatrus, 368
Souls, pre-existence of, 301; nature of, 103; circumscription of, 21, 22, 87; transmigration of, 260, 301
Spartel C., 120
Spermologos, 9, 279
Spheres, the crystalline, 8; the nine, 300; revolution of, 135
Stephanus (an abbot), 245
Stephen (first martyr), 218, 226-7
Substantia, 233
Suez, 142
Sun, size of, xviii, xxiii, 244-252; circle of, 321-2; daily course of, 41, 43, 132-4, 340
Sun-dials, 245; degrees how marked on, 311
Sur, or Shur, 143
Surat, 367
Susiana, 37, 58, 59
Syria, 57, 68, 120
Syênê, 245, 249

Tabernacle prepared by Moses, xv, 6, 24, 26, 43, 97, 110, 114, 122, 254; description of, 138-161;. outer and inner, 150-1; door of, 151; curtains of, 147; court of, 154; veil of, 153; pillars of, 147-9; table of, 31, 46, 152; a pattern of the world, 145, 149
Tablet of Basanite with Greek inscription, 57-9
Takazze R., 60-62
Tamieion, 351
Tana, lake, 52, 60, 61
Tangaitae, 62
Taprobanê, *see* Ceylon
Tartarus, 260
Taurelaphus, or bull-stag, 359
Temple (of Jerusalem), 99, 100, 117-8, 383
Tennent, Sir E., quoted, 364, 368, 370
Testimony, Ark of the, 111, 146
Teucer (the Locrian), 380
Thaddaeus, 72
Tharseis (Tarshish, Tartessus), 36
Thebaïd, 20
Theodorus (of Mopsuestia), ix, 25
Theodosius (B. of Alexandria), x, quoted 352-3

Theophilus, St. Luke's disciple, 221-2
Theophilus (B. of Alexandria), 333-4
Thêres (Thracians), 35, 36
Thessalonians, the, 229
Thibet, 48
Thomas of Edessa, 24
Thevenot, ii, 364, 368
Thulê, 49
Tiama, 61
Tiamo, 61
Tibareni, the, 35
Tigrê, 60, 61, 62, 65
Tigris, R., 41, 49
Timaeus, 379, 380
Timotheus the younger, x, 353; quoted 354-7
Timothy, 230
Titus, 230
Tongues, the gift of, 225
Toupha, 360
Tower of Babel, *see* Babel
Trebizond, 120
Tree of Knowledge, 329, 341; of Life, 166
Trinity (the divine), 233, 258
Trinquemala, 365
Troglodytes, 36, 54, 57, 69
Tropics, the, 43
Tubal, 35
Turtle, the, 363
Twelve months, circle of the, 318-9, 322-3, 325
Tyrians, antiquities of the, 380
Tzinitza (China), 48, 49, 366

Unicorn, the, 360-1
Urim and Thummim, 155

Virgins, parable of the ten, 210

Walls, the, joining earth and heaven, 30
Wise Men of the East, the, 197
Woman, creation of, 109-110
World, creation of the, 83; figure of the, 129-137, 261-2

Xenophanes, 75
Xisuthrus, 375

Year, length of the, 321-2
Yemen, *see* Arabia Felix
Yule, Sir H., xiii, xvii, xx, xxi, 119, 120, 367

Zaa, 62, 66
Zachariah, 153, 210
Zechariah, 205
Zephaniah (Sophonias), 202
Zerubbabel, 204, 205
Zingabênê, 61
Zingium or Zingion, 38, 39, 52
Zodiac, the, 324
Zone, the torrid, 249
Zoroaster, 72
Zôskales, 65
Zulla, *see* Adulê

LONDON:
PRINTED AT THE BEDFORD PRESS, 20 AND 21, BEDFORDBURY, W.C.

THE HAKLUYT SOCIETY
1897.

President.
SIR CLEMENTS MARKHAM, K.C.B., F.R.S., Pres. R.G.S.

Vice-Presidents.
THE RIGHT HON. THE LORD STANLEY OF ALDERLEY.
REAR-ADMIRAL SIR WILLIAM WHARTON, K.C.B.

Council.

C. RAYMOND BEAZLEY, ESQ., M.A.
COLONEL G. EARL CHURCH.
THE RIGHT HON. GEORGE N. CURZON, M.P.
ALBERT GRAY, ESQ.
ALFRED HARMSWORTH, ESQ.
THE RIGHT HON. LORD HAWKESBURY.
EDWARD HEAWOOD, ESQ., M.A.
ADMIRAL SIR ANTHONY H. HOSKINS, G.C.B.
VICE-ADMIRAL A. H. MARKHAM.
A. P. MAUDSLAY, ESQ.
E. DELMAR MORGAN, ESQ.
CAPT. NATHAN, R.E.
ADMIRAL SIR E. OMMANNEY, C.B., F.R.S.
CUTHBERT E. PEEK, ESQ.
E. G. RAVENSTEIN, ESQ.
HOWARD SAUNDERS, ESQ.
CHARLES WELCH, ESQ., F.S.A.

Honorary Secretary.
WILLIAM FOSTER, ESQ., BORDEAN, HOLLY ROAD, WANSTEAD, N.E.

Bankers in London.
MESSRS. BARCLAY & CO., 1, PALL MALL EAST.

Bankers in New York.
MESSRS. MORTON, BLISS, & CO., CORNER OF CEDAR AND NASSAU STREETS.

Agent for distribution, &c., of Volumes.
MR. B. QUARITCH, 15, PICCADILLY, W.

Annual Subscription. - One Guinea (in America five dollars).

THE HAKLUYT SOCIETY, established in 1846, has for its object the printing of rare or unpublished Voyages and Travels. Books of this class are of the highest interest and value to students of history, geography, navigation, and ethnology; and many of them, especially the original narratives and translations of the Elizabethan and Stuart periods, are admirable examples of English prose at the stage of its most robust development.

The Society has not confined its selection to the books of English travellers, to a particular age, or to particular regions. Where the original is foreign, the work is given in English, fresh translations being made, except where it is possible to utilise the spirited renderings of the sixteenth or seventeenth century.

More than ninety volumes have now been issued by the Society. The majority of these illustrate the history of the great age of discovery which forms the foundation of modern history. The discovery of AMERICA, and of particular portions of the two great western continents, is represented by the writings of COLUMBUS, AMERIGO VESPUCCI, CORTES and CHAMPLAIN, and by several of the early narratives from HAKLUYT's collection. The works relating to the conquest of PERU, and to the condition of that country under the Incas, are numerous and of the highest value; similar interest attaches to STRACHEY'S

Virginia Britannia, DE SOTO'S *Discovery of Florida*, and SIR ROBERT SCHOMBURGK'S edition of RALEIGH'S *Discoverie of Guiana*. The works relating to AFRICA already published comprise BARBOSA'S *Coasts of East Africa*, the *Portuguese Embassy to Abyssinia* of ALVAREZ, and *The Travels of Leo the Moor*. Notices of AUSTRALIA, INDIA, PERSIA, CHINA, JAPAN, etc., as they appeared in early times to European eyes, both before and after the discovery of the Cape route, are also included in the series, a well-known example being the work on *Cathay and the Way Thither*, contributed by a former President, SIR HENRY YULE. The search for the North-west and North-east Passages is recorded in the narratives of JENKINSON, DE VEER, FROBISHER, DAVIS, HUDSON, BAFFIN, etc.; whilst more extensive voyages are signalised by the great names of MAGELLAN, DRAKE, and HAWKINS.

The works selected by the Council for reproduction are printed (with rare exceptions) at full length. Each volume is placed in the charge of an editor especially competent—in many cases from personal acquaintance with the countries described—to give the reader such assistance as he needs for the elucidation of the text. Whenever possible, the interest of the volumes is increased by the addition of reproductions of contemporary portraits, maps, and other illustrations.

As these editorial services are rendered gratuitously, *the whole of the amount received from subscribers is expended in the preparation of the Society's publications.*

The subscription should be paid to the Society's Bankers on the 1st January in each year. This entitles the subscriber to receive, free of charge, the current publications of the Society. Usually two volumes are issued each year; but it is hoped to add from time to time a third volume, whenever the state of the funds will permit. Members have the sole privilege of purchasing sets of the previous publications; and the more recent of the Society's volumes are also reserved exclusively for its subscribers. In addition, they are allowed a special discount of 15 per cent. on the volumes permitted to be sold to the public. It may be mentioned that the publications of the Society tend to rise in value, and those which are out of print are now only to be obtained at high prices.

The present scale of charges for back volumes is as follows:—

To MEMBERS,—*Complete sets of back publications*, omitting Nos. 1, 2, 3, 5-10, and 10, to be sold for . . . . net £33.

N.B.—*Most of the out-of-print volumes have been, or are being, reprinted as later volumes of the series.*

Nos. 76, 77, 79-87, 90-98, at . . . . net 10s.
Nos. 88, 89, at . . . . . net 15s.

To THE PUBLIC GENERALLY. *A limited number of single copies* as follows:—

Nos. 23, 26, 29, 31, 34, 40, 47, 50, at . . . . 8s. 6d.
Nos. 21, 24, 28, 30, 35, 46, 48, 51, 53, 55, 56, 58, 60 to 75 and 78, at . 10s.
Nos. 20, 27, 33, 38, 39, 41 to 45, 49, 52, 57, at . . . 15s.
Nos. 54 and 59, at . . . . 20s.

⁎⁎ Subject in case of Members to a discount of 15%.

A list of works in preparation is given at page 9. The Secretary will be happy to furnish any further information that may be desired.

Gentlemen desiring to be enrolled as members should send their names to the Secretary. Applications for back volumes should be addressed to MR. QUARITCH.

WORKS ALREADY ISSUED.

1 · The Observations of Sir Richard Hawkins, Knt.,
In his Voyage into the South Sea in 1593. Reprinted from the edition of 1622, and edited by Capt. C. R. DRINKWATER BETHUNE, R.N., C.B.
(First Edition out of print. See No. 57.) *Issued for* 1848.

2—Select Letters of Columbus,
With Original Documents relating to the Discovery of the New World. Translated and Edited by R. H. MAJOR, Esq.
(First Edition out of print. See No. 43.) (1847.) *Issued for* 1849.

3—The Discoverie of the Empire of Guiana,
By Sir Walter Raleigh, Knt. Edited by SIR ROBERT H. SCHOMBURGK, Phil.D. (1848.)
(First Edition out of print. Second Edition in preparation.) Issued for 1850.

4—Sir Francis Drake his Voyage, 1595.
By Thomas Maynarde, together with the Spanish Account of Drake's attack on Puerto Rico. Edited by W. D. COOLEY, Esq. (1849.)
Issued for 1850.

5 · Narratives of Early Voyages to the North-West.
Edited by THOMAS RUNDALL, Esq. (1849.)
(Out of print.) Issued for 1851.

6 - The Historie of Travaile into Virginia Britannia,
Expressing the Cosmographie and Commodities of the Country, together with the manners and customs of the people, collected by William Strachey, Gent., the first Secretary of the Colony. Edited by R. H. MAJOR, Esq. (1849.)
(Out of print.) Issued for 1851.

7 Divers Voyages touching the Discovery of America
And the Islands adjacent, collected and published by Richard Hakluyt, Prebendary of Bristol, in the year 1582. Edited by JOHN WINTER JONES, Esq. (1850.)
(Out of print.) Issued for 1852.

8 A Collection of Documents on Japan.
With a Commentary by THOMAS RUNDALL, ESQ. (1850.)
(Out of print.) Issued for 1852.

9 The Discovery and Conquest of Florida,
By Don Ferdinando de Soto. Translated out of Portuguese by Richard Hakluyt; and Edited by W. B. RYE, Esq. (1851.)
(Out of print.) Issued for 1853.

10 - Notes upon Russia,
Being a Translation from the Earliest Account of that Country, entitled Rerum Muscoviticarum Commentarii, by the Baron Sigismund von Herberstein, Ambassador from the Court of Germany to the Grand Prince Vasiley Ivanovich, in the years 1517 and 1526. Two Volumes. Translated and Edited by R. H. MAJOR, Esq. Vol. I. (1851.)
(Out of print.) Issued for 1853.

11- The Geography of Hudson's Bay.
Being the Remarks of Captain W. Coats, in many Voyages to that locality, between the years 1727 and 1751. With Extracts from the Log of Captain Middleton on his Voyage for the Discovery of the North-west Passage, in H.M.S. "Furnace," in 1741-2. Edited by JOHN BARROW, Esq., F.R.S., F.S.A. (1852.) *Issued for* 1854.

12—Notes upon Russia.
Vol. 2. (1852.) *Issued for* 1854.

13 Three Voyages by the North-East,
Towards Cathay and China, undertaken by the Dutch in the years 1594, 1595 and 1596, with their Discovery of Spitzbergen, their residence of ten months in Novaya Zemlya, and their safe return in two open boats. By Gerrit de Veer. Edited by C. T. BEKE, Esq., Ph.D., F.S.A. (1853.)
(See also No. 54.) Issued for 1855.

14-15—The History of the Great and Mighty Kingdom of China and the Situation Thereof.
Compiled by the Padre Juan Gonzalez de Mendoza. Reprinted from the Early Translation of R. Parke, and Edited by SIR GEORGE T. STAUNTON, Bart. With an Introduction by R. H. MAJOR, Esq. 2 vols. (1853-54.)
Issued for 1855.

16—The World Encompassed by Sir Francis Drake.
Being his next Voyage to that to Nombre de Dios. Collated with an unpublished Manuscript of Francis Fletcher, Chaplain to the Expedition. Edited by W. S. W. VAUX, Esq., M.A. (1854.)
Issued for 1856.

17—The History of the Tartar Conquerors who subdued China.
From the French of the Père D'Orleans, 1688. Translated and Edited by the EARL OF ELLESMERE. With an Introduction by R. H. MAJOR, Esq. (1854.)
Issued for 1856.

18—A Collection of Early Documents on Spitzbergen and Greenland.
Edited by ADAM WHITE, Esq. (1855.)
Issued for 1857.

19—The Voyage of Sir Henry Middleton to Bantam and the Maluco Islands.
From the rare Edition of 1606. Edited by BOLTON CORNEY, Esq. (1855.)
Issued for 1857.

20 Russia at the Close of the Sixteenth Century.
Comprising "The Russe Commonwealth" by Dr. Giles Fletcher, and Sir Jerome Horsey's Travels. Edited by E. A. BOND, Esq. (1856.)
Issued for 1858.

21 The Travels of Girolamo Benzoni in America, in 1542-56.
Translated and Edited by ADMIRAL W. H. SMYTH, F.R.S., F.S.A. (1857.)
Issued for 1858.

22 India in the Fifteenth Century.
Being a Collection of Narratives of Voyages to India in the century preceding the Portuguese discovery of the Cape of Good Hope; from Latin, Persian, Russian, and Italian Sources. Edited by R. H. MAJOR, Esq. (1857.)
Issued for 1859.

23 Narrative of a Voyage to the West Indies and Mexico,
In the years 1599-1602, with Maps and Illustrations. By Samuel Champlain. Translated from the original and unpublished Manuscript, with a Biographical Notice and Notes by ALICE WILMERE. (1859.) *Issued for* 1859.

24 Expeditions into the Valley of the Amazons
During the Sixteenth and Seventeenth Centuries; containing the Journey of Gonzalo Pizarro, from the Royal Commentaries of Garcilasso Inca de la Vega; the Voyage of Francisco de Orellana, from the General History of Herrera; and the Voyage of Cristoval de Acuna. Translated and Edited by CLEMENTS R. MARKHAM, Esq. (1859.) *Issued for* 1860.

25—Early Indications of Australia.
A Collection of Documents shewing the Early Discoveries of Australia to the time of Captain Cook. Edited by R. H. MAJOR, Esq. (1859.)
Issued for 1860.

26—The Embassy of Ruy Gonzalez de Clavijo to the Court of Timour, 1403-6.
Translated and Edited by CLEMENTS R. MARKHAM, Esq. (1859.)
Issued for 1861.

27—Henry Hudson the Navigator.
The Original Documents in which his career is recorded. Edited by GEORGE ASHER, Esq., LL.D. (1860.) *Issued for* 1861.

28—The Expedition of Ursua and Aguirre,
In search of El Dorado and Omagua, A.D. 1560-61. Translated from the "Sexta Noticia Historiale" of Fray Pedro Simon, by W. BOLLAERT, Esq.; with an Introduction by CLEMENTS R. MARKHAM, Esq. (1861.)
Issued for 1862.

29—The Life and Acts of Don Alonzo Enriquez de Guzman.
Translated and Edited by CLEMENTS R. MARKHAM, Esq. (1862.)
Issued for 1862.

30—Discoveries of the World
From their first original unto the year of our Lord 1555. By Antonio Galvano. Reprinted, with the original Portuguese text, and edited by VICE-ADMIRAL BETHUNE, C.B. (1862.) *Issued for* 1863.

31—Marvels described by Friar Jordanus,
From a parchment manuscript of the Fourteenth Century, in Latin. Edited by COLONEL H. YULE, C.B. (1863.) *Issued for* 1863.

32—The Travels of Ludovico di Varthema
In Syria, Arabia, Persia, India, etc., during the Sixteenth Century. Translated by J. WINTER JONES, Esq., F.S.A., and Edited by the REV. GEORGE PERCY BADGER. (1863.) *Issued for* 1864.

33 The Travels of Cieza de Leon in 1532-50
From the Gulf of Darien to the City of La Plata, contained in the first part of his Chronicle of Peru (Antwerp, 1554). Translated and Edited by CLEMENTS R. MARKHAM, Esq. (1864.) *Issued for* 1864.

34—The Narrative of Pascual de Andagoya.
Containing the earliest notice of Peru. Translated and Edited by CLEMENTS R. MARKHAM, Esq. (1865.) *Issued for* 1865.

35 The Coasts of East Africa and Malabar
In the beginning of the Sixteenth Century, by Duarte Barbosa. Translated from an early Spanish manuscript by the HON. HENRY STANLEY. (1866.)
Issued for 1865.

36-37 Cathay and the Way Thither.
A Collection of all minor notices of China, previous to the Sixteenth Century. Translated and Edited by COLONEL H. YULE, C.B. Two Vols. (1866.) *Issued for* 1866.

38—The Three Voyages of Sir Martin Frobisher.
With a Selection from Letters now in the State Paper Office. Edited by REAR-ADMIRAL COLLINSON, C.B. (1867.)
Issued for 1867.

39—The Philippine Islands,
Moluccas, Siam, Cambodia, Japan, and China, at the close of the 16th Century. By Antonia de Morga. Translated from the Spanish, with Notes, by the LORD STANLEY of Alderley. (1868.) *Issued for* 1868.

40—The Fifth Letter of Hernan Cortes

To the Emperor Charles V., containing an Account of his Expedition to Honduras in 1525-26. Translated from the Spanish by DON PASCUAL DE GAYANGOS. (1868.) *Issued for* 1868.

41 The Royal Commentaries of the Yncas.

By the Ynca Garcilasso de la Vega. Translated and Edited by CLEMENTS R. MARKHAM, Esq. Vol. 1. (1869.) *Issued for* 1869.

42—The Three Voyages of Vasco da Gama,

And his Viceroyalty, from the Lendas da India of Caspar Correa; accompanied by original documents. Translated and Edited by the LORD STANLEY of Alderley. (1869.) *Issued for* 1869.

43—Select Letters of Christopher Columbus,

With other Original Documents relating to his Four Voyages to the New World. Translated and Edited by R. H. MAJOR, Esq. 2nd Edition (see No. 2). (1870.) *Issued for* 1870.

44 History of the Imâms and Seyyids of 'Omân,

By Salîl-Ibn-Razîk, from A.D. 661-1856. Translated from the original Arabic, and Edited, with a continuation of the History down to 1870, by the REV. GEORGE PERCY BADGER. (1871.) *Issued for* 1870.

45—The Royal Commentaries of the Yncas.

Vol. 2. (1871.) *Issued for* 1871.

46—The Canarian,

Or Book of the Conquest and Conversion of the Canarians in the year 1402, by Messire Jean de Bethencourt, Kt. Composed by Pierre Bontier and Jean le Verrier. Translated and Edited by R. H. MAJOR, Esq. (1872.) *Issued for* 1871.

47—Reports on the Discovery of Peru.

Translated and Edited by CLEMENTS R. MARKHAM, Esq., C.B. (1872.) *Issued for* 1872.

48—Narratives of the Rites and Laws of the Yncas.

Translated and Edited by CLEMENTS R. MARKHAM, Esq., C.B., F.R.S. (1873) *Issued for* 1872.

49—Travels to Tana and Persia,

By Josafa Barbaro and Ambrogio Contarini; Edited by LORD STANLEY of Alderley. With Narratives of other Italian Travels in Persia. Translated and Edited by CHARLES GREY, Esq. (1873.) *Issued for* 1873.

50 Voyages of the Zeni

To the Northern Seas in the Fourteenth Century. Translated and Edited by R. H. MAJOR, Esq. (1873.) *Issued for* 1873.

51—The Captivity of Hans Stade of Hesse in 1547-55,

Among the Wild Tribes of Eastern Brazil. Translated by ALBERT TOOTAL, Esq., and annotated by SIR RICHARD F. BURTON. (1874.) *Issued for* 1874.

52—The First Voyage Round the World by Magellan.

Translated from the Accounts of Pigafetta and other contemporary writers. Edited by LORD STANLEY of Alderley. (1874.) *Issued for* 1874.

53—The Commentaries of the Great Afonso Dalboquerque,

Second Viceroy of India. Translated from the Portuguese Edition of 1774, and Edited by WALTER DE GRAY BIRCH, Esq., F.R.S.L. Vol. 1. (1875.) *Issued for* 1875.

54—Three Voyages to the North-East.
Second Edition of Gerrit de Veer's Three Voyages to the North-East by Barents. Edited by Lieut. KOOLEMANS BEYNEN, of the Royal Dutch Navy. (1876.) *Issued for* 1876.

55—The Commentaries of the Great Afonso Dalboquerque.
Vol. 2. (1877.) *Issued for* 1875.

56—The Voyages of Sir James Lancaster.
With Abstracts of Journals of Voyages preserved in the India Office, and the Voyage of Captain John Knight to seek the N.W. Passage. Edited by CLEMENTS R. MARKHAM, Esq., C.B., F.R.S. (1877.) *Issued for* 1877.

57—The Observations of Sir Richard Hawkins, Knt.,
In his Voyage into the South Sea in 1593, with the Voyages of his grandfather William, his father Sir John, and his cousin William Hawkins. Second Edition (see No. 1). Edited by CLEMENTS R. MARKHAM, Esq., C.B., F.R.S. (1878.) *Issued for* 1877.

58 The Bondage and Travels of Johann Schiltberger,
From his capture at the battle of Nicopolis in 1396 to his escape and return to Europe in 1427. Translated by Commander J. BUCHAN TELFER, R.N.; with Notes by Professor B. BRUUN. (1879.) *Issued for* 1878.

59 The Voyages and Works of John Davis the Navigator.
Edited by Captain ALBERT H. MARKHAM, R.N. (1880.) *Issued for* 1878.

The Map of the World, A.D. 1600.
Called by Shakspere "The New Map, with the Augmentation of the Indies." To illustrate the Voyages of John Davis. (1880.) *Issued for* 1878.

60-61—The Natural and Moral History of the Indies.
By Father Joseph de Acosta. Reprinted from the English Translated Edition of Edward Grimston, 1604; and Edited by CLEMENTS R. MARKHAM, Esq., C.B., F.R.S. Two Vols. (1880) *Issued for* 1879.

Map of Peru.
To Illustrate Nos. 33, 41, 45, 60, and 61. (1880.) *Issued for* 1879.

62 The Commentaries of the Great Afonso Dalboquerque.
Vol. 3. (1880.) *Issued for* 1880.

63 The Voyages of William Baffin, 1612-1622.
Edited by CLEMENTS R. MARKHAM, Esq., C.B., F.R.S. (1881.) *Issued for* 1880.

64 Narrative of the Portuguese Embassy to Abyssinia
During the years 1520-1527. By Father Francisco Alvarez. Translated and Edited by LORD STANLEY of Alderley. (1881.) *Issued for* 1881.

65—The History of the Bermudas or Somer Islands.
Attributed to Captain Nathaniel Butler. Edited by General Sir J. HENRY LEFROY, R.A., K.C.M.G. (1882.) *Issued for* 1881.

66-67 The Diary of Richard Cocks,
Cape-Merchant in the English Factory in Japan, 1615-1622. Edited by EDWARD MAUNDE THOMPSON, Esq. Two Vols. (1883.) *Issued for* 1882.

68—The Second Part of the Chronicle of Peru.
By Pedro de Cieza de Leon. Translated and Edited by CLEMENTS R. MARKHAM, Esq., C.B., F.R.S. (1883.) *Issued for* 1883.

69 The Commentaries of the Great Afonso Dalboquerque.
Vol. 4. (1884.) *Issued for* 1883.

70-71 The Voyage of John Huyghen van Linschoten to the East Indies.
From the Old English Translation of 1598. The First Book, containing his Description of the East. Edited by ARTHUR COKE BURNELL, Ph.D., C.I.E., and Mr. P. A. TIELE, of Utrecht. (1885.) *Issued for* 1884.

72-73— Early Voyages and Travels to Russia and Persia,
By Anthony Jenkinson and other Englishmen, with some account of the first Intercourse of the English with Russia and Central Asia by way of the Caspian Sea. Edited by E. DELMAR MORGAN, Esq., and C. H. COOTE, Esq. (1886.) *Issued for* 1885.

74 The Diary of William Hedges, Esq.,
Afterwards Sir William Hedges, during his Agency in Bengal; as well as on his Voyage out and Return Overland (1681-1687). Transcribed for the Press, with Introductory Notes, etc., by R. BARLOW, Esq., and Illustrated by copious Extracts from Unpublished Records, etc., by Col. Sir H. YULE, K.C.S.I., R.E., C.B., LL.D. Vol. 1, The Diary. (1887.) *Issued for* 1886.

75—The Diary of William Hedges, Esq.
Vol. 2. Sir H. Yule's Extracts from Unpublished Records, etc. (1888.) *Issued for* 1886.

76-77—The Voyage of François Pyrard to the East Indies,
The Maldives, the Moluccas and Brazil. Translated into English from the Third French Edition of 1619, and Edited by ALBERT GRAY, Esq., assisted by H. C. P. BELL, Esq. Vol. 1. (1887.) Vol. 2, Part I. (1888.)
Issued for 1887.

78— The Diary of William Hedges, Esq.
Vol. 3. Sir H. Yule's Extracts from Unpublished Records, etc. (1889.)
Issued for 1888.

79—Tractatus de Globis, et eorum usu.
A Treatise descriptive of the Globes constructed by Emery Molyneux, and Published in 1592. By Robert Hues. Edited by CLEMENTS R. MARKHAM, Esq., C.B., F.R.S. To which is appended,

Sailing Directions for the Circumnavigation of England,
And for a Voyage to the Straits of Gibraltar. From a Fifteenth Century MS. Edited by JAMES GAIRDNER, Esq.; with a Glossary by E. DELMAR MORGAN, Esq. (1889.) *Issued for* 1888.

80 The Voyage of François Pyrard to the East Indies, etc.
Vol. 2, Part II. (1890.) *Issued for* 1889.

81 The Conquest of La Plata, 1535-1555.
I.—Voyage of Ulrich Schmidt to the Rivers La Plata and Paraguai. II.—The Commentaries of Alvar Nunez Cabeza de Vaca. Edited by DON LUIS L. DOMINGUEZ. (1891.) *Issued for* 1889.

82-83—The Voyage of François Leguat
To Rodriguez, Mauritius, Java, and the Cape of Good Hope. Edited by Captain PASFIELD OLIVER. Two Vols. (1891.)
Issued for 1890.

84-85—The Travels of Pietro della Valle to India.
From the Old English Translation of 1664, by G. Havers. Edited by EDWARD GREY, Esq. Two Vols. (1892.) *Issued for* 1891.

86—The Journal of Christopher Columbus
During his First Voyage (1492-93), and Documents relating to the Voyages of John Cabot and Gaspar Corte Real. Translated and Edited by CLEMENTS R. MARKHAM, Esq., C.B., F.R.S. (1893.) *Issued for* 1892.

87—Early Voyages and Travels in the Levant.
I.—The Diary of Master Thomas Dallam, 1599-1600. II.—Extracts from the Diaries of Dr. John Covel, 1670-1679. With some Account of the Levant Company of Turkey Merchants. Edited by J. THEODORE BENT, Esq., F.S.A., F.R.G.S. (1893.) *Issued for* 1892.

88-89—Voyages of Captain Luke Foxe and Captain Thomas James
In Search of a North-West Passage, in 1631-32: with Narratives of Earlier N.-W. Voyages. Edited by MILLER CHRISTY, Esq., F.L.S. Two Vols. (1894.) *Issued for* 1893.

90—The Letters of Amerigo Vespucci
And other Documents relating to his Career. Translated and Edited by CLEMENTS R. MARKHAM, Esq., C.B., F.R.S. (1894.) *Issued for* 1894.

91—The Voyage of Pedro Sarmiento to the Strait of Magellan, 1579-80.
Translated and Edited, with Illustrative Documents and Introduction, by CLEMENTS R. MARKHAM, Esq., C.B., F.R.S. (1895.) *Issued for* 1894.

92-93-94—The History and Description of Africa,
And of the Notable Things Therein Contained. The Travels of Leo Africanus the Moor, from the English translation of John Pory (1600). Edited by ROBERT BROWN, Esq., M.A., Ph.D. Three Vols. (1896.) *Issued for* 1895.

95 The Discovery and Conquest of Guinea.
Written by Gomes Eannes de Azurara. Translated and Edited by C. RAYMOND BEAZLEY, Esq., M.A., F.R.G.S., and EDGAR PRESTAGE, Esq., B.A. Vol. I. (1896.) *Issued for* 1896.

96—Danish Arctic Expeditions.
Book 1. The Danish Expeditions to Greenland, 1605-07; with James Hall's Voyage in 1612. Edited by C. C. A. GOSCH, Esq. (1897.) *Issued for* 1896.

97 Danish Arctic Expeditions.
Book 2. Jens Munk's Voyage to Hudson's Bay in 1619-20. Edited by C. C. A. GOSCH, Esq. (1897.) *Issued for* 1897.

98—The Topographia Christiana of Cosmas Indicopleustes.
Translated and Edited by J. W. McCRINDLE, Esq., M.A., M.R.A.S. *Issued for* 1897.

OTHER WORKS UNDERTAKEN BY EDITORS.

A Journal of the first Voyage of Vasco da Gama. Translated from the Portuguese, with an Introduction and Notes, by E. G. RAVENSTEIN, Esq. (*In the Press.*)
The True History of the Conquest of New Spain, by Bernal Diaz. Translated from the Spanish, and Edited by Vice-Admiral LINDESAY BRINE.
A Reprint of 17th Century Books on Seamanship and Sea Matters in General. Edited, with Notes and an Introduction, by H. HALLIDAY SPARLING, Esq.
Histoire de la Grande Isle Madagascar, par le Sieur De Flacourt, 1661. Translated and Edited by Captain S. PASFIELD OLIVER.
Raleigh's Empire of Guiana. Second Edition (see No. 3). Edited, with Notes, etc., by EVERARD F. IM THURN, Esq.
The Voyages of Cadamosto, the Venetian, along the West Coast of Africa, in the years 1455 and 1456. Translated from the earliest Italian text of 1507, and Edited by H. YULE OLDHAM, Esq., M.A., F.R.G.S.

The Voyages of the Earl of Cumberland, from the Records prepared by order of the Countess of Pembroke. Edited by W. DE GRAY BIRCH, Esq., F.S.A.

The Voyage of Alvaro de Mendaña to the Solomon Islands in 1568. Edited by CHARLES M. WOODFORD, Esq.

De Laet's Commentarius de Imperio Magni Mogolis (1631). Translated and Edited by Sir ROPER LETHBRIDGE, K.C.I.E., M.A.

The Voyages of Willoughby and Chancellor to the White Sea, with some account of the earliest intercourse between England and Russia. Reprinted from Hakluyt's Voyages, with Notes and Introduction by E. DELMAR MORGAN, Esq.

The Journal of Sir Thomas Roe during his Embassy to India, 1615-19. Edited by WILLIAM FOSTER, Esq., B.A.

Dr. John Fryer's New Account of East India and Persia (1698). Edited by ARTHUR T. PRINGLE, Esq.

The Expedition of Hernan Cortes to Honduras in 1525-26. Second Edition (see No. 40), with added matter. Translated and Edited by A. P. MAUDSLAY, Esq.

The Letters of Pietro Della Valle from Persia, &c. Translated and Edited by CAPTAIN M. NATHAN, R.E.

The Voyage of Sir Robert Dudley to the West Indies and Guiana in 1594. Edited, from Sloane MS. 358 in the British Museum, by GEO. F. WARNER, Esq., M.A., F.S.A., Assistant Keeper of Manuscripts.

The Journey of Pedro Teixeira from India to Italy by land, 1604-05; with his Chronicle of the Kings of Ormus. Translated and Edited by W. F. SINCLAIR, Esq., late I.C.S.

WORKS SUGGESTED FOR PUBLICATION.

J. dos Santos. The History of Eastern Ethiopia. 1607.
The History of Ethiopia, by Manoel de Almeida.
Travels of Friar Rubruquis.
Travels of the brothers Sherley in Persia.
The Travels of Ralph Fitch in India and Burma, 1583-91.

LAWS OF THE HAKLUYT SOCIETY.

I. The object of this Society shall be to print, for distribution among its members, rare and valuable Voyages, Travels, Naval Expeditions, and other geographical records, from an early period to the beginning of the eighteenth century.

II. The Annual Subscription shall be One Guinea, payable in advance on the 1st January.

III. Each member of the Society, having paid his Subscription, shall be entitled to a copy of every work produced by the Society, and to vote at the general meetings within the period subscribed for; and if he do not signify, before the close of the year, his wish to resign, he shall be considered as a member for the succeeding year.

IV. The management of the Society's affairs shall be vested in a Council consisting of twenty-one members, viz., a President, two Vice-Presidents, a Secretary, and seventeen ordinary members, to be elected annually; but vacancies occurring between the general meetings shall be filled up by the Council.

V. A General Meeting of the Subscribers shall be held annually. The Secretary's Report on the condition and proceedings of the Society shall be then read, and the meeting shall proceed to elect the Council for the ensuing year.

VI. At each Annual Election, three of the old Council shall retire.

VII. The Council shall meet when necessary for the dispatch of business, three forming a quorum, including the Secretary; the Chairman having a casting vote.

VIII. Gentlemen preparing and editing works for the Society, shall receive twenty-five copies of such works respectively, and an additional twenty-five copies if the work is also translated.

LIST OF MEMBERS.

1897.

Aberdare, Lord, Longwood, Winchester.
Adelaide Public Library, per Messrs. Kegan Paul, Trench, Trübner & Co.
Admiralty, The (2 *copies*).
Advocates' Library, Edinburgh.
All Souls College, Oxford.
American Geographical Society, 11, West 29th-street, New York City, U.S.A.
Amherst, Lord, of Hackney, Didlington Hall, Brandon, Norfolk.
Antiquaries, the Society of, Burlington House, Piccadilly, W.
Army and Navy Club, 36, Pall-mall.
Athenæum Club, Pall Mall.
Baer, Joseph & Co., Messrs., Rossmarkt, 18, Frankfort-on-Maine.
Bain, Mr., 1, Haymarket, S.W.
Bank of England Library and Literary Association.
Barclay, Hugh G., Esq., Colney Hall, Norwich.
Barlow, R. Fred., Esq., 15, Ambrose-place, Worthing, Sussex.
Barrow, J., Esq., F.R.S., F.S.A., 17, Hanover-terrace, Regent's Park.
Basano, Marquis de, per Messrs. Hatchard's, Piccadilly, W.
Baxter, James Phinney, Esq., 61, Deering-street, Portland, Maine, U.S.A.
Beaumont, Rear-Admiral L. A., 3, Sloane-gardens, S.W.
Beazley, C. Raymond, Esq., 13, The Paragon, Blackheath, S.E.
Belhaven and Stenton, Col. the Lord, R.E., 41, Lennox gardens, S.W.
Bellamy, C. H., Esq., F.R.G.S., Belmont, Brook-road, Heaton Chapel, near Stockport.
Berlin Geographical Society.
Berlin, the Royal Library of.
Berlin University, Geographical Institute of (Baron von Richthofen), 6, Schinkelplatz, Berlin, W.
Birch, W. de G., Esq., British Museum.
Birmingham Central Free Library.
Birmingham Library (The).
Bodleian Library, Oxford (*copies presented*).
Bonaparte, H. H. Prince Roland, 10, Avenue d'Jéna, Paris.
Boston Athenæum Library, U.S.A.
Boston Public Library.
Bowdoin College, Brunswick, Maine, U.S.A.
Bower, Capt. H., 17th Bengal Cavalry, Stirling Castle, Simla, India.
Bowring, Thos. B., Esq., 7, Palace Gate, Kensington, W.
Brewster, Charles O., Esq., University Club, New York City, U.S.A.
Brighton Public Library.
Brine, Vice-Admiral Lindesay, 13, Pembroke-gardens, Kensington.
British Guiana Royal Agricultural and Commercial Society, Georgetown, British Museum (*copies presented*). | Demerara.
Brock, Robert C. H., Esq., 1612, Walnut-street, Philadelphia.
Brodrick, Hon. G., Merton College, Oxford.
Brooke, Thos., Esq., Armitage Bridge, Huddersfield.
Brooklyn Library, Brooklyn, U.S.A.
Brooklyn Mercantile Library.
Brown, Arthur W. W., Esq., 39, Norfolk-square, Hyde Park, W.
Brown, General J. Marshall, 218, Middle-street, Portland, Maine, U.S.A.
Brown, H. T., Esq., Roodeye House, Chester.
Brown, J. Allen, Esq., 7, Kent-gardens, Ealing.
Brown, J. Nicholas, Esq., Providence, R.I., U.S.A.
Buda-Pesth, the Geographical Institute of the University of.
Burgess, Jas., Esq., C.I.E., LL.D., 22, Seton-place, Edinburgh.
Burns, J. W., Esq., Kilmahew, Dumbartonshire.

Buxton, E. North, Esq., Knighton, Buckhurst-hill.
Cambridge University Library.
Canada, The Parliament Library.
Cardiff Public Library, Cardiff (J. Ballinger, Esq., Librarian).
Carlton Club, Pall-mall.
Carlisle, The Earl of, Naworth Castle, Bampton, Cumberland.
Cawston, Geo., Esq., Warnford Court, Throgmorton-street, E.C.
Chamberlain, Right Hon. Joseph, M.P., 40, Princes-gardens, S.W.
Chetham's Library, Hunt's Bank, Manchester.
Chicago Public Library.
Christ Church, Oxford.
Christiania University Library.
Church, Col. G. Earl, 216, Cromwell-road, S.W.
Cincinnati Public Library, Ohio, U.S.A.
Clark, J. W., Esq., Scroope House, Cambridge.
Cohen, Herr Friedrich, Am Hof 22, Bonn, Germany.
Colgan, Nathaniel, Esq., 1, Belgrave-road, Rathmines, Dublin.
Colonial Office (The), Downing-street, S.W.
Collingridge, George, Esq., Hornsby Junction, New South Wales, Australia.
Congress, Library of, Washington, United States.
Conway, Sir W. Martin, The Red House, Hornton-street, W.
Cooper, Lieut.-Col. E. H., 42, Portman-square, W.
Copenhagen Royal Library.
Cora, Professor Guido, M.A., 74, Corso Vittorio Emanuele, Turin.
Cornell University.
Corning, C. R., Esq., care of Messrs. Spencer Trask & Co., 10, Wall-street, New York, U.S.A.
Corning, H. K., Esq., Villa Monnet, Morillon, Geneva.
Cortissoz, Royal, Esq., Editorial Room, *New York Tribune*, New York, U.S.A.
Cow, J., Esq., Montredon, Arkwright-road, Hampstead, N.W.
Cruising Club, The, Adelphi Hotel, Adam-street, W.C.
Curzon, Right Hon. George N., M.P., 4, Carlton-gardens, S.W.
Dalton, Rev. Canon J. N., per Messrs. Williams & Norgate, Henrietta-street.
Danish Royal Naval Library.
Davis, Hon. N. Darnell, C.M.G., Georgetown, Demerara, British Guiana.
Derby, The Earl of, 25, St. James's-square, S.W.
Detroit Public Library, Michigan, U.S.A.
Dijon University Library, Rue Monge, Dijon.
Doubleday, H. Arthur, Esq., 2, Whitehall-gardens, S.W.
Dresden Geographical Society.
Ducie, The Earl, F.R.S., Tortworth Court, Falfield.
Dundas, Captain Colin M., R.N., Ochtertyre, Stirling.
Dunn, John, Esq., 1, Park-row, Chicago, U.S.A.
Eames, Wilberforce, Esq., Lenox Library, 890, Fifth-avenue, New York, U.S.A.
Edinburgh Public Library.
Edwards, T. Dyer, Esq., 5, Hyde Park-gate, Kensington Gore, S.W.
Edwards, Mr. Francis, 83, High-street, Marylebone, W.
Ellsworth, James W., Esq., 1820, Michigan-avenue, Chicago, Ill., U.S.A.
Elton, Charles I., Esq., Q.C., F.S.A., 10, Cranley-place, Onslow-square, S.W.
Faber, Reginald S., Esq., 10, Primrose Hill-road, N.W.
Fanshawe, Admiral Sir Edw., G.C.B., 74, Cromwell-road, S.W.
Fellows Athenaeum, per Messrs. Kegan Paul, Trench, Trübner, & Co.
Field, W. Hildreth, Esq., 923, Madison-avenue, New York City, U.S.A.
Fisher, Arthur, Esq., St. Aubyn's, Tiverton, Devon.
Fitzgerald, Edward A., Esq., per Mr. Jas. Bain, 1, Haymarket, S.W.
Foreign Office (The).
Foreign Office of Germany, Berlin.
Forrest, G. W., Esq., The Knowle, Brenchley, Kent.
Foster, William, Esq., Bordean, Holly-road, Wanstead.
Georg, Mons. H., Lyons.

George, C. W., Esq., 51, Hampton-road, Bristol.
Gladstone Library, National Liberal Club, Whitehall-place, S.W.
Glasgow University Library.
Godman, F. Ducane, Esq., F.R.S., 10, Chandos-street, Cavendish-square, W.
Gore-Booth, Sir H. W., Bart., Lissadell, Sligo.
Gosset, Major-General M. W. E., C.B., 21, Suffolk-street, Pall Mall, S.W.
Göttingen University Library.
Grant-Duff, Sir Mountstuart Elphinstone, G.C.S.I., 11, Chelsea Embankment, S.W.
Gray, Albert, Esq., 12, Culford-gardens, Chelsea, S.W.
Gray, M. H., Esq., Silvertown, Essex.
Grosvenor Library, Buffalo, U.S.A.
Guildhall Library, E.C.
Guillemard, Arthur G., Esq., Eltham, Kent.
Guillemard, F. Henry H., Esq., The Old Mill House, Trumpington, Cambridge.
Haig, Maj.-General Malcolm R., Rossweide, Davos Platz, Switzerland.
Hamburg Commerz-Bibliothek.
Harmsworth, A. C., Esq., Elmwood, St. Peter's, Kent.
Harvard College, Cambridge, Massachusetts.
Hawkesbury, Lord, 2, Carlton House-terrace, S.W.
Heap, Ralph, Esq., 1, Brick-court, Temple. E.C.
Heawood, Edward, Esq., M.A., F.R.G.S., 3, Underhill-road, Lordship-lane, S.E.
Hervey, Dudley F. A., Esq., per Messrs. H. S. King & Co., 45, Pall-mall.
Hiersemann, Herr Karl W., 3, Königsstrasse, Leipzig.
Hippisley, A. E., Esq., care of J. D. Campbell. Esq., C.M.G., 26, Old Queen-street. Westminster, S.W.
Hobhouse, C. E. H., Esq., The Ridge, Corsham, Wilts.
Horner, J. F. Fortescue, Esq., Mells Park, Frome, Somersetshire.
Horrick, Mrs. Perry, Beau Manor Park, Loughborough.
Hoskins, Admiral Sir Anthony H., G.C.B., 17, Montagu-square, W.
Hoyt Public Library, per Messrs. Sotheran and Co., Strand.
Hubbard, Hon. Gardiner G., 1328, Connecticut-avenue, Washington, D.C.
Hudson, John E., Esq., 125, Milk-street, Boston. Mass., U.S.A.
Hull Public Library (W. F. Lawton, Esq., Librarian).
Hull Subscription Library.
India Office (21 copies).
Inner Temple, Hon. Society of the (J. E. L. Pickering, Esq., Librarian).
Ismay, Thos. H., Esq., 10, Water-street, Liverpool.
James, Walter B., Esq., M.D., 268, Madison-avenue, New York.
Johns Hopkins University, Baltimore, U.S.A.
Johnson, General Sir Allen B., 60, Lexham-gardens, Cromwell-road, S.W.
Jones and Evans, Messrs., 77, Queen-street, Cheapside, E.C.
Keltie, J. Scott, Esq., 1, Savile-row, W.
Kelvin, Lord, F.R.S., LL.D., The University, Glasgow.
King's Inns Library, Henrietta-street, Dublin.
Kimberley Public Library, per Messrs. Sotheran and Co., Strand.
Kleinseich, M., National Library, Paris (2 copies).
Leeds Library.
Lehigh University, U.S.A.
Leipzig, Library of the University of, per Herr O. Harrassowitz, Leipzig.
Lewis, Walter H., Esq., 11. East 35th-street, New York City, U.S.A.
Liverpool Free Public Library.
Liverpool Geographical Society (Capt. D. Phillips, R.N., Secretary), 14, Hargreaves-buildings. Chapel-street. Liverpool.
Loch, Lord, G.C.B., G.C.M.G., 44, Elm Park-gardens, S.W.
Loescher, Messrs. J., & Co., Via del Corso, 307, Rome.
Logan, Daniel, Esq., Solicitor-General, Penang, Straits Settlements.
Logan, William, Esq., The Priory, St. Andrews, Fife.
London Institution, Finsbury-circus.
London Library, 12, St. James's-square.

Long Island Historical Society, Brooklyn, U.S.A.
Lopez, B. de B., Esq., 22, Chester-terrace, Regent's Park, N.W.
Lucas, C. P., Esq., Colonial Office, S.W.
Lucas, F. W., Esq., 21, Surrey-street, Victoria Embankment, W.C.
Luyster, S. B., Esq., c/o Messrs. Denham & Co., 27, Bloomsbury-square, W.C.
Macgregor, J. C., Esq., Ravenswood, Elmbourne-road, Upper Tooting, S.W.
Macmillan & Bowes, Messrs., Cambridge.
Manchester Public Free Libraries.
Manierre, George, Esq., 184, La Salle-street, Chicago, Ill., U.S.A.
Manila Club, The, per Mr. J. Bain, 1, Haymarket, S.W.
Margesson, Lieut. W. H. D., R.N., H.M.S. Buzzard.
Markham, Vice-Admiral Albert H., F.R.G.S., 19, Ashburn-pl., Kensington, W.
Markham, Sir Clements, K.C.B., F.R.S., 21, Eccleston-square, S.W.
Marquand, Henry, Esq., 160, Broadway, New York, U.S.A.
Massachusetts Historical Society, 30, Tremont-street, Boston, Mass., U.S.A.
Massie, Admiral T. L., Chester.
Maudslay, A. P., Esq., 32, Montpelier-square, Knightsbridge, S.W.
McClymont, Jas. R., Esq., 201, Macquarie-street, Hobart Town, Tasmania.
Mecredy, Jas., Esq., M.A., B.L., Wynberg, Stradbrook, Blackrock, Co. Dublin.
Melbourne, Public Library of.
Meyjes, A. C., Esq., Rose-cottage, Sudbury, Middlesex.
Michigan, University of, per Messrs. H. Sotheran & Co., 140, Strand, W.C.
Milwaukee Public Library, Wisconsin, per Mr. G. E. Stechert.
Minneapolis Athenœum, U.S.A., per Mr. G. E. Stechert, 2, Star-yard, W.C.
Mitchell Library, 21, Miller-street, Glasgow.
Mitchell, Wm., Esq., 14, Forbesfield-road, Aberdeen.
Molyneux, Lieut.-Col. Edmund, F.R.G.S., Warren Lodge, Wokingham, Berks.
Morgan, E. Delmar, Esq., 15, Roland-gardens, South Kensington, S.W.
Morris, H. C. L., Esq., M.D., Gothic Cottage, Bognor, Sussex.
Morris, Mowbray, Esq., 59A, Brook-street, Grosvenor-square, W.
Moxon, A. E., Esq., Farncombe-place, Godalming, Surrey.
Munich Royal Library.
Nathan, Captain, R.E., 11, Pembridge-square, W.
Natural History Museum, Cromwell-road, per Messrs. Dulau & Co., Soho-sq.
Naval and Military Club, 94, Piccadilly, W.
Netherlands, Geographical Society of the, per Mr. Nijhoff, The Hague.
Nettleship, E., Esq., 5, Wimpole-street, Cavendish-square, W.
Newberry Library, The, Chicago, U.S.A.
Newcastle-upon-Tyne Literary and Scientific Institute.
Newcastle-upon-Tyne Public Library.
New London Public Library, Conn., U.S.A.
New York Public Library, per Mr. B. F. Stevens.
New York State Library, per Mr. G. E. Stechert, 2, Star-yard, Carey-st., W.C.
New York Yacht Club, 67, Madison-avenue, New York City, U.S.A.
New Zealand, Agent-General for.
Nicholson, Sir Charles, Bart., D.C.L., The Grange, Totteridge, Herts, N.
Nordenskiold, Baron, 11, Tradgardsgatan, Stockholm.
North Adams Public Library, Massachusetts, U.S.A.
Northbrook, The Earl of, G.C.S.I., Stratton, Micheldever Station.
North, Hon. F. H., C 3, The Albany, W.
Northumberland, His Grace the Duke of, Grosvenor-place, S.W.
Nutt, Mr. D., 270, Strand, W.C.
Oliver, Captain S. P., Findon, near Worthing.
Oliver, Commander T. W., R.N., 16, De Parys-avenue, Bedford.
Ommanney, Admiral Sir Erasmus, C.B., F.R.S., 29, Connaught-sq., Hyde Park.
Oriental Club, Hanover-square, W.
Parmly, Duncan D., Esq., 160, Broadway, New York.
Payne, E. J., Esq., 2, Stone Buildings, Lincoln's Inn, W.C.
Peabody Institute, Baltimore, U.S.
Peckover, Alexander, Esq., Bank House, Wisbech.

Peech, W. H., Esq., St. Stephen's Club, Westminster.
Peek, Cuthbert E., Esq., 22, Belgrave-square, S.W.
Petherick, E. A., Esq., 2, Harley-place, Marylebone-road, N.W.
Philadelphia Free Library, U.S.A., per Mr. G. E. Stechert, 2, Star-yard, W.C.
Philadelphia, Library Company of, U.S.A.
Poor, F. B., Esq., 160, Broadway, New York, U.S.A.
Poor, Henry W., Esq., 45, Wall-street, New York, U.S.A.
Portico Library, Manchester.
Pringle, Arthur T., Esq., Madras, c/o. Messrs. G. W. Wheatley & Co., 10, Queen-street, Cheapside, E.C.
Pym, C. Guy, Esq., 35, Cranley-gardens, S.W.
Quaritch, Mr. B., 15, Piccadilly, W.
Raffles Library, Singapore.
Ravenstein, E. G., Esq., 2, York Mansions, Battersea Park, S.W.
Reform Club, Pall-mall.
Rhodes, Josiah, Esq., Heckmondwike, Yorkshire.
Richards, Admiral Sir F. W., G.C.B., United Service Club, Pall-mall, S.W.
Riggs, E. F., Esq., Washington, U.S.
Ringwalt, John S., Jr., Esq., Mt. Vernon, Ohio, U.S.A.
Rittenhouse Club, 1811, Walnut-street, Philadelphia, U.S.A.
Rockhill, W. W., Esq., care of Mr. B. F. Stevens.
Rose, C. D., Esq., 6, Princes-street, E.C.
Royal Artillery Institute, Woolwich (Major A. J. Abdy, Secretary).
Royal Colonial Institute (J. S. O'Halloran, Esq., Sec.), Northumberland-avenue, W.C.
Royal Engineers' Institute, Chatham.
Royal Geographical Society, 1, Savile-row, W. (*copies presented*).
Royal Scottish Geographical Society, Edinburgh (John Gunn, Esq., Librarian).
Royal United Service Institution, Whitehall-yard, S.W.
Russell, Lady A., 2, Audley-square, W.
Rutherford, Rev. W. Gunion, M.A., Westminster School, S.W.
Ryley, J. Horton, Esq., 308, Coldharbour-lane, Brixton, S.W.
Satow, H. E. Sir E., K.C.M.G., 104, The Common, Upper Clapton, E.
Saunders, Howard, Esq., 7, Radnor-place, Gloucester-square, W.
SAXE-COBURG AND GOTHA, H.R.H. the Reigning Duke of (Duke of Edinburgh), K.G., K.T., etc.
Science and Art Department, South Kensington.
Seawanhaka Corinthian Yacht Club, 7, East 32nd-street, New York, U.S.A.
Seymour, Vice-Admiral E. H., C.B., 9, Ovington-square, S.W.
Signet Library, Edinburgh (Thos. G. Law, Esq., Librarian).
Silver, S. W., Esq., 3, York-gate, Regent's Park, N.W.
Sinclair, W. F., Esq., late Indian C. S., c/o Messrs. H. S. King & Co., Pall Mall, S.W.
Smithers, F.O., Esq., F.R.G.S., Dashwood House, 9, New Broad-street, E.C.
Société de Géographie, Paris.
Sotheran, Messrs. H., & Co., 140, Strand, W.C.
South African Public Library.
South Australian Legislature Library.
Springfield City Library Association, Mass., U.S.A.
Stairs, James W., Esq., c/o Messrs. Stairs, Son and Morrow, Halifax, Nova Scotia.
Stanley, Lord, of Alderley, Alderley Park, Chelford, Cheshire.
St. Andrew's University.
St. John, N. B., Canada, Free Public Library (J. R. Buel, Esq., Chairman).
St. Louis Mercantile Library, per Mr. G. E. Stechert, 2, Star-yard, W.C.
St. Martin's-in-the-Fields Free Public Library, 115, St. Martin's-lane, W.C.
St. Petersburg University Library.
Stephens, Henry C., Esq., M.P., Avenue House, Finchley, N.
Stevens, J. Tyler, Esq., Park-street, Lowell, Mass., U.S.A.
Stevens, Son, & Stiles, Messrs., 39, Great Russell-street, W.C.
Stockholm, Royal Library of.

Strachey, Lady, 69, Lancaster-gate, Hyde-park, W.
Stride, Mrs. Arthur L., Bush Hall, Hatfield, Herts.
Stringer, G. A., Esq., 248, Georgia-street, Buffalo, N.J., U.S.A.
Stubbs, Captain Edward, R.N., 13, Greenfield-road, Stoneycroft, Liverpool.
Surrey County School, Cranleigh.
Sydney Free Library, per Mr. Young J. Pentland, 38, West Smithfield, E.C.
Taylor, Captain William R., 1, Daysbrooke-road, Streatham Hill, S.W.
Temple, Lieut.-Col. R. C., C.I.E., Pioneer Press, Allahabad, India.
Thin, Mr. Jas., 54, 55, South Bridge, Edinburgh.
Thomson, B. H., Esq., North Lodge, Ascot.
Tighe, W. S., Coalmoney, Stratford-on-Slaney, Co. Wicklow.
Toronto Public Library.
Toronto University.
Transvaal State Library, Pretoria, Transvaal, South Africa, per Messrs. Mudie.
Travellers' Club, 106, Pall-mall, S.W.
Trinder, H. W., Esq., Northbrook House, Bishops Waltham, Hants.
Trinder, Oliver Jones, Esq., Mount Vernon, Caterham, Surrey.
Trinity College, Cambridge.
Trinity House, The Hon. Corporation of, Tower-hill, E.C.
Troop, W. H., Esq., c/o Messrs. Black Bros. & Co., Halifax, Nova Scotia.
Trotter, Coutts, Esq., Athenæum Club, S.W.
Trübner, Herr Karl, Strasburg.
Turnbull, Alex. H., Esq., 7, St. Helen's-place, Bishopsgate-street, E.C.
Union League Club, Philadelphia, U.S.A.
Union Society, Oxford.
United States Naval Academy.
University of London, Burlington-gardens, W.
Upsala University Library.
Van Raalte, Charles, Esq., Aldenham Abbey, Watford, Herts.
Vienna Imperial Library.
Vignaud, Henry, Esq., U.S. Legation, 59, Rue Galilee, Paris.
Wahab, Colonel G. D., Knowle, Godalming.
Ward, Admiral Hon. W. J., 79, Davies-street, Berkeley-square, W.
Warren, W. R., Esq., 81, Fulton-street, New York City, U.S.A.
Washington, Department of State.
Washington, Library of Navy Department.
Watkinson Library, Hartford, Connecticut, U.S.A.
Watson, Commander, R.N.R., Ravella, Crosby, near Liverpool.
Webb, Captain Sir J. Sydney, The Trinity House, E.C.
Webb, William Frederick, Esq., Newstead Abbey, Nottingham.
Webster, Sir Augustus, Bart., Guards' Club, 70, Pall-mall.
Western Reserve Historical Society, Cleveland, Ohio, U.S.A.
Wharton, Rear-Admiral Sir W. J. L., K.C.B., Florys, Princes-road, Wimbledon Park, S.W.
Wildy, A.G., Esq., 14, Buckingham-street, W.C.
Wilson, Edward S., Esq., Melton Grange, Brough, East Yorkshire.
Wisconsin State Historical Society.
Wohlleben, Mr. Th., Great Russell-street, W.C.
Wood, Commander R. T., R.N., 2, Esplanade, Whitby, Yorkshire.
Worcester, Massachusetts, Free Library.
Yale College, U.S.A.
Young, Alfales, Esq., Salt Lake City, Utah, U.S.A.
Young, Sir Allen, C.B., 18, Grafton-street, W.
Young & Sons, Messrs. H., 12, South Castle Street, Liverpool.
Zürich, Bibliothèque de la Ville.

www.ingramcontent.com/pod-product-compliance
Lightning Source LLC
Chambersburg PA
CBHW031957300426
44117CB00008B/807